Robert Menzies

BY THE SAME AUTHOR

Paul Keating: the big-picture leader

The Dismissal: in the Queen's name
(with Paul Kelly)

Rudd, Gillard and Beyond

The Whitlam Legacy (ed.)

For the True Believers: great Labor speeches
that shaped history (ed.)

Looking for the Light on the Hill:
modern Labor's challenges

The Wran Era (ed.)

The Hawke Government: a critical retrospective
(ed. with Susan Ryan)

Robert Menzies

the art of politics

TROY BRAMSTON

To Melissa /
with best wishes /
Troy B~~~~
2019.

SCRIBE

Melbourne • London

Scribe Publications
18–20 Edward St, Brunswick, Victoria 3056, Australia
2 John St, Clerkenwell, London, WC1N 2ES, United Kingdom
3754 Pleasant Ave, Suite 100, Minneapolis, Minnesota 55409, USA

First published by Scribe 2019

Typeset in Garamond Premier Pro by the publishers

Printed and bound in Australia by Griffin Press, part of Ovato

Scribe Publications is committed to the sustainable use of natural resources
and the use of paper products made responsibly from those resources.

9781925713671 (Australian edition)
9781912854561 (UK edition)
9781950354009 (US edition)
9781925693508 (e-book)

Catalogue records for this book are available from the National Library of
Australia and the British Library.

scribepublications.com.au
scribepublications.co.uk
scribepublications.com

To Paul Kelly, colleague and friend,
who set the standard for writing about Australian politics

Contents

PART IV

Afternoon Light: 1966–78

Politics is both a fine art and an inexact science. We have concentrated upon its scientific aspects — the measurement and estimation of economic trends, the organisation of finance, the devising of plans for social security, the discovery of *what* to do. We have neglected it as an art, the delineating and practice of *how* and *when* to do these things and, above all, how to persuade a self-governing people to accept and loyally observe them. This neglect is of crucial importance, for I am prepared to assert that it is only if the art of politics succeeds that the science of politics will be efficiently studied and mastered.

—Robert Menzies, *The New York Times Magazine*, 28 November 1948

PREFACE

Robert Menzies Unplugged

IN May 1972, journalist Frances McNicoll began a series of interviews with Robert Menzies at his post–prime ministerial office, located on the 14th floor at 95 Collins Street, Melbourne. These extraordinary interviews have never been fully revealed until now. Menzies talked at length about his upbringing, reflected on political events, policies, and personalities, offered political lessons drawn from his experience, and candidly assessed his prime ministerial successors. These interviews — eight conducted in May 1972 and another in December 1973 — are of historical significance. They show Menzies like never before. He is surprisingly frank, offering unvarnished thoughts about all manner of subjects, events, and people in the twilight of his life. These interviews will amaze and astonish readers, provide new insights into Menzies' life and legacy, and add immeasurably to our knowledge of our political history.

A fortnight after Menzies' death in May 1978, McNicoll wrote an article for *The Bulletin* magazine that disclosed the former prime minister's poor opinion of Harold Holt, John Gorton, and Billy McMahon.[1] These comments from Menzies were drawn from the interviews, but they represented only a fraction of his remarks recorded on reel-to-reel tapes and later transcribed. Another article, for *The Australian Women's Weekly*, divulging further comments by Menzies from the interviews, was published in July 1982.[2] But this vast trove of interviews has not been completely utilised.[3] Moreover, McNicoll's correspondence, notes, and research with and about Menzies, his family, colleagues, and staff have not all previously been made public. Ownership of the interviews transferred to the Menzies Foundation in the early 1990s, with restricted access. They have been made available for this book by the Menzies Foundation, and with the approval of the Menzies family.

McNicoll married Vice Admiral Sir Alan McNicoll, who knew many people in politics, the public service, and the media, in 1957. (Journalist David McNicoll was her brother-in-law.) In 1959, she met Menzies at a dinner party, and they became friendly. She subsequently worked for *The Economist* magazine in London and in Australia, and in 1969 was commissioned by Menzies to write his official biography. In 1972, this arrangement was confirmed, and McNicoll was given access to Menzies' papers at the National Library of Australia. Menzies also stipulated in his will that McNicoll was to have exclusive access to the papers for the first three years after his death, and the family extended this for a further year, until 1982. This gave her sole access to his papers for ten years. Menzies refused requests for interviews and access to his papers by prospective biographers; understandably, they saw little point in competing with McNicoll, and their books were not written.

She conducted considerable research, but never managed to produce more than a few scraps of handwritten notes and what seems to be one typescript draft chapter. Her papers, also at the National Library of Australia, are a mess. It is a tragic story. McNicoll was evidently overwhelmed by the task, and the book never appeared. 'The family gave up on me,' she claimed in 1991. 'They wouldn't give me the papers anymore. I gave up in high disgust because I'd done a lot of work on it.'[4] She died in 1993.

By 1983, the Menzies family had indeed become concerned about the progress of the biography. So had publisher William Collins. Repeated reassurances from McNicoll, who revelled in her status as 'official biographer', were unconvincing.[5] McNicoll was awarded multiple grants worth $10,000 — about $70,000 in today's value — by the Australia Council to write the book.[6] The Menzies papers had been opened to the public in 1982, and two years later, the Menzies family agreed with Melbourne University Press that academic Dr Allan Martin be commissioned to write the biography. Martin's book was expected to be published in 1987.[7] However, he said it was not 'official', and assured readers that his 'independence' was 'absolute'. The first volume, *Robert Menzies: a life*, was published in 1993, and the second in 1999.[8] Martin did not use McNicoll's interviews with Menzies. Nor did he delve far into her papers. Martin did not interview Menzies or McNicoll.

Journalist Allan Dawes also began a biography of Menzies. But that manuscript was left incomplete in the 1950s. I have also made use of Dawes' manuscript and his interviews with Menzies. Another biographer, Ronald Seth, also interviewed Menzies for his short biography, *R.G. Menzies*, published in 1960.[9] But Menzies had a poor opinion of Seth's book. The only other biography published in Menzies' lifetime, Kevin Perkins' *Menzies: the last of the Queen's men*, was thought by the subject to be littered with errors.[10] Percy Joske, a friend and colleague at both the Bar and in parliament, curiously characterised his biography of Menzies as an 'informal memoir'.[11] Cameron Hazlehurst's *Menzies Observed* stressed that it was 'biographical' but not 'a biography'.[12]

In this book, I offer a new biography of Menzies that incorporates these previously undisclosed interviews, coupled with full access to his personal papers, including hundreds of documents that have not been drawn upon in other works. For example, I was granted unrestricted access to Menzies' correspondence with his sister, Belle Green. And I have discovered fragments of memoirs, personal notes, letters, reports, and verse that have not been used by other historians or biographers. I also draw on my own interviews with Menzies' daughter, Heather Henderson, and several of Menzies' former colleagues, such as John Carrick, Jim Forbes, Doug Anthony, and Ian Sinclair; public servants Lenox Hewitt and Richard Woolcott; and his staff, William Heseltine and Tony Eggleton.

This biography largely follows a chronological approach, but it also contains focused chapters that examine the political, policy, and personal aspects of Menzies' life. I have not attempted to re-do what Allan Martin did extensively, and often brilliantly, over two volumes of biography. Nor have I focused on the broad sweep of the Menzies era, as John Howard has impressively done, surveying Australian politics until 1972.[13] This book, rather, offers a fresh account of Menzies' full life, informed by rich new source material and complemented by other personal and public papers, newspaper reports, and a range of books of history and biography. I rely more on new material than that which is already well known to chronicle and analyse Menzies' life. It is in the marshalling of this material, much of it new and in Menzies' own voice and hand, that I have tried to address what he thought was the 'truly formidable task' facing 'the serious historian' — understanding his or her subject. 'How is he to see the man himself, and understand his mind, and be influenced by his personality?' Menzies asked in 1970.[14] So, with these new archival sources, this book examines the people and events that shaped Menzies' public and private life, as well as the policy and political issues that he grappled with, and provides an assessment of his legacy. It also considers his personality, character, and principles.

Too often, Menzies has been viewed as a caricature. Some see him as the personification of statesmanship in the 20th century, and lionise and laud him without criticism. To others, he is snap-frozen in time as a stuffy Edwardian figure not in tune with the emerging Australia of the 1950s and 1960s. Or he is remembered with scorn and derision as an appeaser, a forelock-tugging British Empire toady or 'Pig-iron Bob' who let the country drift, resting on its laurels with policy settings on autopilot. He is described by Liberals as either a conservative, a liberal, or a centrist. In truth, Menzies is a far more complex, nuanced, and interesting figure. He is more substantial than his critics allow, and has more faults than his admirers accept. He deserves a fuller and more balanced account of his life, and an assessment of his legacy, within the context of the times in which he lived. That is the purpose of this biography. With the Liberal Party commemorating its 75th anniversary in 2019, a new study of Robert Menzies' life and legacy, and how he practised the art of politics, could not be timelier.

Life and Legacy

WHEN Sir Robert Gordon Menzies retired in the summer of 1966, he bestrode the Australian political stage like a colossus. He had served as prime minister over two separate terms, from 1939 to 1941 and from 1949 to 1966. He had been a minister in state and federal politics. He was then, and still is, the country's longest-serving prime minister, and the only one to have resigned at a time of his own choosing, undefeated, in the post-war era. He was the principal founder of the Liberal Party of Australia in 1944. He led the party to seven straight election victories. He presided over a nation imperilled by war and prosperous in peace. He was a politician who was admired and respected at home and abroad, although not universally loved. He had immense authority and stature. Australians viewed him as a safe, trusted, and reassuring leader.

He even *looked* prime ministerial. He was over six feet tall, had a bulky 20-stone frame, fleshy jowls, short silvery-grey hair, and piercing blue eyes underneath black bushy eyebrows — that could intimidate all on their own — which gave him a commanding presence. He wore buttoned-up double-breasted suits, usually with a crisp white shirt, dark tie, and pocket handkerchief. He smoked big fat cigars, mixed a lethal martini, and liked a Scotch whisky in the evening. He often wore a felt homburg hat and carried walking sticks, some engraved with 'R.G.M.' This sartorial elegance augmented his gravitas and presence. He spoke in a mellifluous voice with crisp expressiveness that was British in tone but uniquely Australian in its inflection. He filled any room, was often imposing, and almost always the centre of attention. For a generation who had grown accustomed to reading about him in the newspaper, hearing him on radio, and watching him on television, Menzies was *the* prime minister.

When Menzies exited the prime ministership at the age of 71, the tributes recognised his longevity, electoral success, and policy achievements. These included striking a blow against sectarianism by providing financial assistance to non-government schools; investing significant sums in universities and colleges, coupled with scholarships for students; forging new trade links in Asia; developing Canberra as the national capital; and cementing the US alliance with the ANZUS Treaty. He governed during the great post-war boom that saw the economy turbocharged with strong economic growth, rising living standards, expanding home ownership, national development, and a huge influx of migrants from Britain and Europe. It was a time of relative economic stability and prosperity. He left his mark on the world stage, and enjoyed friendly relations with a dozen US presidents and British prime ministers, and visited more Asian countries than any of his predecessors.

He was a traditionalist and a sentimentalist, but not a reactionary; he was a cautious reformer. Menzies advocated liberalism within a conservative economic and social framework. He saw 'the basic philosophy' of liberalism as encouraging free enterprise and advocating for the individual, for his or her liberty and freedom, from which all social gains and advantages stemmed.[1] He was a believer in Keynesian economics, a promoter of the family as the most important social unit, and a crusader against communism. He cherished the British legal tradition, the monarchy, and the Westminster system of government. He ran a methodical cabinet process and respected the advice of public servants, although he could be brutal with ministers if he thought they were not across their brief. He was also pragmatic, shrewd, and attuned to public thinking. He led a government, he said, that was 'progressive' and 'forward-looking', and never used the word 'conservative' to describe his philosophy. 'The prime duty of government,' he argued, 'is to encourage enterprise, to provide a climate favourable to growth, to remember that it is the individual whose energies produce progress, and that all social benefits derive from his efforts.' This was the standard he set and, in large part, met.[2]

Menzies believed in the duty of public service. He was a man of decency and integrity. He developed genuine friendships across the political divide with John Curtin and Ben Chifley — a notion almost completely foreign in modern politics. He was a superb speaker who excelled in parliamentary debate and could give grand orations. He enjoyed the cut and thrust of election campaigning, especially parrying interjectors at town hall meetings with clever and often wounding wit. But the other side to his skills as a political warrior was that many saw him, often accurately, as vain, arrogant, and aloof. He could be patronising and condescending. He was accessible to backbench MPs, but rarely offered praise, encouragement, or promotion. He did little to groom and mentor a new generation of Liberals, and that became evident soon after his departure. Interestingly, his closest colleagues and family say that behind the image of the master performer was, in fact, a very shy and deeply sensitive man.

But no prime minister gets everything right. His first term as prime minister (1939–41) ended in humiliation, but warrants a reassessment. His most significant mistake during his second term (1949–66) was his government's decision to send combat troops to Vietnam — a war that was never properly understood, doomed from the start, ended in catastrophic failure, and later divided Australians. His greatest political misstep was his attempt to ban the Communist Party of Australia, which saw him depart from his liberal principles, and was rejected by the voters. His mission to reverse Egypt's nationalisation of the Suez Canal was a failure. He pioneered Australia's most important long-term trading relationship with Japan, but never supported recognising China, even though other countries were beginning new diplomatic relations with it. His flattery of the monarchy, and his acceptance of imperial honours — the Order of the Thistle, and the post of Lord Warden of the Cinque Ports — seemed somewhat outdated by the 1960s. His views on race, whether to do with Aboriginal Australians, the White Australia policy, or racial segregation in South Africa, remain jarring today. Yet these views, however misguided, reflected those of many born 125 years ago.

While Menzies eased wartime economic restrictions and defeated Ben

Chifley's plans for nationalisation, the economy remained firmly shackled to highly regulated capital, labour, and product markets. Yet the economy roared through the 1950s and 1960s, delivering a 'golden age' for Australia, even though policy management was often characterised as 'stop-go'. There was the 'horror budget' of 1951 to deal with an inflationary surge, and a recession in 1952–53. Then a period of muddled policy led to the government inducing a 'credit squeeze' in 1961. The budget, for most of the period, was in deficit. The top marginal tax rate on incomes was 67 per cent, or higher, in the 1950s and 1960s. Many of Menzies' policies reflected the political consensus of the times, but they would later be jettisoned by both major parties. But even in the mid-1960s, there were some, such as Donald Horne in his ironic book, *The Lucky Country*, who recognised that Australia's economic and social policy settings needed to change.[3] The Deakinite Federation-era policies of industry protection, centralised industrial relations, and White Australia remained largely in place.

Debate over Menzies' life and legacy has never settled. Interpreting Menzies is core business for every Liberal leader. Liberals such as John Howard and Tony Abbott have continued to invoke him as the epitome of conservatism, while Malcolm Fraser viewed him as the personification of what it means to be a liberal. For Malcolm Turnbull, he was a political centrist. Scott Morrison steered a middle path, and said, 'The things that we believe in today are the things that he believed in then.'[4] Yet Menzies' true philosophical bearing remains contested within the party he led longer than anyone else. He was never popular among intellectuals, who see him as an Edwardian with a fawning attitude to the monarchy and the British Empire, and clinging to outdated views on race, women, and Aboriginal Australians. They say he achieved little, but reaped the benefits of global economic growth. To the working class, he was 'Pig-iron Bob' or 'Ming the Merciless', never to be trusted or forgiven, and an appeaser to boot. And to Labor, he used the communist bogey to exploit divisions in its ranks, and got lucky at the 1954 and 1961 elections when he won a majority of seats but a minority of the two-party-preferred vote. While Menzies' successes are frequently challenged by his critics, his failures are routinely defended by his staunchest admirers.

That is why it is important to place Menzies within the context of his times. He was born in the small wheat town of Jeparit, about 350 kilometres north-west of Melbourne, in 1894 — the last prime minister born in the nineteenth century. He had a Scottish and English inheritance that infused his outlook on life. As a young boy, his ambition was to be a barrister. When he was about the age of ten, a phrenologist came to the school and proclaimed that, for sixpence, he could tell what the future held for each of the young students. This form of pseudo-science claimed to be able to discern personality traits by studying the contours of the skull. The phrenologist, a tall man of slim build with greying beard and muttonchop whiskers, wore a dark suit with a white shirt and a thin black-ribbon bow tie. He sat next to the teacher's desk at the front of the classroom, and each child was called up to him. The phrenologist ran his fingers over the bumps on their heads, examining the shape of the skull overlying the brain, and then recorded his impressions on a piece of paper. When his hand lifted off the young Menzies' head, he proclaimed that the boy would become 'a barrister and public speaker'.[5]

After school, Menzies raced home to tell his mother. 'That's what I'm going to be!' he said. The family, however, could not fund the university education he needed to become a lawyer. So young Robert looked for scholarship opportunities. His mind was set on bringing the phrenologist's vision to fruition. 'My course was charted and my mind clear, provided that I could win enough free passages, that is, scholarships and exhibitions, to bring me to port,' Menzies said.[6] James and Kate Menzies, his parents, encouraged his education. His uncle Sydney Sampson urged him to read books from the local Mechanics' Institute. He won scholarship after scholarship, and excelled at schools in Jeparit, Ballarat, and Melbourne. At university, his star shone brightly and he collected many glittering prizes.

His father, two uncles, and father-in-law had been elected to parliament, so politics was in the blood. Yet Menzies insisted that he never had any ambition to be prime minister from a young age. 'I had never even heard of the prime minister when I was a small boy in Jeparit,' he said later in life. 'And if I had, and know as much as I do now, I'd probably have stayed in Jeparit.'[7] He wanted to be a lawyer. And while at the Bar, he aspired to be chief justice of Victoria. This was the happiest time in his life, he recalled, having been mentored by leading barrister Owen Dixon.[8] He made a name for himself when he dazzled the High Court and won, single-handedly, the landmark Engineers' Case in 1920. Yet he gave up a promising law career for government service. Menzies insisted that he saw politics as a 'public duty' and that he 'owed a great deal to my country', given the educational opportunities that had been afforded to him.[9] But there was another reason.

His older brothers, Les and Frank, had enlisted for the First World War, and the family decided not to send another son abroad. As a result, Menzies was branded a coward for not enlisting. This, he said in a previously unpublished interview, had 'a very searing effect on my mind'. So he decided to go into politics, viewing it as 'public service of some kind', to erase the perceived stain on his name. 'I just had to do something to justify my existence,' he recalled. Not enlisting, and the attacks that came with it, continued to affect him deeply. One of the reasons he went to London during the Second World War, and stayed for months while his colleagues were growing restless at home, was to show people that he was not without courage. He was chasing his demons. Menzies said he had to show the world that he was 'not yellow'.[10]

Menzies succeeded at his second attempt to get elected to the Victorian state parliament in 1928. He was soon a minister, then deputy premier, and then Canberra called. He was persuaded by prime minister Joe Lyons to run for the seat of Kooyong with the promise of becoming attorney-general and, possibly, his successor. Menzies hesitated at first, but then made the plunge, and his star continued to rise. But Menzies fell out with Lyons and resigned from cabinet on a matter of policy, as he had done in state politics. He was seen by his colleagues as intelligent but too proud. When told by a colleague in 1941 that he did not suffer fools gladly, he replied, perhaps in jest, 'What do you think I am doing now?'

When Lyons died in 1939, Menzies seized the leadership of the United Australia Party and became prime minister. Soon, the nation was at war. Menzies' first government helped to lay the foundations of Australia's war effort. The Second Australian Imperial Force was raised, diplomats were dispatched to foreign capitals, local war production was stepped up, forces were sent to fight overseas, and he remonstrated with Winston Churchill in London about the importance of defending Singapore. But he could not unite his party or his cabinet, or galvanise the nation, and so he resigned. It looked like a humiliating end to a dazzling career.

But Menzies was not yet finished with politics. He knew he had to change in order to rehabilitate his standing. He also knew that the UAP, beholden to business interests, was finished as a political force. In 1944, Menzies initiated a conference of 18 centre-right organisations, which resolved to form the Liberal Party of Australia. He was the most important figure in the formation of the new party and in the development of its structure, philosophy, and policies. But there were still some who doubted the party could 'win with Menzies' as leader. Although the 1946 election was a disappointment, Menzies persevered and seized on the issue that would, more than any other, catapult him back to power: Labor's plans for nationalisation. He had learned from his earlier mistakes — a virtue essential in any successful political leader — recognising especially the need to work more collegially with others and to be less brusque and overbearing. At the 1949 election, Menzies led the Liberal Party to a landslide victory, and went on to govern until he retired in 1966.

MORE than fifty years after Menzies departed from the political stage, it is time for a new perspective on this larger-than-life political figure who dominated government for so long, who continues to inspire many, and who also still attracts the most fervent of critics. His upbringing in Jeparit, the influence of his family, his schooling and university education, and his time as a lawyer tell the story of a Protestant middle-class boy with gleaming potential and a determination to make what he could of his life. In state and federal politics, we see another Menzies emerge — filled with ambition and intelligence, and unafraid to take risks, but held back by his poor relations with his colleagues, who never trusted or liked him very much. His first prime ministership ended in resignation and rejection, but it led to the formation of the Liberal Party, the development of a new political creed, and a pathway back to power. His lengthy second prime ministership reveals yet another Menzies as he grappled with many complex issues at home and abroad during a period of political turmoil, and saw him cycle from victory to near-defeat on two occasions, only to consolidate again and again, and retire undefeated.

Perhaps Menzies' most contemporarily relevant legacy is how he practised politics rather than the enduring nature of his policies. Learning the art of politics came only after hard work, self-reflection, and determination. Menzies knew what he stood for, and could communicate it clearly. He was a talented administrator of government who prized the cabinet process and respected the public service. He was a shrewd political tactician and campaigner who was unrivalled on the stump and achieved a record seven straight election victories. He was a brilliant parliamentary debater, public speaker, and broadcaster. He was, without doubt, the driving force behind the creation of the Liberal Party. He was a good manager of the party, and gained and kept its trust for more than two decades. And he understood that an effective relationship with the Country Party was essential to stable and effective government.

It is time to revisit and reassess the personal and the political aspects of Menzies' life. This is an important exercise, not only for the Liberal Party, but also for a better understanding of our political history. It is almost two decades since a full-life biography of Menzies was published. For too long, the vast Menzies papers and the interviews he conducted in the final years of his life have been ignored or forgotten by historians. Memories of the Menzies era are fading. At the time of writing, only three ministers from his government survive, and only one is a Liberal.[11] Those who cast a vote for the Liberal Party while Menzies was prime minister are mostly long gone; the youngest are in their mid-70s.[12] There is much to learn from Menzies. 'Study history,' Winston Churchill counselled a young student in 1953. 'In history lie all the secrets of statecraft.'[13] Therefore, it is also time for a new generation, whatever their politics, to look at the life of Menzies fairly but rigorously, and without partisan idolatry or mockery, and to learn of it anew.

PART I

The Boy from Jeparit:
1894–1926

CHAPTER 1

Jeparit

IN the spring of 1966, Robert Menzies returned to his birthplace of Jeparit, some 350 kilometres north-west of Melbourne. The occasion was the unveiling of a plaque affixed to the base of a 70-foot steel spire with an illuminated purple thistle atop that had been erected in his honour. It was a grand occasion. Jeparit's small population of 770 more than trebled to see Menzies, who had retired as prime minister earlier that year. Members of the Menzies family — including Dame Pattie and his siblings, Frank Menzies, Sydney Menzies, and Belle Green — were also in attendance. Crowds lined the streets and waved enthusiastically as Menzies' black chauffeur-driven car zoomed past, with its Cinque Ports banner affixed to the front. There were three pipe bands and two brass bands to herald his arrival. Speeches were made by the local shire president and councillors, and the federal MP for Mallee, Winton Turnbull.[1] The small Wimmera township had not witnessed anything quite like it before.

'This is rather an overwhelming sort of occasion,' Menzies said, as he stood next to the spire, smartly dressed in a dark double-breasted suit with silver tie and pocket handkerchief. On this sunny day beneath a wide, blue country sky, he spoke movingly about his childhood:

It was a great place in which a family might grow up. There are some advantages in not being in the middle of the hustle of a city, and one of the great advantages was that we lived in a community, almost every person in which we knew ... We acquired some moral and spiritual standard which perhaps we might not have acquired in a more turbulent and bustling community, and so I look back on all this and it is with great pleasure.

Menzies told the crowd of about 2,000 people who had gathered on the corner of Charles Street and Sands Avenue that Sunday, 18 September 1966, that it was in Jeparit he learned about public service, duty, and honour. He spoke about the importance of learning, of reading books and studying to improve one's lot in life. And he highlighted the family and community values he had gained as a boy that shaped him as a man:

We lived at home, we became fond of reading for each other and discussing matters with each other. This produced a very well-knit family atmosphere and had encouraged me, in particular, to be a student. And if I had not been a student, then I certainly would never have encumbered the political landscape ... we got to learn something about the things that mattered in the world.

He paid tribute to his parents, James and Kate Menzies. 'What I did for Jeparit is of no significance compared to what my parents did for Jeparit,' he said. Menzies remembered his early school days, folding and hand-delivering the local newspaper, and some of the local townsfolk. He mentioned the drought that wrought hardship in 1902, and recalled Lake Hindmarsh as the 'pride and joy' of the town, and also how his father had helped to establish the railway link from Jeparit to Lorquon. 'The Railways Standing Committee came to Jeparit and I found myself, as a small boy, looking at Members of Parliament for the first time and thinking how wonderful it must be to be a Member of Parliament.' Jeparit, he said, had a formative influence.

It was a deeply personal moment for the man Jeparit called their 'most famous son'. The spire, it was said, symbolised the rise of a local schoolboy who, because of his hard work, had reached 'the highest post in the land'. Menzies said he found the occasion to be very moving. Local chemist Fred Raven's *History of the Menzies Family in Jeparit*, published by the Chamber of Commerce, was presented to Menzies. Congratulatory telegrams were read aloud to the large crowd. Kids perched on fences or climbed trees to catch a glimpse of him. After the spire was officially unveiled, 82-year-old Albert Williams, who had given Menzies the job of newspaper delivery-boy, led the crowd in a spontaneous rendition of 'For He's a Jolly Good Fellow'. The town buzzed with excitement.[2]

ROBERT Gordon Menzies was born in a small room at the back of the family's general store in Jeparit, Victoria, on 20 December 1894. Of the five children born to James Menzies and Kate Menzies (née Sampson), he was the fourth, and the third son. He was named Robert after his paternal grandfather, and Gordon was given as his second name, after British army officer General Charles George Gordon. Both James and Kate were the children of migrants. They were a close-knit family who believed in middle-class Protestant values such as hard work, thrift, self-respect, independence, and community service. James was a coach painter and later a storekeeper. Kate also worked in the store and ran the family home. Their first three children — Les, Frank, and Belle — were born in Ballarat. Robert and Sydney were born in Jeparit, where the family had moved in late 1893.

In the early 1890s, Jeparit was 'a small township with a main street and a few score houses', Menzies recalled.[3] The population grew to around 200 by the end of the decade. Mostly, it was hot, windy, and dusty. At the time, Australia was enduring an economic depression. Menzies said his birth had been 'ushered in by the greatest series of bank failures in the history of the State of Victoria'.[4] The Menzies family owned and operated a general store that sometimes had financial difficulties during these years. His mother served behind the counter, and his father focused on the sale and servicing of farm machinery. Local farmers were regularly extended credit until they could raise enough funds to pay for goods bought at the store, placing the Menzies family under added financial pressure. They also had to pay high interest charges on accounts held with Melbourne merchants.

James's patchy health had prompted Sydney Sampson, his brother-in-law, to suggest that he move to Jeparit for the warmer weather. Sampson was the owner of the general store and publisher of the local newspaper, the *Jeparit Leader*. (He later sold the newspaper to Albert Williams, who employed 'Young Bobbie' to fold and deliver the 250 copies around town each week.) James and Kate took his advice, and bought the store. The shop was on the corner of Roy and Charles Streets, fronting a wide dirt thoroughfare, with an awning that stretched across a wooden pathway to the roadside, opposite the Hopetoun House Hotel. The signage above the entrance read 'James Menzies' in bold white writing, and on either side there were smaller signs that advertised drapery, boots, and shoes. The family lived in the back of the store, having expanded it for accommodation, for several years until James built a standalone house on the corner of Charles and Hindmarsh streets, behind the store.

In the year the Menzies family relocated to Jeparit — an Aboriginal term for 'home of small birds' — the population was estimated to be around 55. While Victoria, like the rest of the nation, was struggling through a depression, Jeparit was relatively unscathed compared to other country communities around Australia. The town was expanding with a growing population, and soon there were new businesses, a chapel, and a railway that connected it to Ballarat and Melbourne. By 1911, the population reached over 800 citizens. But there were the usual ups and downs of country life to be endured. The banks of the Wimmera River burst and the town was flooded in the year the Menzies family arrived. Farming survived several disappointing seasons through the 1890s. And in 1902 the town was gripped by drought.[5]

Jeparit was dotted with small wooden houses and businesses. There were scarcely any trees in the centre of town. Water came from rain captured in galvanised-iron tanks. There was no sewerage. There was no electricity: candles and gas lanterns provided light. About eight buildings comprised the Roy Street shopping centre: a bank, a bakery, a butcher's shop, the Mechanics' Institute, the Hopetoun House Hotel, a timber yard and residence, and two general stores. Newspapers from Melbourne arrived in town three times each week, but two days late, with news from around Australia and the world. Menzies would have been aware of, and observed, Aboriginal people, some of whom were living outside of town, and at the nearby Ebenezer Mission Station, near Antwerp.

It was an isolated but not lonely existence. Young Robert had a happy, fulfilling, and mostly carefree childhood. There were plenty of birds, horses, emus, and kangaroos in and around the town. Running through the streets, climbing the few trees, or playing in the rivers and streams, the children of Jeparit had little awareness of some of their parents' struggle to make ends meet during trying times. 'They had no inkling of their parents' dour struggle for economic survival,' wrote Allan Martin. 'They played football and a rustic form of hockey, with paper sticks and empty jam tins for balls; they yabbied, fished and swam in Lake Hindmarsh and the Wimmera River.'[6]

The young boy gave early signs of the future politician. By the age of ten, Robert was already known as a 'soap-box' orator. Perhaps he was emulating his father, who was a local councillor. 'He could talk about anything, and people would listen,' recalled Jeparit resident Laurie Binns. 'As a kid, he'd get up on a box and make a speech. Anything they asked, Bob could always answer. It was predicted at the time he'd be prime minister one day.' Alma Cameron remembered Robert as 'a really nice boy' from 'a lovely family' who had a distinctive head of hair with corkscrew curls.[7]

For the first decade or so of Robert's life, he knew only Jeparit. In 1905, he moved to Ballarat to continue his schooling, and lived with his paternal grandmother. In 1910, Robert enrolled at Wesley College in Melbourne. By 1909, Kate had moved to East Melbourne, and James, who would contest a seat in the state parliament, would follow in 1910. A 640-acre farm in Jeparit, which James had bought for £200, was leased on a share basis to farmers for several years until it was sold for a bonanza of £2,080. These funds would allow the family to relocate to Melbourne.

BY early 1966, bureaucratic red tape, design difficulties, and construction problems had delayed the raising of the spire. The council hoped it would be unveiled while Menzies was prime minister, and the problems had become the talk of the town and occasionally spilled into the local press. It was to be located on the edge of the town's reserve and showground, now to be called Sir Robert Menzies Park. But the embarrassment for the local council and the township was forgotten when the former prime minister returned home and was greeted with a gala celebration.

It was a moment of great pride for Jeparit. A committee had been established to oversee the project as a civic initiative. A crowded public meeting in July 1965 had given it enthusiastic approval, and the necessary funds were raised by the community. The plaque unveiled by Menzies more than fifty years ago is a reminder of the boy from Jeparit who became Australia's longest-serving prime minister:

> This spire has been erected by the people of Jeparit and district, to honour Sir Robert Menzies. This spire symbolises the rise to world recognition of a boy who was born in Jeparit and who rose by his own efforts to become Australia's Prime Minister and a statesman recognised and honoured throughout the world.

CHAPTER 2

Family

TO Robert Menzies, the family and their home embodied 'the real life' of the nation. 'The home is the foundation of sanity and sobriety; it is the indispensable condition of continuity; its health determines the health of the society as a whole,' he said. In Menzies' broadcast about 'the forgotten people' in May 1942, he explained that the walls, windows, and heating of even a great house did not necessarily make a home. 'My home is where my wife and children are,' he said. 'The instinct to be with them is the great instinct of civilised man; the instinct to give them a chance in life — to make them not leaners but lifters — is a noble instinct.'[1] This is an insight into Menzies' conception of family, home, and community — all three were inexorably linked. It was at home with his family where he absorbed values that informed and sustained his approach to public life.

Menzies' parents, James and Kate, had different temperaments and outlooks on life. James was stern, earnest, and pious. Kate was also hard-working and industrious, but more outwardly loving and kind, and had a great sense of humour. James and Kate seemed to complement each other. They both had ambitions for their children, encouraging their schooling and wider learning with books, discussions, and community involvement. Robert admired his older brothers, Les and Frank, but was closer to his sister, Belle. Sydney was born more than a decade after Robert. The two people who had the most formative influence on young Robert were his mother, Kate, and her brother, Sydney, his uncle.[2]

The Menzies family, who hailed from Scotland, were rural tenant farmers, known as crofters. James's father, Robert, was born on 23 May 1831 at Greenock East, Renfrewshire; his mother, Elizabeth Menzies (née Band), was born on 23 November 1834 in Dairsie, Fife. Robert migrated to Australia from Dumfries in 1855, hoping to make his fortune on the goldfields. He married Elizabeth in Collingwood, Victoria, on 11 November that year. Robert opened a small business that sold machinery to miners, and, with Elizabeth, had ten children. James was the fourth, born in Ballarat on 9 August 1862. When James was aged 16, his father died after a short illness, leaving the family in dire financial circumstances. James had won a scholarship to study art overseas, but this plan had to be abandoned to support the family.

Kate Sampson was born on 6 November 1865 in Creswick, Victoria. She was one of nine children born to John Sampson and Mary Jane Sampson (née Organ), who both came from Cornwall in England. John was born on 2 March 1834 at Gulval; Mary was born on 1 September 1831 at Penzance. Mary died when Kate was 12. John, who remarried, was a dedicated unionist and a founding member of the Miners' Association with the legendary W.G. Spence in 1872. Sampson had led a miners' strike in support of higher wages in Creswick, which gained considerable notoriety. Sampson was the first president, and Spence was the secretary, of the Miners' Association — the forerunner to the Australian Workers' Union. Sampson's union activities later got him sacked and banned from working in the mines.

After his father's death, James Menzies secured an apprenticeship as a coach-painter — creating decorative art on horse-drawn vehicles and locomotives — with Phoenix Foundry, located in Ballarat. He later established his own coach-painting business. After the family moved to Jeparit in late 1893, he took over the general store and also acted as a selling agent for H.V. McKay and Wilson & Bolton. McKay had invented the stripper harvester, which transformed wheat harvesting. James painted and decorated the first one produced, and gave it its famous name — the Sunshine Harvester.[3]

James dedicated himself to Jeparit's community life with boundless energy. He served as a Dimboola shire councillor (1898–1912), and was president for two terms (1901–1902 and 1911–1912). He was the first signatory on a petition to the Victorian governor to formally proclaim Jeparit as a township in 1902. He was elected to the seat of Lowan in the Victorian Legislative Assembly in 1911 and held it until 1920, when he was defeated by a Country Party candidate. He was a member of the Commonwealth Liberal Party, formed by Alfred Deakin and Joseph Cook, and then of the Nationalist Party. James was also a lay preacher at the Jeparit Methodist Church. He returned to Jeparit to lay the foundation stone for the new Methodist church in August 1925.

James Menzies was of medium height and solid build, with a distinguished full moustache and hair that had turned silver-grey by middle age. Menzies described his father in an interview with journalist Allan Dawes, who was writing his biography, in the early 1950s:

> My father was a very intense man. He was a very devoutly religious man ... he possessed by and large no real humour. Life was too serious for that and certainly [he had] no verbal dexterity or wit. But he had great character, he was enormously generous and devoted. He would work himself almost to death for anybody else or to redress an injustice ... he was the most dynamic and the most public-spirited and the most politically informed man.[4]

The relationship between James and Robert, as father and son, was often difficult. James suffered from depression, was both 'dogmatic and intolerant', and prone to losing his temper. Robert described his father as having a 'nervous tension' that sometimes made family life difficult. 'We were not a little frightened of him, and found our regular refuge in the embracing arms of our mother who afforded us the comfort of her own understanding, balance, and exquisite humour,' he recalled.[5] James was often emotional in public, particularly when giving impassioned and earnest speeches, either as a politician or a preacher, which sometimes embarrassed his son. Robert decided that he would eschew showing emotion in public, and instead favoured 'cold' and 'logical' expression in his speeches.[6]

The final two decades of James Menzies' life, after moving to Melbourne, were spent as a statistical officer and tariff adviser for BHP, from 1926 to 1945. Lenox Hewitt, who would later serve as deputy secretary in Treasury

(1962–66) during the Menzies era, met James Menzies while working as a trainee at BHP in the mid-1930s. The two men became close friends. 'We used to eat our luncheon sandwiches together and talked throughout,' Hewitt told me in an interview. They often discussed policy issues and political matters, and their respective families. Robert Menzies had been prime minister by the time Hewitt left BHP to work in the public service. Hewitt recalled there being a strained relationship between James and Robert. 'My impression was that Menzies senior had little to do with his son, of whom he was immensely proud,' he said.[7]

In James Menzies' final years, while continuing to work at BHP, he also spent time as president of the Menzies Home for Boys in Frankston. He was an important and respected member of the local community, as he had been in Jeparit. James died, aged 83, on 1 November 1945 at home, 65 Wellington Street, Kew, Victoria.[8]

Robert's relationship with his mother, Kate, was more loving and affectionate. Kate's calming personality balanced James's frequent insensitivity, irritability, and eruptions of temper. Kate was far less judgemental, and often displayed a wicked wit. She had a 'calm' and 'beautiful' face, her son recalled. Life was not easy for her, nor for any married woman with children in a small country town, but she never complained. 'She was always the first port of call for those who needed comfort,' her son recalled.[9] Menzies further described her temperament to Dawes:

> She was a woman with the most serene religious faith, but she had a perfectly divine sense of humour ... she had an exquisite capacity to look back on some incident that had been sheer misery to her when it happened and to make it most absurdly funny in retrospect. She had a mind of beautiful simplicity and clearness. She was calm, she was tactful, she was judicial. She had a wonderful faculty for seeing the other side.[10]

James and Kate had met in Ballarat, and married on Christmas Day 1889. They could not have been more different, yet Robert said they balanced each other as parents. 'Where he was explosively intolerant, she was calm, human and understanding and in the end, with patience, would secure a victory for sweet reasonableness,' Robert recalled.[11] Kate died, aged 80, on 30 June 1946, also at home in Kew.[12]

In August 1972, journalist Don Whitington's *Twelfth Man?* was published.[13] He claimed that Robert Menzies' character was 'cultivated by matriarchal pressures that never relaxed through his formative years'. In other words, Whitington argued that Kate Menzies' overbearing presence and ambition for her son were critical to his entering politics and aspiring to be prime minister. The book angered the Menzies family, as it misunderstood Kate's temperament and influence on her son Robert.

Frank Menzies, the second son of Kate and James, was the first to respond after Whitington's book was serialised in *The Age*. 'Nothing could be further from the truth,' he wrote to the newspaper. 'Our home was certainly not a matriarchal institution. Anyone who knew my father would know that. Mother regarded and treated her five children as equally dear to her. Of course, we all shared the family pride in Bob's academic achievements. Far from coveting political greatness for him, my mother deplored his entry into and his experiences in public life.'[14]

Next to respond was Belle, daughter to James and Kate, in an interview with John Hamilton in *The Herald*. 'This man Whitington has painted a ridiculous picture,' she said. 'My parents were a marvellous couple. My father James was emotional and artistic. He should have been an artist. My mother Kate was a very calm, balanced person. When Bob became prime minister for the first time, people would ask her, "How's your son?" She would reply: "Which son? I have four." There was no favouritism. She shared her love equally among us.'[15]

The Menzies family prized hard work, self-discipline, integrity, private morality, and public duty. 'My grandparents were morally absolute,' Heather Henderson, Robert Menzies' daughter, told me in an interview for this book. 'They made sure they went to the Methodist Church every weekend, but morality was all they lived — honesty, decency, all of those things — and my father's father had a great feeling of civic responsibility.' If Robert stepped out of line, he would be harshly punished. 'Grandpa beat with a strap, and my father said he would be burning so much on his bottom that he had to sit on a cold tin trunk to recover.'[16]

James Menzies was a staunch Presbyterian in Ballarat, but became a Methodist in Jeparit. (There was no Presbyterian church in Jeparit.) James seemed to blend the strict Calvinism of Presbyterianism with the more emotional temperament fostered by Methodist teachings.[17] He was a lay preacher, and the Menzies children read passages of the Bible aloud every day at home. As for his own faith, Menzies described himself as a 'simple Presbyterian'.[18] Later, when Robert was in state politics, he found the family's firm adherence to Presbyterian values to be too narrow-minded, intolerant, and prejudiced. These are strong words. But in a previously unpublished interview, Menzies recalled attending the opening of a Catholic school in his state electorate, which was also attended by Archbishop Daniel Mannix:

> I was born in a household of people whose memories I revere but they were the most bigoted people in the world, and for Robert to go and be seen on the same platform as that man Mannix was an unthinkable offence. My father was violently upset, my mother was, my uncles were, they had a family gathering about it and I was practically hauled up and I remember saying: 'Well, I understand what you feel but you are overlooking one thing. I am the Member for East Yarra — Presbyterians, Anglicans, Roman Catholics, Brahmins for all I know. There may be a few Muslim men in this electorate for all I know. Certainly a few Jews in this electorate. I think you have forgotten I am the Member for the lot — and consequently any of them who are of repute and respectable who want me to do something, I will do it if I can.'[19]

Menzies made it clear he was not 'the Member for the Presbyterians'. The family accepted his point of view, even if they were not entirely happy with it. This incident had a marked impact. Menzies recalled that it 'did me a lot of good', because he felt in his youth that he had been 'indoctrinated with a sectarian feeling' that was manifestly wrong in a free, pluralistic society. 'From that time on, I just hated all forms of sectarianism and so it did me good.'[20] This is a significant insight into Menzies' thinking, and it helps to explain his later decision to provide funding for non-government schools in 1963. In his long public life, Menzies never tolerated religious bigotry or prejudice.

THE first son born to James and Kate was James Leslie ('Les') Menzies in November 1890. Les served in the First World War, and later became a highly regarded public servant and was posted to New York and Wellington. Frank Gladstone Menzies, named after British prime minister William Gladstone, was born in Ballarat in January 1892. He, too, served in the First World War. Frank became a distinguished lawyer, and was crown solicitor in Victoria from 1926 to 1954. James and Kate were blessed with a daughter, Isabel Alice, known as Belle, born in May 1893. Sydney ('Syd') Keith Menzies was born in July 1905, more than a decade after Robert. Syd had a successful career as a managing director of a manufacturing company.

As an older brother, Frank took a keen interest in Robert. He dispensed advice and encouragement, and later managed Robert's financial affairs. Robert looked upon Frank as more than just a brother: he was a protector, adviser, and friend. 'I feel I'm in a position to tell Bob what he needs to know,' Frank said to his niece, Heather Henderson. As a boy, Frank advised Bob to control his 'bad temper'. As a man, Frank cautioned him about how he dealt with his colleagues. For example, Frank told Bob not to refer to people by their surnames — it may have been customary at the Bar, but in parliament it only fostered a perception that he was arrogant. Although advice such as this was well-meant, it could irritate him. 'I do wish Frank wouldn't lecture me,' Robert later said.[21]

The closest of Robert's sibling relationships was with Belle. She was very attractive and warm-hearted, and had a bubbly personality. 'There was a tremendous bond between them,' Henderson said. 'They were very close, had the same sense of humour, and could talk about anything. Aunty Belle was so very much like my father. As children they were very close in age, and they did a lot of things together.' In 1916, Belle eloped with George Green, and married him before he left to go abroad with the Australian Imperial Force during the First World War. This, according to James Menzies, shamed the family, and he told his daughter to 'never darken my doorstep again'. It was several years before anybody in the family saw her. Robert was the first to reach out to her. 'I can remember Belle saying one day she was broke and looking in the window of the butcher's shop thinking what she would have for dinner,' Henderson said. 'Dad appeared beside her and handed some money over.'[22]

The years after the war were grim for Belle and George. They had three children but struggled to make a living, especially after George's stock-

and-station agency folded in 1929. In subsequent years, with the help of Sidney Myer, she ran a service bureau in the Myer Emporium and worked for *The Argus* newspaper. In 1931, George became trustee secretary for Melbourne's Exhibition Building. After George's death in 1938, Belle succeeded him in this role. She excelled at organising concerts, balls, and exhibitions, and became a notable member of Melbourne society.[23]

For more than 30 years, some of the letters that Robert and Belle wrote to one another have remained sealed among the Menzies papers at the National Library of Australia. Accessed for this book, they reveal that Menzies provided a generous weekly allowance to his sister. By May 1965, it had increased to £7 a week or £364 a year — almost $10,000 in today's value. 'I really hope that this will be enough as I hate the idea of you running short of the proper comforts of life,' he wrote. 'I don't want you to feel in some way indebted to me. I assure you that the debt is on the other side; you have given me a great deal of happiness and that is more important than money.'[24] Pattie did not like Robert sending his sister money. 'He was very generous,' Henderson said. 'This infuriated my mother.'[25]

CHAPTER 3

Student

IN November 1951, nearly two years into his second prime ministership, Robert Menzies returned to Jeparit and visited the school where he had first enrolled, aged four and a half. '2988, the same old number,' Menzies said, noting the school's state designation as he stepped inside. The school register was brought out. 'Robert Gordon Menzies, No. 233, enrolled June 4, 1898,' it read.[1]

Menzies sat at a wooden desk in the rear of the classroom. He raised his hand, pretending to answer a question asked by the teacher. He met Tom Livingstone, who had taught him half a century earlier. His father, John 'Daddy' Livingstone, had been the head teacher at the school. Menzies would later recall that flies always buzzed around the classroom. The headmaster would remain composed if one happened to land on his bald head. Instantly, he would snatch it with his fingers, crush it, and then let it drop to the floor. Classes continued uninterrupted as the dead flies collected around him.[2]

Most of the students walked several miles to school each day, which was initially located within the Mechanics' Institute near the Menzies store on Roy Street. It was later moved to a one-room imported timber structure on a sandy rise in Jeparit, a five-minute walk from the centre of town. Visiting more than half a century later brought back many fond memories for the prime minister. About 30 to 40 students attended the school. There was a strict learning routine, and discipline was meted out on a regular basis for any errant student. Livingstone was remembered for being a tough head teacher who had little hesitation in using the cane or a strap to belt his students for bad behaviour.

For the first three years of his life, Robert had not uttered a single word. (He later claimed that he didn't want to speak up in case he made a mistake.[3]) But by the time he enrolled in school, he was already a talkative, convivial, and self-assured young boy who made a lasting impression. Robert excelled at Jeparit. 'I was the bright boy, so to speak, at the top of the school and nothing more to be learned,' he recalled later in life.[4]

JAMES and Kate Menzies never had much of a formal education. Robert recalled that his father had gone to school in Ballarat until age 14 or 15; his mother had been schooled in Creswick until she was nine or ten years old. 'Yet,' Menzies recalled, 'each of them spoke very well, had a good vocabulary, had a capacity for thought, had an interest in intellectual problems.'[5] At home, they encouraged reading, writing, and discussion. Young Robert recalled that both his parents were avid readers of books, newspapers, and periodicals. The children would often take turns in reading aloud to the family in the evening. Jerome K. Jerome's *Idle Thoughts of an Idle Fellow* (1886), *Three Men in a Boat* (1899), and *Tommy and Co* (1900) were family favourites.[6]

As Robert had shown promise as a student, James and Kate wanted to make sure he made the most of his talents. In 1905, Robert, aged 11, was sent to Ballarat, and enrolled in the Humffray Street State School No. 34 the following year. His sister, Belle, went too. They lived with their widowed paternal grandmother, the dour and devout Elizabeth Menzies, in her small wooden cottage on the western side of town. Three years earlier, brothers Les and Frank had moved to Ballarat and enrolled in the government-run school.

Each day, Robert would walk a mile from his grandmother's house on Dana Street, opposite the insane asylum, to school. Classes finished by 4.30 pm. After dinner at his grandmother's house, Robert devoted himself to study. 'Every evening, regular as clockwork, at twenty past six, I sat down to my homework, and I worked solidly every evening until twenty minutes past midnight,' he recalled. 'I did six hours prep every night, except Sundays, of that first year.'[7] His grandmother, while no intellectual, encouraged Robert. 'Now, Robert,' she would say after dinner had finished, 'get to your book!'[8] Heather Henderson remembers her father referring to his grandmother as 'a mean old woman'.[9]

Ballarat was a world away from Jeparit. This bustling city was lively and energetic. There were many people, tall buildings, trains arriving and leaving, cars zooming along the streets, and lampposts that kept the city illuminated after dark. It was eye-opening for a boy from a small country town. He explored it to the fullest, walking and riding a bicycle around the city. He would use his pocket money to buy boiled lollies from the shops on Sturt Street. There were only a handful of books in his grandmother's house — the Bible, a Presbyterian hymn book, *Pilgrim's Progress* (1678), and *Ingoldsby Legends* (1840) — so young Robert would often borrow books from friends and relatives. He would read them late at night, after his studies, in bed by candlelight.

While living in Ballarat, Bob and Belle would travel east across town to visit their maternal grandfather, John Sampson, the former union activist. Young Robert, in his pre-teen years, would sit with his grandfather and read aloud articles from *The Worker*, published by the Australian Workers' Union. They would then debate the merits of the article, with Robert often taking a contrary view to his grandfather.

At the end of his first year at the Humffray Street State School, aged almost 12, Robert sat the Victorian examination to secure one of 40 state school scholarships offered that year by the state government. The day before the examination, Robert visited a relative. There, he overindulged on gooseberries. 'The result was that when I went into the examination the gooseberries took their toll [on] me and I had to rush out to the loo,' he recalled. 'I managed to get in the meritorious list but that settled me of any chance of getting a scholarship because I missed half the exam.'[10]

After two years at Humffray, Robert, now almost 13, again sat the annual state scholarship examination. This time, he performed brilliantly, setting a state record and placing first. He won a scholarship to attend Grenville College, a private school in Ballarat, commencing in 1908. There were about 35 boys studying at Grenville. There, Robert joined brother Frank, who had earlier won a half-scholarship. Robert worked hard at Grenville, and again recalled studying until after midnight every night other than Sundays. At the end of Robert's first year at Grenville, he passed the Junior Public Examination with stellar results.

While Robert focused on his studies at Grenville, he also met new friends, and enjoyed playing cricket and Australian Rules football, as he had in Jeparit. The team of boys from Grenville did well at cricket, but was hopeless at football. Its nemesis was St Patrick's College, a much larger school, which would stop at almost nothing to secure victory on the field. Robert played in the team with his brother Frank. There was one match that lived on in memory when Grenville was clobbered and only managed to score a single goal, kicked by Robert.

This was a golden era of public speaking, when orators and aspiring orators would stand on soapboxes on street corners or in parks and try to move crowds with the power of their words. At the age of 14, Robert became quite clever at mimicking the Reverend Judkins, 'a mob orator,' who railed against the evils of alcohol. A talent for mimicry, which would continue for the rest of his life, was born. Robert attracted small crowds to see him impersonate the 'extravagant and melodramatic' speaking style, which earned him the nickname 'Judkins' or 'Juddy'.[11]

But not all was going well for Robert. At the end of his second year, he failed the Senior Public Examination. The headmaster, Arthur Buley, had been so impressed with Robert's performance the year before that he overloaded him with more difficult subjects in the second year. Robert worked hard, but it was not enough. 'I didn't get the reward of my labours because I addled my mind,' Menzies recalled later. 'I became so completely confused in my mind that at the end of the year, I didn't pass in a single subject.' It was humiliating. His father, James Menzies, was not impressed. 'The trouble with you, Robert, is that you are a loafer,' he was told.[12]

Young Robert was so despondent that he considered ending his life. When the family gathered at Sandringham at Christmas, he thought about throwing himself off the cliffs. 'This was a blow,' he recalled.[13] Heather Henderson remembers her father telling this sad story. 'It was all too much,' he later told her.[14] However, Robert sat the Senior Public Examination a second time, after taking on a more manageable subject load, and won a scholarship to one of Melbourne's prestigious colleges. He had passed all of his subjects with high marks. Hard work, persistence, and determination had paid off.

Pattie Menzies told Ronald Seth, her husband's biographer, that there is an attribute often found in successful men which is not always appreciated: a commitment to learning instilled at an early age can pay a dividend later. Robert, she said, was always 'a student' with an unquenchable thirst for knowledge and understanding. 'He still works hard as ever he did at gathering knowledge,' she said. 'Success and fame will never come to any man, no matter how clever he is, unless he lays the foundations of hard work as a boy.'[15]

In 1910, at the age of 15, Robert enrolled at Wesley College, a school run by the Wesleyan Methodist Church, in Melbourne. His father had wanted Robert to enrol at Scotch College, but Robert chose Wesley because he knew several boys who were enrolled there. He had not thought highly of the teachers at Jeparit, Humffray, or Grenville. But Wesley's teachers — Harold Stewart (Latin and History) and Frank Shann (English) — left a strong impression. The headmaster, L.A. 'Dickey' Adamson, apparently made no mark on him at all.

At Wesley, he struggled in Mathematics and Science — not his favourite subjects — and did not secure a scholarship to university at the end of his first or second year. 'I'm afraid I wasn't a very brilliant success,' he recalled. 'I just crawled through and didn't get a scholarship, didn't get within cooee of one, and the same thing the second year.'[16] However, he was able to continue on his state school scholarship. Robert focused on his academic studies, and, though he enjoyed watching cricket and football, still showed no particular prowess on the sporting field.

Percy Joske, a contemporary of Menzies at Wesley from 1910 to 1912, remembered that the bright boy from Jeparit and Ballarat did not 'shine' in his first two years. Robert did well in History and English, but, as Menzies himself said, struggled especially in Mathematics, putting at risk his chances of winning a scholarship to university. So he gave up Mathematics and focused on English, French, Latin, and History, and secured a state scholarship (known as an exhibition) at the end of his third year at Wesley.[17] In his final year, in 1912, he was now destined for university.

In these years at Wesley, Robert was remembered as a proud student, brimming with self-confidence and often arrogant. 'He was a gangling type of boy, growing rapidly, with intense energy and tremendous self-assurance, who believed in getting around and making himself known to everybody,' Joske recalled. Within a week of arriving at the school, Menzies had introduced himself to most of the teachers and the 500 or so boys. Menzies had 'charm and good looks' in spades, but he was also 'forceful and determined', with a 'cutting tongue' that could be off-putting. Anyone who disagreed with him was disparaged as 'a dag', which led to Menzies earning the moniker 'Dag Menzies'.[18]

In 1913, Robert began studying for a Bachelor of Laws at the University of Melbourne. This was a time when his personality, character, and values began to fully take shape. He immersed himself in his studies and engaged in many aspects of student life. He was well known on campus. He was tall, at over six feet, handsome, and always well groomed and confident. During these years, he continued to live at home with his parents in Rockley Road, South Yarra. (In the preceding years, the Menzies family occupied several homes in East Melbourne, Camberwell, and South Yarra; in 1917, the family moved again, to a new home in Wellington Street, Kew.[19])

In the first year of what was to be a four-year degree in law, Robert studied English, History of the British Empire, Ancient History, Deductive Logic and Elementary Psychology, and Latin. He was in his element. After the first two years, which were devoted to arts subjects, and also included Political Economy, Robert passed with first-class honours. But he was not successful in gaining an exhibition or scholarship in those first two years. In his third and fourth years, he continued studying law — in particular, property, contracts, and the constitution. In his final examinations, Robert passed his law subjects with first-class honours.

In 1916, Robert was elected president of the Students' Representative Council, president of the Law Students' Society, and president of the Students' Christian Union. He also became editor of the *Melbourne University Magazine*, published three times a year, for which he also contributed articles and wrote verse. He revealed himself to be a strong defender of freedom of speech, an advocate of private enterprise, and a supporter of the British Empire. He enjoyed the writings of G.K. Chesterton, Anthony Trollope, and William Shakespeare, and later Charles Dickens. He also found time to help establish a Historical Society at the university, which hosted roundtable discussions and organised lectures and social events.

While at university, Robert was briefly engaged to be married to Phyllis Lewis. One of her brothers, Owen Lewis, had been at Wesley College at the same time as Robert. Phyllis was an accomplished violinist. They were both academically brilliant, and were involved in a range of campus activities together. Little is known about the short-lived engagement, and Robert never spoke about it. (It is only very briefly mentioned in Allan Martin's biography.[20])

Robert graduated with first-class honours in law in 1916. He went on to complete a Master of Laws, finishing in 1918. He left university having claimed many of the institution's most impressive awards, including the Dwight Prize in British History and Constitutional History (1914); the Jessie Leggatt Scholarship in Roman Law and the John Madden Exhibition in Jurisprudence (1915); the Bowen Essay Prize (1916); and the Supreme Court Judges' Prize (1917).

In 1919, Robert was employed as a sessional academic in the Law School. After university, he began a year working as an articled clerk — essentially an apprenticeship — with a solicitor at a small practice in Melbourne. There was so little to do, remembered Joske, that he spent most of his time visiting other offices and talking to friends. He had so much free time that he was described as an 'articled lark'.[21]

THE First World War broke out in July 1914. Menzies supported Australia sending troops to fight abroad, and also backed conscription for overseas service. He joined the Melbourne University Rifles — a citizens' militia — as part of his compulsory military-training duty, serving four years from 1915 to 1919, and attained the rank of lieutenant. With his two older brothers, Les and Frank, having enlisted in the Australian Imperial Force and being sent abroad, the family decided not to send another son. Syd, aged ten, was still at school. The condition of James Menzies, who was physically unwell and emotionally unstable, was an important factor in deciding to keep one of the older sons at home.

Another reason was Belle's elopement with George Green. When she climbed out of her bedroom window and was married the next day, without her parents' blessing, it nearly killed her father. It was felt that Robert, therefore, needed to stay to help the family. The decision not to go to war was decided at a family conference. James would not allow his daughter to bring Green home to meet the family. She was excommunicated. Menzies recalled in a previously unpublished interview that it was a 'wretched' situation that added to an already difficult decision about which sons would go to war:

> The war broke out and then in due course there was a discussion in the family. My two brothers and myself ... had a talk and it was decided that somebody would have to remain here because of the old man's state — he used to get heart attacks and things like this ... — there ought to be somebody at home to look after the family and that two ought to go, so two went. They picked themselves and they said I was to stay and so I did stay, pretty reluctantly, as you might imagine.[22]

It had been a family decision involving both parents, James and Kate, and the three sons. Menzies, who was the most academically promising of all the boys, devoted himself to study. 'I sweated my blood out at the university,' he recalled. But the decision gnawed at him, and he was soon contemplating whether he should enlist. 'Just as I was getting to the point where I thought, "Well, I can't take this any longer, I must go," my sister crawled out of the window one night and eloped with the fellow':

> The effect on my father was such that, honestly, I was called in to say goodbye to him. He was lying in bed gasping and groaning ... I knew how devoted he was to her and how this would just tear his insides out because she disappeared literally into the outer darkness and was never seen by the family ... the old man was in a bad state and really for some time it looked as if he might peg out at any moment.[23]

The decision not to enlist, and the subsequent criticism throughout his parliamentary career that he was a coward, had a significant impact upon Menzies that may not have been fully appreciated before, largely because Menzies rarely discussed it. This is understandable given the traumatic series of events that engulfed the family: two sons sent abroad to fight in a war, a daughter eloping and being banished from the family, a father so sick and grief-stricken that he nearly died, and young Robert left to look after the family while juggling his studies.

Menzies said he was deeply hurt by the attacks he faced, re-considered his decision not to enlist towards the end of the war, and that it was the decisive event that propelled him into politics. He said that Frank had written to him saying 'you might be released from your promise' and could enlist — but the letter never arrived. Frank confirmed to Frances McNicoll that he sent a letter from France. 'I wrote a letter to my parents saying that I thought he ought to enlist and take a position somewhere without going into the infantry and ... at least he would have taken part,' he said. Frank worried about the decision to keep Robert at home. 'I felt that if he did not go, [as] so many fellows had gone, that it would be used against him.'[24]

After the war, Menzies decided he would redeem his public standing by going into politics. He felt a need to serve his country in another way. He went into politics not to become premier or prime minister, but to erase the perceived stain on his family name. This was the primary motivating force. He thought a few terms in parliament would be a 'tour of duty' of another kind, a service to the nation, that would re-establish his public standing. Then, perhaps, he could return to the law:

Having been the one in the family not able as I believed to go to war, [I] had a strong feeling that I ought to do some public service of some kind and that was the dominating reason why I went into parliament. Thinking in my innocence that I would be able to come in and do a tour of duty for seven or eight years and then give it away.[25]

Pattie Menzies recognised this in an interview with Gerard Henderson. 'I think he wanted to serve,' she said. 'You've got to remember that he was not a returned soldier ... He was hurt that he hadn't been able to do it, and people, not knowing the circumstances, criticised him so severely. I think that was one reason why he wanted to serve in some way in politics.'[26] But Menzies' interview with McNicoll, revealed here, seems to be the only time he ever confirmed it so directly in his own words. Moreover, it was not *one* reason, but *the* reason he went into politics.

Menzies wrote about his decision not to enlist at the time in the *Melbourne University Magazine*. 'I do not think I am either sublimely ignorant, sublimely conceited or sublimely selfish when I said that the path of duty does not always lead to the recruiting depot — duty has to many in this respect been a hard taskmaster.'[27] The AIF was constituted of volunteers. In 1916, faced with declining recruits, Prime Minister Billy Hughes proposed introducing conscription. The conscription debate divided Australians and eventually led to a split in the Labor government. Menzies, while declining to volunteer, supported Hughes on conscription.

But not enlisting in the war became a political problem when Menzies first stood for state parliament in 1928, and it dogged him for the rest of his career. Menzies was often criticised, by his opponents and even by some on his own side of politics, for not having signed up to fight abroad. 'The Right Honourable gentleman had a brilliant military career cut short by war,' firebrand Labor MP Eddie Ward often famously said. The most notorious attack on Menzies' non-war record came from Earle Page in April 1939, which is discussed in a later chapter.

In the twilight of his life, Menzies exposed his true feelings about his lack of war service, which continued to evoke difficult memories. 'This had a very searing effect on my mind,' he said. 'I felt all the time that I just had to do something to justify my existence and that is why … I decided that I ought to go into Parliament … but one way or another, I have been very vulnerable on this matter.' It was to have another important effect on Menzies. It would help explain, he later acknowledged, why he went to England as prime minister during the Second World War and stayed for so long. He felt he had to show that he was 'not yellow'.[28] But that decision contributed to him losing the prime ministership in August 1941.

CHAPTER 4

Barrister-at-Law

ROBERT Menzies was admitted to the Victorian Bar in May 1918. He took rooms at Selborne Chambers in Melbourne, and was accepted to read with barrister Owen Dixon, who later became chief justice of the High Court of Australia. (Menzies would retain his room in Selborne Chambers for the rest of his life, renting it to young up-and-coming lawyers.) To become Dixon's pupil gave him a considerable leg-up in the competitive profession. During the next few years, Menzies developed a particular interest in constitutional and industrial law, and worked busily to establish his own legal practice, taking briefs for cases and providing opinions on request. He appeared as Dixon's junior in dozens of cases before the Supreme Court of Victoria and the High Court before Dixon was appointed to the bench of the High Court in February 1929. Menzies also appeared regularly on his own to argue cases. He explained:

> It is the practice of a newly called barrister to 'read' in the chambers of some leading junior ... He reads the briefs that come in; he is encouraged to discuss them with his chief. He is, of course, free to accept briefs of his own, and if he is lucky, as I was, gets a few. But his great advantage is that he sees a busy junior at work and at close quarters. The law comes alive for him. He begins to know how little he knows and what a world of difference there is between academic learning and the same learning when applied to the tangled facts of life.[1]

In 1919, Menzies appeared before the High Court for the first time in the case of *Troy v. Wrigglesworth*. The brief had come to him after the senior counsel became unwell and was unable to run the case. It concerned an army driver who had been caught speeding but pleaded he was transporting a patient to hospital. Menzies argued that the case should have been heard by a Police Magistrate's Court rather than a summary court composed of two justices of the peace. Menzies appealed the case to the full High Court. A majority of judges, including Edmund Barton, agreed, and a retrial was ordered. Menzies had impressed the judges with his first appearance. 'I congratulate you on the great ability with which you have conducted your case,' said Justice Gavan Duffy. There was another person who was surprised — James Menzies. 'It seems that I've underestimated Bob,' he told Kate.[2]

In 1920, aged 25, Menzies cemented his name as a lawyer when he argued the Engineers' Case — *The Amalgamated Society of Engineers v. Adelaide Steamship Co. Ltd* — before the High Court. The landmark case considered whether the Commonwealth's conciliation and arbitration powers could be applied to members of the Amalgamated Society of Engineers, who worked for state-owned enterprises. The union wanted employees working in a West Australian government-run sawmill and machine shop to come under a federal industrial award. Menzies, as a junior counsel, acted alone in the case representing the union.

The case ran for a week. Menzies was up against an all-star line-up of prominent counsel from various states, including John Latham and H.V. 'Doc' Evatt, briefed to support Western Australia against the Engineers. Menzies convinced a majority of judges that the scope of federal powers could be applied to the states. This judgement represented a departure from earlier court rulings and had far-reaching consequences. 'No man in the whole history of the High Court ever had a greater chance to win a colossal success and he seized the opportunity,' wrote Percy Joske.[3]

Eminent constitutional scholar Geoffrey Sawer analysed how Menzies approached constitutional law, differing from his mentor Dixon and his rival Evatt:

> From the Engineers' Case of 1920, which remade a good deal of Australian constitutional history, down through the Oil Cases and

the James Cases, Menzies left his mark on constitutional doctrine. He lacked the historical learning of Dixon, but made up for it by a much better sense of contemporary social reality. He lacked the passion for justice of Evatt, but made up for it by a fluency and wit which Evatt lacked.[4]

In retirement, Menzies reflected on his great rivalry with Evatt, which would last more than 40 years in the law and politics. 'He was in fact the worst advocate I ever appeared against,' Menzies said. 'I am not meaning to say that he was without grey matter, he was not; or that he was without legal knowledge, he was not by any means without legal knowledge. But as an advocate he did not leave the barrier.' Menzies thought Evatt often rambled and struggled to get to the point in his courtroom presentations.

In December 1930, the Labor government appointed Evatt to the High Court. Prime Minister James Scullin, who was away in London at the time, opposed the decision, but felt powerless to override the caucus. Menzies privately described the appointment of Evatt as 'an awful piece of jobbery'. But, at least outwardly, Menzies was magnanimous, and took Evatt to lunch in Melbourne to congratulate him. After lunch, as they were about to go their separate ways, Evatt told Menzies that his wife, Mary Alice, had one regret. 'She said to me: "I wish you could have won a case against Mr Menzies before you were appointed,"' Evatt said. 'But Bert, this is nonsense,' Menzies replied. 'I would assume that it is about 50–50 because the advocate does not make the case, the case makes the advocate's argument, and you must be on the right side half of the time.' But Evatt was not convinced. 'Oh no, it's true,' he replied. Menzies thought this was 'pathetic', and could not believe it was true, but decided to check his fee book. He was astonished to find that Evatt was correct. 'This thing had rankled in his mind,' Menzies recalled.[5]

FLUSH with his success in the Engineers' Case, Robert Menzies married Pattie Maie Leckie on 27 September 1920 at the Kew Presbyterian Church in Melbourne. The officiating clergyman, Reverend Ringland Anderson, told the congregation that 'the bridegroom of today will one day be prime minister'.[6] Bob and Pattie first met in 1910, and were reacquainted at a party in 1919. 'You're Pattie Leckie,' he apparently said to her. 'You used to make eyes at me in church.'[7] They talked all evening, and Robert walked Pattie home. Their courtship continued. Within a few months, they were engaged. Robert was 25, and Pattie was 21. They had much in common. Pattie was independently minded and not afraid to voice her opinions. Both of their fathers were politicians. They would be married for almost 60 years.

Pattie was born on 2 March 1899 at Alexandra, in rural Victoria. She was the eldest daughter of John William Leckie and May Beatrix Leckie (née Johnston).[8] Leckie was the son of James Leckie, born in Scotland, and Mary Leckie (née Reilly), born in Ireland. Pattie had two younger sisters, Con and Gwen. May Leckie tragically died during childbirth when Pattie was just 11 years old, in 1910. The family moved to Melbourne, where Pattie boarded at Presbyterian Ladies' College and Fintona. Her father later married journalist Hattie Martha Knight in April 1917.

After a promising Australian Rules football career, Jack Leckie took over the family farming business and general store. In 1912, he established a small printing and manufacturing business. Leckie served on the Alexandra Shire Council, including a term as president, from 1900 to 1911. He was elected to the Victorian Legislative Assembly seat of Benambra in 1913, and served a term in the House of Representatives as the Member for Indi from 1917 to 1919. Leckie later became a Victorian senator, serving from 1934 to 1947, first under the United Australia Party's banner and then the Liberal Party's. He was also a minister in the first Menzies government. He died on 25 September 1947.

Robert and Pattie moved into his flat in Wellington Street, Kew, where he had lived after university. They moved twice, to houses in Gellibrand Street and Charles Street, before settling into their longstanding home at 10 Howard Street, Kew.[9] They had three children: Kenneth Leckie Menzies (born on 14 January 1922), Robert Ian Menzies (12 October 1923), and Margery Heather Henderson (3 August 1928). (Another child, before Heather, was stillborn.) While Menzies focused on building his law practice, he also made time to spend with his family. Sundays were a day for family activities with Pattie, Ken, Ian, and Heather, such as going for picnics. Holidays were also marked out on the calendar as time to spend with the family. A holiday home at Mount Macedon was bought in 1929 and became a popular retreat.[10]

Menzies worked very long hours — usually no less than 80 in a typical week. He would be up early, work in his Melbourne chambers, often attend meetings with clients or court appearances, and keep toiling late into the evening. There was little downtime. Menzies described his years in the law, before politics, as his 'first love', and he enjoyed the heavy workload. Those who knew Menzies in these years recalled his performances at Victorian Bar dinners at venues like the Mitre Tavern, where gentle ribbing among the lawyers regularly took place. Menzies was often parodied with 'I'm only a State School boy from Jeparit but my footsteps will echo in the sands of time.' Menzies enjoyed being cut down a peg, and he often repaid in kind.[11]

He thought it was important to build a network in Melbourne's legal, business, and political circles. Menzies was, it has been said, a 'club man'. He joined the Savage Club, the West Brighton Club, and the K.K. Club. He was also a member of the Freemasons, like prime ministers Earle Page, Arthur Fadden, John McEwen, and John Gorton. Menzies did not, however, join the Melbourne Club, a bastion of the Victorian establishment. It was thought that a small number of club members held against him the decision not to serve in the First World War, and his candidacy was not pursued by his proposers. (He subsequently declined a renewed offer to put him up for membership in 1939 when he became prime minister.[12])

Allan Martin describes this period in Melbourne as one of 'ferment', when young men 'wanted to bring a new sense of public responsibility' to bear in the state, and engaged in study groups, lectures, and debates. Menzies, now earning a good income, felt a responsibility to make a contribution to public life.[13]

BOB and Pattie Menzies, as they became known, were a prominent political couple. During Robert's 40-year political career, she was almost always by his side at home and abroad. Pattie conversed easily with kings and queens, as she did with everyday Australians. She often attended

Robert's major speeches and political meetings, some of which made her uncomfortable. 'My husband can cope very well with all types of meetings, but sometimes I get a bit concerned when he tackles a hostile electorate,' she said. When she wasn't travelling with him, Pattie would listen to his speeches on radio, and read newspapers to keep up with political news. Pattie also took a keen interest in 'the social sphere' of the Liberal Party, and became president of the Australian Women's Liberal Club, which was 'a meeting place for women interested in politics'.[14]

'I think she did enjoy politics,' recalled daughter Heather Henderson. 'She was good at the social side in terms of getting along with people. She made very good speeches. She was very good at talking to people and travelled a lot around Australia. She was very interested in politics and had her views on what went on.'[15] However, there were 'pros and cons' to political life. Running the Lodge, for example, could be stressful. 'There was a lot she didn't enjoy, but a lot of it she did,' Heather said.[16] Pattie formed quick and often harsh judgements about people, and they were hard to shake. 'My mother never forgave anybody for whatever they had done wrong, but my father did immediately.'[17]

As in almost any marriage, there were tensions from time to time. Henderson was reluctant to speak too frankly about this, but she did acknowledge that her mother could be a difficult person and was not always as supportive of her father as perhaps she could have been. Allan Martin thought Pattie felt 'intellectually inferior' to Robert, and that this helped to explain her occasional prickliness.[18] Their personalities were different. Whereas Pattie was domineering and assertive, Robert tended to avoid confrontation. Pattie also resented Robert's relationship with Belle. 'They hated each other,' Henderson said. 'My mother didn't like Belle. She was jealous of her because Dad was so fond of her.'[19] Belle, who had an outgoing and lively personality, may have overshadowed Pattie. When Pattie was overseas, Belle acted as 'official hostess' for functions held at the Lodge while Robert was prime minister.[20] This would not have pleased Pattie.

PART II

Rise, Fall, and Redemption: 1926-49

CHAPTER 5

Spring Street

BY the mid-1920s, Robert Menzies was gravitating towards a career in politics. 'Politics were in my blood,' he told his biographer Ronald Seth. 'It would, I think, have been strange indeed if, with my background of public service, I had not wanted to take part in public affairs too.'[1] A step towards a career in politics came when he spoke at the launch of the 'No' campaign opposing the referendum on industrial relations being put to voters by Stanley Bruce's federal government. The proposed constitutional changes were designed to deal with growing industrial conflict, and would see the Commonwealth Arbitration Court granted the power to hear and resolve disputes.

Menzies, at the age of 31, addressed an audience of over 500 people, mostly businessmen, at the Prahran Town Hall on the evening of 16 August 1926. He was reported as saying that the power to deal with industrial matters 'resided in the states', and he did not want to see a new federal body emboldened that would also lead to increased litigation:

Many people thought industrial matters related to the fixing of hours and wages, but they went much further. The question of how far industry should be responsible for men who fell ill, the question of unemployment and how it was to be cured, and to what extent industry should insure its units against unemployment were some of the matters the people were now asked to hand over to this irresponsible, independent, and therefore undemocratic body, which federal parliament intended to create.[2]

While Menzies' argument in the Engineers' Case had resulted in expanding Commonwealth powers over the states, here Menzies advocated the right of the states to continue to determine industrial matters. He found 'no compelling reason' for industrial powers to be 'handed over' to the federal government. But as Menzies continued his argument, he encountered spirited opposition from the floor. He argued that the federal government was encouraging striking workers to take their grievances to court. Menzies said 'the master and the men', and indeed, 'the whole public', were concerned by this. This prompted an interjection:

A voice: Who are the masters and the employees but the public?
Your logic is not sound.
Mr Menzies: My logic may not be perfect, but my common sense
is right.
The same voice: It is rubbish.

Menzies — not yet expert in dispatching interjections — continued his argument against 'the litigation method of dealing with disputes'. He said 'the sovereignty of parliament' and 'the principles of democracy' would be undermined by the proposals of the Bruce government.

Menzies' uncle Sydney Sampson was there to hear the debut political speech from the young lawyer. Sydney had encouraged his nephew's interest in reading as a young boy, and pressed him to study books at the Mechanics' Institute in Jeparit. 'He had a big influence on me,' Menzies said. '[He] would walk up and down the garden path and ask me questions as if I was his equal in age and experience — knew exactly how to talk to a boy.'[3] But uncle Sydney was not impressed with the speech. 'Robert, as an address to the High Court it was perfect,' Sydney said as he drove his nephew home. But political speechmaking was different from courtroom advocacy. 'You must learn that when you are making political speeches on the platform you must repeat, and repeat, and repeat ... you can't leave an audience with more than two or three clear things in their minds ... so that in the long run they carry your message away with them.' To sum up, the speech was 'in the lowest possible class', Sydney told a chastened Robert.[4]

Menzies, while disappointed, later saw the speech as an important step on his pathway into politics. He learned from it. Polite applause and a critique from his uncle did not deter him. After all, Menzies was no stranger to political life. His father, James Menzies, had been the Member for Lowan in the Victorian Legislative Assembly from 1911 to 1920, and before that a councillor of Dimboola Shire from 1898 to 1912. His uncle, Hugh Menzies, had been a Stawell borough councillor between 1894 and 1906. And uncle Sydney Sampson had been the Member for Wimmera in the House of Representatives from 1906 to 1919. Menzies continued to speak in favour of the 'No' case around the state. He began to consider whether he could make a bigger mark on the political stage.

In late 1927, Menzies declared his intention to stand for the Legislative Council seat of East Yarra at the election to be held on 2 June 1928. He enjoyed being a lawyer, and thought he could continue practising if he were an upper house MP, where the duties were less onerous than those in the lower house. He had also at one time thought he might like to be the chief justice of Victoria. The decision to give up a full-time law career would come at a financial cost to the family, as he was earning around £10,000 a year by the late 1920s — around $800,000 in today's value. Menzies recalled telling his legal mentor, Owen Dixon, the news. 'Well, Menzies, it is probably easy to convert a good lawyer into a good politician; but re-conversion is impossible!' he said.[5]

Menzies joined the Nationalist Party, which had been formed following the merger of the Deakin–Cook Liberal Party and Billy Hughes' breakaway National Labor Party in February 1917. The Nationalists were fiercely patriotic and the custodians of the liberal-conservative tradition that had its genesis in the party fusion of 1909. Menzies was not part of the Melbourne political or business establishment. His parents had been small-business proprietors, and enjoyed a comfortable middle-class lifestyle, but were not wealthy. Menzies' schooling and university was made possible by his winning of scholarships. He worked hard, in school, at university, and as a lawyer, and resented any suggestion that he was carried along by God-given talent, or family fortune and connections.

The East Yarra province included suburbs such as Toorak, Kew, and Malvern. Menzies' opponent was George Swinburne, a local community leader and former state minister. He was also a Nationalist candidate. Journalist Desmond Robinson was on hand in late 1927 to hear Menzies address a meeting in the basement of the Hawthorn Town Hall. 'The young man's speech was not a world-beater,' Robinson recalled, 'but ... a pleasure to listen to.' Menzies was 'a young barrister whose effervescent appearances in court, forensic skill and sense of timing and style were already attracting attention in important places', Robinson remembered. When the campaign event had concluded, Menzies drove the reporter back to his Melbourne office, a gesture of kindness that he did not forget.[6]

Menzies recalled that during several of his speeches, he was asked: 'It's all right you talking about this and that, why didn't you go to the war?' Menzies decision not to enlist became a political problem. It was a smear ruthlessly deployed by Swinburne's supporters to undermine his candidature. Menzies acknowledged that he hesitated to answer these attacks clearly and strongly. It was a family decision not to send him to war, he simply replied, again and again. Menzies failed to win the election, losing by a considerable margin of 9,127 votes to 5,451. He had thought he would be beaten, and was not sure if he would stick with politics. 'I had great hesitation as to whether I should stand again,' he recalled later in life. 'I had been through the muck once and that was enough.'[7]

But Menzies could not shake the feeling that he had something to prove. The defeat seemed, in time, to embolden him. On 6 October 1928, he stood again for East Yarra, this time at a by-election. The election had been caused by the death of Swinburne, who had collapsed in parliament while preparing to speak on a Bill on 4 September 1928. The sitting had been suspended while attempts were made to resuscitate Swinburne, but he died soon after. It was only three months since his election.

There were only two candidates contesting the seat, the other being Edward Rigby, a Hawthorn solicitor, councillor, and community leader. Menzies addressed town hall meetings all over the electorate. He spoke on street corners, pressed his case through newspapers, and made direct appeals to business and community leaders for support. One of the key issues was the proposed Greater Melbourne Council, which would replace several small municipal councils, which Menzies opposed. He also advocated greater support for university education and more funding for agricultural education and research.[8]

The election was declared on 9 October outside the Hawthorn Town Hall: Menzies had easily defeated Rigby by 6,902 votes to 4,045. Menzies was jubilant. The election had been conducted in 'a most friendly spirit', he said. He promised to serve the electorate as faithfully as his predecessor, Swinburne, had done. The voter turnout had been low, perhaps only 20 per cent, and Menzies thought there might need to be 'some measure of compulsion' to vote in the future to provide for 'proper representation' in parliament. Later that night, Menzies was sworn in on the floor of the Legislative Council.[9] He was 33 years old.

It did not take Menzies long to adjust to life as a politician. Robinson recalled that he made an immediate impact in parliament 'with his quick wit, razor-sharp tongue, clear logical mind and mastery of the art of public speaking'.[10] Menzies' star rose fast. He became a minister without portfolio when the Nationalists, led by William McPherson, formed a government with the support of the Country Progressives. But when the government, under pressure from the Country Progressives, agreed to continue to provide financial support to loss-making rural enterprises in July 1929, Menzies resigned from cabinet. His friend Wilfrid (Billy) Kent Hughes also resigned as cabinet secretary. This was not an unpopular position to take for young MPs representing metropolitan seats, but it put them on the outer with many of their colleagues.

Menzies reflected with amusement on his resignation at a time when he was young, brash, and intolerant, and when 'everything was black and white':

The day came when the question arose as to whether we ought to keep maintaining one of these inland freezing works ... as a business proposition it was ludicrous to keep on throwing good money after bad. There was no hope of recovering the position and two or three of us took a strong view of it and said, 'This is nonsense, we ought not to do this.' And then old Jack Pennington piped up and said, 'Well, all I know is that if you don't do this, my seat's a goner.'[11]

Menzies then told McPherson that the decision, essentially, was whether or not the cabinet would agree to pay £150,000 to hold Pennington's seat. The cabinet, after further discussion, agreed to provide the funds to keep the freezing works open. Menzies felt he had no other option but to resign:

> I called on old McPherson after the meeting and said, 'Well, I am sorry, Mr Premier, but this is not my idea of how the government ought to run. I sympathise with the position that you are in and I have a great respect for you personally, but this is no good to me. If you don't mind, I resign.'[12]

Menzies refused to support a bank guarantee to keep a loss-making rural business afloat. For the next six months, he focused on his legal work. On 12 February 1929, he was appointed a King's Counsel, then the youngest in Australia. In December, Menzies resigned from the upper house and successfully contested the Legislative Assembly seat of Nunawading. McPherson's government soon lost the support of the Country Progressives, and was routed at the election by Labor, led by Edmond Hogan. Labor formed government.

IN the late 1920s, Menzies became more involved in the internal affairs of the Nationalist Party. He grew increasingly concerned about growing business influence on the party from outside parliament. Menzies joined with others, including Billy Kent Hughes, to form the Young Nationalists. Richard Casey and Harold Holt also joined. This new generation wanted the party to be more democratic and responsive to emerging economic and social issues. They organised debates on policy issues, and gave speeches on street corners and at town-hall meetings. The new grouping won control of the Victorian National Federation, which dominated the party, and Menzies became state president in September 1931. 'We have suffered too much from people who have no political convictions beyond a more or less genteel adherence to our side of politics,' Menzies said. 'We must have people who believe in things, and who are prepared to go out and struggle to make their beliefs universal.'[13]

The United Australia Party was formed at the federal level on 7 May 1931, replacing the Nationalist Party. It was a time of political upheaval and economic turmoil. John Latham, the then leader of the Nationalist

Party, sought to unify the non-Labor forces. Latham offered the leadership of the new party to Joe Lyons, the former Labor acting federal treasurer and premier of Tasmania, who had resigned from James Scullin's cabinet over an economic-policy dispute on 29 January 1931. Menzies joined the new UAP. He was one of several figures who urged Lyons to leave Labor and join the new party, with the prospect of becoming leader, in February 1931. The following month, March 1931, Lyons left the Labor Party.

Several New South Wales Labor MPs loyal to premier Jack Lang also split from the party and sat on the crossbenches. Lyons supported a no-confidence motion against Scullin's government in March 1931, but it survived with the precarious backing of the Lang Labor forces. The Scullin government eventually fell when a no-confidence motion was passed in the House in November 1931. Lyons, like Billy Hughes, was a Labor man who had been embraced by the non-Labor forces to lead a new party. Both were dubbed Labor 'rats'. Lyons led the UAP to an election victory on 19 December 1931 and was sworn in as prime minister on 6 January 1932. Latham became attorney-general in the new government.

On 14 May 1932, the new UAP, led by Stanley Argyle, succeeded in winning government in Victoria. At the age of 37, Menzies was appointed attorney-general and minister for railways, and served in these portfolios from 1932 to 1934. He was also appointed deputy premier. Menzies was never close to Argyle; they eyed each other warily. Menzies had been part of the wave of Young Nationalists elected to parliament who now commanded majority support in the party room. Menzies remembered being asked to join the cabinet again:

> Argyle sent for me and he said, 'Well, Mr Menzies, I am selecting a cabinet and, of course, I must have you in it as Attorney-General.' And I said, 'Yes.' He said, 'You have been very interested in railway problems, I have noticed ... would you like to be Minister of Railways as well?' And I said, 'Yes.'[14]

That was straightforward. But this was not all that Menzies wanted to discuss:

He appeared to think the conversation had ended. And I remember saying, 'Well, I would like to know about some of my fellow Young Nationalists. You know, we have got some pretty good young men in this.' Indeed, so many were there that if I had challenged him for the leadership I would have been elected at that time because of these people but I didn't want it, that would have been silly.[15]

Menzies declined to force the leadership issue, but did succeed in getting a couple of his 'fellows' into the cabinet. Nevertheless, Argyle made it clear he was calling the shots. Pennington, who had won cabinet support for the inland freezing works years earlier, also returned to cabinet. Menzies saw Argyle as having 'the highest motives' but too rigid and artless in his political thinking. Argyle thought Labor was the enemy — a notion that Menzies thought was 'drivel'. Menzies reflected: 'It is vital in politics to be friendly as far as you can be with your opponents and, at any rate, respected by them and never to be unfair.' This was 'elementary' to how Menzies approached politics.[16] Argyle objected to Menzies' friendship with Labor leader John Cain Sr, and told him to end it. Menzies refused, and told Argyle what he thought:

In the political field, in the cabinet field, I am your devoted follower, but you don't control my private life, or my private friendships. I happen to think that man is a very good man, and his wife, and we both like them very much and we had them for dinner and I will have them again. You mustn't think that you can control that aspect of my life, if you don't mind.[17]

Menzies carried out a root-and-branch review of his portfolio, and decided upon a strategy to reduce debt held by the state's railways to put it on a more efficient footing. He proposed to write off about £60 million in debt to the Treasury. He also questioned the viability of continuing to give farmers cheap rates to transport wheat in order to make it economical. This was a costly subsidy, and it contributed to the railways' debt problem. But there was opposition from some cabinet members to abolishing the subsidy, especially given competition from the road-transport industry. Menzies also proposed regulating the freight industry so that trucks would be licensed and charged fees for using the roads, while railway freight would be better organised to maximise returns. Argyle did not like Menzies' reforms, nor did Country Party MPs, but he won support to introduce them into the parliament. Menzies recalled an arduous debate in the parliament that stretched for days and days, but the legislation was eventually passed, to the surprise of some in the government.

Menzies was pleased with the reforms, which he said saved the regional railways, and reduced state debt and operating costs. 'That was my greatest achievement in state politics,' he recalled. But he also learned a valuable lesson. 'It is a great mistake to think that politics is a conflict between two sets of ideas,' Menzies said later. 'It is not. It is usually a conflict between [a] well-recognised set of ideas and just an unreasoning negative on the other side.'[18]

WITHIN a few years of entering state politics, Menzies was on a pathway to the premiership. He served as acting premier in 1934. He had made a strong impression on politicians and bureaucrats when attending the Premiers' Conference held in Melbourne that year, when he had spoken eloquently about constitutional matters. He was seen as intelligent and capable, but also as self-centred and somewhat aloof from his colleagues. He liked to refer to fellow MPs by their surnames, which came across as conceited. Menzies later explained that he had referred to Owen Dixon, his legal mentor, as 'Dixon', and in turn was referred to as 'Menzies'. But this would not work in politics. 'I saw nothing wrong in addressing everybody by their surname,' Menzies recalled of his time in state parliament. 'After a while I found that no one wanted to talk to me.' He raised it with the clerk of the House. 'Well,' the clerk said, 'if Jack Smith is a politician you can call him Mr Smith or Jack, but you can't call him Smith.' So Menzies changed how he addressed fellow MPs.[19]

Nevertheless, he was still said to have little time for people he judged to be inferior. During a debate in parliament, Menzies was told: 'The trouble with you is that you have a superiority complex.' Menzies replied: 'Considering the company I keep in the place, it is hardly surprising.'[20] When Menzies gave a speech that referred to prime minister Jim Scullin as 'a small grocer' who could not understand matters of high finance, he was chided by his father, who was in the audience. 'It is rather shameful,' James Menzies said to his son. 'Quite wrong.'[21] While at the Bar, and during his years in state politics, Menzies attracted the sobriquet of 'Ming'. This was said to have derived from the pronunciation of the Menzies clan in Scotland as 'Ming-ees'. It later transposed itself to the name of the oriental villain in the Flash Gordon comic strips and movie serials: 'Ming the Merciless'.

In these years, not yet 40, Menzies was learning the art of politics. He gained critical skills in how to campaign and deal with constituent matters. He had valuable experience as a minister. He was beginning to understand how to win debates in the party room, in cabinet, and in the parliament. While aware that his personal relations with MPs were affected by his overbearing manner, arrogance, and sense of self-importance, he did little to change his ways. Still, aligned with the Young Nationalists and playing a more prominent role in internal party affairs, Menzies was seen as having a big future in state politics. He was also increasingly being touted for a career in federal politics. He had ruled out running for several federal seats, including Ballaarat (as it was then spelt), formerly held by Alfred Deakin, and where Menzies had attended school. But the idea continued to turn over in his mind. When the federal seat of Kooyong became vacant, he faced a difficult choice. The eventual decision he made was not taken lightly nor quickly.

CHAPTER 6

Canberra

AHEAD of the September 1934 federal election, John Latham retired from parliament, citing ill-health. (He later went on to become chief justice of the High Court of Australia.) Latham's retirement created a vacancy in the Melbourne seat of Kooyong, where Robert Menzies lived with his family. Joe Lyons, who had been impressed with Menzies and counted him as among his strongest supporters, encouraged him to stand for the seat. Lyons offered to make Menzies attorney-general if he made the switch to the national parliament. 'Latham's retiring,' Lyons told Menzies. 'He can't take it any longer. You can get the nomination for Kooyong, I am sure. Will you come and be Attorney-General?'[1]

Menzies thought this was 'a dazzling offer'. But he did not immediately seize it — in fact, he declined. It was 'almost' his 'life's ambition', at that stage, he said, to be the federal attorney-general, but he worried about the impact on his family life. It would also mean giving up his law practice. Menzies went home and told Pattie about the conversation with Lyons. She encouraged him to grab the opportunity. 'In which parliament do you do the most work for the country?' Pattie asked him. 'Canberra, of course,' he replied. 'Go and ring him up and tell him you have changed your mind,' she said.[2] On 23 July 1934, Menzies announced that he would stand for Kooyong, having won the endorsement of a convention comprising the United Australia Organisation, the Young Nationalists, and the Australian Women's National League, meeting at the Glenferrie Masonic Hall.[3]

It is likely that Lyons offered Menzies a further incentive to seal the deal: a promise to succeed him as prime minister before the next election. Enid Lyons later wrote in her memoirs that Joe did indeed want Robert to succeed him: 'Joe had envisaged for himself only a short term of office, and in Menzies saw a man to whom he could confidently hand over.'[4] The leadership of any party can only be decided by its MPs, but Lyons' promise of endorsement could be of great advantage. Menzies first had to be elected, of course, and he comfortably took the seat of Kooyong for the UAP at the general election on 15 September 1934. Menzies won 61.7 per cent of the primary vote, which was down from Latham's 76.5 per cent at the previous election. Stanley Argyle, the Victorian premier, was happy to see Menzies leave Spring Street. 'Thank God we have got rid of him,' he told a federal minister. 'You're welcome to him.'[5]

Lyons had led the UAP to power. On 12 October 1934, Menzies was sworn in as attorney-general and minister for industry, both portfolios previously held by Latham. The cabinet met after the swearing-in, and attended a dinner party with the governor-general, Isaac Issacs. The question of the deputy leadership of the UAP was repeatedly raised in party meetings, but deferred by Lyons for more than a year. (Latham had been deputy leader.) Lyons favoured Menzies for the position, but there was far from unanimous agreement about this from MPs. This is an indication of how many in the party room viewed Menzies at the time — with suspicion. Archdale Parkhill, the minister for defence, was Menzies' main rival for deputy leader. Others, such as treasurer Richard Casey and former prime minister Billy Hughes, also featured in media speculation. Eventually, on 4 December 1935, Menzies was elected deputy leader.[6]

On 2 November 1934, Menzies stood in the House of Representatives to give his first speech. He called for a new examination of the most pressing economic and social problems confronting Australia. 'When we are not in office, we all too frequently regard the task of thinking as unnecessary and, indeed, as irrelevant; and when we are in office we are so busy that we have little time for thinking,' he said. 'The result is that thinking about large problems tends to be discounted.' He called for both sides of politics to 'pool all of our mental resources' and work together to address 'the greatest problems that confront us'.[7]

The speech was praised by some in the media, but many in parliament, including in his own party, remained sceptical about the new Member for Kooyong. Yet Menzies quickly gained a reputation as a hardworking minister who was confident, clever, and articulate. He was always seen as a future prime minister. Menzies got on well with Lyons, but thought he sometimes lacked the superior administrative abilities needed to be a successful prime minister. For example, cabinet business was not often efficiently managed or focused, and key decisions were delayed while others were not sufficiently resolved. While Lyons was popular and likeable, he was not an intellectual heavyweight. Menzies, as a result, grew increasingly impatient with Lyons.

Many years later, Menzies recalled Lyons giving him advice one day on how to address an audience. 'You are a wonderful speaker, but couldn't you roughen it up a bit?' Lyons suggested. 'It would go better with the crowd. Make a grammatical error.' Menzies would never countenance such an idea. 'I always make speeches to what I think is the highest factor in the audience of people who will be critical and judge. If I were found performing a shabby trick like that, I would lose the respect of all the people of whose respect I value,' Menzies replied. 'I will speak as myself.'[8] While Menzies was right never to underestimate the intelligence of his audience, it was this sort of brusque response that irritated his colleagues.

Menzies clashed with other ministers in cabinet, especially those from the Country Party, and developed a reputation for having a prickly personality. From the outset, he did not get on with Earle Page, whose parochialism and high-pitched voice especially grated. Menzies did not seem to be able to hide his poor opinion of his colleagues. While Menzies was smart and urbane, and respected for his political talents, few MPs were enthusiastic supporters, let alone real friends. A number of issues and events only seemed to harden his reputation for arrogance and strong-headedness.

In late 1934, Czech writer and peace activist Egon Kisch was invited to Australia to speak at an All-Australian Congress Against War and Fascism to be held in Melbourne. Kisch, a communist, was denied entry into Australia because he was deemed to be a risk to national security. But when his ship arrived, he jumped overboard and came ashore. Menzies launched legal action to have him deported, winning the first round of litigation, and Kisch was legally detained on the ship. But Kisch appealed to the High Court, with H.V. 'Doc' Evatt presiding, and was successful. This was a blow to Menzies, who seemed to have reacted too harshly in what many saw as an attempt to stifle free speech. Eventually, Kisch agreed to leave Australia in return for the government ending further legal action and paying his court costs.

At the end of 1938, there was a growing dispute at Port Kembla, south of Sydney, where wharf labourers were refusing to load 23,000 tons of pig-iron being exported to Japan aboard the steamer *Dalfram*. The Waterside Workers' Federation argued that the pig-iron would be used by Japan against China, and could also be used against Australia if there was a war. In November 1938, the cabinet agreed to introduce a licensing system — the so-called 'dog-collar act' — requiring any waterside worker to pay for a licence to work on the wharves if the strike was not broken. The workers refused to accept this, and remained on strike for nearly three months. By early 1939, around 7,000 miners and wharf labourers were out of work. On 11 January 1939, Menzies went to Wollongong to talk with the parties. He was met with huge protests. Eventually, after another meeting later that month, an agreement was reached that the workers would load the pig-iron on the proviso that it would be the last shipment. Menzies was called 'Pig-iron Bob' — an epithet that lasted for the rest of his political career.

IN February 1935, Menzies sailed to England aboard the *Otranto* for the silver jubilee of King George V. He spent seven months abroad building relationships with senior politicians, civil servants, leading barristers and judges, and members of the royal family. Menzies was in his element, and it confirmed all of his dreams about England. He loved being in London. He went to the theatres, galleries, and lecture halls. He dined in expensive restaurants, and drank in exclusive clubs. It was where the common law had derived from and where the Westminster tradition was born. He addressed the Empire Parliamentary Association. He met Ramsay MacDonald at Downing Street; lunched separately with Stanley Baldwin, Neville Chamberlain, and Anthony Eden; sat in the cabinet room; and visited the prime minister's country home, Chequers, for a weekend. He also visited the Menzies clan in Scotland. Gray's Inn elected him as an honorary bencher. And he appeared before the Judicial Committee of the Privy Council, and won his first case — *Paper Sacks Ltd v. Cowper*.

There was one person he met who was unforgettable: Winston Churchill. Menzies had first laid eyes on Churchill when he was speaking in the House of Commons. On 26 May 1935, when visiting cabinet secretary Maurice Hankey, Menzies and Hankey walked next door to Chartwell. Churchill was in the swimming pool. 'There in the middle of it was what appeared to be a miniature Rock of Gibraltar but it was only Winston lying on his back in the pool,' Menzies remembered. Churchill was not happy to be ordered out of the pool by his wife, Clementine, but was introduced to Menzies, and they spent the afternoon together. He thought Churchill's greatest virtue was his 'indomitable courage' and his 'unrivalled gifts of expression'. His greatest vice? 'He was a little bit inclined to be unforgiving,' Menzies said in 1967. 'He didn't forget an enemy but he equally didn't forget a friend.'[9]

In February 1936, Menzies returned to England and again appeared before the Judicial Committee (twice). He was back in London for the coronation of George VI and Elizabeth as king and queen, which took place at Westminster Abbey on 12 May 1937. Menzies was appointed to the Privy Council the following year. He was sworn in as a privy councillor in full-dress uniform on 23 June 1938 at Buckingham Palace — his fourth visit to London in three years. During these visits, he participated in official talks with ministers and officials about trade and investment. On 21 July, Menzies travelled to France for the unveiling of the war memorial at Villers-Bretonneux.

In the last week of July 1938, Menzies visited Germany under Nazi rule, and met several government and party officials. He discounted the threat of war, and told journalists that Germany's intentions were purely defensive. He thought there was little chance of an impending attack on France or Britain. 'I do not believe war is possible in Europe,' he said.[10] Many in the Lyons cabinet, including Menzies, supported the British government's policy of appeasement towards Adolf Hitler. They endorsed Chamberlain bowing to Hitler's demands at Munich. '[The] Czechoslovakian problem is not a question on which war for the British Empire can justifiably be contemplated,' Lyons told the British government.[11] The ultimate purpose of the policy of appeasement, with memories of the horrors of the First World War still very fresh, was to avoid conflict at almost all cost.

Menzies wrote to his sister, Belle, on 6 August 1938, sharing his impressions of Nazi Germany. This letter has not, it seems, been previously published. He noted the huge expenditure on roads and public works, the lack of trade unions and a free press, and thought the 'general physique' of athletes, despite their training, was 'inferior' to that of Australians. During his stay, he met with 'official and semi-official' people in government, and dined with the siblings and cousins of senior Nazi politician and military commander Hermann Goering:

> I don't think they really want war, for they know it will be the end of themselves as well as others, but at the same time they have lived for so long on real and imaginary grievances that they are in a very unhealthy state of mind. Incidentally, I think they have far more justice on their side over the Sudeten problem than the Czech government, which is, I think, behaving badly; but their position would be considerably improved if they could only learn to laugh about some of their problems instead of working themselves up into a fanatical condition of making, or listening to public speeches.[12]

Menzies thought the Goering family were 'extremely friendly' and had 'a real German desire to be at peace with England'. But he cautioned that a 'misunderstanding' of the British character 'might easily lead them to misjudge the consequences of a too-aggressive policy on their part'. Menzies supported the aspirations of the Sudeten Germans, and thought that if a 'fair settlement' could be reached, there might be 'an excellent prospect of ten years' peace' in Europe. Menzies was not uncritical of Nazi Germany. Yet he concluded this letter with a degree of praise for Hitler, who had lifted 'the German spirit' among his people:

> It must be said that this modern abandonment by the Germans of individual liberty and of the easy and pleasant things of life has something rather magnificent about it. The Germans may be pulling down the churches, but they have erected the state, with Hitler as its head, into a sort of religion which produces a spiritual exaltation that one cannot but admire and some small portion of which would do no harm among our somewhat irresponsible populations.[13]

Nazi Germany had earlier annexed Austria, on 12 March 1938. Hitler continued to speak of a 'Greater Germany' that included Sudeten Germans in Czechoslovakia. On 15 September — just six weeks after Menzies' letter — Neville Chamberlain met with Hitler and agreed to Nazi Germany's accession of the Sudetenland. Menzies reflected the views of the British and Australian governments, which thought that the complaints of the Sudeten Germans were legitimate and that Hitler's ambitions were limited. This was a significant misjudgement. But Menzies, like Lyons and Chamberlain, was far from alone in making it. John Curtin, leading a Labor Party with strongly pacifist elements, also supported appeasement.[14]

THE Lyons government was re-elected on 23 October 1937. Lyons was the first prime minister to lead his party to three successive election victories, and he remained popular with voters. As a father of 12, he cultivated a homespun image, and cleverly used radio to broadcast directly to Australians. His nickname was 'Honest Joe'. His wife, Enid, was an admired prime ministerial spouse who balanced raising her children with official duties and campaigning for her husband. But over time, Lyons' health began to deteriorate. He was overly sensitive to criticism, often second-guessed himself, struggled to deal with party and cabinet divisions, and had difficulty in managing the stresses and strains of the prime ministership.

Within the government, there were growing difficulties. In January 1932, the UAP had initially formed government without being in coalition with Earle Page's Country Party. But a coalition government was formed in November 1934, after the September election that year when the UAP lost several seats. Wanting to shore up the government's position, and cognisant of Lyons' growing unhappiness and possible retirement, Page and Richard Casey periodically tried to persuade Stanley Bruce to relinquish his post as high commissioner in London and return to Australia to take up politics again. Labor won 11 seats under its new leader, John Curtin, at the October 1937 election. The opposition was proving to be more united and effective in parliament than it had been for a long time. There were also occasional leaks from cabinet and unhappiness in the party room. Thomas White resigned from cabinet on 8 November 1938, claiming that Lyons was being unduly influenced by 'two prominent ministers' with 'ambitions toward leadership' — known to be Menzies and Casey.[15]

With the ever-present conjecture about Lyons' future, largely because of his declining health, it was often reported that Menzies was his most likely successor. In April 1936, Lyons wrote to Menzies flagging his intention to retire, and said that he wanted Menzies to succeed him.[16] But there was resistance inside the UAP and the Country Party to Menzies. The controversy over pig-iron shipments to Japan in 1938–39 had not helped his image. Some thought Casey or Billy Hughes should take over from Lyons when he retired. Others mentioned New South Wales premier Bertram Stevens as a possible successor. In January 1939, Lyons surprisingly offered the prime ministership to Bruce, who accepted it on the proviso that Lyons would recommend it to the governor-general and serve in his cabinet. But the next day, Lyons changed his mind.[17]

Lyons, it was clear, no longer saw Menzies as the man to replace him. A few months earlier, on 24 October 1938, Menzies had given a speech at the Constitutional Club in Sydney. He argued that Australia lacked 'inspiring leadership' like that seen in 'dictator countries', and that a new national spirit was needed to deal with defence preparedness and economic challenges. The speech underscored a sense of drift in the government, and won newspaper editorial support. Some interpreted it, though wrongly, as an endorsement of totalitarian leadership. The speech was, however, seen by some in the UAP as a veiled attack on Lyons. To believe that it was not designed to undermine Lyons, an observer then or now would have to accept that Menzies was foolish in making such a speech — and Menzies was no fool. Menzies, however, assured Lyons of his support. Still, it led to a no-confidence motion being moved by Labor in the House of Representatives, which was defeated.[18]

Enid Lyons saw Menzies' speech as an attack on her husband, and was enraged by it. Later, she reflected on the growing tensions between her husband and Menzies. She saw Menzies as torn between his 'desire' for the prime ministership and his 'loyalty' to Lyons. 'A young ambitious man convinced of his own power to serve his country well, and the loyalty he owed the leader who had given years of self-less service, but whose capacity for further leadership he genuinely doubted,' was how she saw Menzies' predicament. 'I could not accept any theory of misreport or misinterpretation' of Menzies' speech, she said. 'I was brimming over with righteous wrath.' She remained indignant about Menzies' speech for the rest of her life.[19]

On 14 March 1939, Menzies resigned from the Lyons cabinet. It was less than six months after his damning speech on leadership in Sydney. Menzies argued that the failure to implement the *National Insurance Act* — a scheme that provided social-security support and pensions — was a betrayal of voters, and justified his resignation. The government had been divided over the scheme for months. Finally, cabinet decided to repeal old age, widows', and orphans' pensions, and to focus on redesigning the scheme to provide family medical benefits. Menzies was said to be on the verge of resigning three months earlier when the scheme was thought to have been indefinitely postponed.

'I frankly do not think we can expect to be taken seriously if we start off again with conferences and drafting committees at a time when we have already so notoriously failed to go on with the Act which represents two years of labour, a vast amount of organisation and considerable expenditure of public and private funds,' Menzies said in a statement. He emphasised that his resignation was not to be interpreted as criticism of Lyons or any other member of the government. Menzies, the deputy leader of the UAP, was praised by some in the media for taking a principled stand based on policy. But others saw a man playing political games and too eager to become prime minister.[20]

Many Country Party MPs were opposed to the national insurance scheme, as they believed it favoured those living in the major cities. Richard Casey, who had secured passage of the Bill through the parliament in 1938, had briefed ministers on growing opposition to the scheme among influential members of the UAP. The clerk of the House of Representatives, Frank Green, recalled that Lyons was being pressured to dump the scheme by the Melbourne financial group known as the 'Temple Court Group', which effectively controlled the UAP.[21]

On Good Friday, 7 April 1939, Lyons died at St Vincent's Hospital in Sydney. He had suffered a heart attack while driving from Canberra to Sydney, where he was to open the Royal Easter Show. He was 59 years old. 'I should never have left Tasmania,' Lyons told Green not long before. 'I had good mates there, and was happy, but this situation is killing me.'[22] Joe agreed with Enid only weeks earlier that he would resign.[23] The death of the prime minister — the first Australian prime minister to die in office — ignited a power struggle within the government. The UAP was left without a leader or deputy leader. Earle Page, the leader of the Country Party, moved quickly. Armed with advice from the new attorney-general, Billy Hughes, he suggested to Governor-General Lord Gowrie that he be commissioned prime minister until the UAP could elect a new leader. Page had acted as prime minister under Bruce and Lyons. Within five hours of Lyons' death, Gowrie acceded to Page's advice and swore him in as prime minister on a caretaker basis. If Menzies had remained deputy leader of the UAP, he may have had a claim to the prime ministership.

In any event, Page was determined to stop Menzies. (Page had form on this score, as he had edged Hughes out of office in favour of Bruce in 1923.) Page told Gowrie he would resign once the UAP had chosen a new leader, but added that if they chose Menzies, he would not serve in cabinet. Now, with Lyons gone, Page stepped up his efforts to encourage Bruce to return to Australia and become leader of the UAP and prime minister. Page contacted Bruce, who was on a ship headed for California, and had several 'radio telephone' talks with him. Bruce, who was considering taking up the tantalising suggestion, insisted he be able to form a government with MPs from any party. The appeals to Bruce continued right up until the eve of the UAP ballot to select a new leader, and had Casey's backing. Page even took the extraordinary step of announcing that he would resign his northern New South Wales seat of Cowper so that Bruce could enter the House of Representatives.[24] The businessmen who exercised influence inside the UAP also tried to stop Menzies; they mostly favoured Bruce or Casey.

There was considerable speculation about who would succeed Lyons as UAP leader and Page as prime minister. Newspapers focused on Casey or Hughes, then aged 76, as the most probable. Menzies, then on the backbench, was initially seen as an outsider. '[Mr Menzies] has been mentioned as a likely candidate but his prospects are not regarded as bright as those of Messrs. Hughes and Casey,' a typical newspaper report said.[25] Nevertheless, *The Age* and the Melbourne *Herald* called for Menzies to be made prime minister. Other newspapers threw Percy Spender and Geoffrey Street into the mix of candidates. The weekend after Lyons' death, a report suggested that Hughes was ahead on the counting with 20 votes in the party room, Menzies having just nine votes and Casey four.[26]

A week on from Lyons' death, the tide had turned in Menzies' favour. His pitch to MPs on the phone and in person was yielding results. The choice, it seemed, had narrowed to a contest largely between Hughes and Menzies. But the day before MPs were scheduled to return to Canberra for the ballot, Bruce's name reappeared as a candidate. 'UAP leaders will now definitely include Mr Bruce as a candidate for leadership and for the prime ministership,' it was reported on 17 April. Bruce had the backing of Page, New South Wales premier Stevens, and Casey, who had, apparently, withdrawn from the contest. Casey was said to be planning to put Bruce's name into contention at the party-room meeting. 'The choice of the party will thus lie between Mr Bruce and the former attorney-general (Mr Menzies) — the candidacy of Mr Bruce having greatly weakened Mr Hughes' prospects,' reported *The Herald*.[27] Menzies was confident: he told Owen Dixon on 13 April that he expected to win the party-room ballot and become prime minister.[28]

In this febrile atmosphere, the UAP met — 11 days after Lyons' death — at 11.00 am on 18 April 1939. Menzies was staying at the nearby Hotel Canberra, and while walking to Parliament House he tripped and fell, badly injuring himself. He was taken to Canberra Hospital for examination. With MPs unaware of Menzies' mishap, the meeting went ahead. But within minutes, MPs were dramatically interrupted by a messenger with news of Menzies' fall, and it was decided to reconvene the meeting at 2.00 pm. Menzies left the hospital and made his way back to Parliament House, his arm resting in a sling.[29]

Casey informed the meeting that Bruce was prepared to be a candidate for leader, provided he would be given the freedom to constitute an all-party government. This idea was an affront to many MPs who could not countenance surrendering ministries to Labor, and they almost immediately rejected it. Casey, rebuffed, thereupon decided to nominate himself for the leadership. There were now four candidates for leader: Menzies, Casey, Hughes, and Thomas White, a surprise late entry.

(White was a former minister for trade and customs, and a son-in-law of Alfred Deakin.)

Each candidate addressed the party room, with special microphones and speakers having been installed for this purpose. There were three ballots over several hours, which took the meeting into the evening. Page sent word to the meeting that if the party elected Menzies, the Country Party would not serve in coalition with the UAP. With 41 MPs present, they began to cast their votes. White was eliminated on the first ballot, and Casey on the second ballot. The third and final ballot set Menzies against Hughes. Menzies emerged triumphant with a narrow margin of victory of just four votes — 23 to 19.[30] No decision was made on electing a deputy. (Prior to the meeting, Menzies considered himself 'technically' still the deputy leader of the party, as it had not been 'formally' considered by the party room before Lyons' death.[31])

The party room cheered when Menzies' election was announced. A motion of congratulations was put and carried unanimously. It was reported that when parliament resumed the following day, the new party leader would have to sit on the backbench, as he was not a minister. Following the ballot, Menzies asked Page to reconsider his position and maintain the UAP–Country Party coalition. Page refused, and continued to press Bruce to reclaim the prime ministership, even though the UAP had chosen Menzies as its leader. Menzies formed a government with the confidence that the Country Party members, while not formally in a coalition with the UAP, would not vote to bring it down. But Menzies led a divided party, the coalition was broken, and war in Europe was imminent.

But Page was not yet done with Menzies. On 20 April 1939, Page stood in the House of Representatives and gave an electrifying speech that sought to demolish Menzies' chances of becoming prime minister. Page unleashed a bitter personal attack, identifying 'three incidents' that, he said, should disqualify Menzies from the prime ministership. He suggested that Menzies had been cowardly for not having enlisted in the First World War. (Page had enlisted in the AIF in February 1916.) Second, he labelled Menzies' Constitutional Club speech, lamenting a lack of 'inspiring leadership', as a direct attack on Lyons. And third, he said Menzies' resignation from cabinet had upset Lyons so much that it contributed to his death. Moreover, he argued that Menzies did not have the capacity to unite the nation and lead it during a period of heightened tensions abroad and economic challenges at home.

Page's poisonous speech was met with loud interjections of 'shame' from government and opposition benches. Page would not serve in a Menzies-led government, and the Country Party would not sit in coalition with the UAP. But Page had gone too far. The speech led to Page, rather than Menzies, being criticised by UAP and Country Party MPs. Arthur Fadden was appalled. He and three other Country Party MPs — Bernie Corser, Tom Collins, and Oliver Badman — temporarily left the party room. It is not surprising that the speech Page delivered to the House is not the version immortalised in *Hansard*, which differs from several newspaper accounts, and is likely to have been amended by Page for the official parliamentary record. Page had miscalculated. He did not stop Menzies from becoming prime minister, and he would lose the leadership of his own party five months later. But he nevertheless damaged Menzies, and the bitterness that his speech unleashed would contribute to the instability that plagued Menzies' first prime ministership.

Menzies, like everyone, was stunned by Page's vitriol. Menzies responded to each of the allegations. 'This kind of attack is very disagreeable,' he replied in parliament. 'It is the sort of attack that is made, and in my case has been made, time and again … I shall exhibit none of those miserable attributes that have been suggested by the Prime Minister in the most remarkable attack that I have ever heard in the whole of my public career.' He insisted that his speech to the Constitutional Club had not been critical of Lyons, and that the deceased prime minister did not see it that way. He explained that his resignation from cabinet over national insurance was because of a commitment he had given to his electorate, and represented 'one of the more respectable actions of my public life'. He defended his non-enlistment during the First World War because of his family circumstances, and corrected Page for falsely claiming that he had resigned from the 'military forces' in 1915. (He had served in the Melbourne University Rifles and held a commission for the mandatory period of service.) 'Is this not getting down pretty low?' Menzies said.

Pattie Menzies was sitting in the gallery when Page delivered his broadside. She did not hear all of it because she promptly stood up as the attack unfurled, glared at him for a period, and then left the chamber.

Pattie never spoke to Page again, nor even acknowledged him in person. Kate and James Menzies were shocked by the accusation of wartime cowardice directed at their son. It had been a family decision, Kate said to *The Daily Telegraph*. 'Bob was keen to go, but father and I got to him and we pleaded with him to stay home,' she said, aged 73. 'We told him again that two sons from a family was as much and more than a country expected ... We told Bob that we needed someone at home to look after us. Even with all this it was hard to convince him not to go ... I think that is why he was perhaps the bravest of all my boys.'[32]

Menzies' non-enlistment continued to be raised by some in his own party, by the opposition, and in the media from time to time, and it had a searing impact upon him. Bill Hayden was elected as the Labor MP for the seat of Oxley, in Queensland, in 1961. He told me it was often a topic of scuttlebutt in the lobbies of Parliament House. Hayden, taking his cue from Eddie Ward, also used it as an interjection one day, and soon regretted it. 'I said he had a promising military career cut short by the outbreak of war,' Hayden recalled in an interview for this book. 'But it was cheap and nasty, and I should not have done it. Reg Pollard, who had served in World War I, and Frank Crean, both came over to me and said, "You were very unfair to Menzies." Reg said, "Two members of Menzies' family had been sent to the front, which was two more than any family should have to send." I was sorry about that.'[33]

IN March 1972, six years after Menzies retired, Enid Lyons was preparing to publish a further volume of her memoirs. Her first memoir had not criticised Menzies. Now that they were both out of politics, this time it would be different. Enid Lyons wrote to Menzies while he was residing at the Mercy Hospital in Melbourne recovering from a stroke, and enclosed a chapter from her forthcoming book. Enid Lyons wrote that Menzies, driven by an overweening ambition, had been grossly disloyal towards her husband. She reflected on Menzies succeeding Lyons as UAP leader, writing that 'the man who had caused him so much hurt succeeded Joe as leader of the party'.[34]

'Your charge of disloyalty astonishes me,' Menzies furiously replied from his hospital bed. The speech he had given in October 1938 'was not a speech about my leader at all', Menzies protested. His resignation from the ministry in March 1939, citing the national insurance scheme, was not calculated either. He again explained that he could not break any promises to his constituents that would have left him vulnerable at the next election. He concluded in an angry tone, saying that 'two people looking at or participating in a series of events can quite honestly come out of the process with entirely different understandings on what has gone on'.[35] Indeed, but Menzies was ambitious, and impatient with Joe Lyons' reluctance to hand over the prime ministership, as he had promised to do.

Menzies had dispatched his reply just before he sat down with Frances McNicoll for the first in a series of interviews for her planned biography. 'It is a poor thing,' he said, clearly irritated with Enid Lyons. 'I am sorry for her in a sense because I think she must be very hard up.' Menzies speculated that she had been offered 'a large sum' of money to publish an extract from the book in *The Sunday Australian*. It was about revenge for her dead husband as much as it was about making money, Menzies implied. 'That's a rum thing, isn't it?' he said. 'It will do her a lot of harm.'[36]

Menzies talked frankly to McNicoll about his relationship with Page, who had tried to stop him becoming prime minister in 1939. In short, Menzies and Page despised each other. It was a clash of personality more than anything else, he explained. Page was a difficult person to get along with. He had an excitable, giggly, and sometimes indecipherable manner of speech, often punctuated with 'You see, you see.' Menzies thought Page was a fool:

I don't blame Page for not liking me because I was conscious of his eccentricities and would occasionally be silly enough to let him know that I understood them. That was a great mistake. With more experience, perhaps, I wouldn't have done it.[37]

Menzies recalled attending a conference in London with Page in mid-1938. The officials could not understand a word of what Page was saying. The officials asked Menzies to translate, which he did:

I got pretty fed up with this one day, and I must have gone off pop,
and said to Page: 'If I am to attend these meetings, I jolly well have

to know what we're there to discuss so that at least I will have a few clear ideas because, quite frankly, Page, I never know what you are talking about. 'Oh, you see, you see, that was the trouble, you see, my mind is so quick that I think so fast that it is faster than my tongue and the result is that the speed of my mind overwhelms my powers of expression,' [Page replied.] I laughed at him and said: 'No doubt about it, Page, you flatter yourself.' And that was the beginning of the end. [A] very tactless thing to say, although it was completely true.[38]

A letter from Helen Page — Earle Page's daughter-in-law — to Ken Menzies in December 1979 provides another perspective on Page's acerbic parliamentary speech:

I happened to be Sir Earle Page's secretary in April 1939 and typed the fateful speech for the eighth or ninth time, taking the paragraph in and out many times. Everybody involved at the centre like Lady Page, Tom Paterson, myself, advised against this, knowing that it would reflect more on himself for using it than your father. But Archie Cameron, who was a very militaristic Highland non-gentleman with very authoritative urges, kept on at him until he persuaded him. I happened to be standing behind your mother in the chamber that day and saw her colour change, so I know what she went through on that occasion. Of course, there was nothing anyone close to him could do — he was such a strong-willed man, but he regretted it for the rest of his life.[39]

When Page's memoir, *Truant Surgeon*, was posthumously published in 1963, the speech denouncing Menzies was inexplicably omitted. He only mentioned that he had referred to Menzies' 'public record' and questioned whether it 'qualified him' for the prime ministership.[40] Two years earlier, Page recontested his northern New South Wales seat of Cowper at the election on 9 December 1961. He had held the seat since December 1919 — more than 40 years — and was then 81 years old. Page fell ill during the campaign, and died 11 days later, at 8.00 am on 20 December 1961. The family did not tell him that he had lost his seat to Labor's Frank McGuren.[41]

CHAPTER 7

Wartime Prime Minister

ROBERT Menzies was sworn in as Australia's 12th prime minister at Government House, Yarralumla, by the governor-general, Lord Gowrie, on the morning of 26 April 1939. He was 44 years old. It was less than five years since he had been elected to the federal parliament. The Menzies-led UAP would initially govern alone, without the Country Party. The cabinet, which had been announced two days earlier, met briefly that afternoon at Parliament House. It included a former prime minister in Billy Hughes, a future prime minister in Harold Holt, and a future governor-general in Richard Casey. Menzies told Gowrie that he thought his government might only last six weeks.[1]

James and Kate Menzies flew to Canberra to be with their son for the opening of parliament on 3 May. It was the first time they had been on an aeroplane. It was also their golden wedding anniversary. 'This is the proudest and most delightful day of my life,' James, aged 76, told *The Daily Telegraph*. 'I am not surprised to find myself in this position. I know Bob, and I have always known that he would rise to the top, whether he chose law or politics as his career.' Kate was emotional. 'I am thrilled beyond words,' she said. 'I am too happy to say much beyond that today is an eventful one for me. My son is prime minister. It is my golden wedding anniversary. And I made my first flight.'[2]

Menzies made a radio broadcast to the nation following his swearing in. He began, unusually, by addressing his shortcomings. 'Fellow

Australians,' he said. 'Today I am introducing myself to you as your prime minister. I come after Mr Lyons, a leader who had your affection and respect — a simple and understanding man. I come as one who has been freely accused of grave defects — aloofness, superiority, and one thing and another. The truth is that my apparent aloofness is just one of the fantastic ideas that obtain currency.'

He then spoke about his background and upbringing. 'I am a singularly plain man, born in the little town of Jeparit, on the fringe of the Mallee, educated at Ballarat, in a state school, and then by scholarship at a public school and Melbourne University. Apart from having parents of great character, intelligence and fortitude, I was not born to the purple. I have made my own way, such as it was and is, and I want you to believe me when I say that I do not hold the prime ministership as an occasion for foolish vanity. I find in it a responsibility so great that it might well deter better men than I can ever hope to be.' He asked Australians for their prayers, tolerance, and support.

Menzies was humbled by the honour of becoming prime minister. Messages of congratulations flooded Menzies' office, he was feted at civic receptions hosted by the lord mayors of Sydney and Melbourne, and leading newspapers and magazines profiled the new family as they moved into the Lodge on 23 May. The parliament met for six weeks through May into mid-June. Eager to establish his authority and demonstrate that the new government had a plan for the nation, the prime minister and several of his ministers conducted a national tour to discuss their policies. It was a promising start.

However, despite the initial national goodwill, Menzies faced an exceedingly difficult time as prime minister. The UAP remained divided, and within the party there were substantial doubts about Menzies' capacity to lead. The hostilities between Menzies and Page remained barely concealed. The UAP could not command a majority of seats in parliament until a new coalition agreement was struck on 14 March 1940 with new Country Party leader Archie Cameron. Yet much worse was to come: Menzies would face among the gravest challenges of any prime minister, as Europe was soon at war, and danger loomed in the Asia-Pacific.

AT 9.15 pm on Sunday, 3 September 1939, Menzies addressed the nation on radio to announce that Australia was at war with Germany. Warnings from Britain and France to Germany to halt its aggression towards Poland had been ignored. As the clock ticked past 11.00 am in London on 3 September, a state of war between Britain and Germany came into existence. Nearly one million Australians would serve in the Second World War, fighting in Europe, Africa, the Middle East, Asia, and the Pacific between 1939 and 1945. The announcement by Menzies, made shortly after war had broken out, would herald transformative changes in Australian society, economy, and politics.

'Fellow Australians,' Menzies began. 'It is my melancholy duty to inform you, officially, that in consequence of a persistence by Germany in her invasion of Poland, Great Britain has declared war upon her and that, as a result, Australia is also at war.' As Australians anxiously huddled around their radios to listen to Menzies, he said there was 'no harder task' for a political leader than to inform a nation that they were at war. 'In the bitter months that are to come, calmness, resoluteness, confidence, and hard work will be required as never before,' he said. 'May God in His mercy and compassion grant that the world may soon be delivered from this agony.'

Menzies cabled British prime minister Neville Chamberlain to tell him that Australians were 'deeply moved' by his announcement that Britain was at war. Chamberlain replied in a 'personal' cable to Menzies. 'It is the greatest encouragement to us in these difficult hours to know that the Commonwealth government are with us,' he said.

Menzies' broadcast would be criticised for implying that because Britain had declared war on Germany, Australia was automatically at war. Indeed, Australians could be forgiven for thinking that this was exactly what he meant. Was Australia not an independent nation, able to decide whom it went to war with and under what terms?

Dr Brendan Nelson led the Liberal Party from 2007 to 2008. He was a minister in the Howard government, and is now director of the Australian War Memorial. Nelson told me that Menzies was mistaken in leaving the impression that Australia was a compliant ally. 'Menzies' statement implied that Australia went into the war because Britain was at war, but this is misleading,' Nelson said. 'The prompt response to the

British announcement wasn't really an automatic reaction. We were an independent nation, and we made the announcement independently.'[3]

In accordance with the policy of the British and Australian governments, Menzies supported an accommodation with Adolf Hitler's Nazi Germany. This was a policy designed to keep Britain and its dominions out of war by negotiating with Germany, but also not failing to prepare for possible war. Once Germany had invaded Poland on 1 September 1939, and then ignored a British–French ultimatum to withdraw, a state of war existed. Menzies, however, continued to explore the possibility of appeasement towards Germany after it had invaded Poland. He was despairing about the course of events and wondering at this late stage whether war could be avoided, given that the horrors of the First World War remained an active memory for so many Australians.

Menzies wrote to Stanley Bruce, Australia's high commissioner in London, on 11 September 1939, advocating appeasement.[4] This letter was first made available for public access in October 1972 and published in the *Documents on Australian Foreign Policy: 1937–49* series in 1976. In his letter to Bruce, marked 'Secret', Menzies argued for a peace deal to be struck with Hitler. He envisaged Chamberlain reaching a settlement with Hitler to avoid war that allowed Germany to keep Danzig and a corridor through Poland. Menzies doubted that Hitler wanted 'a first class war', and thought a Polish corridor could be easily conceded:

> I feel quite confident that Hitler has no desire for a first class war, and that until the Polish debacle is complete he will not be disposed to assume the offensive against either France or Great Britain. It seems to me that when he has finished with Poland he will say to Great Britain and France — 'Well, it is all over now; I have beaten the Poles and you haven't been able to do anything about it and you cannot do anything about it now; but I am a magnanimous fellow. I don't propose to annex Poland. I will simply re-take the corridor and Danzig and, for the rest, I will be prepared to be a guarantor with yourselves of the integrity of Poland proper'.

Menzies told Bruce this presented Britain and its dominions with a choice to either say 'Yes' or 'No' to German aggression. If the answer was 'No', Menzies predicted that 'millions of British and French lives will be lost'. But for what purpose? Menzies wrote that 'nobody really cares a damn about Poland', and Germany really had 'an almost unanswerable case' to claim the corridor. He said it was 'indefensible' to dictate to the German people what kind of government they should have:

> What positive action could be taken in relation to Poland I admit I do not know. All I know is that I feel profoundly disturbed because Germany has always seemed to me to have an almost unanswerable case in relation to the corridor ... I know that you feel much the same as I do, and I know that there is probably no answer to it all — except just to go on fighting until the other country goes down into a state of starvation and riot in which the seeds of another war, in which my grandchildren will fight, are sown. But at the same time, I see no sanity in it.

In later life, Menzies knew this letter did not reflect well on him, so he was furious when Billy McMahon's government released it, along with other war records from the period, without his consent. 'By what authority did your government release to the press a communication expressly marked "private and confidential" from me to Bruce in 1939?' Menzies wrote to McMahon on 24 October 1972.[5] Menzies was not satisfied with McMahon's reply, which he described as 'a long, wheedling sort of thing, a contemptible letter'.[6] 'My idea of what is private and confidential apparently is different from the view entertained by Mr McMahon,' he said in a note dictated for his files. 'This, of course, was to say the least of it, an act of gross discourtesy.'[7]

Only part of this extraordinary letter was included in the official *Documents in Australian Foreign Policy: 1937–49* series published by the Department of Foreign Affairs. In a further two pages, Menzies unburdened himself to Bruce about domestic politics. These pages contain Menzies' unvarnished opinions about his colleagues and the opposition. He did not think he could work effectively with Earle Page. He regarded Billy Hughes as a 'pathetic' figure. Archie Cameron was 'completely irresponsible' and 'intensely vain'. Richard Casey was angling to be sent to Washington. Menzies was worried about the defence of Singapore, and reluctant to send Australian troops to Europe or the Middle East. He thought John Curtin was content to remain opposition leader for the duration of the war. Yet he was optimistic:

> Page gave me an unexpectedly good start by making a martyr of me, though he did not think so at the time, and I certainly thought that his attack upon me would have worked like beavers, and I think I can say that today my government has a better public than any government has had for the last four years. The cabinet is united and loyal, though for obvious reasons my own work and responsibilities are incessant.

It is strange that Allan Martin decided not to include this significant and revealing letter in his biography of Menzies.[8] John Edwards discovered the full letter in Bruce's papers in 2001, and wrote about it in his book *John Curtin's War*, published in 2017.[9] At the time, Gerard Henderson argued that Menzies 'did lack judgement on this issue' of appeasement. But he made the equally valid point that a similar view was held by many in Britain and Australia at the time.[10]

THERE were five prime ministers during the Second World War. This six-year period, from 1939 to 1945, was one of the most turbulent in Australian politics. Menzies lost the confidence of his cabinet, and his party, and resigned. The Country Party was riven with division, and its leader, Archie Cameron, was also deposed. Arthur Fadden's government fell on the floor of parliament. John Curtin, battling inner demons and ill-health, died. Frank Forde, prime minister for eight days, lost a party ballot to remain in office. And Ben Chifley was reluctantly thrust into a job he thought he might not be suited to. A minority government existed, mostly, until 1943. The United Australia Party collapsed. The Liberal Party of Australia was formed in 1944.

Despite this instability, Australia managed to prosecute a war, plan for the peace, and hold fast to its democratic principles. 'It was a time when Australia's political class and leadership were at its finest,' Brendan Nelson said. 'Given the immense price that had been paid, unlike other nations, we maintained our commitment to democracy. We had a much greater polarisation of political opinion during that wartime period. Australians actively engaged in, and were respectful of, our democratic political processes.'[11]

Within days of the announcement of war, the Menzies government put the nation on a war footing. Compulsory military training was reintroduced. Enlistment for a volunteer Second Australian Infantry Division, comprising 20,000 men, was announced. Plans were made to expand the air force. The 6th Division of the AIF began its departure from Australia for the Middle East in January 1940. Curtin opposed this decision on the basis that it might leave Australia vulnerable 'should a dire emergency arise' in the Asia-Pacific. He led a Labor Party with strong pacifist elements and opposed to conscription, which was likely to be imposed if troops were sent abroad. The government also raised and sent the 7th and 9th Divisions to the Middle East and North Africa. The Australian navy engaged in battles against Italy in the Mediterranean in mid-1940, but the army did not participate in battle until it fought the Italians and Germans in the Mediterranean, North Africa, and the Middle East in mid-1941.

Meanwhile, at home, a *National Security Act* provided new regulatory powers to marshal resources for the prosecution of the war. Price controls and petrol rationing were introduced. There were greater restrictions placed on railways, road transport, and shipping. Progress was slow, however, and Australians were not galvanised by the dangers abroad or the risks in its own region. The need to rally the nation was probably not helped by Menzies' insistence that it was 'business as usual' in this early phase of the war. Newspaper editorials lashed the government through 1940–41 for not mobilising fast enough. Facing increased losses of troops abroad and with armaments becoming quickly depleted, Menzies appointed the chief executive of BHP, Essington Lewis, to take charge of the department responsible for munitions and to harness the efforts of private industry. On 17 June 1940, with the government worried about possible subversive activities, the Communist Party of Australia was banned.

In June 1940, after France fell, a deeply troubling assessment of the Japanese threat to Australia was discussed at a war cabinet meeting. The chief of the general staff, Brudenell White, said it would be futile to resist an invasion because Australia was ill-equipped to do so. Nobody, including Menzies, challenged this inescapable yet brutally frank view. The fear was that if Japan attacked Australia, or imperilled her with sea power, Australia would have to accept defeat if the United States or Great Britain could not come to her aid. Curtin had repeatedly warned about war with Japan, and had questioned whether British forces in Singapore were strong enough to resist an invasion force. At an uncertain time, both Menzies and Curtin sometimes struggled to fully understand the strategic challenges facing Australia and how to respond to them. For example, before Japan bombed Pearl Harbor, Curtin supported striking a 'face-saving arrangement' with Japan. Before and after Britain declared war, Menzies supported appeasing Germany.[12]

Menzies' views about Australia's foreign policy within the framework of the British Empire had evolved. While he did not support the notion of 'dominion independence', he said in his first broadcast as prime minister that 'Australia must regard herself as a principal providing herself with her own information and maintain her own diplomatic contacts with foreign powers'. This was a departure from established policy. Menzies was concerned about the security of Australia. More to the point, he had increasing doubts about the stated British commitment to protect and defend 'the Far East' and Australia if Japan were to enter the war.

Menzies conveyed his concerns to Bruce in London at the outset of the war. 'I have had a growing feeling for some time that though the Far East is a major problem to us, it is a relatively minor one to Whitehall,' he wrote in September 1939.[13] These concerns continued to be conveyed to London, but were met with unconvincing statements of general reassurance. The British high command told Menzies that the 'danger' to Australia was 'remote'. Menzies told Bruce 'there is a very strong impression here that our interests are being overlooked', and asked him to pass this on to the British government, in February 1940.[14]

Menzies was reluctant to send Australian troops to fight in Europe while the danger of conflict in the Asia-Pacific loomed. But when New Zealand acceded to a request to send troops to the Middle East, Menzies felt he had little option but to agree to send the 6th Division in November 1939. He instructed Richard Casey in London to tell the British government that Australia did so 'under protest' because there was 'a quite perceptible disposition to treat Australia as a colony' and not as a government that should be able to 'determine' if and when it sent troops abroad.[15] The Menzies government authorised the deployment of troops to Europe and the Mediterranean.

But Menzies sought a more independent role for Australia within this framework of imperial defence. He insisted upon the right of the Australian government and its military commanders, having consulted with the British leadership, to determine where its forces were to be deployed. In reality, he would find this easier said than done. Menzies also insisted on Australia dispatching its own diplomatic representatives to the United States (Richard Casey), Canada (William Glasgow), Japan (John Latham), and China (Frederic Eggleston). These diplomats would represent Australia's interests and transmit vital information back home.

From the start of the war, Menzies understood that Australia's survival, should war break out in the Asia-Pacific, might well depend on the assistance of the United States. Menzies cabled Bruce on 15 September 1939, just days after Germany invaded Poland. 'An Australian minister to the United States could perform an invaluable function if he were able to contribute towards a better British/American understanding and in particular the development of a growing sense of American responsibility for the integrity of another white and English-speaking country on the Pacific Basin,' Menzies argued. He asked Bruce to consider the appointment to Washington. 'I may tell you confidentially that so seriously do I regard this matter that before war broke out I gave serious consideration to whether I should not resign prime ministership and go to America myself.' This is a significant statement that testifies to how important the United States was to the future of the Asia-Pacific, but it is highly doubtful Menzies would have given up the prime ministership to become an ambassador.[16]

IN the morning of 13 August 1940, a Royal Australian Air Force Lockheed Hudson plane crashed into a hill when flying to Canberra, and claimed the lives of Brudenell White, the chief of the general staff, and three cabinet ministers: James Fairbairn, Henry Gullett, and Geoffrey Street. Menzies was utterly devastated. These ministers had been among his most trusted supporters in the party room, and he regarded them as friends. The three ministers who perished had voted for Menzies over Hughes in the last leadership ballot, which he had won by just four votes. The loss of these men, as Menzies would himself acknowledge, would have far-reaching political consequences the following year.[17] Menzies paid tribute to his 'close and loyal friends' in the House of Representatives on 14 August. 'It is my sad duty at this stage to speak particularly of our late colleagues, who were not only great servants of our country, but also the daily friends of all of us,' he said.

On 27 August, parliament was dissolved for an election to be held on 21 September. Australians would go to the polls in wartime. It was the first of two general elections that would be fought on the central theme of Australia's wartime strategy. Backlighting the election campaign were concerns about the prosecution of the war and divisions in the government that were often given full expression in daily newspapers. Menzies made his pitch for re-election on 2 September at Camberwell in Melbourne. 'On September 21st the people of Australia will be asked to elect a new parliament,' Menzies said. 'The prime responsibility of that parliament will be to conduct Australia's part in the most critical war in history, to lead our people to a complete victory, and to lay the foundations of a just peace. You will all realise without words of mine the grave responsibility you will discharge at the polling booths. It is no over-statement to say that our people as electors have never been called upon to make a choice of such enormous significance.'

Menzies often had a difficult relationship with the media. He did not have good relations with several proprietors, and had little respect for many press gallery journalists. He did not trust them, and made little attempt to get to know them or satisfy their need for information. Don Whitington recalled that, in his first year as prime minister, Menzies would hold two meetings with journalists most days, one at around lunchtime and the second in the late afternoon or early evening:

> His relations with most journalists were distant and patronising. He had a habit of criticising the way they dressed to attend his conferences, of reflecting on their style of writing or the interpretation of some event. He could be scathing, and often was.

He made few efforts to charm the men who were presenting him to the Australian public through the columns of the metropolitan and country press.[18]

But Menzies could lay on the charm when he needed to, as on one occasion in 1939, when he lunched with journalists in Launceston, and they tore apart crabs and drank beer from longneck bottles. It is not surprising, though, that Menzies remained a somewhat enigmatic political figure in 1940. He had only been in federal politics for six years. His reputation was as a hardworking, intelligent, and capable man, but who was also arrogant with a cutting wit. *The Australian Women's Weekly* travelled with Menzies to try to get a better understanding of him:

> Besides natural charm and courtly manners, Mr Menzies has created for himself a sort of 'stage presence'. This stage presence can be awe-inspiring, boyish and winning, or weary and in need of sympathy, according to the impression Robert Menzies wants to create. If he hadn't chosen politics, he would have been a fine actor. His voice is delightful to listen to in conversation, though in public it sometimes sounds querulous. He smokes beautiful cigars, and smokes them in a more expansive and expensive way than any cigarette smoker I've ever seen. He manages to look well-groomed even after all-night journeys on trains, wears nice ties, good shoes on his small feet, and is very well tailored.[19]

On his return to Australia in May 1941, Menzies introduced a single daily meeting, rather than two, with journalists. In response to complaints, Menzies said that neither Churchill nor Roosevelt held daily press conferences. In short, he did not like the media, and if he could get away with seeing them less often, he would. 'Menzies could be awkward, even discourteous, in his daily contacts with the press, and there were frequent complaints about his rudeness,' noted Clem Lloyd. 'The Menzies of the early war period was more different and less assured than the commanding figure of later years.'[20]

The September 1940 election result was a disappointment for Menzies. In the House of Representatives, the UAP and the Country Party won a combined 36 seats, Labor won 32, and the breakaway Lang Labor Party won four. The government had lost its majority, in what was widely interpreted as threadbare confidence in the government's prosecution of the war. Two Victorian independents — Arthur Coles and Alexander Wilson — now held the balance of power. Coles and Wilson could usually be counted upon to support vital legislation and procedural votes, but the four Labor MPs aligned to former New South Wales premier Jack Lang joined Curtin's Labor Party in February 1941, boosting its tally to 36 seats.

Earle Page agreed to join the cabinet after the election, and became minister for commerce. But there were continuing divisions in the Country Party. At a post-election party-room meeting on 15 October 1940, Cameron, Page, and McEwen nominated for the leadership. Cameron walked out of the meeting, outraged that he was being challenged by a former leader as well as a potential one. He returned, withdrew his nomination, and left again. Page and McEwen tied in three separate ballots with eight votes each. Cameron, who did not vote, could have broken the tie. The question of leader was then put off to conduct a ballot for deputy, which was won by Arthur Fadden, who, it was then agreed, would act as an interim leader.[21] Cameron subsequently resigned from cabinet. He described the Country Party as 'a stew of simmering discontent, spiced by insatiable personal ambitions and incurable animosities'.[22]

On 15 September 1939, Menzies had announced the formation of a war cabinet of six ministers to make decisions on matters affecting the conduct of the war. The appointment of a secretariat was an important innovation, and decisions were now properly recorded to improve the efficiency of business. After the election, on 28 October 1940, Menzies also established the Advisory War Council. Menzies repeatedly implored Curtin to join an all-party government of national unity, as British Labour led by Clement Attlee had done. But Curtin refused, believing it was important that a government unite behind a common set of political and policy principles. No such unity was possible between Labor and the UAP.

The Advisory War Council comprised all members of the war cabinet plus four members of the opposition, including Curtin. Most of these meetings were held either in Parliament House or at Victoria Barracks in

Melbourne. The meetings were chaired by Menzies. During the Second World War, nine current, former, or future prime ministers were members of the Advisory War Council at various stages, often overlapping: Menzies, Hughes, Page, Fadden, Curtin, Forde, Chifley, McEwen, and Holt.

EAGER to ensure that Australia's voice was heard in London, Menzies spent four months abroad from January to May 1941, and also visited Dublin, Washington, and Ottawa for official meetings, to give speeches, and to attend receptions. He had experienced difficulties with Neville Chamberlain, who did not seem to give Australia's interests a high priority. This had worsened when Winston Churchill became prime minister in May 1940. Churchill had little regard for the British dominions, let alone the views of many in his cabinet and some in the civil service. Menzies did not have a high opinion of Churchill before he became prime minister, describing him as 'a menace' and 'publicity seeker' who was 'lacking in judgement'.[23]

Menzies wrote to Churchill demanding to be kept informed of matters of major importance that involved Australian troops. Following the fall of France in June 1940, Australian forces were involved in a failed attempt to recapture the French-African port of Dakar. Menzies cabled Churchill to complain about not being properly informed of this action. 'It is absolutely wrong that [the] Australian government should know practically nothing of [the] details of engagement and nothing at all of [the] decision to abandon it until after newspaper publication,' he said. 'I have refrained from any public criticism but privately can tell you that absence of real official information from Great Britain has frequently proved humiliating.'[24]

Menzies departed Sydney on 24 January 1941 aboard the *Corinna* Qantas Empire Flying Boat. He was the first Australian prime minister to fly overseas. It was a long journey that allowed for visits to Singapore, Jakarta, and Bangkok, and ten days in the Middle East, where he met with Australian troops. In London, Menzies met political leaders, military top brass, and senior Whitehall officials. He visited Number 10, sat in on war cabinet meetings, and stayed at Chequers, the prime minister's country home.

In London, Menzies warned about Japan, urged that Singapore

be reinforced, and requested new aircraft and munitions. The British, however, were not persuaded to change their strategy. Churchill argued that the priority was the war in Europe and that it could not divert resources to the Asia-Pacific. But Menzies argued that reinforcement of Singapore's defences would be vital to repelling any future aggression by Japan. In any event, Churchill informed Menzies that he did not want to agitate against Japan without a commitment from the United States that it would enter the war.

Menzies' encounters with Churchill in cabinet were seldom pleasant. They clashed over strategy and operations, especially to do with Greece, and rarely saw eye-to-eye. The Greek campaign was a disaster that resulted in a considerable loss of Australian and New Zealand lives. Menzies had sought assurances from Churchill that Australian troops deployed to Greece would be properly equipped and that Allied gains made in North Africa were secure. Churchill did not approve of Menzies meeting with the Irish prime minister, Eamon de Valera, hoping to persuade him to join the war. Menzies did persuade Churchill to maintain a proportion of the United States naval fleet, which was being shifted from the Pacific to the Atlantic. But it was not, overall, a successful visit.

Menzies kept a detailed diary of his travels abroad in 1941.[25] This is a remarkable record. Yet Menzies later said he was somewhat embarrassed about the 'intolerance and hasty judgements' evident in his jottings, and said his executors would do him 'a good service' if they burned them.[26] The diary revealed that his opinion of the British prime minister see-sawed. 'Churchill grows on me,' Menzies wrote on 24 February. 'He has an astonishing grasp of detail and ... knows of dispositions and establishment quite accurately.' Menzies found Churchill utterly dominant in the war cabinet, where nobody else dared speak more than a few sentences. 'Does this denote great clarity and directness of mind in all these ministers or has Winston taken charge of them?' Menzies queried.

By 14 April, Menzies had no doubt about Churchill's dominance. 'The [War] Cabinet is deplorable — dumb men most of whom disagree with Winston but none of whom dare to say so,' he diarised. 'This state of affairs is most dangerous. The Chiefs of Staff are without exception Yes Men, and a politician runs the services. Winston is a dictator; he cannot be overruled, and his colleagues fear him. The people have set him up as something little less than God, and his power is therefore terrific.' Menzies made these views freely known to politicians, officials, and diplomats while in London.

Yet Menzies was often greatly impressed by Churchill, especially as he reflected on his London wartime experiences in later years. He described how once, with German planes flying overhead, ministers were awaiting Churchill's arrival in the cabinet room at 10 Downing Street. Churchill, wearing his siren suit, walked in and took his seat in silence. He removed the cigar from his mouth and turned his light, bright, blue eyes towards the men seated around him. 'Gentlemen, we have the signal honour of being responsible for our country at a time of deadly danger,' Churchill said. 'We will proceed with the business.' Their backs straightened, and their hearts swelled and beat a little faster.[27] He was courage manifest.

Moreover, Menzies and Churchill enjoyed each other's company while dining, drinking, smoking, and talking together outside formal meetings. Menzies spent several weekends with Churchill at Chequers, where there was a passing parade of guests for lunch and dinner. The two men discussed politics, literature, and sport, and while they had many disagreements, and could both infuriate each other, an affection of sorts developed between them that lasted for the next two decades. In later years, Menzies revelled in telling stories about his encounters with Churchill, and did a terrific impersonation of him. Andrew Roberts, Churchill's eminent biographer, told me that 'Churchill loved Menzies', and there was, over time, a respect, admiration, and affection that developed between them.[28]

The Blitz was a dangerous time to be in London. France had fallen. Britain was under bombardment. The imperilled island was under the threat of invasion. There were frequent blackouts, air-raid sirens blaring out over the night sky, and sandbags piled up around buildings. Menzies gave many speeches about the war — almost 100 in total — including to the House of Commons. During his ten weeks in London, Menzies lodged at the Dorchester Hotel. He also stayed with the royal family, visited the wounded in hospital, and met with politicians, civil servants, and businessmen. He was well received in the press. While it was not the same as in 1935, evidently, he still found time to enjoy himself, and he made a favourable impression. British Conservative Party politician Henry 'Chips' Channon recorded in his diary meeting Menzies on his way to London: 'He is jolly, rubicund, witty, only 46 with a rapier-like intelligence and gifts as a raconteur.'[29]

On 4 March, Menzies had dinner with Labour leader Clement Attlee and Labour ministers in the national government. 'Very interesting talk about Labour [sic] in Australia,' Menzies recorded in his diary. 'Real answer — Irish. They all agree. Attlee, at close quarters, earnest, upright and intelligent. Labour Party must have a theory to succeed. Importance of trained men in civil service. Folly of Australian Labour in resisting university graduates. My own philosophy.'

Menzies also noted his impressions of London and its people in his handwritten diary. 'London is drab and grey,' he wrote on 11 March. 'There is a tough and determined spirit, but the colour and gaiety have gone ... sandbags in the doorways; ground floor windows bricked up; death around the corner.' Making his way to Downing Street on 17 April, Menzies described the scene: 'I see many people who are drawn, black under the eyes, and shaken.' Menzies' mood, understandably, varied during his stay in London. A visit to a local hospital where wounded Australian soldiers were being treated on 13 February lifted his spirits. 'I see, talk to, and shake hands with 200 Australian wounded — all palpably pleased to hear a voice from home, and all amazingly cheerful,' he wrote.

It was dangerous walking around London, but a risk he felt compelled to take. Menzies' failure to enlist during the First World War was on his mind. He was, it is not an exaggeration to say, troubled that he was viewed by some in Australia as cowardly. So he visited Australian troops in Tobruk, and insisted on being taken to Benghazi, close to the action. By walking along the streets and over the ruins of fallen buildings, he thought he might offer a degree of reassurance back home to those who questioned his fitness to lead a nation at war. This was a remarkable admission made by Menzies himself in a previously unpublished interview in his retirement years:

It had a subsidiary effect on me in the Second World War. I was going over to have a look [and] to discuss various things in Great Britain in [sic] the end of 1940 or early '41 ... when I landed in Cairo I said: 'I must be — I want to chase our soldiers and at least I will do my best that I am not yellow' ... in England when I got there I then made a point, I put a tin hat on and go down the street while there were still things being dropped, to see what was going on, to get a first-hand view of it, and in Plymouth the same way.[30]

Menzies wanted to demonstrate that he was not a coward for having decided not to enlist. He was, as described earlier, chasing his demons. He had told Pattie there were two principal reasons for his trip: to press the case for the reinforcement of Singapore, and to show Australians that he was not afraid of war. 'I must go,' he said. 'I have got [a] very good reason, strategically, in the position of Singapore. It compels me to go. But I also have another personal reason for going. I must be there when I am in the smell of it.'[31] He had to 'set an example' and show Australians that he would not 'run away from any danger'. It had a profound impact upon him, and he was more than a little frightened. It is a remarkable insight into the real Menzies. Looking back, three decades later, Menzies was pleased that he went:

I was as near to being cracked, as quite a lot of people actively engaged in the fighting forces [were], but I thought it was most important that I should not run away from any danger because, well, there I was and I had to be the prime minister and set an example. So, it had an effect on me. I am not claiming to be a man of great courage or anything of that kind but I don't think I have ever been as quite as bad as they thought.[32]

MENZIES left for the United States and Canada on the evening of 2 May 1941. Eager to establish a rapport with Canadian prime minister Mackenzie King, he addressed the House of Commons — the first non-Canadian to address the parliament — spoke at a Canadian Club luncheon, and met members of the war cabinet. He had extensive discussions with King, who was clearly impressed by him, and recorded his observations in his diary. 'Menzies took this city more or less by storm,' he wrote. 'He is a fine looking fellow, splendid presence, great vigour, and has a wonderful gift for speaking. He has endless confidence in himself, and does not mind putting himself very much into the limelight.' King thought Menzies had 'many of the qualities of a great leader', but also recognised that he was often egotistical and overbearing, 'thinking pretty much of Menzies most of the time'.[33]

Menzies tried to enlist King in his mission to persuade Churchill to hold a 'conference' of dominion prime ministers or establish an 'imperial war cabinet'. Menzies was frank with King about Churchill's dominance in cabinet, the preponderance of 'Yes Men' around him, and the lack of consultation and discussion about war strategy. But King was not convinced. 'It was evident that Menzies felt strongly about this; that he himself would like to be on such a cabinet,' King diarised. 'I sensed the feeling that he would rather be on the war cabinet in London than prime minister of Australia.'[34] King said he liked Menzies 'very much', but thought he might have 'lost ground' back home in Australia, and doubted he could be 'a persuasive leader of the mass of the people'.[35] It was a shrewd assessment.

After spending a week in Ottawa, Menzies arrived in Washington.[36] The purpose of meeting Roosevelt was to press upon him how important the United States would be in the Asia-Pacific should conflict with Japan eventuate. Menzies had urged Churchill to insist on not moving the entire United States' naval fleet from the Pacific to the Atlantic, and a small fighting force was retained. On 10 May, Menzies recorded his impressions of seeing Roosevelt in bed while recovering from a bout of gastritis. 'He looks older and more tired, but my hour with him, with fair give and take of conversation, was most vigorous,' he wrote. Menzies compared Roosevelt with Churchill. 'R. is a little jealous of Winston's place in the centre of the picture,' he recorded. 'I tell him they should have a meeting. R. is not an organiser — very like Winston — and co-ordination of effort is not conspicuous.'

Menzies was left with a private, rather than public, reassurance from Roosevelt and secretary of state Cordell Hull that the United States would come to Australia's aid in the event of Japan entering the war. This was important. 'Roosevelt agreed that we all ought to tell Japan where she gets off, but stops short of actually instructing the USA Ambassador to do so,' Menzies diarised. 'I am left in no doubt (*without words*) that America will not stand by & see Australia attacked. I plead for reality about N.E.I.[37] and Singapore.'

Menzies, like Churchill, wanted the United States to enter the war. 'Public opinion has gone as far as it can without a lead by the president, whose delay becomes disturbing,' Menzies wrote in his diary. 'Roosevelt could decide tomorrow to convoy, and the people would back him. He could probably decide not to, and the people would back him.' Roosevelt was a clever politician, and often concealed his true intentions from even those closest to him. But he had given Menzies a degree of hope. 'Here, and in Britain, we look to the great democracy of the United States and believe we will not look in vain,' Menzies said at the Sydney Town Hall on 26 May 1941. 'The American people want us to win and they will do for us in that cause whatever Mr Roosevelt may lead them to do.'[38] This was seven months before John Curtin's famous 'Australia looks to America' message.

Menzies also filmed his experiences abroad on a hand-held 16-millimetre Kodak camera. It was carried in a brown leather bag with his embossed initials: R.G.M. These films constitute another remarkable record of meetings with prime ministers, politicians, civil servants, and the British royal family. These were, essentially, home movies of his trip. Menzies organised a special screening for Mackenzie King in Canada to view several reels. Back in Australia, Menzies would screen these films for members of his family and also his colleagues, in the government party room at Parliament House.

PATTIE Menzies had warned her husband that being away for so long could result in him being forced out of office within six weeks of his return. 'Well, if you go away,' she told him, 'when you come back you may expect trouble.'[39] Indeed, while Menzies was abroad, opposition to his leadership was brewing at home. Menzies, some journalists argued, enjoyed strutting the world stage while critical issues of war planning and organisation were left to others. Menzies was blamed for the failures in Greece and Crete, and was criticised by ministers for being hesitant in making decisions and not being able to effectively communicate the government's war policies. Criticism from newspapers such as the staunchly conservative *The Sydney Morning Herald* worried ministers. Labor did not make Menzies' task any easier by refusing to join an all-party government and sit in a war cabinet.

In retirement, Menzies named the ministers whom he saw as treacherously 'undermining' him while overseas. 'Holt was not among the resolute people,' he said. 'Artie Fadden was, as usual, a queer mixture of good fellow well met.' Menzies thought Fadden was eyeing the possibility of becoming prime minister. Page was also 'undoubtedly one of the underminers,' he said. Billy Hughes was often involved in party intrigue. There were only three loyal ministers: Philip McBride, George McLeay, and Eric Harrison. They were, Menzies said, 'the three people who maintained their resolute friendship' with him in these difficult days.[40]

As Menzies returned to Australia, he knew what lay ahead. 'A sick feeling of repugnance and apprehension grows in me as I near Australia,' he wrote in his diary on 23 May. 'If only I could creep in quietly into the bosom of the family, and rest there.' When Menzies arrived at Rose Bay in Sydney on 24 May 1941, he addressed the media. 'I come back with one sick feeling — that I must play politics,' he said. Events took their time to play out. Menzies was not in immediate danger of losing the prime ministership, although Percy Spender told him that 'his political grave was being dug' and that it was only a matter of time before he was 'pushed into it'.[41]

The following month, Menzies announced a reorganisation of government departments and ministries. Five new departments designed to improve decision-making were established. New ministries were allocated. A series of parliamentary committees were formed to advise on policy. These changes, however, did little to shore up Menzies' support inside the government. On 28 July, Menzies sought and secured an expression of 'confidence' in his leadership at a meeting of United Australia Party MPs. It was only given grudgingly, and did little to quell growing dissent in government ranks. Menzies was despondent, and began thinking seriously about his future — in or out of politics.

At a meeting of the Advisory War Council on 14 August 1941, Menzies suggested that he take up a position in the British War Cabinet as Australia's permanent representative. This had been supported by the cabinet three days earlier. But Labor opposed the idea. Given the precarious position of the government in the House of Representatives, Labor's support was essential. The idea of a dominion prime minister sitting in the British war cabinet had been raised while Menzies was in London, and he had continued to pursue it with his counterparts Mackenzie King (Canada), Peter Fraser (New Zealand), and Jan Smuts (South Africa). It was also periodically mentioned in the press. Menzies continued to explore the idea, and sent a cable to Stanley Bruce asking if he could sit in the British war cabinet even as an ex-prime minister. It seems that Menzies, who did not want to 'play politics' at home, was looking for an opportunity to return abroad. He sensed, as Spender warned, the end might be near. The options of serving in the British war cabinet, either as prime minister or as an ex-prime minister, were fantasy. Churchill, let alone the other dominion prime ministers, and his own colleagues, did not support it.

Menzies was struggling to unite the cabinet and the UAP behind his leadership. Again, the idea of an all-party government was raised, but Labor was immovable. On 21 August, Menzies told the cabinet that the only practical action he could take was to resign and to recommend that John Curtin become prime minister. He did not see any viable leadership alternative in either the UAP or the Country Party. There was, understandably, strong opposition to handing Curtin the prime ministership on a plate. Instead, Eric Spooner suggested, and it was agreed, that another approach would be made to Curtin to support an all-party government. On 22 August, Menzies wrote to Curtin with this proposal, and suggested that he could become prime minister, or an alternative leader chosen, with the ministries evenly divided between the major parties. 'We feel that our country is entitled to demand that at a time when its present security and future liberty are in the balance no normal political rules or practices should be allowed to stand in the way of strong government,' Menzies wrote.[42]

Curtin replied on the same day, saying that his party room would determine a response. The Labor caucus met on 26 August, and promptly rejected Menzies' offer. Curtin replied that Menzies' letter was evidence 'that you are no longer able ... to provide stability in the government and effective leadership of the nation', and suggested that he resign. This was hardball politics. Curtin insisted that Labor had cooperated with the government through the Advisory War Council and had enabled a workable parliament, but Labor was not responsible for resolving problems within the government. Moreover, Curtin rejected Menzies' suggestion 'that a government led by myself would not be able to secure a workable parliament and political stability'.[43] He would prove the truth of that statement within months.

Menzies thought Curtin would have accepted the offer if it were not for opposition within Labor. 'He had people like Evatt and so on who wouldn't have a bar of that, of course, because they had their own ambitions,' Menzies said later in life.[44] Evatt, indeed ever ambitious and calculating, had written an extraordinary letter to Menzies on 24 May 1941 — the day the prime minister returned to Australia — indicating he would be willing to join the government. He canvassed 'some form of closer association' between the parties being needed, but not 'a national government', which Labor opposed.[45] Evatt was angling for a ministry, or possibly the prime ministership. He had left the High Court and won the federal seat of Barton in September 1940. A year earlier, he had a cup of tea with Percy Spender in his chambers at the High Court in Sydney. Evatt said that an 'all-party government should be formed', and, provided that Labor agreed, brazenly asked if the UAP would support him leading it.[46]

At 2.30 pm on 26 August, Menzies met with several ministers while waiting for Curtin's reply. When it came, it was brutal. Not only did Curtin reject the offer of an all-party government, as stated, but he lashed Menzies' leadership and suggested he resign. Menzies was humiliated, and he was now out of options. The view of many — including Page, Spender, Spooner, McEwen, Holt, and Hughes — was that a new leader was needed. At about 5.00 pm, having received Curtin's reply, Menzies adjourned the meeting until 8.30 pm.

He returned to the Lodge, went for a walk with Pattie, and they talked it over. They agreed that he should resign. Menzies' father-in-law, John Leckie, also agreed. He spoke to his father in Melbourne and asked that a family conference be convened. 'He wanted the corporate wisdom of the family,' brother Frank recalled. A few hours later, the family's view was given: 'Throw in the sponge.'[47]

Menzies went back to Parliament House after dinner. It was as if he was walking to the gallows. 'The discussion this afternoon has shown that I have forfeited the confidence of a majority of my colleagues,' Menzies told cabinet.[48] He said he would resign as prime minister. He said he would not remain in cabinet or seek to go to London and sit in the British war cabinet. The new prime minister, he said, should be chosen by the joint party room.

The cabinet met the following day, 27 August, at 10.00 am, and agreed that no further action would be taken until the parliament had dealt with the Supply Bill and the adjournment debate. Menzies then faced the joint party room at 11.00 am. Menzies was criticised by several MPs, including Bill McCall, William Hutchinson, and Charles Marr. They wanted an assurance that a further meeting would be held that week 'to decide the leadership'. Menzies was not going to give them that satisfaction — he walked out of the meeting before any resolution was made.[49]

Late in the afternoon of 28 August, Menzies called the cabinet together, and reiterated his intention to resign. He recalled that some ministers were 'feeling very sick about the position they had gotten into', but his mind was made up.[50] Cabinet met again after dinner, whereupon Menzies said he would be willing to continue as a minister in the government. This was different from what he had said at the earlier meeting. Menzies announced his intended resignation as prime minister at a meeting of the UAP at 9.30 pm. About an hour later, at 10.30 pm, a joint party-room meeting was held. No UAP MP was deemed suitable to lead the government. Hutchinson and Marr nominated Fadden as prime minister, who was elected unopposed. Waiting outside the meeting was Menzies' private secretary, Cecil Looker. Menzies put his arm around Looker's shoulders. 'I have been done,' he said with tears in his eyes, and quoted a Scottish ballad:

Ile lay mee downe and bleed a-while,
And then Ile rise and fight againe.[51]

Later that evening, Menzies issued a statement outlining the discussions in cabinet and his decision to resign. 'I lay down the prime ministership with natural regret,' he said. 'For years I have given my best to the service of the country, and especially during the two years of war. Foundations have been laid and a national effort achieved, in which, I hope, I shall be permitted to take a proper pride.'[52] The following day, 29 August, Menzies formally resigned as prime minister. He remained leader of the United Australia Party, as well as minister for defence co-ordination.

While battling treachery, deceit, and destabilisation from within, Menzies had only himself to blame. A shrewder politician — which he would later become — would have survived. Journalist Alan Reid thought Menzies could not conciliate his party. 'He had never learned to suffer fools — meaning his intellectual inferiors — gladly,' he wrote.[53] Don Whitington said that Menzies' character hastened his downfall. 'Old hands in federal politics have expressed astonishment at his unusual lack of ordinary political cunning,' he reported.[54] *The Sydney Morning Herald* editorialised that Menzies was a man of 'natural gifts' perfectly suited to national leadership, but argued that no prime minister 'has more clearly shown that the most brilliant qualities of mind are ineffective unless they are associated with an understanding of public psychology, ability to choose adequate assistance and a capacity for teamwork'.[55] This is the art of politics.

Menzies, after a long period of reflection, came to understand this. 'I do not doubt that my knowledge of people, and how to get along with them and persuade them, lagged behind,' he wrote. 'I had yet to acquire the common touch, to learn that human beings are delightfully illogical but mostly honest, and to realise that all-black and all-white are not the only hues in the spectrum.' A great politician learns from their mistakes. 'I might have succeeded better if I had worked less in my office and more in the party room,' Menzies would later say.[56]

Menzies was prime minister for two years, four months, and four days. He was disappointed and frustrated. It was widely judged that his political career, at age 46, was over. He recalled being asked by a priest if he slept well at night and said a prayer before bed. Menzies said he did both. 'My final prayer, as I close my eyes on the pillow, is — to hell with them!'[57] And, in the autumn of 1941, Menzies was already thinking of how he could mount a political comeback. 'I refused to accept defeat as permanent,' he later wrote. 'My unspoken response was that of the small boy — "I'll show them!"'[58]

But Menzies also considered resigning from parliament and leaving politics behind. First, there was the possibility discussed of becoming Britain's minister of state in South-East Asia. Second, another report suggested he could be appointed Britain's ambassador to Washington.[59] Third, Churchill suggested to Curtin that he appoint Menzies as Australia's ambassador in Washington. None of these postings came to pass.[60] In the end, Menzies decided to stay in Australia. He was not yet finished with politics.

Did Menzies aspire to take over from Churchill as British prime minister, as historian David Day claims?[61] There is no firm evidence to support this. But Heather Henderson does recall family discussions about her father possibly pursuing a political career in London. 'My mother said to me once: "Of course people were asking him to stay there. And of course he was flattered. It was very flattering. But he didn't want to stay there. He was Australian. He wanted to be in Australia."' Henderson says that, particularly in the 1930s, a number of politicians and lawyers encouraged him to pursue a parliamentary career in England.[62]

Arthur Fadden was chosen unanimously as Menzies' successor as prime minister at a joint party-room meeting late on 28 August. He was sworn in as prime minister the following day. Fadden had succeeded Cameron as Country Party leader, albeit in an acting capacity, on 15 October 1940. He was confirmed as leader of the Country Party on 12 March 1941. Fadden's government was to rule for just 40 days and 40 nights.

Victorian independent MP Arthur Coles had rejoined the UAP two months before Menzies stood down as prime minister, but promptly resigned, describing Menzies' downfall as 'a lynching organised by mass hysteria'.[63] He returned to the crossbench. Coles and Wilson rejected Fadden's budget in October 1941, causing the government to fall. John Curtin, who had defeated Frank Forde by just one vote to become Labor leader on 1 October 1935, secured the support of Coles and Wilson to form a government and become prime minister. Importantly, Curtin had not used the opportunity presented by the government's divisions to force its collapse. He had waited until the government lost the confidence of Coles and Wilson. He waited for them to come to him, and when they did, he was ready. Curtin was sworn in as prime minister on 7 October 1941.

Menzies resigned as UAP leader on 9 October 1941, having failed to win joint party-room support to become opposition leader. Fadden became opposition leader, a position he held until 23 September 1943.

The UAP elected 79-year-old former prime minister Billy Hughes as its new leader. Hughes had little respect for Menzies, and famously said of him, 'He couldn't lead a flock of homing pigeons.'[64]

HOW well had the Menzies government prepared Australia for war? Menzies had warned Britain about the danger to Australia posed by Japanese imperialism. He sought, and eventually won, greater control over the deployment of Australian forces. He established new diplomatic channels in Washington and Tokyo. He extracted a private, although somewhat vague, commitment from Roosevelt that Australia would not be left alone if the Japanese entered the war. But Menzies' fateful months abroad in early 1941 were a failure, because he was not successful in concentrating British or American attention on the Pacific. It was, in fairness, probably a mission doomed from the start. It was not until 7 December 1941, when Japan bombed Pearl Harbor, that British and American attitudes began to shift. Curtin, while operating in a completely different strategic environment from Menzies, succeeded in this task.

On the home front, important progress was made in marshalling departments, instrumentalities, and industry towards the war effort. The army, navy, and air force were strengthened. But during the months of the 'phoney war', before mid-1940, Menzies had unwisely told Australians that it was 'business as usual', and mobilisation was slow. Key decisions, such as introducing petrol rationing, took months to come into force. A new department to coordinate industry, recalled Frank Green, 'was not actually functioning' at all.[65] Percy Spender, the treasurer and minister for the army, recalled the failure of cabinet to agree on a strategy for 'organising the Australian economy for war', and blamed Menzies, who had 'abandoned any attempt to give leadership to its discussions'. He saw the cabinet as complacent and divided, which left the nation 'insufficiently prepared' by the time France fell in June 1940.[66]

Nevertheless, over a two-year period, Menzies' government laid 'the great foundations' for the later war effort, defence department secretary Frederick Shedden argued.[67] The verdict of Paul Hasluck, the official historian of the war, is also worth noting. 'The accomplishment in organising the nation for war was considerable,' he wrote. But Hasluck added that Menzies 'did not have and could not command the trust or seize the imagination of the people and hence inspire them to an undivided war effort under his leadership'.[68] Curtin also recognised the Menzies–Fadden government's 'constructive work' in training and equipping the army, navy, and air force, and stepping up local war production when he came to office.[69] The upshot is that Menzies was not as bad a wartime leader as his critics suggest, nor was he as good as his supporters insist.

In the final analysis, Menzies could not unify his party or cabinet at a time of war — a key test of leadership. 'Your great trouble, Bob, is that you don't suffer fools gladly,' a senator said to him in 1941. 'And what, pray, do you think I am doing now? Menzies replied.[70] But this was more than just arrogance. John McEwen thought Menzies failed to satisfy the public and the cabinet with his wartime leadership. 'It is possible that Menzies was simply one of those people who are leaders in peace but not in war,' he said.[71] This is an important assessment of Menzies made by the man whom he would later regard as his most effective minister. Curtin maintained the support of his party, governed with a minority parliament, and won a landslide election victory in August 1943. 'In passing over the reins to Curtin,' Fadden recalled, 'I did so with the greatest confidence in his leadership abilities, his wisdom and his general capacity ... There was no greater figure in Australian public life in my lifetime than Curtin.'[72] This, too, is a remarkable testament to Curtin's wartime leadership by a political rival, and an indirectly unfavourable assessment of Menzies.

While in opposition, Menzies was forced to rebut unfounded allegations by Labor's Eddie Ward that his government had, in the event of a Japanese invasion, endorsed a plan to abandon Australia north of Brisbane — the so-called 'Brisbane Line'. During the 1943 election campaign, Curtin was ferocious in his attacks on Menzies and Fadden over their lack of leadership during the opening years of the war. In his election policy speech, he accused them of being 'blind to the danger in the Pacific' and of leaving Australia 'underprepared' and 'almost undefended'. It was strong stuff. Not to be outdone, the opposition accused Curtin of starving troops and failing to adequately defend Australia. This was politics played tough, with no quarter given and none taken. But the voters endorsed Curtin's wartime leadership by giving Labor what was, and remains, its greatest-ever election victory.

CHAPTER 8

'The Forgotten People'

IN May 1942, Robert Menzies was a former prime minister languishing in the political wilderness. He was eager to re-establish his political standing, climb back to power, and invest the non-Labor cause with a new statement of belief. The nation — led by popular prime minister John Curtin — was at war, with its survival imperilled. 'You lose an awful lot of face when you are dumped by your party, by your own government, in the course of a war,' Menzies reminisced later in life. 'Nothing could be more painful or humiliating than that — and it has its public effect.'[1]

Earlier that year, Menzies had begun a series of 15-minute radio broadcasts on a range of topical issues, delivered every Friday night. They required considerable preparation to research and write, and then to read and re-read ahead of delivery. Menzies composed them himself, often in pencil on a yellow legal pad, and worked and reworked them before delivering them live to air from a studio. When listeners in Sydney, Melbourne, and Brisbane tuned their wirelesses to the Macquarie Radio Network at 9.15 pm on 22 May 1942, they heard Menzies outline a philosophy that would guide centre-right politics for generations.

'The time has come to say something of the forgotten class, the middle class who, properly regarded, represent the backbone of this country,' he said. They were neither the 'rich and powerful' nor 'the mass of unskilled people' organised by unions and 'safeguarded by popular law'. Instead, Menzies gave voice to the vast 'unorganised and unselfconscious' group of Australians who represented 'in the political and economic sense the middle class' and who were taken for granted by the major parties. They were 'salary-earners, shopkeepers, skilled artisans, professional men and women, farmers and so on'. These men and women were looking for economic security and opportunity. They were motivated by moral values such as aspiration, hard work, and self-reliance. They were 'lifters', not 'leaners'. They prized family, home, and community. They were, Menzies said, 'the backbone of the nation'.[2]

They were people such as Lyall and Mona Howard, who lived in a modest home at 25 William Street, Earlwood, in south-western Sydney. They owned a service station in Dulwich Hill. The youngest of their four boys was born in 1939. John Winston Howard would become Australia's 25th prime minister in 1996. 'Those broadcasts did represent, as Menzies said, the outline of a political philosophy,' Howard told me. 'He was talking to what I would see as the natural base of the Liberal Party: middle class, small business, home-owners, family-centric. He was focusing very heavily on the individual versus the collective, and on individual enterprise and self-reliance. He certainly appealed to moral values. The great thing about it is that it is a reminder that politics is a contest of ideas and values, and not a public-relations encounter.'[3]

Menzies' 'forgotten people' broadcast is also a reminder of the need for leaders to invest their political missions with purpose, values, and direction. Governments and oppositions need an animating vision for the nation they seek to lead. Leaders must be able to articulate to their supporters, and to the voters, how their principles inform their policies. A clear philosophy gives a party coherence and guidance. It offers a reason to keep the faith. 'The art of politics is to convey ideas to others, if possible, to persuade a majority to agree, to create or encourage a public opinion so soundly based that it endures, and is not blown aside by chance winds,' Menzies argued.[4]

In this broadcast, Menzies spoke of the middle classes valuing 'homes material, homes human and homes spiritual'. He identified the importance of home ownership, family, community, and education. He recognised an independence of spirit exemplified by 'self-sacrifice, by frugality and saving'. He gave voice to the aspirational middle class of Australia, who believed in family, owning their own home, educating their children, serving their community, and taking pride in their work. (It is worth noting that Menzies did not use the term 'the forgotten people', but rather 'the forgotten class', yet his speech was later titled 'the forgotten people'.)

The series of broadcasts took place almost every week from January 1942 to April 1944. There were 105 in total, and the 'forgotten people' broadcast was the 20th in the series. The seminal broadcast was published as a pamphlet in June 1942.[5] A collection of several of the broadcasts, though not in order of their delivery, was published as a book in May 1943.[6] These broadcasts were a critical step in Menzies' political revival, and in the formation of the Liberal Party and its later stability and direction in government. '[Menzies] saw these broadcasts as an opportunity for him to lay out his political credo and his beliefs, and to provide a very solid foundation for his return,' Howard said. 'At the time he delivered these broadcasts, he had every intention of staying in politics.'[7]

Menzies often spoke of 'the revival of liberalism' as one of his most important and enduring achievements in politics. Indeed, the philosophical basis of the modern Liberal Party, formed in 1944, though drawing on elements of liberalism and conservatism, was essentially laid down in the 'forgotten people' broadcast. It became the guiding star. Menzies understood that the non-Labor parties needed to renew their purpose. But to win the battle of ideas, their philosophy and values had to be aligned to a coherent and relevant policy framework. Although he had identified a philosophical roadmap, he needed a new political force to campaign for it. A new political party was required.

Although Menzies' 'forgotten people' broadcast has often been celebrated by the modern Liberal Party, it did not have any significant immediate impact in reviving the fortunes of the non-Labor side of politics. It did nothing at all to help the United Australia Party, and it was delivered more than two years before the Liberal Party would be created. In July 1943, Gallup found that 78 per cent of voters were satisfied or more than satisfied that Curtin was doing 'a good job' as prime minister — an approval rating that no subsequent prime minister has ever bettered.[8] The Curtin government was re-elected in a massive landslide on 21 August 1943, and the Chifley government was comfortably re-elected on 28 September 1946 with its majority only slightly reduced. Nevertheless, Menzies' broadcasts were an important step towards his political resurrection in 1943, the formation of the Liberal Party in 1944, and the eventual defeat of the Labor government in 1949.

One passage in the broadcast took on a particular resonance. Menzies did not want to be forgotten. 'To discourage ambition, to envy success, to hate achieved superiority, to distrust independent thought, to sneer at and impute false motives to public service — these are the maladies of modern democracy, and of Australian democracy in particular,' he said. Was he directing any of this at his parliamentary colleagues who perhaps envied his intelligence and oratorical skills, but misjudged his true purpose for being in politics? 'Ambition, effort, thinking, and readiness to serve are not only the design and objectives of self-government but are the essential conditions of its success,' he said. He was surely thinking about himself. It was a none-too-subtle message to those who might have questioned the virtues of his leadership.

It is no surprise that Menzies had been a critic of Billy Hughes' leadership of the UAP since 1941. The UAP as a parliamentary party had all but vanished as a political force, and hardly ever met when parliament was sitting. In March 1943, when Hughes announced his support for Curtin's limited overseas conscription, he faced 'an open mutiny'. A motion to spill the leadership, which Hughes thought Menzies was ultimately behind, was defeated by 24 votes to 15. While Hughes led a dying party, the wily old man was still a force to be reckoned with. Menzies was part of a faction within the party known as the National Service Group, whose purpose was to reorganise the party under 'new and vigorous leadership' and who called for a raft of new policy measures to address the 'grave anxiety at the recent drift of events'. Hughes rallied his supporters and lashed Menzies, who had been a principal drafter of the policy manifesto, as 'the great self-seeker, the man behind the scenes in every intrigue, the fountain head of every whispering campaign, the destroyer of unity'.[9]

Menzies, at the age of 48, was still often talked about as a 'what might have been'. In the lead-up to the August 1943 election, journalist Edgar Holt penned a portrait of Menzies for *The Daily Telegraph* in Sydney. When he entered state politics in 1928, Menzies 'was confidently named as a future prime minister', he wrote. When Menzies went into federal politics in 1934, his rise up the UAP ranks was 'meteoric'. He had 'the most lucid and disciplined' intellect, and was a debater with 'ideas' and 'wit'. But now, Menzies was 'a rather lonely figure' in federal politics, although 'still head and shoulders above most' others. 'His greatest misfortune is that people don't like him,' Holt wrote. Menzies had a giant ego, and couldn't win the loyalty of his colleagues. 'He has all the gifts — except the political gifts,' Holt concluded. 'In politics he is always the brilliant amateur.'[10] Menzies cut this out of the newspaper and kept it in his files. He knew what he had to do. He had still not fully learned the art of politics.

Menzies was returned in Kooyong at the 1943 election, winning comfortably on preferences, but suffering a sizeable 14.3 per cent primary-vote swing against him. A month later, in the afternoon of 22 September, the UAP met in Canberra. Menzies had decided to stand for leader. Could he make a comeback? This was by no means assured, as the 'old' Menzies still aroused mixed feelings. However, he attracted some press support, and was winning plaudits as a 'brilliant', 'distinguished', and 'gifted' political personality.[11] Hughes, mercurial and cunning as ever, did not declare his intentions about the leadership until the meeting began. He said he would lead the UAP if it continued in a 'joint arrangement' with the Country Party, sparking a lengthy debate. Eventually, Menzies insisted on the meeting determining the leadership without delay.

Those who wanted to nominate for leader were asked to stand up. There were four candidates: Menzies, Allan McDonald, Thomas White, and Percy Spender. (Hughes did not nominate.) The method of election was by exhaustive ballot, whereby the candidate with the least votes was eliminated, and further elections took place until one candidate had an absolute majority. In the first ballot, Menzies received 13 out of 26 votes, and Spender, who received just two votes, was eliminated. In the next ballot, Menzies obtained a slim majority with 14 of 26 votes, with the remainder divided between McDonald and White.[12] Menzies was elected the leader of the party.

Hughes — who would turn 81 three days after the meeting — nominated for deputy leader. Menzies wrote to his friend Lionel Lindsay that he was shocked to see 'the little digger' standing 'in an erect posture' on his left when nominations for deputy were called. Menzies thought he was adjusting his hearing aid and asked, 'You are not submitting yourself, are you?' Hughes looked directly at Menzies and replied, 'Oh yes, brother; for the deputy leadership, certainly brother.' Menzies told Lindsay that Hughes' 'qualifications as an up-and-coming understudy to a leader' were not immediately obvious. But there were no other nominations. Hughes cleared the field and was elected unopposed as deputy leader.[13] (Hughes would be expelled from the UAP on 14 April 1944 for rejoining the Advisory War Council after Menzies had resigned from it, following a dispute with Labor.) The UAP's alliance with the Country Party, still led by Arthur Fadden, ended.

The election result had a sobering impact on Menzies, which prompted further reflection about the need to reconstruct and revitalise the non-Labor forces. Menzies told the meeting at which he was elected UAP leader that the opposition party had to be 'recreated as a living political entity' if it was to survive as an effective force in national politics. In a broadcast two days after his election as leader, Menzies hinted at what lay ahead. He spoke more as the leader of the opposition rather than as the leader of the UAP. He began by noting the disastrous election result and the decision to terminate the coalition with the Country Party:

> Perhaps someday, as reconstruction proceeds, we shall find it possible to create in Australia one non-Labor party with a universal policy and appeal, and perhaps with urban and rural sections. I hope so ... Two criticisms have been levelled at us. One is that we were divided, that we were a collection of competing captains and not a team. The other was that we had no policy for the modern world.[14]

Menzies essentially accepted these criticisms. He then spoke of the disintegration of the Nationalists and the creation of the United Australia Party in 1930–31. This was a sign that Menzies was thinking about the need for a new party if 'reconstruction' could not be effectively achieved. Moreover, he was already thinking about philosophy and policy. He spoke of 'a liberal revival' in Australian politics:

> The work of political reconstruction to which the opposition has now put its hands is not one which can be reformed without team work in the best sense. The essential foundation of a liberal revival

in Australia is a competent and cohesive body of spokesmen in the national parliament ... it is true to say that the non-Labor forces and supporters are vague about their essential political faith ... surely hundreds of thousands of people must have a rich faith in a political doctrine which elevates the importance of the individual, which seeks to expand his powers, which never forgets his social duties ... a political revival campaign is overdue if liberalism is not to die; and a revival campaign requires not only talented preachers but a soul-rousing gospel.[15]

Menzies would soon decide that the UAP could not be remade and could not endure as an effective political party. It was finished. A new political party, a truly liberal party, and one not beholden to special interests, would have to come into being. This was the task that he set himself in 1944.

CHAPTER 9

The Liberal Party of Australia

FOLLOWING the August 1943 election, which had all but decimated the United Australia Party, Robert Menzies began work on a post-mortem. Of the 74 seats in the House of Representatives, Labor won 49 and the UAP won 14. Labor won 49.9 per cent of the primary vote; the UAP, just 22.4 per cent. Menzies knew, instinctively, that the UAP was spent. A document he prepared, which has been located in his papers at the National Library of Australia, served as a blueprint for the new political party he had in mind. Titled 'Some Lessons of the Election' and marked 'confidential', it was sent to several of his parliamentary colleagues. It is a landmark document, often overlooked by historians, in the formation of the Liberal Party the following year. (It is reproduced in the Appendix.)

Menzies wrote that the principal reason for the election defeat — which he termed 'disastrous', a 'debacle', and a 'wreck' — was 'the prestige of Mr Curtin aided as it was by sharp divisions in the opposition'. He called for the earlier selection of candidates, better organisation and on-the-ground campaigning, and a shrewder approach to preferences. He referred to 'the Curtin halo' as a 'legend and personality' cultivated by his press secretary, Don Rodgers. Menzies said he needed his own 'first class press officer'. But Menzies went much further: he recommended the establishment of a new party called the 'Liberal Democratic Party':

The wreck produced by the election gives us a great opportunity if we
are ready to seize it. The name United Australia Party has fallen into
complete disregard. It no longer means anything. Many of my own
strongest supporters in my own electorate decline to have anything
to do with the party as such. It is a great misfortune when the name
of a political party means nothing. The word Labour [sic] does. The
name Country Party is self-explanatory. If we are to build a new party
it must have a name which expresses our true and permanent point of
view; and having got that name we should not chop and change every
few years as we have in the past. My own opinion is that our side of
politics should stand for liberal democracy. After all, this is one of the
natural classifications of political thought, fascist, communist and
socialist being among others. I therefore believe that we should set
about establishing a LIBERAL DEMOCRATIC PARTY.

Menzies argued that this new party must not be 'subservient' to the
Country Party. It should work with other likeminded organisations,
such as the Services and Citizens Party. The new party should not be run
by 'big business', as the UAP was criticised for being. And it should be
established on 'an Australian-wide basis' with a mass membership. He
suggested a federal structure with executives representing local branches
in each state. An organisational head should be appointed, representatives
in key electorates employed, and a public relations officer hired. On-the-
ground campaigning needed to improve significantly. A policy committee
should be formed, a party journal should be established, and candidate
recruitment should begin at once. He had identified the UAP's critical
defects, and spelt out a plan to remedy them. 'The time between now and
the next election is already beginning to run out!' he concluded.

In this document, written in September–October 1943, and sent to
his parliamentary colleagues and other political organisations, Menzies
also suggested that representatives of various parties meet 'freely and
frankly with a view to the abolition of the existing organisations and
the creation of a new one with a clear-cut policy'. This is an important
statement. It shows that Menzies was proposing to bring together the non-
Labor parties to discuss the formation of a new political party at least one
year before the first conference was convened to discuss the creation of the

Liberal Party in October 1944. Moreover, he had sketched out a structure for the new party, a strategy for winning an election, and a philosophical framework to appeal to voters — 'liberal democracy'.[1]

In a broadcast on 29 October 1943, Menzies again called for a 'revival' of liberalism. Menzies said that 'a new movement' with 'great ideas' was needed to mount an effective opposition to the popular Labor government. This new political force could not be the 'socialism' of the left or the 'reactionary capitalism' of the right. 'The choice,' Menzies told listeners, 'is between communism or fascism on the one hand and an enlightened liberal system on the other'. The latter did not support a return to 'unrestricted and ruthless competition', he stressed. This new political thought would emphasise 'individual initiative' as its 'driving quality' and 'motive power'. This ethos of liberalism, Menzies said, was 'an instrument of progress which is of such great value to mankind that to destroy it would be to inflict almost untold hardships upon future generations'.[2]

In the year after the August 1943 election, other politicians and citizens also began turning their minds to the creation of a new political party. As the UAP continued its inevitable collapse, there were attempts in several states to salvage what remained and to merge with other parties on the centre-right. Leaders in the business community also sought to create a cohesive force to oppose Labor. In 1944, a meeting was organised by journalist turned businessman W.C. Robinson, and held at the Melbourne home of mining executive James Fitzgerald. The meeting was attended by leading media proprietors and managers, including Keith Murdoch (from The Herald & Weekly Times), Frank Packer (Consolidated Press), and Rupert Henderson (Fairfax). Menzies was also invited, and was the only politician present. They subsequently met again in Sydney. In Billy McMahon's personal papers, there is an August 1978 memorandum of a conversation he had with Henderson about the meeting. The purpose, Henderson said, was 'the idea of persuading the "various groups" on the liberal side of politics to coalesce'. Menzies agreed with this. Henderson added that 'the concept for the formation of the party was framed by Menzies'.[3]

Menzies was the outstanding political leader on the opposition benches in 1943 and 1944. Gallup found that 44 per cent of UAP or

Country Party voters preferred him as leader, over Arthur Fadden (24 per cent), Billy Hughes (18 per cent), and Earle Page (6 per cent), following the election. But Curtin continued to enjoy consistently stratospheric approval ratings. In August–September 1943, Gallup reported that 72 per cent of respondents were satisfied or more than satisfied with his performance as prime minister. Among Labor voters, Curtin was preferred as the leader by 74 per cent, followed by H.V. 'Doc' Evatt (20 per cent), Eddie Ward (3 per cent), and Jack Beasley (1 per cent). Ben Chifley was not polled as a possible Labor leader.[4]

ON 16 June 1944, Menzies called 23 political representatives from around Australia to a conference in Melbourne to improve the co-ordination of the non-Labor forces. Their immediate focus was the Curtin government's 'Fourteen Powers' referendum on 19 August 1944. The group agreed on a statement of 'common beliefs' to guide policy. Importantly, they also agreed that 'liberal political thought cannot be adequately expressed and the fight for free political institutions cannot be effectively carried on' without a new party and organisation established on a national basis. In the draft statements prepared by Menzies, he urged that 'a conference of interstate and federal parliamentary organisation representatives should be held after the referendum'.[5]

The referendum campaign provided an opportunity for Menzies to argue the case for an enlightened liberal approach to government. Labor was seeking to expand and entrench constitutional powers to reconstruct the post-war economy and society. Menzies seized his opportunity, leading the case for why these new powers would be an unwanted intrusion into the lives of Australians and would centralise power in the hands of the federal government. In part due to his efforts, the referendum failed, and Menzies wanted to capitalise on this success. He told a meeting of the UAP in Canberra that it was time to convene a meeting of non-Labor organisations with the task of creating a new 'nation-wide movement' dedicated to defending and protecting 'democratic liberalism'.[6]

On 7 September 1944, a week later, he wrote to 18 organisations and individuals, inviting them to a special conference in Canberra. 'The time seems opportune for an effort to secure unity of action and organisation among those political groups which stand for a liberal, progressive policy and are opposed to socialism with its bureaucratic administration and restriction of personal freedom,' he wrote. 'I believe it to be most desirable that those of us who share the same broad political beliefs should first see if a basis can be found for unity. A successful outcome to such discussion might quickly and completely alter the current of Australian politics.'[7] There was an enthusiastic response to Menzies' letter. As noted, a number of other political parties and organisations had also sought to form a united opposition to Labor, and had held meetings on this basis, but they had not prospered. Menzies was the leader of the opposition. He had the stature and experience, coupled with the initiative and drive, to make it happen.

The conference would be held from Friday 13 October 1944 to Monday 16 October 1944, but not meet formally on the Sunday. The venue was the Masonic Hall in Canberra. There would be 77 delegates and observers from 18 centre-right organisations. The attendees included representatives from organisations such as the Institute of Public Affairs, the Australian Constitutional League, and the Australian Women's National League. There were state and federal parliamentarians, and officials from political parties such as the Nationalist Party, the Liberal Democratic Party, and the Services and Citizens Party.

On the morning of 13 October, Menzies flew from Melbourne to Canberra. At 3.00 pm, the conference opened. The delegates sat in hardback chairs at wooden trestle tables in the main room of the Masonic Hall. Menzies opened the conference with a lengthy address. At the age of 49, with silvery-black hair and dark, bushy eyebrows, and immaculately dressed in a double-breasted suit, he had, as ever, a commanding presence. 'This conference has been convened in an endeavour to produce unity of organisation among those who do not support socialism as the solution of Australia's political and economic problems,' he began. 'The present condition of what I call liberal political organisation in Australia, particularly on the men's side, is far from satisfactory, and all its implications should at once be considered quite frankly.'[8]

Menzies presented a bleak view of the centre-right political forces around Australia. 'The picture thus presented is one of many thousands of people all desperately anxious to travel in the same political direction but divided into various sects and bodies with no federal structure, no central executive, with no co-ordinated means of publicity or propaganda, and, above all, with no clearly accepted political doctrine of faith to serve as a banner under which we may all fight.' He proposed that a new political party be formed with a federal structure and a mass membership on a national basis. The new party must not be captive to outside groups with vested interests, like the UAP had been, he argued. The Country Party would remain a separate force, but 'co-operation or alliance, or even full organic unity' could be considered in the future. (Fadden recalled that Menzies 'tried to lure' the Country Party into participating in the conference.[9])

Menzies argued that the new party had to have a 'political faith' that would define what it stood for and provide a rallying point for action. He spoke of a party with 'a liberal and progressive faith' that was neither reactive nor negative. It was essential that the party was not seen to be resistant to 'political and economic progress' and 'branded as reactionaries'. The party's task had to be one of proposition, not just opposition. The party could not be an organisation that simply said 'no' or occupied a self-satisfied position as a 'critic' of Labor's policies. 'There is no room in Australia for a party of reaction,' Menzies said. 'There is no useful place for a policy of negation.'

Most of Menzies' speech concerned philosophy and values. A policy document prepared by the Institute of Public Affairs, *Looking Forward*, was extensively referred to.[10] The new party, Menzies argued, had to oppose Labor's 'socialism' and advocate greater freedom, choice, and enterprise. 'I see the individual and his encouragement and recognition as the prime motive force for the building of a better world,' he said. Menzies spoke about security, opportunity, and prosperity for all citizens. And he addressed education, employment, housing, and industrial relations. 'What we must look for,' he said, 'is a true revival of liberal thought which will work for social justice and security, for national power and national progress, and for the full development of the individual citizen, though not through the dull and deadening process of socialism.'[11]

On the Friday evening, Menzies hosted a cocktail party for delegates at the Hotel Canberra. There was an air of excitement, anticipation, and goodwill among the participants as Menzies mingled, and mixed some of the drinks himself. The conference reconvened at 10.00 am on Saturday. Menzies remained in the chair and worked on the sidelines to make sure ideas were freely debated, progress was made, and decisions were taken. On Saturday, a committee was set up to consider the new party's name and objectives, and another was formed to consider the organisational model and constitution. The two committees met informally on the Sunday, and reported when the conference reconvened officially at 10.00 am on Monday.

It was agreed that the name of 'the unified organisation' would be 'the Liberal Party of Australia'. Menzies' draft philosophical objectives circulated days earlier were adopted with only slight modifications. It was noted that a constitution for the new party would take more time to develop. A second conference in coming months was agreed to. In the meantime, a federal council, state branches, and a secretariat would be established without delay.

'The conference just held was remarkably successful,' Menzies enthusiastically told the media. 'All delegates showed a resolute desire that past occasions of difference should be forgotten, and that, in the words of one delegate, "The dead past should be allowed to bury its dead." The emphasis throughout was what one speaker called the need for a positive creed for a positive organisation. This was the keynote. It will be found that the new movement is not established upon any negative ideas.'[12] Menzies departed Canberra for Melbourne by train, leaving late that evening. He could not have been more pleased with what had been achieved, and the role that he had personally played in it.

The media referred to the new political party as 'anti-Labor' or 'non-Labor'. It would take time for 'the Liberal Party' to catch on. Menzies thought the name of the party was essential, because it spoke to its true character and philosophy. 'We were aiming at political progress and power in our own right,' he wrote later. 'We took the name "Liberal" because we were determined to be a progressive party, willing to make experiments, in no sense reactionary but believing in the individual, his rights, and his enterprise, and rejecting the socialist panacea.'[13] An insight into Menzies' thinking can be derived from Keith Hancock in his seminal book *Australia*, which illuminates the politics of the pre-war era. '*Conservative* is a word which has no currency at all; in Australia it signifies *reactionary*,' he wrote. 'Similarly, if a politician declares that he is a *liberal*, his audience will understand that he is by nature *conservative*.'[14]

Whether the Liberal Party was conservative, liberal, or centrist would be debated in later decades. It was not an issue that needed litigating while Menzies was leader. Menzies never used the word 'conservative' to describe the party's philosophy when he led it. 'Australian liberalism inherits the inductive method, as opposed to the doctrinaire approach of socialism,' he explained. 'It is in this sense pragmatic and not dogmatic,' he added. 'Australian liberalism must present itself as the party of action and the party of the future.'[15] At the formal launch of the party on 31 August 1945, in Sydney, Menzies described the Liberals as a 'middle of the road' party that had to appeal broadly to voters.[16]

John Carrick began working as a research officer for the Liberal Party in New South Wales in January 1946. He told me that it was important to place the party's philosophy in the context of its formative years. The party was founded during the Second World War. Labor, some feared, would continue to expand state intervention in the economy and society after the war. There was an alternative vision for Australia guided by a sense of 'liberal democratic post-war idealism' and 'opposition to socialism', he said. The new party wanted to encourage private enterprise, but also recognised there was a role for the state in the economy and society. It wanted to support individual freedom, encourage initiative, and reward self-reliance. It saw the family, and its moral values, as the foundation of society. It had a conservative respect for the nation's traditions, institutions, and shared heritage. And the new party wanted to encourage policies to deliver higher living standards and greater prosperity. This was, essentially, what was meant by 'progressive' liberalism.[17]

Menzies did not see the Liberal Party as projecting a 'doctrinaire political philosophy', but rather a practical and pragmatic 'attitude of mind and of faith'.[18] Former minister Paul Hasluck developed this notion further. 'Although a traditionalist, Menzies was not a conservative in any doctrinal sense,' he argued. 'I do not know what part he had in choosing the name "Liberal" for the new party he formed and led but the name would certainly fit his political creed. His political thinking was in accord with the liberalism of Alfred Deakin and the liberalism of late nineteenth century England. His wartime attitude on such questions as conscientious objectors, censorship, and personal rights and liberties was liberal — much more than that of his successors — and his post-war innovations were in the liberal tradition.'[19]

Menzies advocated liberalism within a framework of state regulation — which testified to his conservatism. 'Menzies, as the benign patriarchal figure protecting the community, continued the Syme and Deakinite tradition, but in a political order that had accustomed itself to the patterns appropriate to a protected and regulated society,' Greg Melleuish has argued. 'Be individual and ambitious but not to excess: this was the trademark of the liberalism of the Menzies era. It is also apparent that the Liberal Party combined this instinctive ideal of liberty, as summed up in the British inheritance, with a fear of socialism and communism. It did not set out a positive ideal of liberalism, and actively discouraged anyone from so doing.'[20]

The founding philosophy of the Liberal Party has, understandably, been interpreted in different ways. Malcolm Fraser saw the party as liberal and not conservative. 'It was never meant to be a conservative party,' Fraser insisted to me.[21] 'Menzies was a thoroughly liberal and progressive prime minister. If you called him a conservative he would regard it as an offence.'[22] John Howard saw the party as a blend of liberal and conservative traditions. Howard said that Menzies, personally, 'was so obviously a conservative' because he wanted to preserve institutions, customs, and practices, but he also had 'a classical liberal view' on many issues.[23] Tony Abbott said he, like Menzies, saw the party as inherently conservative. 'Menzies was a conservative,' Abbott suggested. 'He was someone who cherished a certain set of values, instincts, and intuitions, and he was someone who respected traditions, and he governed very much in those terms.'[24] Malcolm Turnbull described the Menzies-led Liberal Party as centrist. 'He steered resolutely to the centre ground and put his faith in the goodwill, the common sense and the enterprise of his fellow Australians,' he said.[25]

The party's philosophy, argued Menzies, was not meant to be narrowly focused. Andrew Peacock told me that Menzies created a 'broad church' party which is now 'more conservative than it was'.[26] The Liberal Party's federal president, Nick Greiner, argued that Menzies was a 'classical liberal', much like himself, who believed in 'individual freedom' rather

than 'collective power', and 'aspiration' rather than 'equality'. Commenting
on the present, Greiner told me the party could not survive if it was only
a 'small-c conservative or small-l liberal' party.[27] Peter Costello said in an
interview that Menzies did not seek to create a British-style Conservative
Party. 'Menzies came from a pretty humble background,' he said. 'He
was on the conservative side of Australian society and supported self-
improvement, reward for effort, private enterprise.' He described Menzies,
in the context of his times, as a 'mainstream' Liberal. Costello said today
the party is often distracted by phony 'tests' of ideological 'purity', where
Menzies is invoked. 'To try and fit him into today's divisions is historical
madness,' he said.[28] Heather Henderson, Menzies' daughter, said her
father wanted to create a 'liberal' party that was 'forward looking' and not
a 'conservative' party.[29] The Liberal Party's true creed, 75 years on, remains
contested.

The founding date of the Liberal Party would also become a matter
of conjecture. Was it during the Canberra conference held on 13–16
October 1944? Was it the occasion of the second plenary conference, in
Albury, held on 14–16 December 1944? Was it 21 February 1945, when
Menzies announced in parliament that the new party had been formed?
Or was it 31 August 1945, when the party was 'officially launched'
in Sydney? It is time to put this debate to rest. Menzies had no doubt
when the Liberal Party was formed. In his diary on 16 October 1944, the
concluding day of the Canberra conference, he wrote: 'New party: "The
Liberal Party of Australia".'[30]

When delegates arrived at the regional New South Wales city of
Albury, on the border with Victoria, for the second conference to form
the Liberal Party, the media were on hand to record the momentous event.
The conference was scheduled for Thursday 14 December to Saturday
16 December 1944. Men in three-piece suits wearing felt homburg hats
and smoking pipes, cigars, and cigarettes mingled with women wearing
their finest dresses with frilly hats and white gloves. Menzies arrived by
train on the Wednesday morning, the day before the conference began.
In the two months since the Canberra conference, he had drafted a new
constitution and platform. He had consulted widely to make sure it had
broad acceptance before the conference. During the proceedings, he again
worked painstakingly to make sure it was successful. Much was at stake.

The conference took place at Mate's Lounge, on the corner of Dean and Kiewa streets, Albury. Menzies wore a tailored double-breasted grey suit with a white shirt, striped tie, and pocket handkerchief. He stood at a table at the head of the room in front of a large Union Jack flag pinned to the wall. To his left sat Henry Baker, the Tasmanian leader of the opposition, and Eric Harrison, the deputy leader of the federal UAP, from New South Wales. The delegates were seated at several tables. Menzies was introduced by the local state MP, Alex Mair, the former premier.[31] 'Never in my life have I been so alarmed as now at the growing threat to all that is good in our beloved country,' Menzies said in his opening address just after midday on 14 December. 'If I speak of it warningly today, it is because I want to make it clear that political unity among the non-socialist forces is for us, who are its trustees at this moment, not a mere matter of political convenience or opportunity — it represents our great chance to give a means of expression to the deepest feelings of hundreds of thousands of Australians who are frustrated by the present, and who are unhappy about the future.'[32]

Important decisions were made at the Albury conference. The animating purpose of the Liberal Party would be to foster 'the encouragement of individual initiative and enterprise as the dynamic course of reconstruction and progress'. The party would be organised around a national structure, with state branches retaining their autonomy. The federal council would have representatives from state councils, and include the parliamentary leaders — something the Labor Party did not have. A federal executive and secretariat would also be formed. The party organisation would ultimately be responsible for the platform, comprising overarching principles, while the leader and the parliamentary party would make detailed policy. A broad membership, with women equal to men, was a central goal. The conference, at its conclusion midafternoon on the Saturday, formally resolved to constitute the party along these lines.

The character and purpose of the Liberal Party were established at the Canberra and Albury conferences. These would prove intrinsic to its success in federal politics. David Kemp, who served as a minister in the Howard government and was later president of the Liberal Party in Victoria, believes the formation of the party provided 'a stable national organisation' for the promulgation of the 'dominant political tradition' in Australia: liberalism. 'Its emphasis on liberal institutions of government, fundamental freedoms, choice, personal responsibility, freedom of enterprise, and an income safety net better reflects Australian political culture than the ideas of any other party,' he said. This broad philosophy, Kemp insisted, has not changed. 'Liberals are united around the ideas of family, private enterprise, individual freedom, personal responsibility and the safety net,' he said.[33]

Menzies, as in Canberra, was the pre-eminent figure at the Albury conference. He became a member of the provisional federal council and was appointed chair of the policy committee. It was reported that Menzies was now the leader of the parliamentary party, with George McLeay the leader in the Senate.[34] A motion thanking Menzies was carried unanimously at the conclusion of the conference. Menzies was moved by the gesture. 'We have brought into existence for the first time in the history of Australia the Liberal Party of Australia,' Menzies said. 'We have existed for too many years as a series of separate state organisations. This is the first occasion on which those of, broadly speaking, our political way of thought have established themselves on an Australian footing.' It was, he said, not a rebadged UAP or a collection of like-minded political groups, but an entirely new political party.[35] In his diary for 16 December 1944, Menzies wrote 'Liberal Party' and underlined it twice.[36]

On Wednesday 21 February 1945, some two months later, Robert Menzies informed the House of Representatives that the Liberal Party of Australia had been formed. George McLeay made a similar announcement in the Senate. Labor MPs roared with laughter. 'Rose by another name,' one said. 'What, another change in name?' interjected another. Menzies was unmoved. He looked across at government MPs and said, with a smile, 'You may as well laugh while you can.' Earlier that day, MPs gathered to hold the last meeting of the UAP, which became the first meeting of the Liberal Party. The new party was widely reported as just a rebadged UAP, as Labor MPs suggested.[37]

THE next few years would not all be easy for the Liberal Party. By September 1947, less than three years after the party was founded, it would boast an impressive membership of more than 130,000.[38] But first there were organisational challenges. State party branches operated as silos in the absence of an effective federal structure. Campaigning, on-the-ground organisation, finance, publicity, and research were still in their formative stages. The inaugural meeting of the federal council was not held until 29–31 August 1945. At the party's 'official' launch on 31 August in Sydney, Menzies outlined the party's priorities: employment, education, housing, and taxation. He promised a continuation of social-security support, greater assistance for farmers, and a guarantee that returned servicemen and women would be looked after.[39] The party's first federal platform, adopted in 1946, was largely based on this speech.

Meanwhile, John Curtin died on 5 July 1945. He had been suffering from heart disease, chronic illnesses, and exhaustion. A major heart attack in November 1944 caused him to miss several party and cabinet meetings over subsequent months. Frank Forde, Curtin's deputy, had been sworn in as interim prime minister on 6 July, but served only eight days in the job. When Labor MPs met on 12 July, Ben Chifley defeated Forde, Norman Makin, and H.V. 'Doc' Evatt (nominated in his absence) in a ballot for Labor leader. Chifley received an absolute majority of 45 votes to Forde's 16, Makin's seven, and Evatt's two.[40] Chifley, sworn in on 13 July, was the country's fifth prime minister in four years. It had fallen to Chifley to announce 'the war is over' in a nationwide radio broadcast from Canberra at 9.30 am on 15 August 1945.

When Labor sought re-election on 28 September 1946, the Liberal Party was hopeful it would claim government at its first attempt. Menzies' policy speech was delivered on 20 August at the Camberwell Town Hall. He spoke for nearly two hours. He advocated a new government committed to 'liberal democracy', rather than returning a government that wants to 'carry forward in perpetuity the war system which subordinates the individual to the mass'. He spoke in favour of 'the divine restlessness and ambitious enterprise of the individual' who sought a life that was 'free' with its 'horizons wide'. He made no apology for speaking about principles. 'In the long run there can be no high politics unless all parties have a sense of direction,' he said. 'We need to return to politics as a clash of principles, and to get away from the notion that it is a clash only of warring personalities.' He concluded with an upbeat peroration, arguing that 'liberalism brings to you the only real hope of a free, friendly, prosperous and growing Australia.'[41]

The voters took a different view, delivering a setback for the new Liberal Party. The Chifley government was easily re-elected, with Labor winning 49.7 per cent of the vote and 43 seats. The Liberal Party, contesting its first general election, won just 32.9 per cent of the primary vote, and gained only 18 seats. Heather Henderson, Menzies' daughter, said her father was bitterly disappointed by the result. She recalled him answering phone calls from the media after the election, asking for a comment. 'Well, what can you say,' he told them, 'when you've been run over by a steamroller?'[42]

Even before the election, there was speculation in the media about whether the party might fare better with a different leader, such as Richard Casey, who had been abroad since early 1940. 'You'll never win with Menzies,' it was often said. Criticism of Menzies increased after the election. Ahead of the party's federal council meeting on 29 October 1946, Menzies' press secretary, Charles Meeking, warned him what lay ahead. 'It will be surprising if the matter of leadership is not raised in some form at the council meeting,' Meeking wrote in a memo. The party's tax policy had been announced too early, the party's 'propaganda' had not adequately positioned Menzies as a superior leader to Chifley, and there was concern that Menzies had 'hit too hard' against interjectors at public meetings.[43]

As expected, T. Malcolm Ritchie, the party's federal president, highlighted doubts about Menzies' capacity to lead in his draft report to the federal council. '[T]here is a strong section of the people who do not accept his leadership and because of that, and that alone, will have nothing to do with the party,' Ritchie wrote. 'On the other hand, it is clear that Mr Menzies gained in prestige and power during the campaign. He came out of it with an enhanced reputation.'[44] Menzies struck out the criticism of his leadership in his copy of Ritchie's report, and it was not included in the final federal council papers. Yet he was stung by the criticism. When Menzies met with Owen Dixon in January 1947, he told him that he would resign as leader. 'He said that he knew he was the subject of dislike and hostility throughout the community [and] thought perhaps his party [could] not win under his leadership,' Dixon wrote in his diary.[45] Menzies was despondent, and thought yet again his political career might be over.

The doubts about Menzies continued. In July 1947, a Gallup poll found that if someone other than Menzies were leading the Liberal Party, 'it is possible' they could win an election held then. As much as 18 per cent of Labor voters said they would, or perhaps would, have voted Liberal if the party were led by somebody else.[46] In September 1947, with pressure mounting, Menzies resigned as leader and asked anyone to come forward to challenge him. He had decided to lance the boil. He was daring the party either to remove him or get behind him. He issued a statement explaining his actions:

> The leadership of this party during the next two years and thereafter is a matter of first-class importance to all of us. It will have a great bearing upon the future of Australian liberalism. It will have its effect upon the next election, with all its crucial importance in the defence of individual liberty against state dictation and bureaucracy. The choice of leader must therefore be made by the party with a clear mind and without regard to any factor other than the success of the great cause to which we stand pledged and of which we are the chosen political champions.[47]

This was not a fit of pique. Menzies had resolved to relinquish the leadership if he were not fully supported by the party room, the organisation, and the membership. He was prepared to give it all away and hand over to somebody else:

> After years of uncommonly active political life, I am entirely willing to make way for another leader if the judgement of the party so decides. I say to you quite frankly that I can see advantages for our cause in a new lead, furnished by some member of the party not handicapped by the apparently inveterate hostilities which my own years of work have, perhaps by my own fault or perhaps inevitably, thrown up against me. You are to be of easy mind so far as I am concerned. I am quite determined not to stand in the way of a cause to which I have devoted some of the best years of my life, or to resent the sharing by others of the feeling which I have just expressed.[48]

If he could not receive the support he was asking for, Menzies urged that 'a new leader' be chosen. But nobody did challenge Menzies' leadership. The federal council also endorsed Menzies as leader. Casey, seen at the time as a rival to Menzies, pledged his support and became federal president. In December 1947, with Menzies' leadership seemingly secure, a Gallup Poll found that Menzies led Casey by just 41–40 per cent as the preferred leader among Liberal-Country voters. It was not an encouraging sign. While Menzies had fortified his position as leader within the party, he still had to prove himself to voters.[49]

John Carrick had lived through the Depression and then served in the Second World War, during which he had been captured and held prisoner by the Japanese. After the war, he began work as a research officer for the Liberal Party in January 1946 and was appointed New South Wales general secretary in February 1948. Carrick, in what was probably his final interview, said there were substantial doubts about Menzies' capacity to lead the party to victory and effectively in government:

> If Menzies had made a mistake in his relationship with Lyons, it was that people thought he was too strident in his fight to get the leadership. He believed that if you succeed, then you are right. He didn't realise that behind his back were real enemies. He may have been too ambitious, I don't know. But then so was Caesar. Some thought that he was not the right leader. I know that people said his pressure helped Lyons to die. So, there were elements in the Liberal Party who had doubts about him.[50]

Menzies himself acknowledged in a previously unpublished interview that his hold on the leadership of the Liberal Party, especially after the 1946 election, was not assured:

> As late as '46, they were all saying, 'Oh, you can't win with Menzies, you know he has been tried, he won't do it. You can't win with him.' Somebody wanted to have Don Bradman because they thought he would be a wonderful fellow to bring over and be prime minister. Somebody wanted Tom Playford. All sorts of stupid things were going round, and so they were. I was still living under the shadow of being dismissed — services no longer required, in 1941. But I guess when they found the election coming and the way I was going about

it, they began to swing around and by say 1949, [with] the victory, I was the answer [to] the maiden's prayer. It took a long time.[51]

THE decision by the Chifley government to nationalise the banks was just what Menzies needed. It underscored what he had been talking about during the previous four years. Here was a Labor government seeking to impose socialist policies that threatened individual freedom and private enterprise in peacetime. Curtin had been a moderating influence on Chifley, but was now gone. Les Haylen, the Labor MP for Parkes, described the political impact: 'It was Chifley who took the holy ikon of socialism off the walls of caucus and marched with it into the House. The Labor Party, that amorphous mass of conflicting opinions, was trapped. It then had to make a decision — a unanimous decision — or be named forever as a party without the guts to stand for the no. 1 plank of its platform.'[52] Labor, largely out of loyalty to Chifley, supported bank nationalisation.

On 13 August 1947, the High Court ruled that provisions in Labor's *Banking Act 1945* that required local and state governments to use the Commonwealth Bank were unconstitutional. The case had been brought by Melbourne City Council seeking an exemption from the provision, which had only come into force in April 1947. Chifley, who had a vehement distrust of the private trading banks, was outraged. On 16 August, he announced that Labor would nationalise the banks. Menzies labelled this 'fascism', and said that Chifley wanted Australia to become a 'dictatorship'. At Chifley's urging, the caucus endorsed bank nationalisation on 16 September, and the legislation won parliamentary approval on 26 November 1947. It was not a popular policy, with 60 per cent of voters opposed to it.[53]

The legislation was immediately challenged in the High Court. Garfield Barwick acted for the private trading banks, and H.V. 'Doc' Evatt, the attorney-general, acted for the government. The case began on 9 February 1948, after an injunction was instituted to stop the legislation taking effect until the appeal had been heard. On 11 August 1948, after 39 days of hearings, the High Court ruled that key sections of the Chifley government's bank-nationalisation legislation, including the compulsory acquisition of assets and provisions empowering the government to prohibit the carrying-on of business, were invalid. This was a big blow to the government. Chifley appealed to the Judicial Committee of the Privy Council.

Menzies used Chifley's banking proposals to reinforce his warnings about the dangers of socialism. Bank nationalisation, Menzies argued, represented 'the most far-reaching, revolutionary, unwarranted and un-Australian measure' introduced to the parliament. '[It] will be a tremendous step towards the servile state, because it will set aside normal liberty of choice, and that is what competition means, and will forward the idea of the special supremacy of government. That is the antithesis of democracy.'[54] While Chifley's legislation had been invalidated by the High Court, he continued to fight for it until the Privy Council dismissed his appeal, just six months before the election, on 26 July 1949.

Standing for the defence of liberty against an all-powerful state remained the cornerstone of Menzies' appeal to voters. It was having an impact. Menzies' later success in leading the 'No' case during the government's referendum to control rents and prices on 29 May 1948 was another sign that voters were sceptical of Chifley's plans to expand and entrench wartime powers in peacetime. There was now a clear dividing line between Chifley's 'socialism' and Menzies' 'free enterprise'. However, through 1947–48, senior figures in the Liberal Party did not believe electoral victory in 1949 was assured. In November 1947, Richard Casey, the federal president of the party, advised that fundraising, candidate selection, and policy formulation needed to be significantly improved. 'We have got to work out the objectives of the Liberal Party,' he stressed, because 'in their present form they don't mean much to the average man.'[55]

In January 1949, leading public relations firm Hansen-Rubensohn provided a confidential report to the Liberal Party that made for sobering reading. Don Cleland, the party's federal director, circulated it to members of the federal executive. According to the report, the Chifley government's chances of re-election were not to be easily dismissed. The two major parties were evenly poised in the coming election year, with the Liberal Party's prospects having been 'seemingly diminished' in recent months. The Chifley government's 'generosity' with increased social-security benefits and tax concessions had been well received by voters.[56] It was yet another reminder that the Liberal Party's coming victory was seen as anything but guaranteed.

Leadership, Hansen-Rubensohn suggested, would be a decisive factor in the election. 'It is all very well, we suggest, to deride Chifley for his obvious personal shortcomings,' the report said. 'But he has become "typed" in the public mind as a leader of the honest-to-God Australian variety; homespun, maybe a little eccentric in some things and miserly in others; but solid.' Chifley was known and trusted — he was Labor's best asset. Hansen-Rubensohn assessed Menzies as 'a man of brilliance and attainments, possessing every qualification which Chifley lacks'. He was a man of 'known probity' who was 'devoted to the welfare of Australia', but few voters 'feel that they really know R.G. Menzies' like they knew Chifley. They recommended, not surprisingly, a public relations campaign to boost Menzies' image and elevate his 'character' in the minds of voters.[57]

Charles Meeking, Menzies' press officer, tried in vain to have his boss use his considerable talents to develop better relations with journalists. He rarely gave press conferences or one-on-one interviews, let alone background briefings. In 1948, Menzies made light of the typical conversation he had with Meeking about press relations:

Meeking (brightly): Good morning! May I suggest a press conference?
Menzies: You may, but I won't have one.
Meeking: The boys would like one.
Menzies: Curse the boys.
Meeking (doggedly): Well, then, what about a written statement on a burning topic?
Menzies: There are no burning topics.
Meeking (perspiringly): It would be good if you could consent to be photographed while shaving! The Sydney readers ...
Menzies: 'Out damned spot'
Meeking: Well, what can I arrange?
Menzies: To close the door behind you!
Meeking (despairingly): Hell, what a job![58]

The Liberal Party printed and distributed a pamphlet that asked voters, 'How well do you know this man?' It described Menzies as 'a man of the people' who had 'made his own way in life'. His grandfather was a miner, his father was a storekeeper, and he had put himself through school by winning scholarships. 'Through sheer hard work and ability, he early established himself as one of Melbourne's leading counsel.' He was also 'a man of simple tastes' who had 'the typical Australian's love of sport' and was 'a family man'. He was also a 'statesman whose stature is freely recognised' abroad. No mention was made of his time as prime minister or as a state and federal minister; this was about rounding out Menzies' personality.[59]

In April 1949, Cleland sent Menzies three advertisements that would appear in newspapers around Australia. They featured a sober and serious-looking Menzies, with an electoral commitment endorsed with his signature. The first promised to extend child endowment. The second asked voters to choose between 'socialism or a free and fair Australia'. The third was a pitch to trade union members. 'We believe in trade unionism and in the protection by the law of the rights secured by wage earners,' it said. Menzies approved the ads, but didn't like the photo of himself. 'Still think the photograph gets worse and worse,' he told Cleland.[60]

Menzies sought to position the Liberal Party as pro-worker, pro-producer, and pro-consumer. He promised to enshrine the 'freedom of the worker' to 'bargain for better wages' and 'to choose his own job'. He attacked communist-run unions. But with more than 50 per cent of workers being members of unions, the Liberal Party could not afford to be anti-union. When I spoke to John Carrick about this almost 60 years later, he was disappointed that the modern Liberal Party had come to be regarded as anti-union. 'Menzies said there is no war between the boss and the worker — they have identical causes,' Carrick said. 'Unionism is very good in itself. I don't willingly hear any of our people say anything kind about trade unions ... When was the last time you heard anyone say the boss and the worker have the same cause?'[61]

On 10 December 1949, the Australian people voted. Labor had been in power for eight years. Chifley was a respected and admired, indeed loved, prime minister. His government had ushered in the massive post-war immigration program, established the Snowy Mountains Hydro-Electric Scheme, provided financing to General Motors-Holden to manufacture cars in Australia, and founded the Australian National University. But the government kept wartime rationing for too long, there was industrial unrest, and the attempt to nationalise the banks was unpopular. Menzies charged that Chifley was soft on communism. Chifley thought the government would be rewarded for leading the nation through the war and in peacetime. 'My colleagues and I ask that you judge us on our record and on our ability to go on with the job of building Australia into the nation we all want it to be,' Chifley said in his broadcast from Canberra on 14 November.

But there was a mood for change. Menzies led a united party whose membership had swollen to over 155,000 by 1949, he was a dynamic and forceful campaigner, and his team was hungry for victory.[62] He had secured an agreement with the Country Party for cooperation in government. Promises to 'put value back into the pound', to expand the child-endowment allowance, and to end rationing, resonated strongly with voters. While Menzies was confident, he knew that he would be finished in politics if the Liberal Party lost the election. The future of the Liberal Party itself would also be in question. Much was riding on the election outcome.

Menzies had launched his campaign at the Canterbury Soldiers' Memorial Hall in Melbourne at 8.00 pm on 10 November 1949. He told the voters that it was a 'year of great decision' that would have a profound impact on Australia. 'In 1946, you could vote Labor, reasonably supposing that it was a party of reform and not socialisation,' he said. 'In 1949, it is clear that the Labor vote is a vote for the socialist objective and nothing else.' Menzies argued that the contest was between 'the socialist state' offered by Chifley, which subordinated the individual, and 'the ancient British faith that governments are servants of the people'. He promised to dismantle much of Labor's 'socialist' state, energise national development, extend child endowment, reform industrial relations and tackle union militancy, support private enterprise, and ban the Communist Party of Australia.[63]

The polls showed that since the previous election, Labor's bank-nationalisation plan had seen its support fall from 51 per cent of the primary vote to 46 per cent. The government had clawed back some support, particularly with its income-tax policy, but it dipped again due to the seven-week coal strike in the Newcastle region, which was broken when troops were sent in to work the mines.[64] In his final appeal to voters, Chifley said that Labor had 'a record of sterling service' and 'a program for the future economic development' of Australia. Menzies called the election contest 'one of the decisive political battles of Australian history'. He said socialism was the key issue and that the opposition's policy encouraged 'prosperity in industry and business as the best guarantee of full employment'.[65] On the eve of the election, the signs were good for the opposition. A Gallup poll predicated a narrow Liberal–Country Party victory with a combined 48 per cent primary vote to Labor's 44 per cent.[66]

Carrick thought Menzies campaigned superbly. He, like Menzies, saw politics as a battle of principles, values, and ideas. The ideological clash between the two major parties was up in lights in 1949. Menzies articulated a new vision from a new party for a new government. It was a thrilling and exciting time to be a Liberal. 'He was brilliant,' Carrick said of Menzies. 'He had come from an ordinary family and had ordinary values. He had a tremendous ability to articulate things.' Carrick worked tirelessly to build the new party organisation, attract members, recruit candidates, and develop a grassroots campaign. He thought Menzies meshed values and policies into a compelling narrative that won over the voters. 'Menzies, philosophically, was tremendous,' Carrick said.[67]

The election result was a landslide victory for the Liberal Party. The Chifley government had increased the size of the House of Representatives from 74 seats to 121, which made Menzies' victory seem even greater. The Liberal Party received 39.3 per cent of the primary vote, the Country Party won 10.8 per cent, and Labor secured 45.9 per cent. The Liberal Party won 55 seats, the Country Party 19 seats, and Labor 47 seats. The Liberal Party had gained 37 new seats, whereas Labor had gained four. Overall, the two-party-preferred vote was 51–49 per cent in favour of the Coalition.

Governor-general William 'Bill' McKell, who had previously been New South Wales Labor premier (1941–47), and whose appointment to the vice-regal office had been strongly opposed by Menzies, wrote to King George VI about the change of government. The increased size of the parliament had been expected to favour Labor 'and almost automatically ensure the return of Mr Chifley's government', but it was not to be, McKell wrote in January 1950. However, the swing away from the government 'was not as big' as the seats won by the opposition. McKell identified what swung the campaign to the Liberals:

The major issue during the election campaign was the question of a continuance of the government's policy, interpreted as being socialistic in its development ... I feel too, that the fact that Labor had been in office for approximately eight years, mitigated against the government. In this regard, the average Australian is prone to say 'let's give the other side a chance' ... Mr Menzies' personal prestige is extremely high and it is apparent that since he vacated the prime ministership in 1941, he has matured considerably.[68]

As McKell told the King, Menzies was back. It was a triumphant return to power after the humiliation of being effectively forced from office in August 1941. Only Alfred Deakin and Andrew Fisher had previously returned to the prime ministership. Menzies would possess considerable authority in the new government, but he was not yet the giant of Australian politics that he would later become.

Paul Hasluck, who would serve as a minister under Menzies, wrote an assessment in his private notebook about Menzies' standing in 1949. 'Although Menzies had reappeared as the leader and inspiration of the Liberal Party and was mainly responsible for presenting the issues at contest, I do not think that in December 1949 he had yet fully established his popular appeal,' he wrote. 'There were still members of the Liberal Party and a considerable section of the public who had doubts about him and still showed the effects of the many years of disparagement of him. It was a year or two after becoming prime minister that his prestige began to grow.' Hasluck perceptively added: 'The vote in 1949 was a rejection of socialism and of arrogance in government rather than an ardent acceptance of Menzies. Menzies reached his personal zenith later.'[69]

THE Liberal Party was created fit for purpose: winning government and staying in power. It was shaped by Menzies' thoughts about how a party should operate in government, benefiting from his experience of being a minister in state and federal politics. The party's policies would remain within the purview of the parliamentary party. There would be no external organisation, like Labor's federal executive and conference, or its union masters, which could direct MPs. The Liberal leader, not the parliamentary party, would have the authority to select ministers. This concentrated power first in the parliamentary party and then in the hands of its leader. The party had a philosophy, and it had values that would help guide policy-making. 'His importance to the Liberal Party cannot be overestimated,' said Labor leader Arthur Calwell in 1966. 'He founded the Liberal Party, he wrote its platform, he moulded its attitudes and philosophy — he was the Liberal Party.'[70]

Was Robert Menzies the founder of the Liberal Party? He himself was in no doubt that the party would not have been created without him. Menzies *was* the driving force behind the creation of the party. He invited representatives to the Canberra conference, and they came. He defined the party's philosophy, he outlined its structure, and he drafted its constitution. There was no other person who had the initiative, the capacity, and the determination to create the Liberal Party. Others had tried to regroup the non-Labor forces in the war period, but only Menzies' initiative succeeded. This is how Menzies saw it, and, in his retirement years, he was not afraid to say it:

> I had created the party. I had written and invented the whole policy for them, everything was my handiwork ... I was right in the middle of the show.[71]

But Menzies' role in the creation of the Liberal Party has been challenged, most notably by Ernest White and John Cramer. White was a founding member of the Liberal Democratic Party in New South Wales, established in 1943. White became a member of the Liberal Party's federal executive, but resigned in 1945. He stood against the endorsed Liberal candidate in the seat of Warringah in 1954, and lost. In August 1979, White disputed Menzies' role in the formation of the Liberal Party. 'No one man created the Liberal Party,' he said. 'This is a personal insult to me and my many friends who were associated with me in creating the Liberal Party.'[72] The Canberra conference, White argued, was just the culmination of many conferences during 1943–44. Cramer was the Liberal Member for Bennelong (1949–74), and served as minister for the army from 1956 to 1963. 'Menzies did a great job when there was no other alternative for him, but he didn't initiate the thing,' Cramer said.

'Menzies tried his damnedest to stop the founding of the Liberal Party.'[73] There is no evidence to support Cramer's claims.

White wrote to Tony Eggleton, then Liberal Party federal director, on 20 December 1979. He argued that the notion that Menzies was the 'founder' of the Liberal Party was 'factually and historically incorrect'. He traversed the history of the collapse of the UAP and the subsequent formation of the Liberal Democratic Party in New South Wales and other likeminded parties in other states. White wrote that it became necessary to have 'a preliminary conference' in Canberra. He didn't mention who organised it. Indeed, it was apparently 'at this stage' that Menzies became involved and 'took over the chair' at the conference. White argued that 'no one man or group of individuals' formed the party, and stressed that 'the initial effort' came from 'the party organisation'.[74]

White knew this to be misleading. Even before Menzies invited the 18 organisations to the Canberra conference, White had written to Menzies welcoming his leadership in forming the new party. This is an important historical document. 'I note with great satisfaction that you are pressing for an Australia-wide non-Labor political organisation,' White wrote to Menzies on 4 September 1944. 'There is a strong feeling in the Liberal Democratic Party that you are the person most fitted to lead the united non-Labour forces, and to this I heartily subscribe.'[75] And that is precisely the point — it is doubtful that there would have been a successful party formed without Menzies. Menzies was, as White said, 'the person most fitted to lead the united non-Labour forces'. White didn't organise the conference or chair it; he was simply invited to it as a representative of his party.

Yet, Menzies was not the sole founder of the Liberal Party. He himself paid tribute to those who attended the Canberra and Albury conferences. He especially named Elizabeth 'May' Couchman and William Anderson.[76] But Menzies was the leading figure in the party's foundational phase. Writing in *The Argus* after the Albury conference, journalist Creighton Burns noted that the phrase 'Mr Menzies and his party' was prevalent. 'It is indeed Mr Menzies' party,' Burns wrote. 'His initiative, leadership, hard work and persuasiveness have brought it to its present stage. Physically he stood head and shoulders above most of the delegates, and intellectually he undoubtedly did.'[77]

Heather Henderson recalled that the establishment of the Liberal Party 'was the most exhausting time' for her father. 'He worked at it like mad,' she said. 'I remember him travelling all over the place and talking to all the different groups to try and get them to come together. I remember some of them coming to the house in Kew. He believed in it so deeply that he was prepared to potentially run himself into the ground doing it.'[78] It is doubtful that anybody else could have done this, least of all White and Cramer.

Menzies looked back on the formation of the Liberal Party as one of his most important achievements. The party's political success was undisputed. Menzies thought the Liberal Party had also won a great battle of ideology in the post-war years. He thought liberalism had not only been successfully revived and promulgated, but was also influencing the Labor Party under its then new leader, Gough Whitlam. 'It all seems commonplace today,' Menzies wrote on a scrap of paper in early 1967. 'Even the most newly elected leader of the Labor Party in Canberra is advocating pragmatism not doctrinaire socialism. He knows that the latter is as dead as the dodo. The revival of liberalism in Australia has made its permanent mark on Australian political thinking and has influenced even its political opponents.'[79]

CHAPTER 10

Friends and Rivals: Curtin and Chifley

WITHIN a few months of his retirement as prime minister in January 1966, Robert Menzies began work on the first of two volumes of memoirs. They were written by hand in pencil on A4 yellow legal pads. Most of the writing was done at his office in Melbourne, and some at his home in Malvern. In *Afternoon Light* (1967), he wrote portraits of John Curtin and Ben Chifley. The original drafts of these are in Menzies' papers at the National Library of Australia. There were several subtle changes made between the drafting and publication of these essays.

One notable excision from the memoir concerned a suggestion by a Labor MP in 1943, while Menzies was in opposition, that H.V. 'Doc' Evatt and several of his supporters were considering crossing the floor of the House of Representatives. Their plan was to make Evatt leader of the opposition and then vote with the non-Labor MPs to bring down the Curtin government. In his memoir, Menzies said this person spoke on behalf of 'a very prominent member of the government';[1] in his papers, he named the person as 'a man who professed to speak on behalf of Dr H.V. Evatt' with his knowledge.[2] Menzies was suggesting the idea came from Evatt himself.

Menzies, however, would not have a bar of it. 'If that man crosses the floor and, as an opposition leader, moves a vote of no confidence in

Curtin, I will vote for Curtin,' he told this supporter of Evatt. 'If even a few of my friends vote with me, the "sacrifice" will have been all in vain!'[3] This is not only a testament to how Menzies viewed politics, as essentially an honourable battle of ideas rather than a clash of personalities or a contest of political tactics, but underscored his personal relations with Curtin.

It is easy to forget, looking back through a mist of nostalgia, that Curtin and Chifley waged a ferocious political battle during their eight years in power against opponents such as Menzies, Arthur Fadden, Earle Page, and Billy Hughes. It was often brutal and unremitting. But none of this diminished the deep respect and genuine friendship that was shared across the political divide. The 1943 election campaign, when Curtin and Chifley accused Menzies of neglecting the defence and security of Australia, and therefore imperilling its survival, is a notable example.

There was almost a ten-year age gap between Menzies and Curtin. Menzies respected Curtin, admired his personal character, praised his political skills, and described his wartime prime ministership as one of 'notable achievements'. Menzies made the point that Curtin had been able to inspire confidence among his party and among the voters — something that he had been unable to do during his first prime ministership. The two men battled each other as prime minister and opposition leader in public, but they were friends in private. Menzies wrote that Curtin 'loved nothing more than a personal discussion', and that over many years they 'had a regular practice of personal meetings and conversation'.[4]

Menzies recalled sitting with Curtin in his office, away from the public spotlight, talking as friends:

> Curtin didn't want to talk politics all the time. Nobody could understand that half as well as I could. And when he was prime minister, he would occasionally ring through to my office. 'Could you come around for a yarn' and I would go around. He didn't want to talk about the state of business in the House but he would say, 'You know I have been thinking about such and such a problem. Have you given some thought to that?' 'Yes'. 'Well, what do you think about it?' Some general philosophical consideration, you see, sitting there, and we would have a most amiable talk, nothing to do with politics. It refreshed our minds, both of us, and then I went back to resume the rat race.[5]

Elsie Macleod, the daughter of John and Elsie Curtin, recalled her father's relationship with Menzies. 'They had a good relationship,' she said. 'They always seemed to get on quite well ... certainly they seem to have a good, quite a good, friendly relationship. I don't think they let the politics and the fact that they were on opposite sides affect them in other ways.'[6] Not only did they enjoy each other's company, but they also respected each other's differing views. This says much about both men, and about the politics of their time.

In 1944–45, as Curtin's health began to deteriorate, he was often absent from parliament, and missed cabinet and caucus meetings. By mid-1945, there was deep concern among his colleagues and those who admired him across the table that the prime minister was dying. Menzies was one of the opposition MPs who kept in touch with Curtin as the end neared. He wrote an extraordinary letter to the prime minister on 28 June 1945:

> My dear John,
> I am sorry that I have not been able to get over to see you in the last few days. I have, however, been very tied up in the House, in addition to which I have acquired some kind of disease in the throat which I would not want to transfer to you.
> Ben has been doing extremely well and the House is in a good temper so that at least I think you need not give yourself any worry on the parliamentary side.
> My advice still stands: As soon as you get into the necessary condition for a real holiday, have one, and make no decisions until you have had it.
> Kind regards –
> Yours truly,
> Robert Menzies[7]

One week after Menzies' letter, in the afternoon of 5 July 1945, Curtin died. He was 60 years old. Frank Forde, who had been sworn in as prime minister, led the tributes. Curtin was, Forde said, 'a gallant, happy warrior' who was 'a common man' and 'Australia's greatest son'. Five former prime ministers — Hughes, Scullin, Page, Menzies, Fadden — looked on with ashen faces. Menzies also paid tribute to Curtin. 'It was possible, and from my point of view necessary, to attack on political ground[s] John Curtin's politics or his public administration; it was impossible and unthinkable to attack his probity, his honesty of purpose, the man himself,' Menzies said. 'He has left behind him a good name and an honoured memory.'[8]

Curtin had died at the Lodge. After lying in state at King's Hall in Parliament House, his coffin was taken by gun carriage to Fairbairn Airport and flown to Perth for a state funeral. Chifley was too distraught to attend. A long processional march snaked its way from Cottesloe, where Curtin had lived, to Karrakatta Cemetery on 8 July 1945. Menzies and Fadden were among the thousands walking to honour Curtin. 'I don't want all this fuss when I go, Artie,' Menzies said. 'Don't worry, you won't get it,' Fadden replied.[9]

Chifley was sworn in as prime minister on 13 July 1945. He, like Curtin, was a popular prime minister, and he led Labor to a comfortable election victory in September 1946. Menzies, who was then opposition leader, had strong policy differences with Chifley. They attacked each other in parliament, in the press, and on the campaign trail, without giving an inch or sparing a quarter. Menzies' attacks on Chifley's socialist policies were merciless. Chifley countered by accusing Menzies of doing the bidding of big business. But Menzies liked Chifley personally. 'I looked at him across the table for years, and never failed to be fascinated by him,' Menzies wrote. 'He was a man of integrity ... he was an opponent never to be taken lightly.'[10]

Menzies viewed Curtin and Chifley as very different people. 'Chifley was essentially the good unionist,' Menzies said. 'He was a completely devoted union man.' Menzies recalled their shared passion for literature — they had both sat on the Commonwealth Literary Fund committee. 'He was a man who did a bit of reading. To put it in his own homely way, he would say, "When I go home I like to sit in the kitchen and have a bit of a read where it is warm" ... There was a lot of humanity about the old boy and I thought an instinctive good taste in a literary sense.'[11] Chifley was nine years older than Menzies — a factor that, as with Curtin, may have contributed to the respect and regard he had for the two Labor prime ministers.

Chifley continued as opposition leader after his party lost the December 1949 election. He led Labor to a further defeat on 28 April

1951, and on 11 June was re-elected Labor leader at a caucus meeting in Canberra. On 13 June, a Jubilee Ball was held at Parliament House. The red carpet was rolled out from Kings Hall down the steps and out of the building to the footpath below. The men wore black dinner suits, the women wore fancy gowns, Jim Gussey's dance band provided the entertainment, and flowers and palm trees adorned the building. Chifley decided not to attend, and Elizabeth Chifley remained in Bathurst. He was not a drinker, and not much of a dancer. He told Labor MP Fred Daly that he would stay in his room, no. 205, at the Hotel Kurrajong. 'I'm going home to read a couple of westerns,' he said.[12]

Later that night, at about 9.30, Chifley began complaining about chest pains to his secretary, Phyllis Donnelly, who was also possibly his mistress. He had suffered a heart attack just six months earlier. An ambulance was called, and the outlook was immediately recognised as grim. Word got to Evatt, the deputy Labor leader, at Parliament House. 'Fred, come into the library immediately, Chifley's dying,' Evatt told Daly at about 10.00 pm.[13] Menzies was told about Chifley, too. 'If he needs one heart specialist or half-a-dozen, get them,' the prime minister instructed. The ball went on. At 11.00 pm, Don Rodgers, Chifley's press secretary, went up to the press gallery and rang the bell. 'Mr Chifley is gravely ill,' he told the journalists still working ahead of their midnight deadline.[14] By the time Evatt and Daly arrived at the hospital, Chifley was dead. He probably died in the ambulance. At 11.29 pm, an ABC radio news flash brought the grim news to the country. The former prime minister was dead. He was 65.

Meanwhile, the Jubilee Ball was in full swing. When news of Chifley's death reached Menzies in Kings Hall at about 11.50 pm, he was shocked and soon overwhelmed with grief. He wiped his eyes and stepped up on to the stage. Menzies told the band to stop playing — he had an announcement to make. 'It is my sorrowful duty to tell you that tonight, during this celebration, Mr Chifley, former prime minister and leader of the opposition, has died,' he said. There were gasps in the audience. 'He was a great friend of mine and yours, and a great Australian.' The revellers were stunned; many broke down in tears. 'Mr Chifley served this country magnificently for years,' Menzies continued. It was appropriate that the dancing conclude immediately and that people finish their supper and leave, he suggested.[15] Labor MP Clyde Cameron said he never forgot Menzies that night. 'He really lost control of himself and he did not care who saw him.'[16]

Chifley, like Curtin before him, lay in state in Kings Hall. His casket was taken by gun carriage to Fairbairn Airport, where it was loaded onto a plane that flew to Bathurst for his state funeral on 17 June. About 40,000 people attended the service at the Catholic Cathedral of St Michael and St John before he was buried at Bathurst Cemetery. Menzies, who was one of the pallbearers, visited Elizabeth Chifley at her home to pay his condolences. On 19 June, Menzies officially informed the parliament that the opposition leader had died.

I ASKED Heather Henderson about her father's relationship with Curtin and Chifley. 'They got on extremely well,' she said. 'He could have a good argument about some problem or some matter, but that didn't mean he disliked the person he was talking to — quite the opposite. Very often it made them closer. I think that's the way it was with both of those men. Certainly, on a personal level he was actually fond of both Curtin and Chifley.'[17]

Henderson showed me a small polished wooden box that once belonged to her father. He kept it on his desk. It now sits atop a cabinet in her lounge room at her home in Canberra. In it, she said, among other things, Menzies kept letters and notes he had received from Curtin. Menzies wrote one of those letters to Curtin on 29 August 1941, with a biblical connotation, just after he resigned the prime ministership.

> My dear John,
> I have ceased to be prime minister and we shall therefore no longer be opposition members at the table.
>
> I want to thank you for two years and four months in which my task, always difficult, has frequently been rendered easier and at all times been rendered more tolerable by your magnanimous and understanding attitude.
>
> Your political opposition has been honourable and your personal friendship a pearl of great price.

Yours sincerely,
Robert Menzies[18]

This is another extraordinary letter. It shows the friendship between these two men, from different political parties, with differing worldviews and political ambitions, and both competing to be prime minister. Curtin's handwritten reply on 30 August is also astonishing.

Dear Bob,
Thank you for your letter. I appreciate it more than I can say.

On my part I thank you wholeheartedly for the consideration and courtesy which never once failed in your dealings with me.

I wish you good health and fair going. Your personal friendship is something I value, as I hope and know you do, as a very precious thing.

Yours faithfully,
John Curtin[19]

ON 14 September 1964, Menzies gave a lunchtime address to the National Press Club at the Hotel Canberra. Towards the end of his speech, his remarks turned to Curtin and Chifley. He said Curtin had been 'a delightful man' and 'a good friend'. He remembered Chifley as 'a great man' with a sharp mind and impeccable literary judgement. 'As I look back over the 30 years and remember all the people who mattered,' he said, 'I doubt whether I will have many happier memories at the end of my life than recalling them and the work that they did.'[20] Menzies, Chifley, and Curtin were remarkable men. Their ability to put friendship ahead of partisanship, often in the national interest, is a testament to the politics of their era. Those times are, sadly, long gone.

PART III

The Colossus:

1949–66

CHAPTER 11

Return to Power

AT 7.20 am on Thursday 15 December 1949, Robert Menzies departed Melbourne for Canberra onboard a TAA flight. Allen Brown, the secretary of the Prime Minister's Department, met him at the airport, and they had a long discussion later that morning. Brown, who had been appointed by Chifley, was not fully trusted by some MPs in the incoming government. Menzies had an open mind about him, but felt compelled to ask Brown if he was a member of the Labor Party. 'Mr Prime Minister, I would not be seen dead in the Labor Party,' Brown replied. Menzies was relieved. 'And I would not be seen dead in the Liberal Party, either,' he continued.[1] Menzies kept Brown as his departmental head. Menzies also met with William McKell, the governor-general, at Government House, who asked him to form a government.[2] Menzies departed Canberra on a return flight for Melbourne at 7.15 pm that day.[3]

Ben Chifley had phoned Menzies to offer his congratulations on winning the election on Monday 12 December. The next day, Chifley offered his resignation to McKell and advised him to call on Menzies to form a government. The outgoing prime minister had travelled to Canberra from Bathurst the day after the election. Chifley was eager to hand over government as quickly as possible, but would maintain a caretaker administration while Menzies settled on his cabinet.[4] On Thursday, before seeing McKell, Menzies went to Chifley's office in Parliament House. The outgoing prime minister offered the outgoing opposition leader a cup of tea. They had a genial conversation. A photographer was on hand to record the moment for posterity.[5] It was a civil and orderly transfer of power.

On Monday 19 December, Menzies caught the same 7.20 am flight from Melbourne to Canberra.[6] Also onboard the plane were Enid Lyons, Dick Casey, and Thomas White. At 2.15 pm, the new government was sworn in by McKell at Government House. Each minister was handed a bible on which to take the oath of office, and they were then signed personally by McKell as a memento.[7] Menzies had spoken to McKell in person after the election and then wrote formally to him on Saturday 17 December — two days before the swearing-in — with his 'proposed cabinet'.[8]

Menzies had prepared, in his own hand, a list of appointments. He had consulted with Arthur Fadden on Wednesday 14 December at his room in Selborne Chambers in Melbourne.[9] The most senior minister, after the prime minister, was to be Fadden as treasurer, followed by deputy Liberal leader Eric Harrison in defence and post-war reconstruction. Menzies was magnanimous in victory; previous grudges were buried or well hidden. Earle Page, who had tried to stop Menzies becoming prime minister in 1939, was appointed minister for health. Casey, who had long been seen as a leadership contender, was appointed to the works, housing, supply, and development ministries. There was even a place for White, who had challenged Menzies for the leadership of the United Australia Party in 1943 — he became minister for air and civil aviation. (The only amendment to Menzies' handwritten list was to strike out 'works and housing' from Philip McBride's portfolio and give that to Casey.) Others appointed included Percy Spender (external affairs and external territories), Harold Holt (labour and national service, and immigration), John McEwen (commerce and agriculture) and John Spicer (attorney-general). Enid Lyons became vice-president of the Executive Council, but did not hold a ministerial portfolio, which still rankled with her many years later. There were 13 Liberals and five Country Party MPs in cabinet.[10]

The new government made it clear that long-term national development rather than post-war reconstruction would be its emphasis. Accordingly, the post-war reconstruction ministry and department under Harrison was only transitional. The new ministry and department of national development, headed by Casey, was established in March 1950.

The cabinet met at 5.00 pm after the swearing-in, whereupon Menzies emphasised the need for collective responsibility in decision-making and the maintenance of unity. The next day, 20 December, was Menzies' 55th birthday. At 10.30 am, the cabinet met again in Parliament House. After lunch, at 3.00 pm, Menzies went with Brown to be shown into the Lodge. The two previous prime ministers, Chifley and Forde, had not resided there — it had been vacant since Curtin's death in 1945. Chifley lived in a simple room at the Hotel Kurrajong, while Elizabeth Chifley remained in Bathurst. (The Chifleys did, however, use the Lodge for formal occasions, and stayed overnight when they were both in Canberra.) Arrangements were made for Menzies to move into the Lodge in January 1950. In the afternoon, there were meetings with department heads, journalists, and several MPs.[11]

At 7.50 that evening, Menzies made a live broadcast to the Australian people on radio. 'The new government is the government of the nation,' he said. 'We take up our task with no foolish sense of triumph and certainly with no wrong-headed idea that we are the servants only of those who voted for us. We are and must be the servants of all of you. We shall esteem it our simple duty to do justice to all Australians, to cultivate good relations between employer and employee, to regard the great trade unions as our co-operators in the production of industrial justice, and to make ordinary men and women feel that the government is their friend and not their oppressor.'[12]

Over the next decade and a half, Menzies would be a champion of free enterprise and a believer in Keynesian economics rather than laissez-faire capitalism to support full employment and the welfare state. He was a staunch anti-communist, mindful of the dangers of totalitarianism, which had been learned the hard way during the Second World War, and of the continuing threat to liberty at home and abroad.[13] He understood that a prime minister who had respect and authority in his party and cabinet, and in the electorate, could lead a government successfully. In a 1966 ABC television documentary, *Mr Prime Minister*, he identified 'the two greatest sources of prime ministerial power' as the capacity to lead and influence 'the creation of policy', and being the government's 'chief public relations officer'.[14]

ROBERT Menzies' prime ministerial suite was located in the north-eastern corner of the upper floor of Parliament House. There were two smaller offices, for his personal secretary and department head, next to his office. There was a lobby area, several administrative 'cubbyholes' for typists, messengers, and attendants, and a small bathroom. The prime minister's ante-room, essentially a small lounge area, led to the cabinet room and a verandah. It was the ante-room that Menzies would gravitate to in the evenings to mix cocktails for ministers, public servants, and some of his staff, and hold court with stories and anecdotes from a life in law and politics.

The interior of the office did not change much over the 16 years that Menzies occupied it. On the dark wooden-panelled walls there were often a few framed photos, such as of the Queen and Prince Philip, cricketers Don Bradman or Keith Miller, and one of Menzies and Winston Churchill taken in 1941. There was also a painting by Churchill, *Cap D'Antibes*, gifted to Menzies in 1955, and other Australian landscape paintings by Arthur Streeton, that hung on the wall. (Menzies' estate bequeathed the Churchill painting to Parliament House in 1982.) A small bookshelf held volumes of *Hansard*, law books, and William Shakespeare's collected works. There were a few pot plants between several lounge chairs.

Menzies sat in a leather chair behind an ornate maple pedestal desk used by every prime minister since 1927. Atop were often folders and papers, perhaps a book or two, document in and out trays, a telephone, an ashtray for his cigars, and a lamp. He almost always used pencils, and signed letters and official documents with a fountain pen. A small radio would be tuned to the cricket during summer. He was never at ease with the phone, and, if he used it, he held it a foot from his head and often shouted into it. He would smoke cigars — usually Coronas — perhaps half a dozen, during the day. In the evening, Menzies would enjoy a drink in the cabinet ante-room. Before dinner, he would enjoy a potent martini — usually mixed in a glass jug as three parts gin and one part vermouth, plus ice and lemon rind — always stirred and never shaken. In the afternoon, he enjoyed a 'Southerly Buster' cocktail. And he would drink Scotch whisky with soda water and a lump of ice in the evenings.

Menzies routinely worked a 70-hour week. Unlike Chifley, he was not an early starter — he did not often arrive at the office before 10.00 am.

The day usually began with a bath or shower. He would read *The Canberra Times* and *The Sydney Morning Herald* over breakfast at the Lodge before being chauffeur-driven to Parliament House. He would usually go home to the Lodge for lunch, and during his first prime ministership often played a game of snooker with Pattie. He would work in the office through the afternoon, sometimes go home for dinner, and return to the office in the evening. He often worked until 11.00 pm or midnight, or later, and staff would have to be on hand. He would spend Saturday mornings and afternoons in the office, whereas Sundays would be more relaxed, with time set aside for work in the afternoon at the Lodge. By 1966, he had a small staff of around a dozen, mostly recruited from within the public service. He would routinely meet with his private secretary — initially J.R. ('Bob') Willoughby — and his press secretary each weekday morning. The rest of the day would involve a combination of meetings with public servants or ministers, attending cabinet or parliament, occasionally seeing journalists, and dealing with administrative matters. He would usually summon staff to his office with a bell.[15]

Parliament House was a stately, though increasingly cramped, building in those days. It had been designed by John Smith Murdoch as a temporary building to house the parliament and executive offices, and was opened by the Duke of York (later King George VI) in 1927. MPs shared offices, took meals together in the dining room, and relaxed during the evening either in the party rooms, the bars, or the library. The House of Representatives and the Senate chambers were located on opposing sides of the building. In the middle was King's Hall, a hive of activity where MPs, journalists, and the public could bump into each other and talk about politics. The press gallery was located on the top floor, though journalists freely roamed the building. Most Liberal and Country MPs lodged at the Hotel Canberra, while many Labor MPs stayed at the Hotel Kurrajong, both a short walk from Parliament House.

William Heseltine worked as Menzies' private secretary from 1955 to 1959. At that stage, the prime minister had about nine members of staff: a private secretary, personal secretary, press secretary, three typists, two messengers, and an attendant or two. Heseltine had joined the Prime Minister's Department in 1951 and was recommended for the role in Menzies' office by departmental secretary Allen Brown. 'I was extraordinarily anxious about the appointment, and wondered what on earth I was going to talk to this great man about,' Heseltine told me. But they soon developed a rapport, and his esteem for Menzies grew immensely. 'I really loved the old boy and admired him hugely for his great talents both as statesman and politician,' he said.[16]

Tony Eggleton worked as Menzies' press secretary from 1965 to 1966. He recalled his old boss being 'informal' and 'kindly' to staff and public servants. 'Menzies was open to ideas and welcomed advice he may not always agree with,' Eggleton told me. He made it clear that he didn't mind what Eggleton's politics were, and didn't ask.[17] Menzies' first press secretary, Stewart Cockburn, recalled that the staff had 'admiration' and 'real affection' for their boss. He almost never lost his temper, and used his 'impressible wit' to keep the office working harmoniously. 'No matter what his mood, his sense of the comic or the ridiculous would many times a day sweeten an argument, relieve the tension in a threatened confrontation, or relax a nervous visitor.'[18]

Menzies' staff found him unlike the public stereotype of an aloof and arrogant man. While he could be demanding, he was almost always respectful and appreciative, and worked through each day with good humour. Robert ('Buzz') Kennedy, a newspaper, television, and radio journalist, worked as a special assistant to Menzies from 1958 to 1960. 'He was a kindly, thoughtful, and gentle boss,' Kennedy recalled. 'People just didn't believe me.'[19] Menzies was essentially a shy man, and not always comfortable with confrontation. One of the implications of this, argued Heseltine, was that he sometimes criticised people behind their back rather than to their face. While not diminishing his overall admiration for Menzies, Heseltine described this as 'a weakness of character'.[20]

Two of Menzies' most important personal staff were Eileen Lenihan and Hazel Craig. Lenihan had worked as secretary to Richard Casey and then Joe Lyons, and continued working for Menzies when he became prime minister in 1939. She worked for Menzies from 1939 to 1951. Lenihan performed all manner of duties, including taking shorthand minutes of meetings, writing letters, organising his diary, seeing to visitors, and answering the phone. Menzies called her 'Lennie'. In 1951, concerned about the pace of work and her health, she became private secretary to the attorney-general, John Spicer.

Hazel Craig began work in the Prime Minister's Department in 1934. She went on to work on the staff of five prime ministers: Lyons, Menzies, Fadden, Curtin, and Chifley. Craig continued working for Chifley as his secretary while he was opposition leader, from 1949 to 1951. She then worked on Menzies' staff from 1951 to 1966, taking over from Lenihan, and continued working for Menzies in his retirement until 1976. Menzies called her 'the boss'. When she retired, Menzies gave her a silver tray on which he had engraved: 'A splendid secretary and faithful friend.'[21] Craig had become part of the family. As a sign of Menzies' appreciation and affection for her, in his will he stipulated that she was to be left $3,500 — about $18,000 in today's value.[22]

Lenihan and Craig, who worked for Menzies and Chifley at the same time, were friends. In 1950, they went on a six-month holiday to England, Scotland, and Ireland. They were described as 'two women who probably know more of what goes on behind the scenes in Australian politics than anyone but the two men whose private secretaries they are'.[23] It is another testament to the friendships across the political divide that existed then. Lenihan and Craig continued to be the closest of friends for the rest of their lives. When Lenihan died in September 1990, Craig posted a notice in *The Canberra Times*. 'LENIHAN, Eileen G,' it read. 'On Sept 2 at Sydney. Long-time good friend of Hazel Craig.'[24] Hazel Craig died in May 2013 at the age of 98.

THE Prime Minister's Department was not established until 1911, as an initiative of prime minister Andrew Fisher. Initially, the department was an administrative and coordination agency within government rather than concerned with policy matters. During the First World War, Billy Hughes had the Prime Minister's Department take on a policy role. However, policy work within the department was sporadic until the 1940s, including during Robert Menzies' first prime ministership, but expanded when Ben Chifley established a secretariat to coordinate cabinet business in 1949. By the time Menzies became prime minister again, the department had further enlarged its policy and administrative functions. Fin Crisp, who headed the Department of Post-War Reconstruction and was later a professor of politics, said these developments, which were further consolidated under Menzies, 'undoubtedly strengthened the hand of the prime minister' within government.[25]

Chifley had appointed Allen Brown as departmental secretary in August 1949, and he continued in the position under Menzies until December 1958. John Bunting succeeded Brown in January 1959, continuing until Menzies' retirement in January 1966, and then served under Harold Holt and John McEwen. There was a strong central bureaucratic influence over government during the Menzies period — key secretaries were referred to as the 'seven dwarves'. This influence declined in subsequent years, due to several factors such as ministers relying less on the bureaucracy, new and competing sources of policy advice, the introduction of personal staff, and structural changes to the bureaucracy that dispersed this power across departments and increased the authority of ministers over public servants.

Menzies maintained a close relationship with departmental heads. He looked to them for policy advice, sought their feedback on how ministers were performing, and also elicited their views on each other. He invited them to drinks in his office, had them for dinner at the Lodge, and occasionally took them to lunch at one of Melbourne's prestigious clubs. Menzies also wanted to develop the professionalism of the public service and encouraged the facilitation of university graduates into its ranks, having been impressed by the calibre of staff in Whitehall and Washington. An important step was the establishment of a committee charged with inquiring into public service recruitment headed by Richard Boyer, the chairman of the Australian Broadcasting Commission, in September 1957.

During the 1950s, the cabinet system became more efficient and better coordinated: a formal agenda was prepared, submissions were required to be circulated three days in advance, and decisions were properly recorded and followed up. The Prime Minister's Department also began to provide written briefs to Menzies on every submission presented to cabinet.[26] Menzies said departmental assistance in scrutinising submissions meant that, combined with his own study, he 'was extremely well informed' and had an advantage over other ministers.[27] Menzies described how he approached cabinet. 'What I said no doubt carried a good deal of influence,' he explained. 'But the first thing I think is for a prime minister to make it clear to his ministers that each of them with something to say will be heard.' He would guide the discussion. When he felt a consensus had emerged, he would summarise and then say, 'Well, I agree with that, boys, we ought to do it.'[28]

Heseltine remembers that Menzies placed a 'high priority' on advice from ministers and public servants, and saw the cabinet process, with full and frank discussion, as fundamental to good government. 'He really looked to his public servants for advice,' Heseltine said. 'Ministerial offices weren't full of advisers and staffers. Ministers had their private secretaries and a small private office. The advice came from cabinet colleagues and senior public servants. He was very good at receiving advice, respected it, but didn't always take it, of course.'[29]

Lenox Hewitt worked in the Department of Post-War Reconstruction during the Chifley government, and, after a posting in London, returned to Australia and joined the Treasury in 1953. He served as first assistant secretary (1955–62) and deputy secretary (1962–66). Hewitt told me that he occasionally attended cabinet, supporting secretary Roland Wilson. 'Menzies conducted cabinet meetings impressively,' he recalled. 'He was dignified and appropriate in proceedings.' Hewitt said Menzies had 'a dignified relationship' with Wilson, and was especially close to Brown and Bunting, whom he judged as 'central' to the work of the Menzies government.[30]

Menzies argued that the prime minister was *primus inter pares* — first among equals — within the cabinet. Yet his intelligence, experience, and political authority, plus his large physical size, meant that he could be imposing in meetings. Still, Menzies ran a largely collegiate cabinet process. Meetings were almost always held in the cabinet room, near the prime minister's office in Parliament House. Periodically, tea, coffee, and biscuits would be brought to meetings. Ministers would break for lunch or dinner, and usually enjoy a drink in the ante-room afterwards. As most ministers sucked on cigarettes or cigars, proceedings would often be conducted in a fug of thick smoke. The workload steadily increased. In 1950, cabinet met 158 times, considered 237 submissions, and made 456 decisions. By 1965, cabinet met 159 times, considered 618 papers, and made 785 decisions.[31]

Ministers, personally chosen by the prime minister rather than elected by the party room, owed a special loyalty to Menzies. But it was more than just patronage that resulted in a mostly unified cabinet with few leaks over a 16-year period. Howard Beale recalled that Menzies had 'a strong personality', and in cabinet demonstrated his 'good mind, excellent political sense and timing, and was lucid and eloquent in exposition'.[32] Journalist Don Whitington noted that Menzies' cabinet was initially made up of young ex-servicemen 'with a desire to serve and obey, expecting and even welcoming discipline and leadership from a man they had admired from a distance while he was breathing life into the new Liberal Party'.[33] Another factor that may have contributed to building cohesion and unity is that many in cabinet in 1949 — apart from Enid Lyons and Neil O'Sullivan — were Masons. The Masonic fellowship was an important form of male bonding, particularly among Protestants, during this era. It is also worth noting another unique characteristic of the first Menzies cabinet: all of its members, other than George McLeay, Hubert (Larry) Anthony, and Harold Holt, were subsequently knighted. (Lyons was made a Dame.)

But Lyons argued that Menzies' 'aura of personal dominance' had an 'intimidating' and 'inhibiting' effect on other ministers.[34] This has been a common complaint of Menzies' cabinet style — that ministers were too afraid to challenge him and rarely dissented, and that he almost always got his way. Menzies rejected the idea that he was 'a dictator in cabinet'. He said this demeaned his ministers and that if it were true he should have been given credit for all of the government's achievements. 'The legend is false,' he insisted.[35] Most of his ministers, in their memoirs and later interviews, agreed.

John Gorton was well aware of Menzies' reputation for being 'curt and cold' with some ministers. Nevertheless, 'Personally, I found him to be entirely approachable, very warm hearted, ready at all times to help if one got into trouble,' he recalled.[36] Garfield Barwick was also impressed by Menzies in cabinet. 'He was a good chairman, anxious to obtain the views of its members,' he remembered. 'Rarely was his own view put forward before discussions had taken place, though doubtless on most occasions he had one.'[37] Beale also rejected the notion that Menzies was a 'dictator' in cabinet. 'In important matters there was a full discussion in which all who wished to speak had a chance to,' he recalled. Beale also said Menzies did not always get his way. 'Well, gentlemen,' Menzies would say, 'I do not agree with you but that is your decision.'[38] Yet Beale also noted that when Menzies felt he was right, and unchallenged, he would sometimes 'wound and humiliate' his colleagues with a cutting remark.[39]

John Bunting also recalled that Menzies gave leeway to his ministers, and welcomed debate and discussion. He rejected the notion that Menzies was a 'dominating' presence, but did acknowledge he had a 'pre-eminence'. He often used his intellect and experience to state firmly where he stood. Menzies did not favour consensus-based decisions, because not every opinion was deserving of equal weight, but he did listen to different views and sought broad agreement on decisions. No votes were taken. 'He achieved orderliness and purpose and result, and all in an atmosphere of informality,' Bunting recalled.[40]

Frank Jennings, who served as Menzies' private secretary from 1963 to 1966, also recalled that Menzies did not always get his own way. He remembered when Menzies once lost a debate to Country Party leader John McEwen, he was so cranky that he left the cabinet room and returned to his office to cool down. He reached for his volume of William Shakespeare's works, and found consolation in the Bard's writings. 'He'd come out of the cabinet and he was reading Shakespeare to settle himself down,' Jennings remembered. 'He did this for half an hour or so and then he went back into cabinet ... so his relaxation, or getting himself together, it was to come out and read Shakespeare.'[41]

For the most part, Menzies left ministers to run their portfolios with minimal intervention. Consequently, some of the important policy initiatives during the Menzies government came from ministers themselves rather than from prime ministerial intervention or initiative. John McEwen was essential in delivering the trade treaty with Japan. Percy Spender was vital in negotiating the ANZUS Treaty and the Colombo Plan. Earle Page played the lead role in the national health scheme. Paul Hasluck was important in the development of Papua New Guinea and overseeing the introduction of a parliament, judiciary, public service, and local elections. Menzies allowed Garfield Barwick latitude in developing trade practices legislation to address price-fixing and collusion, but it had a tortuous path into law given cabinet opposition to it, and the watered-down version made it through the parliament only after Barwick was on the High Court. Barwick also delivered reform to marriage and divorce laws — after a free vote of MPs in parliament — which introduced a no-fault dissolution of marriage after the parties had been separated for five years.

Menzies thought it was vital that the prime minister be able to choose his ministry to establish their authority, and indeed there was much change in the ministerial ranks between 1949 and 1966. A notable sacking was Billy Kent Hughes in 1956 due to statements he had made on Taiwan that contradicted government policy. 'He had a certain vanity about him,' Menzies recalled. 'He was always more interested in the thing he was not responsible for than the thing he was responsible for.'[42] Les Bury was sacked in 1962 for suggesting Britain's entry into the Common Market would not be significant for Australia. 'Certainly no political talent at all,' was how Menzies described Bury in a later interview. 'He was like a small boy who was lost in a strange world.'[43] Yet Bury returned to the ministry the following year. Allen Fairhall was dumped as minister for the interior and works in 1958, but returned as minister for supply in 1961. Only two ministers who were alongside Menzies when he chaired his first cabinet meeting after returning to government in 1949 were there at his last cabinet meeting in 1966: Holt and McEwen.

In 1956, a two-tier ministry was introduced, which required a change to legislation. The cabinet would comprise senior ministers, and an outer ministry would comprise junior ministers, who would attend cabinet meetings if there was a matter that related to their portfolio. This was an important innovation; only Gough Whitlam's cabinets (1972–75) since then have included all ministers. But one of the complaints about Menzies was that his cabinets were increasingly filled with old men; he did little to promote younger men into the cabinet or outer-cabinet ranks. Among the names often mentioned who deserved promotion were Jo Gullett, Bill Wentworth, and Charles Anderson. In Menzies' later years, a ginger group that included Malcolm Fraser, Bert Kelly, Don Chipp, Jim Killen, and others often raised issues in the party room, but were denied promotion. Billy Snedden became a minister after nearly nine years in parliament, and Jim Forbes after seven years. Chipp thought the 'quality' of ministers in Menzies' final years were 'mediocre to say the least'.[44] Naturally, this view was not shared by Menzies. 'I have not heard of any man who was fit for cabinet rank who didn't secure it,' Menzies insisted, looking back in retirement.[45]

One young MP who bided his time on the backbench for more than a decade was Malcolm Fraser. Years later, this still rankled with him. Fraser told me that he had indicated his desire to be appointed to the ministry after the 1961 or 1963 election. 'I was getting agitated about not being appointed to the ministry, given I had been there since 1955,' Fraser said. 'I made it clear to Harold [Holt] when he became prime minister that if there was not a spot in the ministry, then I would leave parliament and make way for someone who could be appointed.'[46]

When Hubert (Larry) Anthony died suddenly in July 1957, his son Doug Anthony succeeded him in the seat of Richmond at a by-election in September. He was no stranger to Canberra, given his father had held the seat for almost 20 years and had served under Menzies during both of his prime ministerships. As a kid, Anthony would run through the corridors, pester the cooks in the kitchen for a snack, and roller-skate on the lower floor. He would talk to the men shovelling coal into the boilers, roam through the dining room and library, and wander into the prime minister's office when Menzies first occupied it. And he often talked to Billy Hughes, Joe Lyons, Earle Page, Arthur Fadden, John Curtin, and Ben Chifley.

As a young MP, Doug Anthony thought Menzies was impressive in parliament, had a powerful intellect, and knew how to manage the joint party room. But after several years in parliament, Anthony found being a backbencher somewhat boring. 'I don't know if I could have stayed if I wasn't made a minister,' he said in an interview. 'I actually was thinking about what else I could do.' In March 1964, Menzies phoned Anthony at home on his farm in northern New South Wales and said he was appointing him minister for the interior, outside cabinet. 'I was just flabbergasted; I could hardly speak,' Anthony recalled. 'I said, "Thank you very much, Prime Minister." And he said, "Well, that will keep you out of mischief now."'[47]

Anthony saw Menzies chair cabinet and cabinet committee meetings. 'In cabinet, he was sound and listened to people,' Anthony remembered. 'But he could be difficult, arrogant, and proud when trying to get a decision to go one way or another. Menzies used to just make people look like a fool if they were not on top of their portfolio — and I think he liked to do that to people. Very seldom did I hear him regret anything he had said or done. He was a proud man. He could be vile, too, and knock people about. I remember one minister presented a proposal that he hadn't prepared very well, and Menzies picked up a few paragraphs and asked, "What do you mean by that?" The minister could not respond. Menzies had a very quick mind and was a clever study of people. If he said, "Bring that back to the next meeting," that was really embarrassing.'[48]

Ian Sinclair was appointed minister for social services in February 1965, having only been elected to parliament in November 1963. (John McEwen had been instrumental in his promotion to the outer ministry.) Sinclair also attended several cabinet and cabinet committee meetings, which enabled him to observe close up how Menzies operated. 'I got on well with Menzies,' Sinclair told me. 'He always had an idea of who was on his side and who wasn't. He certainly had an idea of his own status, but he was an effective persuader.' Sinclair recalled that Menzies was a good chair of meetings — he was focused, organised, and efficient. 'He was very logical, and I found him quite interesting to negotiate with and to talk to on issues,' Sinclair said.[49]

Dr A.J. 'Jim' Forbes won the South Australian seat of Barker in October 1956. Menzies appointed him minister for the army in December 1963. 'I was very much in awe of Robert Menzies when I first started, and the more I got to know him, the higher my opinion of him was,' Forbes recalled in an interview. 'He was head and shoulders above everybody else.' Forbes found Menzies to be accessible and often encouraging, which was not always the case with other MPs. Forbes' appointment to the ministry came as he turned 40, and he was given the task of reintroducing national service. He recalled it was a difficult decision because nobody wanted to see their sons, brothers, or friends conscripted, but he argued it was necessary to deal with a 'manpower problem'. Although it attracted public opposition, Forbes said Menzies assured him the government would stand by the decision. 'He was a very straight shooter and you felt you knew exactly where you were with him,' Forbes said. 'He would stick with you. He wouldn't give you the sack just because you've made the government unpopular.'[50]

THE Liberal Party would meet in the government party room on Wednesday mornings when parliament was in session, with Menzies seated behind a table at the front of the room and presiding. All ministers would be required to attend; they would sit behind the prime minister in green leather chairs, or around the sides of the room. 'His conduct of the meetings was impeccable,' recalled Alick Downer. He spoke little and listened a lot. The meetings were an opportunity for backbenchers to raise questions and sometimes objections to policy decisions. 'If attacked, as sometimes happened, he would deliver a reasoned reply, but he refused to be provoked to anger,' Downer said. 'He aimed throughout these proceedings to achieve a consensus, to avoid a vote.'[51]

Don Chipp won the Melbourne seat of Higinbotham in December 1960. Most MPs, Chipp said, regarded Menzies as above mere mortal status. 'Whenever he walked into the party room or the House of Representatives a change came over the Liberals similar to that in a fifth form classroom when the headmaster appears,' he wrote. There was a 'total obedience' towards Menzies. Political success bred loyalty.[52] Billy Snedden, who held the Melbourne seat of Bruce (1955–83), also recalled that Menzies listened intently but did not say much in party meetings. He would sit at the table, leaning on his elbow, taking notes with a passive face. 'I will look at this myself,' [Menzies] would say when a difficult issue arose, remembered Snedden. 'Once he had decided what to do, he would say, "This is the way it is going to be."' He always carried the day.[53]

Jim Killen, who was elected to the Brisbane seat of Moreton in December 1955, described his first party-room meeting. 'The level of noise lowered, the door opened and in came the great man,' he remembered. 'Clapping and cheering broke out and reached a crescendo as the large Menzies frame moved like a pageant towards his seat at a table at the top of the room.' Menzies sat down. 'He raised his right arm, the palm opened as though he was giving his own distinctive blessing upon all of us, when all he was doing was asking for silence. He got it.' Menzies then addressed the MPs: 'I am glad you are all here. There were those who were consumed with pessimism that we would not be back. Let's say they were in error.' The early-election gamble had paid off. 'Well,' Menzies said next, 'I suppose we must have a leader. Who is there who is available?' he asked. There was laughter. 'What, no takers? Well, it looks as though, poor mutt that I am, I'll have to be your leader of sorts.' Killen said the applause was deafening.[54]

While Menzies rarely, if ever, offered praise or encouragement to backbench MPs, he was accessible. He was always available for backbench MPs to raise issues or seek help with a constituency matter. An appointment would usually take a day or two to be arranged. 'Upon being shown into his office,' recalled Downer, 'he received one with encouraging courtesy, listened intently to the case you advanced, never seemed in a hurry to close the interview, appeared glad you had come to see him.'[55]

Three of Menzies' most important relationships were with his two treasurers, Arthur Fadden (1949–58) and Harold Holt (1958–66), and also John McEwen, who served as minister for commerce and agriculture (1949–56), and trade and industry (1956–66). Fadden had previously served as treasurer, and as prime minister at the same time, in the period 1940–41. He delivered 11 budgets — a record only surpassed by Peter Costello's 12th budget in 2007. Fadden and Menzies generally got on well; they rarely disagreed on policy. Menzies, for the most part, let Fadden have the lead role in economic-policy formulation. Fadden, who was known to enjoy a drink, could often be found in the non-members' bar in Parliament House. Legend has it that on more than one occasion he delivered the budget while moderately intoxicated and swaying slightly from side to side, sometimes steadied by a supporting prime ministerial hand. Lenox Hewitt recalled that Fadden was 'a very capable treasurer', but thought Menzies had 'a sort of contempt for Fadden'.[56]

Holt had long been seen as Menzies' heir-apparent, and was elected deputy leader two years before becoming treasurer. Sam Holt told me that his father was 'a loyal deputy' to Menzies, admired and respected his leader, and patiently waited for when the opportunity of succession arose. 'He certainly got on extremely well with Menzies,' Sam said. 'There was a suitable age gap between them, which shaped their relationship to a degree, and I think Menzies sort of regarded him a bit as a protégé.'[57] Despite suggestions in the party, and in the media, that Holt should be replaced following the 1960–61 credit squeeze, Menzies kept him on. There was no serious rival to Holt as Menzies' successor by January 1966. But there were limits to the Menzies–Holt partnership. 'They were both Victorians and they had worked together for many years,' William Heseltine, Menzies' private secretary, recalled. 'I don't think it was quite as easy a relationship as it was with dear old Eric Harrison.'[58] Heather Henderson added, 'He got on well with Harold, and he liked him, but I don't think he had huge respect for him.'[59]

Overall, Menzies had generally friendly relations with his ministers. But Fadden recalled that Menzies 'had a tendency to take his loyal friends for granted and impose on their loyalty', and seldom offered words of 'congratulation, appreciation, gratitude, mateship or warm-hearted encouragement'.[60] Menzies was personally closest to Harrison, who served as deputy leader of the Liberal Party (1945–56) before he resigned from parliament to again become high commissioner to London (1956–64). Harrison, elected to the Sydney seat of Wentworth in 1931, provided critical support to Menzies in New South Wales. Holt, frequently described in the media as charming and handsome, succeeded Harrison as deputy leader. But it was a close-run thing. The exhaustive ballot to succeed Harrison was contested by Holt, Richard Casey, Philip McBride, and Bill Spooner. Casey and McBride were eliminated early, and Holt only defeated Spooner by two votes.[61]

The minister whom Menzies admired the most was John McEwen, leader of the Country Party from 1958; Menzies described him 'as formidable in his own right' and by far 'the ablest minister I had'.[62] Menzies also greatly respected Paul Hasluck, explaining that he kept him in the portfolio of territories for so long because 'he was essential' and 'wonderful' in that role. Menzies later appointed Hasluck as minister for external affairs, a role where he also did 'such marvellous work'.[63] It is no wonder that Menzies thought Hasluck was the best candidate to succeed Holt as Liberal leader.

In retirement, Menzies reflected negatively on Percy Spender, who had served as minister for external affairs (1949–51). He regarded 'little Percy' as 'a lawyer of the second order' who shrewdly used the Colombo Plan to boost his ambitions for higher office. 'We read in the papers that Mr Spender had now produced an idea, the Colombo Plan [which] had got to be known as the Spender Plan, for helping backward people,' Menzies said. When questioned by the cabinet for details, Spender replied, 'It is only an idea, it is only a notion, and I would be very glad to have it filled in.' Menzies then recalled that the cabinet 'filled it in for him'. Menzies agreed with Fadden's description of Spender as 'the butcher bird' who 'flies through the window, makes a mess on the table and flies out again'. Menzies found Spender to be intelligent, lively, and a good speaker who 'did very well in America' as ambassador (1951–58), but always aspiring to higher office. 'His ambition was, of course, overwhelming,' Menzies said.[64]

Privately, Menzies also had a poor view of Casey, another presumptive rival, who would serve as a minister during both his prime ministerships, and be gifted diplomatic and vice-regal posts. When Menzies first became prime minister in 1939, he demoted Casey from Treasury to Supply and Development. Menzies appointed Casey as ambassador to the United States in February 1940. Casey later complained to Winston Churchill that he had been 'kicked out'.

In a previously unpublished interview, Menzies remarked: 'He said that to Winston, no doubt about it ... I took a pretty poor view of that.' In 1941, Casey pressed Menzies to organise for him to be given the Order of the Companions of Honour (CH). 'You know, old man, I would like to have a CH,' Casey told Menzies. The prime minister was unimpressed: 'Dick was always on the make and he always thought that with all his qualities, which are quite real, he always had the typical rich man's outlook that the world was his oyster and that he only had to reach for it and it was his.'[65] In December 1949, Menzies returned Casey to the supply and development portfolio, and also gave him works and housing. In April 1951, Casey was appointed minister for external affairs.

Menzies did not think highly of Casey as minister for external affairs. 'He had enormous industry but no judgement,' Menzies said later in life. He also resented Casey's extensive diary-writing. Casey would soak up everything, from policy debates in cabinet to political discussions in the party room and gossip from the corridors of power, and put it in his diary. These would often be circulated to other ministers. 'He always had a rather pernickety mind — that is why he always had these silly diaries,' Menzies said. 'All the little details had to go down. That attracted his mind. But on the big ones, no, not a penetrating mind.' Menzies came to a final, damning, conclusion about Casey. 'His great trouble is that it rankles in his mind that although he had a tremendous career, he was never prime minister.'[66] It was a harsh assessment.

There was one minister whom Menzies came to especially despise: Billy McMahon, whom he privately called 'Little Willie' for leaking cabinet deliberations to the media. Menzies saw cabinet solidarity and ministerial responsibility as one of the cornerstones of parliamentary democracy. In retirement, Menzies said McEwen would sometimes have 'a whistle in the ear' of a journalist about cabinet. 'The only fellow who really deliberately sneaked was McMahon, who would go down to Sydney on the Friday and be closeted at lunch with [*The*] *Sydney Morning Herald* or [*The*] *Daily Telegraph* and would then proceed to give them a description of the cabinet business of the week, ball [by] ball, each item being altered suitably in his own favour.' He thought McMahon was 'a worm' and 'a stupid rogue', because his leaking was so obvious.[67]

Menzies recalled summoning McMahon to his office after catching him leaking on 23 September 1959. McMahon was then minister for labour and national service. 'Now look, there is this story in the press, and you gave it to them, didn't you?' Menzies barked at McMahon. 'Don't deny it. It is idle to deny it because I know you have given it to them, didn't you?' McMahon, unable to refute it, responded, 'Well, yes.' But he insisted the matter was not important. 'Cabinet secrecy is always important,' Menzies scolded him. 'It embraces all matters, and you have been guilty of an abominable offence.' Menzies had a summary of their conversation written up, and McMahon verified it. Menzies put it in an envelope and then placed it in his safe.[68]

This 'note of conversation' is kept in Menzies' prime ministerial papers at the National Archives of Australia. It concerned the leaking of a cabinet submission on the budget by Hugh Roberton, the minister for social services, to Keith Wilson, who was a member of the backbench social services committee:

> *I said*: 'Did you tell Mr Wilson the substance of the proposal made by Mr Roberton to cabinet?'
> *He said*: 'Yes, because I thought it important to show Mr Wilson that such proposals were not new.'
> *I said*: 'That means that in substance you have conveyed to a private member the nature of a proposal made in cabinet room by a minister, and have indicated that it was rejected by cabinet.'
> *He said*: 'Yes.'
> *I said*: 'How long have you been a minister?'
> *He said*: 'Eight years.'
> *I said*: 'This is an outrage. I will consider this position.'[69]

McMahon was put on notice. 'If ever I have real reason to suppose that you have been up to these hanky-panky tricks again,' Menzies warned, 'I will first of all dismiss you. I will walk straight into the House and I will tell the House why you have been dismissed. And if necessary I will table the stuff in [the envelope] and that will be the end of your beautiful career. Now push off and don't forget it.'[70]

IT has often been suggested that Menzies shrewdly manoeuvred to have any potential rival dispatched to an overseas posting or given a plum job at home. The roll call of those apparently with the leadership baton in their knapsack who were moved on is impossible to ignore. Richard Casey, only four years older than Menzies, who had been made minister to the United States in March 1940, had long been regarded as a leadership alternative. Menzies did not support Casey's bid for the deputy leadership of the Liberal Party in September 1956, and he left parliament in April 1960. Thomas White, who was married to Vera Deakin, one of Alfred Deakin's daughters, and had stood for leader of the UAP against Menzies in April 1939 and September 1943, was appointed high commissioner to London in June 1951. Percy Spender, another minister with a high profile and large ambitions, who had also previously sought to be UAP leader, was made ambassador to the United States in May 1951. Howard Beale, who was no pushover in cabinet, and who also aspired to higher office, was made ambassador to the United States in March 1958. Garfield Barwick, a brilliant lawyer seen as a next-generation leader, but who had differences with Menzies over foreign policy and trade practices legislation, was appointed chief justice of the High Court in April 1964.

Ian Sinclair acknowledged there were rivalries within the Liberal Party, and said it was well known that Menzies carefully managed his relationships with Casey and Barwick, in particular. 'The rivalries within the Liberal Party had been going on forever,' Sinclair said. 'Menzies felt that Barwick might see himself as a future leader.'[71] But Menzies rejected the suggestion that he removed potential rivals. 'This idea that I could not bear a brother near the throne is, I think, pretty silly,' he said in retirement.[72] Spender denied he had been moved on, arguing he was unwell and planning to retire anyway before the Washington appointment.[73] Menzies did send Casey to Washington in 1940, when there were doubts about his leadership. But when Casey was made governor-general in 1965, he had already quit parliament to sit in the House of Lords. And Barwick, too, said in his memoirs that although he felt Menzies saw him as his successor, he decided not to stand for leader if the job became vacant.[74]

In his personal papers, Menzies left an account of how Barwick was appointed chief justice. Barwick met Menzies at Kirribilli House on the morning of 25 March 1964. Owen Dixon was due to retire from the High Court the following month. 'Barwick raised with me the question of his own position,' Menzies recorded. 'He told me that he had never relinquished his judicial ambitions and that they were stirring in him at this time.' Barwick claimed in his memoirs he told Menzies he was 'prepared to go [to the High Court] if the cabinet felt that way', but did not press the issue.[75] Barwick was feigning modesty. They met again on 20 April, and, according to Menzies' contemporary note, Barwick said 'he would like his name considered for the chief justiceship'. In any event, Barwick had decided to leave parliament at the next election. Menzies said that Barwick, at some stage, 'had some ultimate ambition to be my successor'.[76] Barwick told Frances McNicoll that Menzies had, for a time, seen him as his preferred successor as Liberal leader and prime minister.[77]

Menzies canvassed senior ministers on possible candidates for chief justice, and Barwick was at the top of the list. After lunch on 23 April, sitting in Menzies' Parliament House office, Barwick was given the good news of his appointment. Menzies denied placing any pressure on Barwick about his future, and rejected the suggestion in the media that they had disagreed on foreign policy. 'This must have been a difficult choice but it was his to make and he made it,' Menzies wrote. Curiously, Menzies wrote that if he were in Barwick's position, he was not sure that he would have chosen the bench over the possibility of being prime minister. 'Barwick is a man of remarkable intelligence; he didn't make his decision in a hurry, but he made it himself without pressure or influence of any kind.'[78]

In any event, Menzies' leadership was never under serious pressure during his second term as prime minister, and nobody did challenge his position. There were reports in 1950–51, though, concerning party-room talk about replacing Menzies with Spender.[79] This should not be overstated, but nor should it be ignored. In the early years of the government, especially considering the failed referendum to ban the Communist Party and the disappointing 1954 election result, Menzies was not in an impregnable position. Old doubts resurfaced about his leadership. But, in time, Menzies consolidated his position and towered over any potential rivals in cabinet. The argument that Menzies worked, Machiavelli-like, to dispatch rivals to coveted postings at home and abroad is thus difficult to sustain. However, moving prickly opponents and potential leadership contenders — such as Casey, White, Spender, Beale, and Barwick — to other fields did strengthen Menzies' position within the government.

ROBERT Menzies understood that a cooperative relationship between the Liberal and Country parties was instrumental to effective government, political stability, and electoral success. Menzies never considered the idea of breaking the coalition with the Country Party. He had learned from bitter experience in state politics and also in federal politics, namely with former Country Party leader Earle Page, about the importance of working effectively with the junior coalition partner. Although Menzies had put Page back in cabinet, he could not be trusted. 'Page, who hated the Liberal Party more than he hated the Labor Party, was a constant problem,' Menzies said. 'You never knew what he was up to.'[80]

Menzies trusted McEwen, and they worked well together. Menzies recalled that McEwen occasionally made veiled threats to break the coalition. Menzies did not think McEwen was ever serious, but when an issue of difference arose, he made sure it was dealt with satisfactorily. 'You might postpone the problem, or delay it or get around it in some way,' Menzies explained.[81] When it came to appointing a cabinet, Menzies said 'the leader of the Country Party selected the fellows he wanted unless I objected to them', which happened on one or two occasions. 'Now, I won't have that man,' Menzies would tell McEwen, and they agreed on an alternative.[82] McEwen recalled in retirement that the secret to his relationship with Menzies was 'mutual respect'. He added, 'Menzies' great attributes were his intellectual capacity and his political acumen, as well as his considerable strength of purpose and character.'[83]

Ian Sinclair recalled the Menzies–McEwen partnership. 'Menzies was the chairman, and McEwen was the managing director,' he said. 'If there was ever a problem, they were always resolved between the two leaders.'[84] Journalist Alan Reid later wrote that Menzies had better judgement than many of his Liberal colleagues who feuded with McEwen. 'Patiently and with uncharacteristic tolerance of viewpoints, with which he cannot possibly have agreed, [Menzies] has been remarkably successful in keeping the strain between the two parties to the coalition at a viable minimum.'[85]

When asked at his farewell press conference on 26 January 1966 what his achievements were, Menzies noted two on the 'political' side of things: the formation of the Liberal Party, and the coalition with the Country Party. 'I look back with great satisfaction on the fact that there's been a fruitful and constant alliance with the Country Party,' Menzies said. 'We have for all those years been a joint government ... it's not always easy to have a marriage of this kind.'

THERE were five governors-general during Menzies' second prime ministership, four of whom he recommended for appointment. Menzies rarely spoke about the appointment of governors-general or how he thought they comported themselves in the role. In a previously unpublished interview, Menzies argued that governors-general should be known to the monarch, and therefore likely to be British-born. 'I always had a strong feeling that other things be equal, we ought to get somebody who was personally known to the Queen and, therefore, somebody in Great Britain because it kept the links going,' he said. 'To appoint an Australian for the sake of having an Australian would, in the long run, be fatal because it would mean that every superannuated minister had a claim to be governor-general.'[86] Yet, by the 1940s, polls showed that most Australians supported an Australian as governor-general.[87]

Menzies said this approach guided the appointment of the 13th governor-general, Sir William Slim, who held office from May 1953 to February 1960. Menzies thought Slim was the 'best governor-general we have ever had', but they did disagree on some matters. The next appointment was brief: William Morrison (Viscount Dunrossil), who held the office from February 1960 to February 1961. Morrison had been Speaker of the House of Commons. He left parliament at the October

1959 election due to poor health. It was not surprising that he was frequently ill during his term as governor-general, and he died in office on 3 February 1961. It was not a wise appointment.

There was a considerable delay until William 'Bill' De L'Isle was appointed in August 1961. De L'Isle was the Queen's personal choice, and her favourite Australian governor-general, whom she had met during his time as a minister in Winston Churchill's government.[88] But Menzies had a poor opinion of De L'Isle. 'He was, to put it bluntly, a rather conceited fellow,' he said. 'He was always a faint disappointment.'[89] When Menzies raised the appointment of a new governor-general with the Queen in March 1961, he did not have De L'Isle high on his list — he was fourth out of six possible names. Menzies cabled John McEwen with his thoughts. He suggested, in order of preference, the Duke of Hamilton, Lord Cobham, Lord Evershed, then De L'Isle, and also the Earl of Dudley and the Duke of Beaufort. It was to remain a very British appointment.[90]

When De L'Isle was preparing to vacate the office three years later, Menzies said there was 'a great feeling in the cabinet that we ought to have an Australian'. But he remained unconvinced. Menzies could not think of any 'distinguished man' in Australia 'who was known to the Queen'. Several names did eventually emerge. But Menzies' first choice — retired Vice-Admiral Sir John Collins — declined the appointment.[91] Menzies then suggested Richard Casey. In January 1960, Casey had been appointed to the House of Lords. Over dinner at the Savoy Grill in London, Menzies said to Casey: 'Would you like to be governor-general? It would crown your career.' Casey asked for time to think about it, and agreed the following day. Casey was only the third Australian to serve in the vice-regal post, after Isaac Isaacs (1931–36) and William McKell (1947–53), who had been recommended by Labor prime ministers James Scullin and Ben Chifley respectively. Casey served as governor-general from May 1965 to April 1969. Menzies thought Casey 'did very well' in the role.[92]

ROBERT Menzies served a second term as prime minister for 16 years, one month, and eight days, from 19 December 1949 to 26 January 1966. He had previously served as prime minister for two years, four months, and four days, from 26 April 1939 to 29 August 1941. In total, he was prime minister for 18 years, five months, and 12 days. He is Australia's longest-serving prime minister, and is also the oldest-serving, having retired at the age of 71.

Some aspects of the modern prime ministership were cemented during Menzies' second term. The prime minister's office, though not significantly different from that under Curtin or Chifley, did increase slightly in size. While there were no political or policy functions undertaken, the staff were integral to the functioning of government, and had a strong loyalty to the prime minister. They travelled with him, they joined him at the Lodge for dinners, and he trusted them implicitly. When combined with Menzies' considerable administrative talents — such as managing paperwork, focusing his time, running a cabinet and making decisions, and coordinating ministers and public servants — this ensured a smooth running of the government.

Menzies was, as noted, an effective chair of cabinet. An innovation was providing briefs on every cabinet submission to Menzies. Processes were also streamlined so that an agenda was prepared in advance, submissions were circulated three days before meetings, and decisions were better recorded. Menzies allowed ministers to have their say, did not intervene in their portfolios unless there were problems or he had a particular interest in the area, and was effective in guiding discussions towards outcomes. Introducing an inner cabinet served to centralise the prime minister's influence within the scope of a group of senior ministers, increasing Menzies' authority. As a Liberal leader, he was further helped by being able to appoint ministers without needing party-room approval.

Menzies encouraged a public service that was highly professional, truly independent, and willing to give frank and fearless advice. There was no 'night of the long knives' when his incoming administration sacked a haul of public servants seen to be favourable to the previous government. Menzies kept on Prime Minister's Department secretary Allen Brown, external affairs department secretary John Burton (later appointed high commissioner to Ceylon), and Commonwealth Bank chief H.C. 'Nugget' Coombs, all of whom had been personally close to Ben Chifley or H.V. 'Doc' Evatt. The Prime Minister's Department, under Brown and Bunting, took on a broader policy role and became more influential within government. The department, which always reflects the prime minister's interests, played key roles in Menzies' university-funding initiatives, in providing state aid to state schools, and in the development of Canberra.

The consequence was that these changes in the institutional apparatus of executive government helped Menzies to consolidate his prime ministership and provide stable government. When coupled with his stature as founder of the Liberal Party and his election successes, his communication skills and parliamentary dominance, his careful management of the Liberal Party and relations with the Country Party, and his ability to exploit the divisions in, and highlight the differences with, Labor, it is no wonder that by the mid-1950s many were referring to Menzies' prime ministership as the 'Ming Dynasty'.

CHAPTER 12

The Art and Science of Politics

IN November 1948, Robert Menzies wrote an article for *The New York Times* on the art and science of politics.[1] 'Politics is both a fine art and an inexact science,' he argued. Politicians focused on the science of politics, 'the discovery of what to do', but neglected the art of politics, which was the 'practice of how and when to do these things'. Without mastering both, nothing of lasting value could be achieved.

Many in today's political class — politicians, staffers, party officials, pollsters, advertising gurus, and consultants — are skilled in the technical aspects of politics. They are knowledgeable, and understand key policy challenges. They can write learned articles and competently deliver a speech replete with facts and figures. They are expert in using scientific tools such as statistics, focus groups, and opinion polls. Some are adept at parliamentary procedures. They can write political advertisements, devise clever campaign tactics, use Facebook and Twitter, spin the media, and carry out routine campaign functions and the basic administration of government.

What they lack is a talent for the art of politics. This includes building consensus and understanding the importance of compromise. Being able to interpret public opinion and to persuade with effective advocacy. Formulating a long-term strategy. Knowing how to grease the wheels of government to work in their favour. Having a capacity for the hard slog of policy development and consultation with stakeholders. Being prepared to take risks and champion a long-term agenda, however unpopular it might be in the short-term. Or possessing the gift of oratory, the ability to give an inspiring speech or an interesting interview free of jargon, clichés, and key lines repeated in rote form.

All politicians must have an instinctive feel for the public mood. It can be studied through polls and focus groups, but it must also be discerned. Menzies, governing at a time when there were few reliable scientific measurements of public opinion, drew on his experiences, reading, and observation to judge when to seek to change public opinion and when to follow it. Tony Eggleton, his press secretary, said this was one of Menzies' strengths as a politician. 'He had a skill for reading the community,' Eggleton said. 'He had this strong feeling about the man in the street, the ordinary people, and governing for the majority of the people.'[2]

Menzies' predecessor, Ben Chifley, thought voters made up their minds which way to vote well before the traditional five-week election campaign was underway. Menzies had a convivial drink with Chifley before they faced off at the 1946, 1949, and 1951 elections. 'Bob, here we are, facing another campaign,' Chifley said to Menzies on one occasion. 'You'll go and work like a horse trying to convince people to vote for you. I'll then go and try and convince them to vote for me. And all this when they've already made up their minds. Bob, it's all a bloody nonsense.' But Menzies knew that the electorate was becoming 'more sophisticated', that the issues were 'bigger and more complicated' than before, and that an increasing number of voters would determine their choice during the campaign.[3]

So Menzies developed the necessary skill of reading the electorate, trying to gauge political feeling, and coming to understand which issues were driving their voting preferences. He did not always possess supreme political judgement — almost no politician ever has — but Menzies thought he could understand the mind and mood of the electorate better than most others. His record election victories attest to this. 'I suppose I have a political nose,' he told a journalist in November 1963. 'It's something that comes with time. If I want to know what the sound, solid majority of Australians think, I try and find out what the skilled tradesman is thinking, a man with a job and with responsibility. He represents what Australians are thinking.'[4] This penetrates to one of Menzies' strengths: although he had little in common with everyday Australians, he had a capacity to empathise with their values, instincts, and aspirations.

A year after Menzies' essay on the art of politics was published, he led the Liberal Party to its first election victory in what was to inaugurate a record 23 years in government. While the Menzies era from 1949 to 1966 was not always one of policy innovation, and his success was in part due to Labor's lacklustre leadership and internal divisions, his political success cannot be disputed. How Menzies practised politics — how he saw the role of opposition, how he campaigned, how he communicated, how he operated in parliament, how he managed the party room and cabinet, and how he dealt with the media — is instructive. As Menzies himself argued, 'It is only if the art of politics succeeds that the science of politics will be efficiently studied and mastered.'

ESSENTIAL to Robert Menzies' political resurrection after the ignominy of losing the prime ministership in 1941 was his capacity to learn from his mistakes. Menzies recognised that in his public manner and in his private dealings with colleagues, he needed to change. This did not mean inventing a persona, or losing his authenticity and credibility, but adapting how he presented himself to voters and his fellow MPs. He was more aware of his imposing presence, of his commanding intellect and his inability to suffer fools gladly, and recognised the need to be more collegiate, understanding, and respectful of others. He began to make these adjustments when he returned to lead the United Australia Party in 1943.

Menzies spent six years as opposition leader, from 1943 to 1949. He understood that the art of opposition is not always to oppose, but to oppose selectively, to find things to support, and to propose alternative courses of action. This took two forms. First, Menzies supported much of the Curtin and Chifley governments' policies. 'No government is always wrong on everything,' Menzies argued. 'The opposition must choose the ground on which it is to attack. To attack indiscriminately is to risk public opinion, which has a reserve of fairness not always understood.'[5] There was a political dividend to be reaped in offering support for government initiatives. He did not want to be seen as an endlessly whining, carping, complaining political leader who tested the patience of voters.

Second, the opposition is an alternative government and should present itself as such. Menzies argued that promises made by an opposition could come back to haunt them in government. It was unwise, he said, to make a promise that could not be carried out. 'A quick debating point scored in parliament against some government measure will be a barren victory unless you are confident that, in office, you would not be compelled to do, substantially, what the government is doing.'[6] In other words, don't create a rod for your own back. An opposition should be strategic, tactical, and clever. Accumulating baggage should be avoided. Menzies would not often lead the most ferocious attacks against the government in parliament. He would leave much of that to others, as Howard Beale recalled, quarantining his contributions to big issues to foster his image 'as the high-minded statesman'.[7]

Menzies also recognised that a party which loses an election should scrutinise what went wrong, and identify how to remedy it. This must include leadership, policy, and the party organisation. 'You must never lose sight of the end result to which all your activities must be directed,' he said.[8] There might be a need for new leadership, new candidates, new personnel, new processes, and new policies. 'It must be regarded as a great constructive period in the life of a party,' Menzies argued, 'not a period in the wilderness, but a period of preparation for the high responsibilities in which you hope will come.'[9] One of the biggest mistakes for a party to make, he said, was to fight an election on the issues of the past.

He understood the need to carve out a different philosophical and policy approach from Labor. The Liberal Party would become the principal vehicle for renewing the non-Labor forces after the collapse of the United Australia Party. Menzies had started to talk about political convictions and policy ideas in his regular radio broadcasts, beginning in early 1942. The seminal speech, though not recognised as such at the time, was the 'forgotten people' broadcast. By presenting a different set of philosophical values and policy ideas, Menzies established a contrast between the Liberal Party and the Labor Party. This was fundamental in fashioning the choice for voters seven years later, in 1949.

Menzies led the Liberal Party in eight general election campaigns: 1946, 1949, 1951, 1954, 1955, 1958, 1961, and 1963. He had also led the UAP to the 1940 election. These later elections were contested over different political battlelines and policy issues, and with three very different Labor leaders: Ben Chifley, H.V. 'Doc' Evatt, and Arthur Calwell. He won most of these elections comfortably, but there were two close calls: in 1954 and in 1961, when the Coalition was returned with a minority two-party-preferred vote but a majority of seats.

Menzies also had a fair dose of political luck. He benefited from the defection of Vladimir and Evdokia Petrov ahead of the 1954 election, which aroused fears of communism, and the death of John F. Kennedy prior to the 1963 election, which underscored national security concerns. The Labor split in 1954–55 and the creation of the Democratic Labour Party, which directed preferences to the Coalition, also helped considerably. And he shrewdly exploited Labor's 'faceless men' scandal concerning the proposed United States naval communications station, and its opposition to state aid for education, in 1963. Menzies went to early elections in 1951, 1955, and 1963, when Labor was vulnerable, to maximise his chances of victory. He was lucky, but he also made his own luck.

Menzies enjoyed political campaigning. He relished the adversarial side of politics, provided that it was in pursuit of greater objectives. He did not like politics just for its own sake. But, as John Howard argued, 'he loved political combat', which is 'a necessary ingredient for any successful PM'.[10] William Heseltine, Menzies' private secretary, said he was 'a natural campaigner' who enjoyed the cut and thrust of an election contest. 'It was amazing to hear him in those campaigns making several speeches each day, most of them with a few notes but no written text in his hand, and each one slightly different from the one he had just given,' recalled Heseltine.[11]

Tony Eggleton, his press secretary, remembered that when travelling in the prime ministerial black Bentley, Menzies always sat in the front seat next to the driver. When Dame Pattie was travelling with her husband, they would both sit in the back seat. Before arriving at an event where Menzies would be speaking outside, the car would be stopped just before it reached the destination. Both Menzies and Eggleton would get out of the car, and Eggleton would then liberally apply fly spray over Menzies' shoulders and back 'to discourage the flies from distracting the audience from his speech'.[12]

Heather Henderson, his daughter, often joined him for campaign events in the early 1950s. 'He enjoyed getting up and making those speeches, particularly once people started yelling out,' she recalled. 'It was good fun. He loved speaking. And he loved speaking at universities. He enjoyed talking to the students. He knew they'd interrupt, be irreverent, and all the rest of it, but he loved that. He really enjoyed it. [But] he didn't enjoy the traveling, flying around [and staying] in a different hotel room every night. It was very tiring.'[13]

Town hall meetings were one of the principal means of communicating with voters in the Menzies era. They would be packed with supporters, opponents, and the undecided. People would attend to deliberately disrupt them. Others would be there to hear what he had to say. Some went for entertainment, and brought along sandwiches, tea, and coffee. The audiences were not filtered by political parties in advance. Menzies would give a speech punctuated by cheers, boos, streams of abuse, cat-calls, whistling, laughter, and clapping. Attendees would wave placards with 'Pig-iron Bob' or 'Ming the Merciless' or some other epithet painted on. Sometimes eggs or tomatoes would be thrown. Police would be on hand to eject the interjectors. Menzies was in his element, and rarely fazed. He gained a reputation for his acerbic wit, which was not always to his advantage, even if it won laughs.

His responses to interjections became legendary. 'I wouldn't vote for you if you were the Archangel Gabriel,' a woman once shouted at Menzies. 'If I were the Archangel Gabriel, madam, I'm afraid you would not be in my constituency,' he replied. When asked if he would 'consult the powerful interests that control you' when selecting a cabinet, Menzies replied, 'Yes, but please keep my wife's name out of this.' When an interjector made a garbled attack, Menzies replied, 'I did not catch your words, sir, if indeed they were words.' A miner once shouted, 'Tell us all you know, Bob — it won't take long!' Menzies looked at him and replied, 'I'll tell you everything we both know — it won't take any longer.' On another occasion, a woman kept interrupting from the front row. 'Madam, I'm sure your husband is very glad you are here today,' he said. When the police grabbed one scruffy lout at a meeting in his electorate, Menzies said, 'Surely, you're not going to throw out my friend, Senator Gorton.'

Menzies did not always like to be reminded of his exercises in vituperation. It was often recalled that when a man yelled out at a public meeting, 'Watcha gonna do with 'ousing, Bob?' he replied, without missing a beat, 'Put an "h" in front of it.' This and other witticisms were collected by Ray Robinson in a book titled *The Wit of Sir Robert Menzies* published in 1966.[14] Menzies told the publisher, Leslie Frewin, that he 'felt it sounded bad' and was 'a little unhappy about its inclusion'. But it was too late — the book had already gone to print.[15] Arthur Fadden, the leader of the Country Party (1940–58), thought Menzies' speech-making helped the Coalition win election after election, but there was also a downside. 'His speeches sometimes gave the impression that he did not care if he walked over dead bodies and created the feeling that he was talking down to people less perfect than himself.'[16]

But, for the most part, his audiences enjoyed the repartee. Towards the end of his prime ministership, Menzies frequently engaged with students, who would attend his town hall meetings, campaign rallies, and campus events. Rod Lyall, a student at the University of Western Australia, recalled an attempted prank when Menzies was awarded the honorary degree of Doctor of Letters on 29 April 1964. He and a friend suborned a girl, who was to sing in the choir for the ceremony at Winthrop Hall, to conceal beneath her gown a crown they had purloined from the university drama society's property box. She was to wait in the wings after the choir had finished. As Menzies received his degree, she approached him with the crown in her hand. The purpose, Lyall remembered, was to make light of Menzies' perceived 'arrogance'. She said: 'In the name of the people of Australia, I offer you this royal crown.' The audience sat in stunned silence. Menzies took the crown from her and put it on and off his head three times, and then, to the astonishment of all, he quoted William Shakespeare's *Julius Caesar*:

> You all did see that on the Lupercal
> I thrice presented him a kingly crown,
> Which he did thrice refuse.

There was a slight pause. The girl was shocked; she had been upstaged by Menzies. The audience began to laugh and applaud. There were cheers. The prank had failed. 'You could not but admire his presence of mind and how it illustrated his wit and brilliant way of dealing with interjectors,' Lyall said.[17]

Menzies was a superb parliamentary speaker, political orator, and campaign debater. He understood that a prime minister has to be able to articulate the government's policies and philosophy, and mesh these within an overall narrative. Menzies had a perfect sense of timing, could raise and lower his voice for maximum effect, and could readily marshal a mix of facts and figures, and anecdotes and witticisms to make his point. He had a gift for making complex issues easy to understand, and reinforcing a clear, often simple, message. He could be stern and serious, or easily switch to self-deprecating humour and witty asides. In parliament, in town halls, on formal occasions, at party meetings, on the campaign trail, and on radio and television, he had a gift for speechmaking. It was a talent honed by observation, reading, and rehearsal.

In the 1930s and 1940s, Menzies was a regular speaker at the Central Methodist Mission's 'Pleasant Sunday Afternoon' talks held at Wesley Church in Melbourne. Organised by Irving Benson, the lectures attracted a large audience and were often broadcast on radio stations 3LO and 3DB. The talks were wide-ranging and, although not often overtly political in nature, they did tend to advocate the need for spiritual renewal, the importance of individual liberty, and the values of Western civilisation. These gatherings were an important part of Menzies' community outreach and helped in the development of his public speaking. He addressed the afternoon gatherings during his prime ministership, through to the 1960s.

Jo Gullett, who held the Victorian seat of Henty (1946–55), thought Menzies to be the supreme orator and debater of his time. 'He is without equal, at least in the English-speaking world,' Gullett wrote in 1958. 'He is master of every debating tactic and has histrionic or dramatic ability of a high order. In this he is much aided by his appearance. For he looks like a Roman senator, imposing, yet not austere, the face softened by his white hair, the famous eyebrows giving it mobility and expression. His voice is about as good as a speaking voice can be, fairly light but penetrating and flexible.'[18]

As a boy, John Howard listened to Robert Menzies on the radio, and later heard him deliver a speech to a rowdy audience of 1,800 at the Rivoli

Theatre in Hurstville in September 1951. He had high praise for Menzies as a speechmaker. 'He had such a commanding voice, cultivated but not posh,' Howard remembered. 'It was an attention-grabbing voice that had an authority which I thought was hugely impressive. He could command an Australian audience in a magnificent way.'[19]

Menzies composed his major speeches by longhand in pencil on lined yellow legal pads, which his staff later typed for him. A line of sharpened pencils would always be kept on the desk. He often wrote fluently, without corrections or alterations, from page to page. For speeches to be delivered at party or campaign events, or when debating in parliament, he would often have smaller pieces of paper with headings and dot points that would allow for extemporaneous presentation. The night before a major speech, Menzies would read poetry. 'It gave a sense of balance in the words and refreshed one's vocabulary,' he told Barry Jones in February 1968. 'Relying, as I always did on the moment for the choice of language, it wasn't a bad thing to have a little bit of poetry in one's subliminal consciousness.'[20]

Heseltine recalled how Menzies prepared speeches. 'He would do it all himself by hand,' he said. 'Seldom did he dictate anything. He did occasionally to Hazel [Craig], if she was there, but if not, one of the other girls would come up in fear and trembling to take it.'[21] Eggleton remembered that Menzies gave a laser-beam focus to the writing of speeches, and hated to be distracted. Menzies did not like the telephone. If it rang while he was in a meeting, reading, or writing a speech, he would urge Eggleton or somebody else to answer it. 'Laddie,' Menzies would say, 'answer the phone, would you.'[22]

Menzies did not like speechwriters. 'I never employed a speechwriter myself,' he said. 'I had an obstinate objection to having other people's words put into my mouth.'[23] While Menzies did prepare most of his speeches, he sometimes used drafts provided by his department. Geoff Yeend, who served as Menzies' private secretary (1952–55), thought the notion that Menzies wrote all of his own speeches was a 'myth'. In a private letter to Frances McNicoll, he wrote: 'He certainly wrote all the important ones but on much of the routine stuff — second reading speeches in parliament etc. — he used what was prepared for him — on occasion completely untouched.'[24]

Parliament, to Menzies, was the manifestation of democracy. He had enormous respect for the traditions of parliament, and mastered the techniques of effective speechmaking, debating, and sparring across the despatch box. He studied the standing orders, and understood the rules and procedures of debate. He thought it was in parliament that a prime minister and a government gained respect and credibility. If a prime minister, and a government, could not draw authority from parliament, they had little hope of convincing the voters.

Menzies saw two things vital for a prime minister in parliament. First, 'they must be listened to' and be able 'to speak with a note of authority'. He thought the McMahon government had 'no authority' and, as a result, was slipping behind the opposition and could not 'capture public support'. The second thing Menzies stressed was that any statement made to the parliament had to be 'immaculately correct'. An error suggested the speaker was being sneaky, or lying, and as a result their credibility would be damaged. 'A government must respect the opposition by never lying to it or deliberately misleading it,' he said. 'Under those circumstances, you will get the business of the House through.' Menzies summed up his approach to parliament. 'We knew what we wanted to do,' he reflected. 'We had a clear-cut program and we got on with it and, on the whole, we maintained a large volume of public support and the opposition knew this.'[25]

Menzies saw parliamentary performances as a key way to judge the effectiveness of a politician. He would often listen to ministers speak on a Bill, and paid close attention to their presentation in Question Time. Parliament, for Menzies, was also theatre. A good speech or response to a question could raise the morale of the government benches, demoralise the opposition, and impress the press gallery watching from above the Speaker's chair. Journalists Wallace Brown and Peter Bowers recalled that at the commencement of Question Time, Menzies would often take a blank piece of paper and draw up a scorecard to rate the performances of his ministers. 'At the end of Question Time, he would always deliberately fold and tear this score sheet into tiny pieces and, grinning and raising an eyebrow, drop it into the wastepaper basket, so that nobody ever knew what his assessment was,' Brown wrote.[26]

ROBERT Menzies never had a particularly good relationship with the media. He initially avoided the informal briefings and friendly relations practised by his predecessors, John Curtin and Ben Chifley. He was often uncomfortable around newspaper reporters, because he never fully trusted them. 'In his relations with newspapermen, Menzies was neither easy nor professional,' recalled journalist turned Liberal Party public relations man Edgar Holt. 'He could be charming and amiable with individual journalists, but he was not at ease with the press as an institution or with journalists as a tribe.'[27]

Stewart Cockburn served as Menzies' press secretary from 1951 to 1954. Menzies had not employed a press secretary for the first 18 months of his prime ministership, as he felt little need for one. He was, after all, an effective proponent of his government's philosophy, principles, and policies. He addressed parliament, gave speeches in public, and used radio extensively. He spoke with authority, and anything he said made news. Eventually, Menzies decided that he needed a press secretary to handle media enquiries. When interviewed for the job, Cockburn, a journalist, volunteered that he was a Labor voter. 'I'm not interested in how you vote, my boy,' Menzies responded. 'All I want to know is: Can you do the job? Will you be loyal?' Cockburn assured Menzies that he could.[28]

Cockburn helped to develop better relations between Menzies and the press gallery. He recommended that Menzies provide an occasional off-the-record 'background talk' to journalists, and Menzies agreed.[29] Cockburn became an effective conduit between the press and the prime minister, but it was not an easy job. Menzies thought Cockburn looked like he had the weight of the world on his shoulders, and called him 'Atlas'.[30] Over time, under later press secretaries Hugh Dash and Ray Maley, Menzies talked more frequently to journalists on and off the record, held press conferences, and occasionally granted one-on-one interviews. But his suspicion of, and often hostility towards, the media remained.

Geoff Yeend recalled that Menzies was generally well served by a succession of press secretaries. 'I think his problem was more his unwillingness to accept that he needed anyone to build or improve the image,' he recalled.[31] Given this, it was not surprising that Hugh Dash succeeded Cockburn as press secretary, serving from 1954 to 1960. Dash was a former newspaper sportswriter who had worked for *The*

Daily Telegraph. He was a larrikin who enjoyed telling stories and having a drink with Menzies in the evenings. Menzies adored 'Hughie', but he was not very helpful with press relations. Dash died at home, aged 53, on 27 June 1960. Menzies was shocked. 'Hugh Dash was a most experienced journalist and to me a most faithful assistant and friend,' he said in a statement. 'I shall miss him most grievously.'[32]

Ray Maley, a former bureau chief for *The Sydney Morning Herald*, served as Menzies' press secretary from 1960 to 1964. He quickly developed a rapport with Menzies, became a valued member of staff, and put relations with the press gallery on a more professional footing. But on 29 September 1964, Maley dropped dead during a function in King's Hall. He was 51 years old. 'Ray had a close and intimate knowledge of both politics and the press,' Menzies wrote to his widow, Jean, in retirement. 'His advice to me was always based on a close understanding of the problems involved, and, I have no doubt, saved me from many errors during the time that he was with me.'[33] Len Owens became Menzies' acting press secretary for a few months after Maley's death.

Tony Eggleton had been the navy's public relations officer, and had impressed Menzies by his handling of the collision of the destroyer *Voyager* with the aircraft carrier *Melbourne* during an exercise off Jervis Bay, New South Wales, on 10 February 1964. The *Voyager* was sliced in half, and 82 lives were lost. The navy's top brass wanted to keep the tragedy under wraps, but Eggleton would not have it, and phoned the press gallery himself to alert them. Menzies, however, was not told of the disaster — he learned about it listening to ABC radio the next morning. It was the navy's worst peacetime disaster, and nobody told the prime minister. Menzies was furious, and promptly ordered a royal commission.[34]

John Bunting recommended Eggleton to Menzies as press secretary. Eggleton accepted, finding himself occupying a small office in a corridor adjacent to Menzies' suite, M85, which previously had been a men's toilet. (It had also been used by Maley and Dash.) Eggleton recalled how Menzies dealt with the media in his final year in office. 'He didn't see many journalists individually, and was happy for me to brief them with advice from the department on issues, and only involve him if it was necessary,' he said. 'Occasionally, he would say we should have a press conference. He would sit at his desk, and the journalists would sit around in a semi-circle and have questions and answers with the PM.'[35]

Eggleton said Menzies did not like being 'door-stopped' by journalists on his way in and out of Parliament House. He liked to exit the building down a side passageway, near his office, in the evening. On one occasion, Menzies was stopped by Jack Allsopp of the Melbourne *Sun* and asked a few questions as he was getting into a car. Menzies was furious, and scolded Allsopp. But he regretted it, and phoned Eggleton later from the Lodge. 'I feel that I was a bit harsh with him,' Menzies told Eggleton. 'What do you think I should do?' Eggleton suggested inviting him for morning tea. Menzies agreed. Allsopp was stunned by the courtesy.[36]

Menzies despised *The Sydney Morning Herald*, which had broken with decades of tradition and supported Labor at the 1961 election. In the lead-up to that election, Menzies penned a parody of how *The Sydney Morning Herald* would report his death. He shared it with family, friends, and colleagues:

We announce today, without gloating but not without satisfaction, the death of the former prime minister Robert Gordon Menzies.

As a newspaper of record, we feel it to be our duty to convey this news to the public. But as an independent newspaper of rare and discriminating judgement, we feel it to be equally our duty to speak the truth concerning the deceased statesman.

Fairness, our constant watchword, requires that we should record that Mr Menzies' notorious failure stemmed from two circumstances for which he was not entirely to blame. He was not born of wealthy parents. He was not born in Sydney.

Possessed as he was by a certain rudimentary native intelligence, he clearly set out to overcome, though alas without much success, these initial disabilities. In particular, he acquired and practiced a certain skill in words which led — as we feel bound to concede it — to a somewhat singular lucidity of speech. This made him difficult to misreport. But we have never been deterred by difficulties; in this connection our readers will share our pride in the way in which we overcame them ...

Perhaps the late statesman's greatest error was his obstinate refusal to acknowledge that the 'fourth estate' if we may recall that immortal phrase, is the real ruler of the nation. Being of a reactionary and fundamentally uneducated mind, he retained an atavistic belief that political power belongs to elected persons and not to those chosen by providence to be newspaper proprietors. This was a fatal error.[37]

Journalist Wallace Brown recalled that Menzies respected most of the journalists in the press gallery, and tolerated the others. He enjoyed warm relations with former Test cricketer Jack Fingleton, and was often seen talking politics and sport with him around Parliament House. Menzies did not like Ian Fitchett, who wrote for *The Age* and then *The Sydney Morning Herald*. Fitchett had compared Menzies to 'Ming the Merciless', the villain from the *Flash Gordon* comic book and movie serial. After the *Herald* backed Labor at the 1961 election, Menzies passed Fitchett in King's Hall. 'I'll make you eat crow, Fitchett,' Menzies said. 'I'll have your guts for garters.' Fitchett replied: 'As long as they are garnished with the sauce of your embarrassment, prime minister.' Brown recalled another journalist asking Menzies for an interview after a long flight from overseas. 'Mr Menzies, I am from the Sydney *Mirror*,' the reporter said. 'My boy, you have my deepest sympathy,' Menzies said as he walked on.[38]

Jon Gaul was a reporter for the Sydney *Daily Mirror* and the Melbourne *Sun* from 1959 to 1964, and political correspondent for *The Canberra Times* from 1964 to 1969. 'When Menzies arrived at Parliament House in the morning, three of us from the afternoon papers would wait for him at the top of the steps,' Gaul told me in an interview. 'He would "feed the chooks" while he walked along the corridor to the prime minister's office, giving us some tidbit or other which was enough for a tabloid story.' It was a subtle way of managing the media. 'Menzies was a natural thespian,' Gaul added. 'He was a superb performer in the parliament, very good on radio, and on television he would sit there and look at the camera — he adapted to it much better than almost anyone, I'd say, up to Bob Hawke.'[39]

In a previously unpublished interview, Menzies reflected on several newspaper proprietors. 'The little dogsbody, the editor of *The Sydney Morning Herald*, [Rupert] Henderson, he didn't like me,' he said. 'I thought he was a silly rabbit. And Fairfax, Warwick Fairfax, was a sort of vague and wandering fellow and he didn't care for me. As a matter of fact,

ABOVE: Roy Street, Jeparit, around 1895, the year after Robert Menzies was born. It was mostly hot, windy, and dusty. About eight buildings lined the main street, and the small town was home to just 200 by the end of the 1890s. (*Museums Victoria*)

RIGHT: James Menzies, an apprentice coach-painter, took over the general store in Jeparit in 1893. He dedicated himself to the community life of Jeparit and served two terms as shire president. (*Jeparit and District Historical Society*)

ABOVE: Kate Menzies, who was more loving and affectionate than James, worked in the general store and ran the family home. (*Jeparit and District Historical Society*)

LEFT: James Menzies' store, on the corner of Roy and Charles streets, Jeparit. Robert Menzies was born in the back of the store in 1894. (*Wimmera Mallee Pioneer Museum*)

LEFT: The four Menzies children born to James and Kate — Frank, Belle, Robert in the front aged about eight, and Les. (*RG Menzies Papers, National Library of Australia*)

BELOW: Robert Menzies, aged about 14, back row far right, photographed in a schoolboys football team in Jeparit around 1909. The Menzies family had all left Jeparit by 1910. (*Wimmera Mallee Pioneer Museum*)

ABOVE LEFT: Robert Menzies in his graduation robes at the University of Melbourne, where he collected many impressive awards and graduated with degrees in law in 1918. (*Jeparit and District Historical Society*)

ABOVE RIGHT: Frank and Les Menzies, the brothers who enlisted in the First World War. Robert, who did not enlist, said later in life that his primary motivation for going into politics was to serve his country another way. (*Jeparit and District Historical Society*)

ABOVE: Robert Menzies, made the youngest King's Counsel in Australia in 1929, cemented his name as a barrister in the Engineers' Case in 1920. *(News Corp Australia)*

RIGHT: Robert Menzies around the time of his election to the Victorian State Parliament in 1928 — his star rose fast in politics. *(News Corp Australia)*

ABOVE: Robert Menzies, seated fifth on the left, appointed Victorian attorney-general, meeting with the ministry after being sworn in by William Irvine, seated in the middle. *(RG Menzies Papers, National Library of Australia)*

ABOVE: Joe Lyons, at the head of the table, chairs a cabinet meeting in Canberra in 1938, with Robert Menzies, attorney-general, seated to his left, as Billy Hughes makes a point. *(News Corp Australia)*

LEFT: Robert Menzies in full Privy Council uniform, having been sworn in at Buckingham Palace in London in 1938. *(RG Menzies Papers, National Library of Australia)*

RIGHT: Robert Menzies' 'melancholy' nationwide radio broadcast announcing that Australia was at war with Germany in 1939. *(News Corp Australia)*

BELOW: Robert Menzies tears apart a crab and downs some longneck beers with journalists from *The Examiner* in Launceston in 1939. *(RG Menzies Papers, National Library of Australia)*

ABOVE: Robert Menzies' initial encounters with Winston Churchill, pictured together at 10 Downing Street, were seldom pleasant, but, over time, they grew to enjoy the company of each other, and Menzies' admiration for the British prime minister grew. *(News Corp Australia)*

ABOVE: Robert Menzies was more than a little frightened being in London during the Second World War but felt he had to show Australians back home that he was not 'yellow'. *(RG Menzies Papers, National Library of Australia)*

LEFT: Robert Menzies filmed many of his travels abroad on a 16-millimetre Kodak camera and would screen them for colleagues, family, and friends at Parliament House. *(News Corp Australia)*

ABOVE: Arthur Fadden's government would rule for 40 days and 40 nights. Fadden, seated next to the Despatch Box, with Billy Hughes alongside, and Robert Menzies on the front bench, listen to John Curtin speak in Parliament in 1941. *(Lloyd Ross Papers, National Library of Australia)*

BELOW: Meeting of the Advisory War Council, which would include nine current, former, or future prime ministers during the Second World War. *(John Curtin Prime Ministerial Library)*

THE RT. HON. R. G.

MENZIES

K.C., M.P.

WILL SPEAK ON

"THE FORGOTTEN PEOPLE"

TO·NIGHT—9.15

ABOVE: Newspaper advertisement ahead of Robert Menzies' landmark 'the forgotten people' broadcast in 1942. *(RG Menzies Papers, National Library of Australia)*

RIGHT: Robert Menzies enjoyed parrying interjectors on the campaign trail and was known for his cutting, often wounding, wit, pictured here in 1940. *(News Corp Australia)*

BELOW: The newly formed Liberal Party of Australia meets in Albury in 1944. *(National Archives of Australia: M3130, 121)*

ABOVE: The newly sworn-in ministry with the governor-general Sir William McKell, seated in the middle, at Government House in 1949. *(National Archives of Australia: M4927, 10)*

RIGHT: Heather Henderson, Robert Menzies, and Pattie Menzies, and the family cat, George, at home in Melbourne after the Liberal Party won a historic victory at the 1949 election. *(News Corp Australia)*

ABOVE: Queen Elizabeth II has reigned during the terms of more than a dozen Australian prime ministers but her closest relationship has been with Robert Menzies, pictured here escorting her into Parliament House in 1954. *(News Corp Australia)*

RIGHT: Robert Menzies meets with Japanese prime minister Nobusuke Kishi, with John McEwen on the right, who negotiated the landmark commerce agreement between Australia and Japan in 1957. *(National Archives of Australia: A1671, JPM4/3)*

LEFT: Robert Menzies met five US presidents in office and enjoyed cordial relations with John F. Kennedy, pictured here in 1963. Kennedy agreed to 'definitely' visit Australia before his term was completed, but was assassinated later that year. *(John F. Kennedy Presidential Library and Museum)*

ABOVE: Robert Menzies answers questions from press gallery journalists in his office at Parliament House. *(National Press Club of Australia)*

BELOW: Robert Menzies was a superb parliamentarian, pictured here facing Labor's Arthur Calwell and Gough Whitlam in the 1960s. *(RG Menzies Papers, National Library of Australia)*

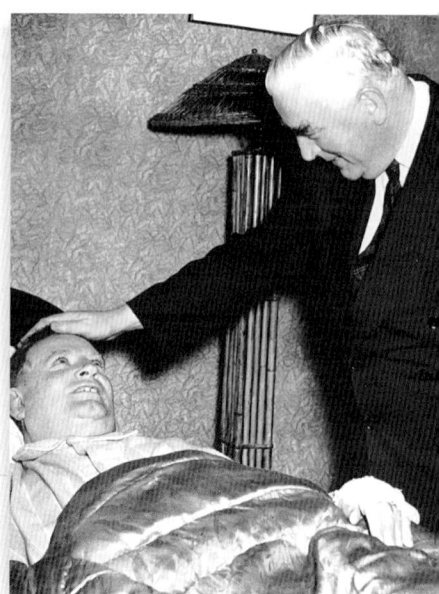

TOP LEFT: Robert Menzies with his long-time deputy and staunch friend and supporter Eric Harrison in London, where he served as high commissioner, 1956–64. *(RG Menzies Papers, National Library of Australia)*

TOP RIGHT: Robert Menzies comforts his treasurer, Arthur Fadden, after a car accident in 1954. *(RG Menzies Papers, National Library of Australia)*

LOWER LEFT: Robert Menzies with his deputy, Harold Holt, in 1962. Holt was a huge disappointment to Menzies when he became prime minister in 1966. *(LJ Dwyer Collection, National Library of Australia)*

LOWER RIGHT: Tamie and Malcolm Fraser with Robert Menzies in Portland, Victoria, 1958. Menzies thought Liberal salvation would only come when Fraser was made leader. *(The Malcolm Fraser Collection, University of Melbourne Archives)*

ABOVE: Robert Menzies returns to his old school in Jeparit, sits at a student desk, and raises his hand to answer a question, with former teacher Tom Livingstone on hand in 1951. *(Jeparit and District Historical Society)*

RIGHT: Pattie and Robert Menzies, and Belle Green, make a triumphant return to Jeparit in 1951. *(Jeparit and District Historical Society)*

LEFT: Robert Menzies valued the advice of public servants, seen here with Prime Minister's Department head John Bunting watching Australia vs England at the Melbourne Cricket Ground, 1965. *(State Library of Victoria)*

TOP: Three generations of the Menz[i]
family gather for a portrait at the Lo[dge]
1965. (National Archives of Australia:
A1200, L84276)

ABOVE: Robert Menzies' personal
bookplate designed by his friend
Lionel Lindsay in 1940. (RG Menzies
Papers, National Library of Australia)

LEFT: William Dobell's portrait of
Robert Menzies for the cover of
TIME magazine in 1960. (National
Portrait Gallery)

ABOVE: Robert Menzies, the master performer, insisted on having 'a nervous pee' prior to his farewell press conference, which was broadcast live to the nation and attracted the then largest-ever television audience, 1966. *(National Archives of Australia: A1200, L53530)*

LEFT: Robert Menzies would usually smoke half a dozen cigars — typically Coronas — during the day. *(RG Menzies Papers, National Library of Australia)*

ABOVE: Robert Menzies installed as Lord Warden of the Cinque Ports at Dover Castle in 1966. *(News Corp Australia)*

LEFT: Robert Menzies' Coat of Arms as Lord Warden. *(RG Menzies Papers, National Library of Australia)*

LEFT: Robert Menzies watches Carlton vs Footscray from the comfort of his Bentley on a special platform installed for hi[m] at Princes Park in Melbourne, 1972. *(News Corp Australia)*

BELOW: Dame Pattie and Sir Robert Menzies at the Kooyong Tennis Centre, mid-1970s. *(Rennie Ellis, State Library of Victor[ia])*

BELOW: Robert Menzies' funeral cortege, led by army, air force, and navy guards of honour, in Melbourne, 1978. *(News Corp Australia)*

I didn't go along to their office and have lunch with them and confide in them as I should have.' In August 1943, Henderson sent Menzies a cheque for £25 — worth about $1,800 today — as a 'contribution' towards his 'election campaign fund' in Kooyong. Menzies promptly sent it back, as it breached his 'golden rule' about not accepting 'monetary assistance' during campaigns.[40]

Menzies did not dislike all newspapers or their proprietors. '*The [Daily] Telegraph* wasn't hostile to me,' he said of the paper owned by Frank Packer. He did not regard *The Age* or the Melbourne *Herald* as especially 'hostile'. And the Murdoch family? 'Keith Murdoch was never among my warmest admirers,' he said.[41] Yet Menzies enjoyed the support of Murdoch throughout the 1930s, who promoted him as Lyons' successor. Menzies appointed Murdoch director-general of information during the Second World War. *The Australian*, founded in July 1964 by his son, Rupert Murdoch, sometimes took a critical editorial line towards the Menzies government.

Menzies' commanding voice was instantly recognisable on radio, the principal means of communication for much of his political career. The Chifley government had planned to introduce television by the end of 1950, but the Menzies government delayed its introduction until September 1956, following a two-year royal commission. By 1956, more than 70 per cent of homes in the United States already had a television set, and Menzies had appeared on television programs in the United States and Great Britain. In time, he saw television, like radio, as a way to sidestep the print media and talk directly to voters. The opening of parliament was broadcast on television for the first time in February 1959, but very few Australians ever saw Menzies perform in the House of Representatives. There was no regular broadcasting of parliament on television, least of all Question Time, during the Menzies government.

'Television gave him all the scope he needed to indulge in his great powers of oratory and use his great ability as an actor, a quality every worthwhile advocate must possess,' argued newsman Ian Fitchett. 'Television emphasised his handsome appearance, his long silver hair and his wild black eyebrows and did not treat too cruelly his heavy jowls. His splendid speaking voice, always his greatest asset, gained new significance. Perhaps even more important was the fact that he developed a friendly

and humorous image on the screen and this did a lot to dissipate what
had generally come to be accepted as an impossibly overbearing manner.'[42]
Menzies' interviews, or at least long excerpts from them, were often
broadcast on television, where the viewers could see the prime minister
parry the journalists' questions. Menzies saw interviews, much like
parliament, as political theatre.

Menzies occasionally sat for interviews on programs on the commercial
stations and on the ABC, and his major speeches and campaign events were
frequently covered by television news programs. Graham Freudenberg,
working for television station GTV9 in Melbourne, persuaded Menzies to
give an hour-long 'report to the nation' after an overseas trip in May 1959.
'I had to come up [to Canberra] to persuade him,' Freudenberg recalled in
an interview. 'He was very reluctant. He didn't like television.' But Menzies
agreed to do the presentation from a Melbourne studio on a Saturday
morning. 'It was a *tour de force*,' Freudenberg said. 'The recording equipment
was very primitive. They had something called telecine, which was a film
[taken] direct from the studio cameras. But the trick was that once you
started, you couldn't stop, you had to do the whole thing.' Menzies had no
notes, but spoke fluently for 50 minutes, with only occasional questions
from actor George Fairfax from the studio control room.[43]

Menzies' election policy speech ahead of the November 1963
election was the first to be broadcast on television; in that campaign,
71 per cent of voters said they had seen one or more of the party leaders
on television.[44] While Menzies successfully used the new medium of
television, and was cognisant of its growing importance in politics,
he did not want to participate in campaign debates. The televised
debates between John F. Kennedy and Richard Nixon in September–
October 1960, ahead of the presidential election, had transformed
politics. The first political debate on Australian television had taken
place in November 1958 between Harold Holt and Billy McMahon,
representing the government, and H.V. 'Doc' Evatt and Arthur Calwell,
representing the opposition. It was telecast by Channel Seven and
moderated by the editor of *The Sydney Morning Herald*, and former
British conservative politician, Angus Maude. In the lead-up to the next
election in December 1961, Holt and McMahon debated Calwell and
Gough Whitlam on television.

'There is an amusing debate going on in the party organisation as to whether it is wise to engage in television debates,' Menzies told his daughter in September 1961. 'Personally, I would not engage in one. You have to develop your own views in a most interrupted fashion, so that you never quite make the point or cover the ground. In addition to this, you advertise your opponents by making them, so to speak, known personalities.' He thought a 'straight television talk' was more effective than debating, and less risky. 'Nixon made Kennedy President of America by conducting nationwide debates with him,' Menzies thought.[45]

One notable incident regarding the media took place in June 1955, when the House of Representatives' Privileges Committee found that journalist Frank Browne had impugned the integrity of Charles Morgan, the Labor Member for Reid, by implying he was involved in 'an immigration racket' offering guaranteed entry into the country in return for payment. The article was published on 28 April 1955 in the *Bankstown Observer*, a Sydney suburban newspaper. On 3 May, Morgan was successful in referring the matter to the Privileges Committee for investigation. The *Bankstown Observer* attacked the decision in an article on 5 May, and lashed Morgan for what it said was a 'cowardly' attack.

On 8 June, the committee reported there had been an attempt to 'influence and intimidate' Morgan with baseless allegations that represented a breach of parliamentary privilege. Browne and the newspaper proprietor, Ray Fitzpatrick, gave evidence to the committee. On 9 June, the House of Representatives agreed with the findings of the report. Menzies moved a motion recommending that a trial take place and that Browne and Fitzpatrick should be summoned before the Bar of the House of Representatives. On 10 June, a wooden bar was placed across the entrance to the House of Representatives, and Browne and Fitzpatrick stood before it. After about 20 minutes, and a short adjournment, Menzies successfully moved that Browne and Fitzpatrick be jailed for breaching parliamentary privilege.

Evatt, however, proposed a fine rather than a jail sentence, but this was not supported. Menzies' motion was carried — 55–11 in the case of Browne, and 55–12 in the case of Fitzpatrick.[46] Three Labor MPs voted with the Coalition — including Gough Whitlam. Browne and Fitzpatrick spent three months in Goulburn jail — a draconian response that betrayed principles which the Liberal Party supposedly upheld. Indeed, Frank Green, the clerk of the House of Representatives, advised there had been 'no breach of privilege', and described the proceedings as 'disgraceful'.[47] But Menzies insisted that anyone who undermined the parliament's integrity could not go unanswered or unpunished. 'The punishment inflicted served as a proper warning to people that the freedom of a newspaper or writer is freedom and not licence, and that it can be lost when it is abused,' he argued.[48]

IN February 1957, just a few months after he was elected deputy leader, Harold Holt wrote a 21-page paper for Menzies titled 'The political situation'. The paper provided an inside assessment of the Menzies government at its mid-point. It was not overly flattering. 'Although comparatively comfortably placed at present, the Menzies government does not enjoy the degree and warmth of public support that its policies, achievements and personnel merit for it,' Holt argued. He said 'there is scope for considerable improvement' in the government's relations with its own backbench, state, and federal party organisations, and also with state MPs. On the bright side, the leadership was 'widely respected', and ministers were 'able and experienced'.[49]

Holt noted 'the parlous plight of our opposition', but warned against complacency. Holt thought the government needed 'an imaginative program' of policies to take to the voters by the time of the next election. 'We still lack a sufficiently large following of devoted people who are wholeheartedly for our principles, and enthusiastic about how we apply them,' Holt wrote. There was recognition that the government had been 'delivering the goods', with 'sustained prosperity, development and full potential', and that it was 'sounder' on finance, foreign policy, and defence. But the government could not afford to rest on its laurels.[50]

As Holt's report reminds us, it would be a mistake to think that Menzies was always dominant. He suffered a significant setback at the December 1961 election, for example, and had to govern for the next two years with only a one-seat majority in the House of Representatives. Menzies never courted popularity, and was acutely conscious that he did not always possess it; in fact, Menzies at no stage reached the heights of popularity enjoyed by John Curtin. The Gallup Poll often showed that, between terms, the Coalition trailed Labor, led first by Evatt and then Calwell, only to recover by election day. This was true of Menzies before winning the 1954, 1961, and 1963 elections. This was also the case with Gough Whitlam (1974), Malcolm Fraser (1980), Bob Hawke (1987 and 1990), Paul Keating (1993), and John Howard (1998, 2001, and 2004).

Menzies was a shrewd practitioner of politics who learned from his mistakes, and could change course on policy, or devise new political strategies to remain in power. This was being pragmatic — a hallmark of any successful political leader. Menzies knew it was more important to be respected than popular. Respect can help a government survive, even when it has a slim majority on the floor of the parliament, whereas popularity can be fleeting and, once it is lost, can lead to disappointment among voters and to panic among MPs. A government needs a more stable foundation for effective political leadership than popularity alone, and that is what Menzies provided.

On 30 November 1954, Robert Menzies became Australia's longest-serving prime minister. He had been in office over two terms for seven years, 15 weeks, and one day — a day longer than Billy Hughes.[51] A month earlier, the Liberal Party had reached ten years since its founding. 'In its ten years, Australia's Liberal Party, formed in unpromising circumstances, has succeeded beyond the dreams of all but its most hopeful supporters,' reported *The Sydney Morning Herald*. The Liberal Party, it argued, 'stands for a fairly weighty hand of government, but one which guides the economy by budget policy and control of credit instead of by the cumbersome system of detailed controls administered by a bureaucracy'.[52]

While there had been the setback of the May 1954 election, and the earlier loss of the referendum in September 1951, Menzies' leadership was secure, and his approach to the prime ministership was largely cemented. This was wholly different from his experience in 1939–41. Menzies was instrumental in the Liberal Party's formation, its electoral success, and its dominance. 'Mr Menzies, once thought too clever to be popular, has become a great vote-winner,' the *Herald* judged. 'That remains important to the Liberal Party, as he does not seem to have any intention of leaving politics.'[53] A year earlier, in April–May 1953, Gallup found that Menzies was preferred prime minister over Evatt by 52–34 per cent.[54]

But a word of caution was sounded about Menzies' dominance that would later — much later — become glaringly evident. 'Menzies has formed and moulded the Liberal Party and led it to its victories. Virtually he IS the Liberal Party,' the *Herald* argued. 'Menzies is unchallenged and probably unchallengeable as long as he likes to remain leader and overshadows his colleagues with his stature, his intellectual grasp of problems, and his frequent and genuine refusal to play for short-term political advantage.' However, the future of the party in the post-Menzies era 'remains obscure', the newspaper foretold. 'There is no sign of a successor who will have Mr Menzies' capacity to overawe his supporters.'[55]

CHAPTER 13

At Home: Domestic Affairs

THE Menzies government was in power during the long post-war boom. Its approach to domestic policy has often been described as 'managed prosperity'. Overall, it was an era of strong economic growth, increasing per capita wages, and rising living standards. Much of the post-war reconstruction plans put in place by the Curtin–Chifley governments were maintained. These included the vast post-war immigration program, the Snowy Mountains Hydro-Electric Scheme, support for local car manufacturing, and approval for a university scholarship and assistance scheme. The Menzies government built on these initiatives with important new policies of its own, especially in education, housing, and national development, and private enterprise was encouraged.

The workforce increased by more than 1 million during the Menzies era — an expansion of around 100,000 new workers every year. Unemployment averaged about 2 per cent. Manufacturing accounted for 30 per cent of GDP and employed 30 per cent of the workforce. Agriculture and mining made up almost 80 per cent of Australia's exports. Certain industries benefited from generous taxation concessions. To facilitate national development, the government funded construction of roads, railway lines, and ports. There was a high level of foreign investment. Home ownership, helped by new lines of bank credit and a home savings grant scheme, increased from 53 per cent in the late 1940s to 71 per cent by the mid-1960s.

The Menzies government favoured an interventionist economic policy, again a holdover from the Curtin–Chifley years, with tightly regulated product, capital, and labour markets. The currency's exchange rate was pegged to the British pound, alongside capital and exchange controls. Australian businesses were protected behind a high tariff wall. (The government did, however, sweep away the structure of quantitative controls on imports in 1960.) While Australia enjoyed full employment for much of the period, there was little foreign labour allowed into the country. The last budget of the Menzies government to be in surplus was in 1952–53. The size of government expanded from 26.7 per cent of GDP in 1949 to 28.4 per cent by 1969.[1] These policies, although they reflected much of the political consensus of the time, are antiquated today.

Donald Horne's critique of the Menzies era, *The Lucky Country*, was published in 1964. It was not a paean to Australia's greatness, but a damning assessment of a country resting on its laurels. The title is often quoted, but the meaning is frequently forgotten. 'Australia is a lucky country run mainly by second-rate people who share its luck,' Horne wrote. 'It lives on other people's ideas, and, although its ordinary people are adaptable, most of its leaders (in all fields) so lack curiosity about the events that surround them that they are often taken by surprise.' Horne thought Menzies had stayed in office for too long, and that Australia lacked imagination and inventiveness. Horne was not offering this critique in hindsight; he was saying it at the time. The Federation-era policies of industry protection, centralised industrial relations, and White Australia remained largely intact, but they would not continue to guarantee Australia's prosperity into the future.[2]

Nonetheless, these policies worked to produce long-run economic growth with low unemployment and mostly low inflation. Yet management of the economy often led to booms followed by sharp corrections. The government initially struggled to deal with an inflationary surge, partly caused by the Korean War, and the continued expansion of the economy. In 1951 and 1956, for example, the government had to take drastic corrective measures, such as increasing income and company tax, to avoid overheating. The economy was in recession in 1952–53. A misreading of conditions and the wrong policy response — characterised as 'stop-go' economic management — induced a credit squeeze in 1960–61.

The creation of the Reserve Bank of Australia, in January 1960, gave the government a more effective monetary-policy tool with which to manage the economy in the future.

The Menzies government was responsible for a number of important social-policy innovations. The age pension was increased from around £2 to £6 per week for single people, and from £4 to £11 for married couples. The property and income means tests were relaxed, and those in retirement who qualified for the age pension increased from around 37 per cent to 53 per cent. Child endowment for the first child under 16 was introduced, and was then extended and increased for subsequent children. The national health scheme provided limited voluntary insurance against sickness that was supplemented with contributions from government. More than 70 per cent of Australians had medical or hospital insurance, with a government subsidy, by the end of the Menzies period. The cost of pensioner visits to their local GP was met by the government.

THE threat of communism permeated the Menzies years, which was often exploited for political purposes. But there was a real threat abroad during the Cold War, and a growing danger at home. In the early 1950s, the government was genuinely concerned that a third world war might break out. We now know that a secret Soviet spy ring was operating in Australia, and only in recent years has ASIO acknowledged that it was penetrated by Soviet spies during this era. There were certainly communist links between scores of Labor Party MPs, local councillors, and officials — some even acted as secret agents or informants for the Communist Party of Australia. However, many of these people were harmless, though misguided, and the influence of spies was exaggerated. It is also true that there were abuses of power by ASIO, and that some Australians were wrongly targeted for innocent associations, or alleged associations, with Soviet persons of interest.

On 27 April 1950, Menzies introduced into parliament the Communist Party Dissolution Bill to outlaw the Communist Party of Australia. 'For some years I and other persons resisted the idea of a Communist ban on the ground that, in time of peace, doubts ought to be resolved in favour of free speech,' Menzies said. But times had changed.

There was now a Cold War, and communism was not only a global threat but also a local one.[3] The legislation would wind up the Communist Party and its associations, and dispose of their property. A union official, public servant, or private individual could be 'declared' as communist and then prohibited either from holding office in a union or a position in the public service. Private property could be seized. The onus of proof would be reversed, so that those accused of being communists would have to prove they were not. This ran against the longstanding legal principle that all persons are innocent until proven guilty.

The Bill was debated at length. Most voters, encouraged by newspapers, were initially supportive. But Menzies faced stiff opposition, including from some within his own party, for being seen to be stifling freedom of speech and association. His cause was not helped when he was forced to admit that he had been in error when he named five union leaders as communists. Nor was his cause further helped when he threatened to 'declare' Labor MPs during a spirited debate with Eddie Ward. Some Labor MPs were opposed to the legislation, particularly its reversal of the onus of proof, but the party's federal executive directed them to allow it to pass through the Senate.

Some opposition amendments were adopted by the government, but passage of the Bill stalled when the House and the Senate, which was controlled by Labor, became deadlocked in June 1950. Menzies reintroduced the Bill three months later, whereupon Labor pushed for further amendments, but these were not supported by the Coalition. Labor remained divided on the Bill. But on 16 October 1950, Labor's federal executive again ordered its MPs to support its passage through the Senate. The Labor Party did not want to fight an election while being accused of being soft on communism. The Bill eventually won Senate approval on 19 October 1950.

The Communist Party and several unions immediately challenged the legislation in the High Court. H.V. 'Doc' Evatt, Labor's deputy leader, acted as counsel for the communist-controlled Waterside Workers' Federation. This was one of many lapses of judgement on Evatt's part, because it looked like Labor was supporting communism, even though he had been motivated to take a stand in defence of civil liberties. On 9 March 1951, after weeks of hearings, the High Court ruled by 6–1 that the *Communist Party Dissolution Act* was invalid, as it breached the constitution. This was a victory for Evatt and a defeat for Menzies. But it was only the opening battle.

Undeterred, Menzies forced a double-dissolution election to try to give the government control of the Senate. The Commonwealth Bank Bill provided the trigger. Menzies wanted to insert a new provision in legislation that would allow for a board of directors, rather than a central director, to run the bank. Labor, which had a Senate majority, opposed it, and the Bill, having previously been rejected by the Senate, was referred to a Senate select committee. The referral was deemed to be the second rejection of the Bill, and, under section 57 of the constitution, this 'failure to pass' became the basis for a double-dissolution election.

Menzies asked the governor-general, William McKell, to grant him a double-dissolution of the parliament — only the second since Federation. Labor was outraged. McKell, a former New South Wales Labor premier, granted Menzies his election for the House and the Senate. On 28 April 1951 — just 16 months after the previous election — the voters went back to the polls. The government lost five seats in the House of Representatives to the opposition, but gained six seats in the Senate, giving it majorities in both houses of parliament. The banking legislation, and amendments to industrial legislation that Labor had opposed, passed the Senate.

On 5 July 1951, Menzies proposed legislation to enable a referendum to be held that, if carried, would amend the constitution so that it would uphold the *Communist Party Dissolution Act* and provide the government with a general power to deal with communism. Menzies led the campaign for the 'Yes' vote. The government needed powers to deal with the communist threat, Menzies argued, and he accused the Labor Party of being soft on communism. But Menzies struggled to make a clear case to voters who were instinctively sceptical about changing the constitution. The question was complex, as it sought powers beyond simply validating the disallowed legislation. Menzies faced public demonstrations organised by communists, unionists, and Labor supporters wherever he went. Some Liberal members were themselves uneasy about the proposed curtailing of civil liberties. Victorian Young Liberal vice-president Alan Missen spoke out forcefully against the proposals, and was expelled from the party's state council.

Evatt, now the opposition leader, led the campaign for the 'No' vote with Labor's full support. Yet how could Labor argue against the referendum, given it had voted for the Communist Party Dissolution Bill? Evatt argued that the power now sought went beyond upholding the legislation. He had a valid point, and reasoned that the laws targeted Australians for what they believed, rather than for what they had done. It was, he argued passionately, a dangerous attack on freedom of speech, thought, and association. Evatt lashed the Menzies government for seeking 'totalitarian methods in order to defeat the totalitarian doctrine of communism'. Evatt was a powerful advocate, and he had a persuasive argument. It was his finest hour.

On 22 September 1951, Australians voted in the referendum. The 'Yes' vote should have easily prevailed. A few months earlier, in June, a Gallup Poll showed a whopping 80 per cent voter support for banning the Communist Party.[4] But the campaign had not gone well for Menzies, and the 'No' case won narrowly. New South Wales, Victoria, and South Australia voted 'No'. Queensland, Western Australia, and Tasmania voted 'Yes'. The overall vote in favour was 2,317,927, and the vote against was 2,370,009. Menzies had been motivated to pursue the referendum because he believed communism was a threat to liberalism. But a majority of voters saw his legislation as a greater threat to liberalism.

Menzies wrote a 'private' letter to the governor-general on 8 October 1951. 'My referendum campaign failed, though by no great margin,' he told McKell. He offered two reasons: Labor's opposition, and the concern that voters had in granting such powers, not to him, but to Evatt if he became prime minister. 'This kind of argument is, of course, quite puerile but the more experience I have of referendums, the more satisfied I am that "the child is father to the man".'[5] It was not a persuasive explanation. The defeat of the referendum, however, enabled Menzies to continue to warn Australians about the dangers posed by communism. It also meant that Labor was perceived as weak on communism. This was no more evident than with Evatt's response to the defection of Soviet diplomat Vladimir Petrov.

In the evening of 13 April 1954, Menzies announced to the House of Representatives that there had been a high-level Soviet diplomatic defection. It was a political bombshell:

Some days ago, one Vladimir Mikhailovich Petrov, who has been Third Secretary and Consul in the Soviet Embassy in Australia since February 1951, voluntarily left his diplomatic employment and made to the Australian government, through the Australian Security Intelligence Organisation, a request for political asylum ... the request has been granted and, following the established diplomatic practice, protection has been provided for Mr Petrov.

There was shock from politicians on both sides of parliament. As Menzies continued, government MPs began cheering. 'Hear, hear,' they said. Opposition MPs were stunned. Some began muttering, 'We're gone, we're gone now.' Several journalists jumped out of their seats and ran to the press gallery to file their stories. Menzies announced that a royal commission would be established to investigate 'espionage activity in Australia'. Labor MP Clyde Cameron remembered returning to the opposition party room, where Eddie Ward jokingly announced, 'I'm Petrovied.'[6]

Labor's leader, H.V. 'Doc' Evatt, was not in the House when Menzies spoke. He had left Canberra that afternoon to attend a dinner at his alma mater, Fort Street High School, in Sydney. Harold Holt had assured Evatt that there was 'nothing important' on the parliamentary agenda that night. Journalist Alan Reid recalled bumping into Evatt after he had spoken to Holt. 'I don't know anything,' Reid told Evatt. 'But I've got a funny feeling that there's something on.' Reid insisted he did not know about the Petrov defection in advance. Evatt checked again with Holt, and with Menzies, and told Reid he had been assured that 'there's nothing of importance on tonight'. So Evatt went to Sydney. When he was told about Menzies' statement concerning Petrov, Evatt believed he had been deceived by Menzies, Holt, and Reid. In any event, later that evening Evatt announced Labor's support for the royal commission. 'If any person in Australia has been guilty of espionage or seditious activities, a Labor government will see that he is prosecuted according to law,' he said.[7]

Menzies was furious with Reid reporting that Evatt had been 'framed' by the Petrov statement in an article published in *The Sun-Herald* on 25 April 1954. He wrote to Fairfax managing director Rupert 'Rags' Henderson, arguing it was 'defamatory', 'highly offensive', and 'untrue'. He rejected the suggestion that the announcement had been timed to coincide with Evatt's absence, or that there was a loose understanding that prime ministers and opposition leaders would confer privately on security matters. In fact, Menzies argued that he had asked his secretary to arrange a meeting with Evatt at 7.40 pm before his planned statement to the House at 8.00 pm. It was only then that he learned that Evatt was not in Canberra. He saw deputy Labor leader Arthur Calwell instead, told him about the statement, and asked for leave to make it. Calwell did not raise any objections.[8]

Reid was censured by chairman Warwick Fairfax, and Henderson, and wrote a grovelling apology to Menzies. 'I acknowledge that [I] should have approached you directly for your answer to the Labor allegations which formed the substance of the article,' he wrote.[9] Henderson replied to Menzies, noting that he 'did not challenge the accuracy of the basic facts', but questioned 'the truth and justification for the inferences drawn'. While noting that Reid should have sought a response, they stood by the article as it was in the national interest.[10]

Vladimir Petrov defected from the Soviet Union and sought political asylum in Australia while he was in Sydney on 3 April 1954. The defection was managed by ASIO deputy director Ron Richards, under the codename 'Operation Cabin 12'. In exchange for embassy files, which contained information about Soviet espionage activities in Australia, Petrov was paid £5,000 — about $170,000 in today's value. Earlier, on 10 February, ASIO director-general Charles Spry had informed Menzies that there could be a defection from the Soviet embassy. The possibility of a royal commission into Soviet espionage was discussed at this time. Menzies was briefed about Petrov's defection on 4 April and also shown the documents that Petrov had given ASIO. These documents implicated Evatt: two of his staff were named, and a third had authored one of the documents. Nine days later, shortly before Menzies addressed the House, he informed cabinet of the Petrov defection and discussed the documents. It was agreed that Petrov would be granted political asylum and that a royal commission into Soviet espionage would be established.[11]

Petrov's wife, Evdokia, did not know her husband had defected. She was escorted to Sydney airport by Soviet Union embassy officials, and boarded a plane to return to Moscow, via Darwin, Singapore, and London, on 19 April. A crowd of anti-communist protestors at the airport — many of them immigrants from Baltic nations — tried to stop her departure. There were dramatic scenes, some of them broadcast on radio, as her Soviet Union handlers bustled her to the plane. Evdokia was upset as, under bright floodlights, police tried to hold back the heaving crowd while the embassy officials were forcing her onto the plane. She lost a shoe on the tarmac.

Meanwhile, Menzies was contacted at the Lodge by Liberal MP Bill Wentworth, who was at the airport. He urged the prime minister to intervene. Wentworth said he had taken statements from some of the protestors, who swore she had asked for help and did not want to return to the Soviet Union. 'I looked her full in the face and I knew what she was feeling, and I also knew that if she went, the election would have been lost,' Wentworth recalled. 'So I went back and rang up The Lodge. At that stage, the cabinet was having its end-of-session dinner. I think they were all fairly well primed. I subsequently heard that there was a debate at the dinner table. Some people, particularly McEwen, said, "Do nothing, let her go." Menzies, however, came round to the position that something had to be done. A message was sent to the plane.'[12]

Menzies contacted Spry to make sure an intervention would be made in Darwin to ask Evdokia if she wanted to seek asylum in Australia. Security officials radioed the captain of the plane, asking him to find out if she would indeed like to stay in Australia. She indicated that she did. Early in the morning of 20 April, the plane landed in Darwin and was met by government officials. There was a struggle with her Russian handlers, who were illegally carrying guns, but Evdokia was separated for talks with Australian officials. Evdokia spoke to her husband, Vladimir, via telephone and requested asylum. It was granted.

These events took place just six weeks before an election, with the opinion polls showing Labor heading for victory. Menzies was accused of smearing Evatt by making him appear to be a communist sympathiser. Menzies did not raise the Petrov matter during the campaign. He didn't need to. It was everywhere in the media, while Arthur Fadden, and other ministers, claimed that Labor was weak on communism. The election, however, was not only about communism, the Petrovs, and Evatt's judgement. The government campaigned on its achievements, including a new health-insurance scheme and an increase in child endowment. Menzies also accused Evatt of proffering unaffordable and inflationary policies that would plunge Australia into economic calamity.

The Menzies government was returned with a seven-seat majority at the election held on 29 May 1954. It was a close-run thing: Labor won more than 50 per cent of the primary vote and gained five seats from the Liberals. Menzies outsmarted Evatt with a clever campaign built on modest promises. The Petrov defection also helped the government win a third term. Labor's near-victory may have contributed to Evatt's increasing paranoia and erratic behaviour. He maintained that the Petrov defection was a grand conspiracy to damage Labor and that he had deliberately not been informed of Menzies' statement to the House on 13 April. It is certainly curious that Menzies did not inform Evatt of his planned statement earlier in the day, given the magnitude of it, and the political impact that he surely knew it would have. And while Menzies denied those charges, he benefited politically from the Petrov defection. The defection also seemed to reinforce what he had been saying about the dangers of communism.

Following the defection of Vladimir and Evdokia Petrov in April 1954, the Menzies government established the royal commission into Soviet espionage in Australia. Evatt continued to argue that the Soviet defection and royal commission were an elaborate conspiracy between ASIO and the Menzies government designed to personally destroy him. While Evatt supported the establishment of the commission, he nevertheless accused the commissioners of doing the government's bidding and uncritically accepting the evidence and testimony by the Petrovs. The commission began its hearings several weeks before the election on 29 May.

In material supplied by the Petrovs, the famous 'Document J', apparently written by communist journalist Rupert Lockwood, named several members of Evatt's staff — Allan Dalziel, Albert Grundeman, and Fergan O'Sullivan — as having communist links. Dalziel had been under ASIO surveillance since the late 1940s. O'Sullivan had supplied the Soviet embassy with an overview of the Canberra Press Gallery, identifying journalists who might be sympathetic to their interests. This was known as 'Document H' presented to the commission. O'Sullivan had written the document while working as a journalist, and when he told Evatt about it on 3 June 1954, he was promptly sacked.

Evatt appeared before the royal commission to defend Dalziel and

Grundeman, and argued that Document J was a forgery. He repeated his claims of a conspiracy. He became increasingly shrill and excitable as the proceedings went on, making a number of outbursts, and the commissioners withdrew his leave to appear on 7 September. This only underscored, in Evatt's mind, the plot against him.

On 14 September 1955, the report of the royal commission was released. It found that documents handed over by the Petrovs were genuine, but no prosecutions were recommended, and the commissioners found nothing to support Evatt's claims of a conspiracy. Evatt criticised the report. On 19 October, Evatt informed parliament that he had written to the Soviet foreign minister, Vyacheslav Molotov, to ask if the Petrov documents were genuine. Labor MPs were stunned; Coalition MPs fell about laughing. Evatt then proceeded to tell the House that Molotov had confirmed that the documents were 'fabricated' and that Petrov was not a spy. The House was in uproar — Evatt was taking the word of the Soviet Union over ASIO and the royal commissioners. Legend has it that Menzies scrawled on a piece of paper: 'The Lord hath delivered him into thy hands.'

No Labor MP knew that Evatt had written to Molotov. 'Evatt was so profoundly shaken by his sad experiences with the Petrov Commission that he became unnerved and dispirited,' his deputy, Arthur Calwell, reflected. 'It all led to his physical breakdown. He thought the Molotov letter would clinch his victory. Instead, it was the cause of his undoing.'[13] Appearing before the royal commission and writing to Molotov were gross errors of judgement. The Labor caucus was now in open revolt, and Evatt fended off challenges to his leadership. Menzies also thought this spelled the end of Evatt. 'Evatt had ruined himself as a real political force,' he wrote later. 'His crowning calamity was his strange invocation of Molotov. The laughter in the House when he made his disclosure was sardonic and sustained, and really disposed of Evatt as a potential prime minister.'[14]

IN April 2011, I interviewed Cyril Wyndham, who served on Evatt's personal staff from 1957 to 1960. He was later Labor's federal secretary (1963–69). He was living in Charlestown, near Newcastle, at the time, and died the following year, on 2 July 2012. His widow, Nola, gave me access to his personal papers, which were gifted to the State Library of New South Wales. 'I admit that Evatt's actions regarding Molotov were naive,' Wyndham told me. '[But] Evatt was betrayed by his staff.' Wyndham pointed the finger at Dalziel, his private secretary of 20 years, who always acted suspiciously. Wyndham said that Dalziel regularly supplied former New South Wales premier Jack Lang's rabble-rousing newspaper, *Century*, with material detrimental to Evatt. 'Dalziel was a treacherous bastard,' Wyndham said.[15]

Evatt resigned the Labor leadership and quit parliament in February 1960 to take up an appointment as New South Wales chief justice. Wyndham kept in contact with Evatt, and went to see him at the time of his appointment to the Supreme Court. They talked about Dalziel. 'I had long suspected that Dalziel was treacherous,' Evatt told him. 'He bludged off me for years.'[16] The royal commission, however, had exonerated Dalziel. The commission's report found that the Soviet embassy was linked to espionage, but no spies were named, and no prosecutions were launched.

British MI5 documents made public in recent years revealed that Australia's intelligence chief, Charles Spry, advised the British government to consider withholding intelligence from Australia if Labor won government. Menzies believed Evatt's judgement represented a security risk. This is extraordinary, but Menzies and Spry may have been more concerned about those close to Evatt, rather than the Labor leader himself, such as those who were on his staff.

In April 2010, a former ASIO official contacted me at *The Australian*. In a series of discussions, he said that Evatt had a tendency to accept uncritically what he was told by people close to him, and was taken advantage of. He doubted that Evatt was a spy; it was more likely that those around him were compromised. He too pointed the finger at Dalziel. 'It is probably a stretch too far to label Evatt as a spy for the Russians,' the former intelligence official said. 'But he was used as an unwitting agent of influence by those around him.' The ASIO official also thought that Evatt was long past his prime by the 1950s. He said that Evatt's state of mind may have presented a security risk. Apparently, he had suffered a mental breakdown and had been institutionalised for a time after serving as president of the United Nations General Assembly in 1948–49. This was not leaked because ASIO officials admired Evatt. 'Many in ASIO regarded Evatt as a genius,' he said.[17]

Menzies' announcement of Petrov seeking asylum in Australia had a dramatic impact and undoubtedly helped the government win a narrow election in May 1954. Similarly, the royal commission and Evatt's blunders helped the government win another election, with an increased majority, on 10 December 1955. Moreover, the split in the Labor Party caused by an internal fight over communist influence helped the Coalition win elections through the 1960s. Taking place during the Cold War, and with evidence of a Soviet spy ring potentially endangering national security, Labor's political problems strengthened the government's hold on office.

IN his retirement years, Robert Menzies looked back on his government's secondary- and tertiary-education policies as among his proudest achievements. 'One of the significant things about this long period of office, one that I recall with great pride and satisfaction, is the dramatic development of the universities and some aspects of secondary education,' he wrote in his memoirs.[18] It is likely, given that Menzies' school and university education were so important in his life, he saw an opportunity to make this a priority during his prime ministership.

About 30 per cent of Australian school students attended non-government schools in the 1950s and 1960s. With about 80 per cent of these students attending Catholic schools, therefore relieving the pressure on the government school system, there were growing calls for state and federal government assistance. In the 1950s, the Menzies government gradually began to increase support for these schools and the parents of fee-paying children by making school fees and donations tax deductible. In the 1960s, the government provided merit-based scholarships for fees and books to encourage students to continue studying in the final years of school.

The catalyst for the major change in school funding arose out of a dispute over who would pay for a new toilet block at a Catholic school in Goulburn, in southern New South Wales. The state government required the school to provide the new facilities, but the school said it did not have the funds to do so. The Catholic Church complained that it was educating children without any financial assistance from the government; what was more, if those students were forced to attend state-run schools, the schools would not be able to cope. So, on 16 July 1962, the Catholic Archdiocese of Canberra and Goulburn closed its schools. Parents turned up at state-run schools asking to enrol their children; of course, they could not all be accepted. After a week, the Catholic schools reopened. The point had been made.

Menzies was taking note of these developments. Catholic voters, particularly in New South Wales, had long favoured the Labor Party. But federal Labor did not support state aid for Catholic schools, and its July–August 1963 conference reaffirmed this position. But the attitude to state aid was different in New South Wales. In June 1963, the state Labor conference voted to support funding for science laboratories in all schools. In September 1963, the New South Wales Labor government sought to introduce funding for science laboratories and a means-tested payment to parents of third-year and subsequent-year students attending school. However, the government was forced to cancel these initiatives when Labor's federal executive ruled in October 1963 that they breached party policy. (Two years later, in August 1965, New South Wales delegates to Labor's federal conference were again defeated when they sought to change policy to support state aid to non-government schools.) Both Calwell and Whitlam supported state aid, but were powerless to challenge the party's federal executive.

Menzies saw an opportunity, and he took it. His government decided to provide financial assistance to secondary schools in the form of grants for buildings and equipment. This was a key announcement in Menzies' policy speech ahead of the 30 November 1963 election. An annual grant of £5 million would be provided to state governments for the building and equipment costs of technical schools, and a further £5 million grant was made available for building and equipment facilities for the teaching of science in secondary schools. This was coupled with a further announcement that 10,000 scholarships would be provided for students to attend the final two years of school. Menzies also pledged 2,500 scholarships for students receiving a technical education.

Menzies recalled going to his office on a weekend to focus his mind on how to address the matter of government funding to non-government schools. 'Now why should we be helping the states with the education burden, which is quite proper, and doing nothing about these people [who] had their own needs and who were serving such an important purpose?' he wondered. 'I then worked out various proposals, which have now gone into operation.' The general view of the cabinet, Menzies said, was that it was a good policy and it would be well received. There was only dissent from one minister: Billy McMahon. 'I think you ought to think twice about this,' McMahon apparently told Menzies.[19]

Menzies was also encouraged by John Carrick, then the general secretary of the Liberal Party in New South Wales. 'Menzies said he wanted to be regarded as a great prime minister for education,' Carrick recalled. He said it was not difficult to persuade Menzies to support state aid, because he instinctively believed in it. But Menzies was cautious. He knew that providing limited funding to non-government schools would be a small step, but also a monumental one. 'I must be cautious about it because I don't want a war to start,' Carrick recalled Menzies saying.[20] Another factor was that the Democratic Labour Party — whose preferences had returned the Menzies government at the previous election — had long supported state aid for Catholic schools.

The provision of state aid for non-government schools and colleges was a major policy advance. The Menzies government hastened the demise of sectarianism in Australia. It was a principled decision that took courage. It forever changed the school education system in Australia. The federal funding of schools on the basis of need, on a recurrent rather than grant basis, was further legislated by the Whitlam government in 1973. 'The state aid controversy was ended in favour of the Catholic Church after a century and a half by two men — Menzies, the self-proclaimed "simple Presbyterian" and Whitlam, the exemplar of the humanist heresy,' wrote Graham Freudenberg.[21]

IN the pre-war period, universities were a responsibility of state governments. This began to change during the Curtin–Chifley era, when grants were provided directly to universities, the Australian National University in Canberra was established, and the Commonwealth Reconstruction Training Scheme provided full-fee university and college scholarships for returned servicemen and women. (Around half the students at universities in 1948–49 were studying under this scheme.) The Menzies government continued and expanded the role of the Commonwealth in these areas, beginning with legislation passed in December 1951 that enabled the Commonwealth to provide direct funding to universities in proportion to that provided by various state governments.

In August 1949, the Chifley government had approved an annual scholarship scheme for 3,000 university and college students. It was to provide fees and a living allowance for talented students from poorer families, and was due to begin in January 1951. In March 1950, the Menzies government announced that it would continue with this scheme. It allowed for bright students from families who could not afford to send their children to university to have their fees met and an allowance provided. Assistance to students continued to grow during the Menzies government. By the end of his prime ministership, in 1966, around three-quarters of students at universities and colleges had their fees paid for via scholarships, bursaries, or cadetships, and many also received a living allowance.[22]

In December 1956, the Menzies government commissioned Sir Keith Murray, the chair of the British University Grants Committee, to head an inquiry into Australia's university system and to identify ways for the federal government to contribute to their development. The Murray Report, presented in September 1957, expressed alarm at the lack of appropriate facilities, the quality of teaching, and the explosion in student numbers. The report, which Menzies tabled in parliament in November 1957, found student enrolments had increased from 16,500 in 1945 to 31,000 in 1956, and were predicted to increase to 70,000 by 1965. (In fact, by 1966, there were 95,000 students enrolled at Australian universities.[23]) The case for increased Commonwealth assistance was evident.

One of the key recommendations implemented by the government was the establishment of a University Grants Committee. The task of this new body would be to advise governments on the type of assistance that was needed and where. While the committee was being established, Commonwealth funds were to be allocated for capital expenditure, academic salaries, and emergency grants. Some of this would be matched by the states. Menzies presented these proposals to cabinet. After some debate, and reservations expressed by treasurer Arthur Fadden, they were endorsed.[24] Between 1958 and 1960, the Commonwealth almost doubled its spending on universities, increasing it to £22 million.

In 1964–65, Leslie Martin, who had been chair of the Australian Universities Commission, presented a further report to government proposing to overhaul the higher-education sector. It recommended the establishment of a two-tier 'binary system' of higher education, with universities and technical colleges being supported to meet national education objectives. This report provided a framework for higher education that lasted until the mid-1980s. The impact of the Menzies government's higher-education policies was significant. In 1955–57, the budget allocated $12 million in grants to universities. By 1964–66, this figure had increased to $117 million.[25] The number of universities doubled from six in 1949 to 12 by 1965. The facilities at universities, the resources they needed, and the quality of teaching and student performance had vastly improved since 1949.

WHEN Robert Menzies was sworn in as prime minister for a second time in December 1949, Canberra was still an underdeveloped Australian city; in fact, sheep still grazed near the provisional Parliament House. There were two administrative buildings, imaginatively named East Block and West Block. The Civic Centre had two colonnaded 'Sydney' and 'Melbourne' buildings for commercial and retail use. There were only a few hotels and two movie theatres, and the airport terminal was a wooden shed. The Australian War Memorial had been opened, but there was no High Court, National Library, or National Gallery, and the National Museum was a long way off. Most public servants were located in Sydney and Melbourne. All in all, it was a far cry from the bustling capital cities that Menzies had visited in Europe, Asia, and the Middle East. But Canberra would be dramatically transformed during Menzies' time. The population of Canberra more than tripled from around 25,000 in the early 1950s to over 90,000 by the mid-1960s.

An important letter in Menzies' papers at the National Library provides an insight into his thinking about Canberra in the early years of his second prime ministerial term. In April 1956, Menzies wrote to Allen Fairhall, the minister for the interior, to express his disappointment at how Canberra was being developed. 'I am not very proud of what has happened to Canberra during my current period of office,' Menzies wrote. He detailed a litany of 'criticisms' that he wanted addressed: poor architecture and design for housing and commercial buildings, traffic-management problems, broken squares of concrete on footpaths, and poor maintenance of the Lodge. Menzies said that the new shops in Civic were 'hideous'. Public buildings were 'squat' and 'flat-topped' — they needed only to add 'a few bales of hay and a goat on the roof' to look as if they were in Suez or Port Said.[26]

It took Fairhall almost six months to reply, and, in a rather desultory manner, he promised that things were being addressed.[27] But later that year a joint parliamentary committee was set up to examine the future of Canberra. The Menzies government established the National Capital Development Commission, tasked with designing, developing, and constructing a modern capital city for Australia. John Overall was appointed as the first commissioner of the NCDC in March 1958. More than 1,000 public servants and their families working in the Prime Minister's Department, Treasury, External Affairs, and Defence would soon move to Canberra. A series of ministers oversaw the development of Canberra by planning new suburbs, roads, and bridges. They funded new public transport links, schools, hospitals, and other government services. Scrivener Dam was completed in September 1963, allowing the waters of the Molonglo River to form Lake Burley Griffin, which was formally opened by Menzies in October 1964.

One of Menzies' important initiatives was construction of the National Library of Australia on the shores of Lake Burley Griffin. In 1960, legislation introduced in parliament by Menzies detached the National Library from the Commonwealth Parliamentary Library. The public were invited to comment on design concepts by the NCDC, and eventually the National Library opened its doors to the public in 1968 (two years after Menzies retired). Menzies played a key role in its construction. He oversaw the appointment of the design team, and gave them the instruction, according to legend, that they were to build 'something with columns' like the marble-and-stone buildings that dotted the landscapes of London and Washington. The National Library was a landmark statement from the government about the importance of national culture, and the value of education and learning.[28]

But one of Menzies' construction initiatives, regrettably, did not come to fruition. In May 1959, the cabinet adopted a plan devised by British architect Baron William Holford to locate a new Parliament House by Lake Burley Griffin. The new Parliament House, he argued, should be located not on the remote Capital Hill but among the people on the shores of the lake. The provisional Parliament House, designed by John Smith Murdoch, had opened in May 1927, and was already over 30 years old. Walter Burley Griffin had suggested the permanent Parliament House be located on Camp Hill, closer to the city, but Menzies was an enthusiast for a Parliament House on the lake. He would have been appalled by the decision of the Fraser government to locate it on Capital Hill, at a cost of $1.1 billion, which Malcolm Fraser later thought was a huge mistake.

Pattie Menzies played an important role in encouraging her husband to develop Canberra. When Menzies gave Doug Anthony the interior portfolio, it meant that he was responsible for Canberra. 'I had to work closely with him,' Anthony recalled. 'I had a big say.' He worked hard on initiating new roads and bridges, and schools and parks. The lake was a priority. But he was aware of Dame Pattie's wrath if something was not right in the national capital. 'Dame Pattie would ring me up and talk to me about someone not getting their garbage collected or the power not being on,' Anthony said. 'We knew we had to get it fixed quick-smart because we didn't want to be in trouble with the prime minister.'[29]

Ian Sinclair also remembered that Dame Pattie took a particular interest in the development of Canberra and would scold her husband if she was not happy with how the city was being planned, organised, or managed. Heather Henderson, who had moved to Canberra in 1951, complained about the poor condition of roads and footpaths as she and her young children moved around the city in the mid-1950s. Menzies would absorb these complaints from his wife and daughter, and promise to do something about it. Their critiques were always the first item of business at any subsequent cabinet or cabinet committee meeting. 'If the garbage hadn't been picked up, or something else wasn't right, we would have a good discussion about that in the cabinet meeting the next day,' Sinclair said.[30]

ROBERT Menzies supported and continued the post-war immigration scheme implemented by the Curtin–Chifley governments in the 1940s. 'It was [Arthur] Calwell's great contribution,' Menzies said. 'It was something that I couldn't have done myself.' He thought the unions would never have accepted a post-war immigration program introduced by a non-Labor government.[31] Menzies acknowledged that the program had contributed enormously to Australia's 'national development' and enriched its 'social life'.[32] He remained a firm supporter of the White Australia policy, but some cracks in it started to appear during his prime ministership.

New migrants were welcomed from selected European countries, but they were deemed to be 'white' and had to be 'assimilated' into Australian life. About 2.5 million migrants came to Australia between 1950 and 1970, and over time more than half were from Europe: Greeks, Italians, Maltese, Germans, and Dutch. As time went by, a greater proportion of Australia's migrant intake came from southern Europe. While Asian students came to Australia under the Colombo Plan, Menzies did not want permanent migrants from Asia. However, the government did allow some relaxation in the policy in the late 1950s, such as by abolishing the dictation test and allowing immigrants from Asia to become permanent residents after they had lived in the country for 15 years. In 1950, those born overseas made up 9.8 per cent of the population; by 1965, this had increased significantly to 18.4 per cent.

But there were some urging the government to remove race as the determining factor in Australia's immigration policy. Hubert Opperman, the former Olympic cyclist, had been elected to the Victorian seat of Corio in December 1949, and became minister for immigration in December 1963. Opperman urged Menzies to move towards a non-discriminatory immigration policy. In September 1964, he proposed ending mixed-race applications based on appearance and allowing a limited intake of 'distinguished and highly qualified' non-Europeans based on their knowledge, skills, and ability to integrate. Cabinet agreed to the first proposal, but insisted it was only an administrative change rather than a shift in policy. It rejected the second initiative.[33]

But in March 1966 — less than two months after Menzies retired — Harold Holt moved swiftly with a major reform to Australia's immigration laws. Opperman announced that applications from non-European migrants to settle in Australia would be mostly based on their skills and qualifications, coupled with their suitability and ability to integrate — essentially, the policy change rejected by Menzies' cabinet.

Menzies reflected the political consensus of the day on the White Australia policy. John Curtin and Ben Chifley supported it. Arthur Calwell, as immigration minister, formally administered it. H.V. 'Doc' Evatt, as external affairs minister, defended it abroad. But by the early 1960s, Menzies' views on race were increasingly out of step with a growing number of Australians, including some in his own cabinet. There was no longer bipartisan support for White Australia by the end of the Menzies prime ministership. It is important to remember that in August 1965, Labor's federal conference abandoned its support for the White Australia policy. But Menzies was unmoveable. His biographer Allan Martin concluded that Menzies believed 'the white man' was 'naturally superior' to those who were 'coloured'.[34]

The Holt government began dismantling the White Australia policy in 1966, and the Whitlam government removed its final vestiges in 1973. It was not until the removal of provisions that allowed overseas posts to assess immigration applications on the basis of skin colour, the deletion of discriminatory provisions in citizenship and immigration laws and assistance programs, and the ratification of international agreements on race that a fully non-discriminatory immigration policy was introduced.[35] Menzies remained concerned about the pace of immigration and the source of new immigrants. 'I think on the whole we have been taking too many,' he said in May 1973. 'There are many incidents which show that people of bad health, people of idle disposition, people who have lived in a semi-civilised condition, they have been brought in with the rake and they are not an asset to this country but only a burden.'[36]

Menzies remained opposed to immigrants from Asia or Africa. 'I am a white Australian,' he said. 'I think our immigration policy has always been fundamentally right, and I think that if we ever modify it by letting in not a handful [of] selected people but a substantial number of people from

Asia or Africa, we will rue the day. We will create in this country the very problems that they are finding almost impossible to deal with in England and quite impossible to deal with in America.'[37] Menzies did not support multiculturalism, nor did he believe that a harmonious society was capable of being built without maintaining the White Australia policy.

BY the mid-1960s, Australians were also becoming more conscious of the conditions in which the Indigenous population lived and their lack of legal rights. However, Menzies showed little interest in policies that concerned Aboriginal Australians. On his first visit to Alice Springs in June 1954, he 'showed no curiosity about the Aboriginal population', biographer Allan Martin wrote.[38] Still, in September 1959, the provision of social services was extended to Aboriginal Australians. In May 1962, Aboriginal Australians were granted the right to vote in federal elections following an amendment to the *Commonwealth Electoral Act 1918*. On 14 and 28 August 1963, bark petitions from the Yolngu people of Yirrkala calling for recognition of their rights to traditional lands were tabled in the House of Representatives. These were important initiatives. It is therefore mistaken to argue, as Martin does, that Aboriginal 'issues' were largely not 'on the political agenda' in Menzies' time.[39]

Indeed, motivated by international criticism of Australia's racially discriminatory laws, Billy Snedden took a submission to cabinet arguing for a referendum that would amend section 51(xxvi) of the constitution, which stipulated that the parliament had the power 'to make laws' with respect to 'the people of any race, other than the Aboriginal people in any state, for whom it is necessary to make special laws'. Snedden recommended removing the words 'other than the Aboriginal race in any state'. This was not supported by cabinet. Menzies later spoke against amending section 51(xxvi) in parliament, arguing, rather unconvincingly, that it was actually 'a protection against discrimination'. The cabinet did support repealing section 127, which would enable Aboriginal Australians to be counted in the census. A Bill proposing a referendum to repeal section 127 was introduced to parliament by Menzies in November 1965. It passed through both the House and the Senate.[40]

Labor leader Arthur Calwell had long supported the Commonwealth having the power to legislate for the benefit of Aboriginal Australians and including them in the census. Labor, accordingly, supported repealing section 127 and amending section 51(xxvi). Harold Holt decided to rework the proposed constitutional referendum, in a clear departure from Menzies. In February 1967, he introduced a proposal to remove section 127 and also remove the words 'other than the Aboriginal race in any state' in section 51(xxvi) — as Snedden had proposed. This overturned the decision of the Menzies cabinet. Labor, with Gough Whitlam now its leader, supported it. (This had been Labor's position since 1961.) The referendum was held on 27 May 1967 — along with a question seeking to alter the balance of numbers in the Senate and the House of Representatives — and was carried with 90.7 per cent voting 'Yes'.

In a previously unpublished interview, Menzies expressed ill-informed views about Aboriginal Australians that are difficult to comprehend today. 'We have created an Aboriginal problem in Australia that did not need to exist at all,' Menzies said in December 1973. 'The Aboriginal is almost the lowest form of human native life.' He said that Aboriginals could not be compared with Maoris or Fijians. Menzies went on to say that he had often 'wondered whether the right thing to do wouldn't have been to mark out a territory and put them into it'.[41] Menzies was 78 when he made these remarks. As absurd as it sounds, he was essentially a neo-Darwinist who believed that 'different races evolved at different speeds', and that there was a hierarchy of races. This was accepted as a scientific fact when Menzies was younger, and it was a view shared by Winston Churchill.[42]

While Menzies should be judged in the context of his times, and as reflecting the views of many Australians of his generation, he was nevertheless out of step with public sentiment on matters of race and immigration by the 1960s. He had stayed too long as prime minister. It is telling that within months of Menzies leaving parliament, cabinet effectively reversed key decisions on immigration and the Indigenous referendum. He lacked empathy and understanding of these matters. But it is going too far to suggest, as one of his biographers, Kevin Perkins, does, that Menzies was a 'white supremacist'.[43] Some important advances for Aboriginal Australians and immigrants were made by the Menzies government, and even greater leaps forward would be made by his immediate prime ministerial successors.

CHAPTER 14

Abroad: Foreign Adventures

ROBERT Menzies conceived of Australia first and foremost as a Commonwealth country, still tied politically, economically, and culturally to the United Kingdom. Yet he forged important diplomatic, security, and economic links with the United States and in the Asia-Pacific region. Key foreign-policy initiatives include the signing of the ANZUS Treaty, the Colombo Plan, and the Australia–Japan Commerce Agreement. But, like all prime ministers, Menzies was not successful in everything. His mission to convince Egyptian president Gamal Abdel Nasser to reverse his nationalisation of the Suez Canal was a failure. He was not able to persuade John F. Kennedy to support the Dutch retaining West New Guinea or to help defend Malaysia in its confrontation with Indonesia. It was a mistake to commit Australian combat troops to the Vietnam War, a conflict he never properly understood and which ended in defeat, but without the consequences of an imperilled Australia that he had warned of. He was reluctant to condemn South African apartheid. And, to some Australians, he seemed too fond of the monarchy and imperial honours.

He was a well-travelled prime minister who developed good relationships with heads of government in the United Kingdom and Europe, in the United States and Canada, and in the Asia-Pacific. He attended many Commonwealth prime ministers' conferences through the 1950s and 1960s, and was a guest at the coronation of Queen Elizabeth II in June 1953. He met with at least nine British prime ministers, from

Ramsay MacDonald to Harold Wilson, visited Number 10 Downing Street, and stayed at Chequers. He met with five United States presidents in office: Franklin Roosevelt, Harry Truman, Dwight D. Eisenhower, John F. Kennedy, and Lyndon Johnson. He visited France, Germany, and South Africa. Menzies also travelled extensively in the Asia-Pacific region, making visits to Japan, Indonesia, Thailand, the Philippines, Singapore, India, Pakistan, Sri Lanka, Papua New Guinea, and New Zealand. Perhaps not since Billy Hughes had an Australian prime minister been as well known on the international stage.

On 20 April 1955, Menzies outlined to the House of Representatives the principles and objectives of his government's foreign policy. First, the government was committed to seeking 'peace' with 'justice'. Second, any involvement in war had to be alongside 'powerful and willing friends'. Third, Australia would 'defend our rights but also the rights of others'. Fourth, the government was committed to raising the living standards of Australians and other nations 'who are struggling towards a life that we have been privileged to enjoy'. Finally, Menzies argued that Australia must 'not interfere with the internal affairs of other people so long as they pursue the same principle'. Guiding these objectives was a commitment to the United Nations and cooperation with the British Commonwealth, and the United States. In the region, Australia would pursue 'good neighbour' policies and the development of 'peaceful trade' between nations.[1]

But on a more practical level, Menzies' foreign policy was based on realism rather than idealism and power-based alliances. 'As a realist and a conservative, Menzies was sceptical of abstract, general schemes,' argued academic, adviser, and ambassador Owen Harries. 'He looked to interest rather than principle as the motive for action, to history and experience rather than abstract reasoning for the basis of sound judgement.' At an inherently dangerous time, Menzies believed it was in Australia's interest to build closer relations with the United States and Britain. 'Such support was our insurance policy,' explained Harries. But he also noted that this approach came at a risk to Australia's own identity and independence in foreign policy.[2]

Richard Woolcott joined the Department of External Affairs in 1951, held several overseas posts, and travelled abroad with Menzies in 1965.

'Menzies did, essentially, focus on his links with Britain and the United States,' Woolcott said in an interview. 'He didn't really think very much about his immediate surroundings. I suppose in the 1950s and 1960s this was logical, but it was not necessarily the right policy for Australia. It doesn't alter the fact that we are in the south-east Asian and south-west Pacific region. But as time passed, I think he was able to see the beginning of a more independent role for Australia in foreign policy.'[3]

THE Menzies government dispatched Australian combat troops abroad in four key conflicts in the 1950s and 1960s: the Korean War (1950–53), the Malayan Emergency (1950–60), the Indonesian Confrontation (1963–66), and the Vietnam War (1962–75). (The latter is dealt with more fully later in this chapter.) In addition to these commitments, in April 1951, compulsory military training for all 18-year-olds began under the *National Service Act*. Those called up for service were required to remain in the reserve military forces for five years. The controversial national service scheme initially ran from 1951 to 1960, by which time more than 500,000 young men had been registered and over 225,000 had received military training. National Service was reintroduced on a selective basis in November 1964.

On 25 June 1950, communist North Korean troops crossed the 38th parallel and invaded South Korea, sparking a war that would run for three years. On 26 July, Menzies announced that Australia would support a United Nations–sponsored mission to defend South Korea: Australia would send three battalions of ground troops, as well as ships and aircraft, as part of a 16-nation effort to liberate South Korea. How they were to be used, Menzies said, would be determined in discussions with the United States.

In explaining the rationale for sending troops to Korea, Menzies argued that Australia had a duty as 'a Christian nation' and because of a desire 'to live at peace with our neighbour', and to 'go the second mile to help him if he is less fortunate than we are'. Menzies privately recognised that supporting Harry Truman, who had sent the bulk of forces to Korea, would help Australia's future relations with the United States. By the time an armistice was signed three years later, 281 Australians had been reported as killed or missing in the war.

On 18 June 1948, the British government declared a state of emergency in Malaya following the murder of three plantation managers by communist guerrillas. Mostly Malayan Chinese, the guerrillas were determined to topple the British colonial government. As the campaign of violence escalated, the British seemed incapable of mounting an effective counter-insurgency operation. In October 1951, the British high commissioner, Sir Henry Gurney, was assassinated. A year earlier, the Menzies government had sent RAAF aircraft and personnel to Singapore to help the British repel the insurgency.

In October 1955, Australia sent a battalion of troops to provide further assistance. Australia's commitment included air support, infantry troops and artillery, and construction and engineering support. In August 1957, Malaya became an independent federation. The leadership of the Malayan Communist Party was eager to reach a negotiated settlement to the conflict, and by the end of 1958 most of the guerrilla groups had surrendered or fled to Thailand. The emergency was declared over on 31 July 1960. Around 7,000 Australian army personnel served in Malaya, with 39 killed and 27 wounded.

With Britain's support, the Federation of Malaysia, which united Malaya, Singapore, North Borneo, and Sarawak, came into effect in September 1963. (Singapore was expelled, and became a separate nation in August 1965.) Indonesia was opposed to the new nation, and, between 1962 and 1966, Indonesia's ultra-nationalist president, Sukarno, pursued a policy of confrontation — *konfrontasi* — towards the new country. With Indonesia mounting cross-border raids from Borneo, Britain wanted Australia to send troops to help defend Malaysia. However, Menzies hesitated. He had sought a reassurance from John F. Kennedy that ANZUS could be invoked if Australia found itself threatened by Indonesia, but received only a vague commitment followed by a highly conditional guarantee. Kennedy also told Menzies that the United States would not be sending troops to defend Malaysia.[4]

The Menzies government eventually agreed to send Australian troops to defend the Malay peninsula, under British command. In January 1965, the cabinet agreed to deploy an Australian troop battalion, field battery, and air squadron to Borneo. Over the next 18 months, a replacement brigade was sent alongside rotating air squadrons, a signals division, and engineers. These Australian forces were committed as part of a larger Commonwealth operation. In August 1966, a peace treaty was signed between Indonesia and Malaysia. During the confrontation, 23 Australians were killed and eight wounded.

When Indonesia's Sukarno came into conflict with the Dutch-held territory of West New Guinea, the Menzies government sided with the Dutch. But as neither Britain nor the United States would support the Dutch retaining its colony, Menzies had to accept the transfer of West New Guinea to Indonesia in 1962. The Kennedy administration understood that a defeat for Sukarno would only bolster the communists in Indonesia, but the Menzies cabinet was now concerned about Australia's vulnerability to a conflict with Indonesia. In this fearful climate, it arranged for the purchase of F-111 planes from the United States in 1963. The idea was that these planes could be used for strikes against Indonesia, possibly even carrying nuclear weapons. In 1964, cabinet considered contingency plans to defend Darwin and Papua New Guinea, and to launch airstrikes on Indonesia, if Australia's security was threatened.

Kennedy's differences with Menzies over Dutch-held West New Guinea threatened to become a domestic political problem one week before the 9 December 1961 election. Rupert Murdoch interviewed Kennedy at the White House on 1 December 1961, and then filed a story about the president's views for his Sydney *Sunday Mirror* newspaper. The report quoted Kennedy as saying the Dutch should 'get out' of West New Guinea, that Laos was 'indefensible', and that he was 'indifferent' to the outcome of the Australian election. Pierre Salinger, Kennedy's press secretary, told Australian ambassador Howard Beale that the story would be 'damaging to Australian–United States relations', so Beale insisted the story be spiked. Murdoch blamed Salinger, who had not told him the meeting was apparently off the record. If the story had been published, it might have influenced the election result, which saw the government returned with only a one-seat majority. 'It's one of the great Australian might-have-beens of Cold War history,' wrote Max Suich, who interviewed Murdoch about it in October 2010.[5]

THE ANZUS Treaty between Australia, New Zealand, and the United States was signed on 1 September 1951 in San Francisco. External affairs minister Percy Spender and United States envoy John Foster Dulles were the architects of this new formal alliance. Menzies knew that Britain's influence and interest in the Asia-Pacific — or Far East — was declining. The need for 'great and powerful friends', as he described Britain and the United States, was paramount. Yet Spender recalled that Menzies was initially 'unenthusiastic' about a Pacific security treaty when negotiations began. 'His view at that time was that, in any case, Australia did not need a pact with the USA since she was already overwhelmingly friendly to us and Australia could rely on her', he wrote in his memoir.[6]

The preamble to the ANZUS Treaty explained that 'no potential aggressor could be under the illusion that any of them stand alone in the Pacific' and made a joint commitment to 'collective defence for the preservation of peace and security'. But the wording of the treaty was, and remains, somewhat vague about the conditions in which either country would come to the aid of the other, and what form it would take. Article II notes that the parties 'separately and jointly by means of continuous and effective self-help and mutual aid will maintain and develop their individual and collective capacity to resist armed attack'. Article IV 'recognises that an armed attack in the Pacific area on any of the parties would be dangerous to its own peace and safety and declares that it would act to meet the common danger in accordance with its constitutional processes'. Menzies noted that there was no automatic requirement for either party, but said this 'does not avoid the conclusion that between contracting parties of good faith it renders common action against a common danger substantially inevitable'.[7]

The British government wanted to be part of the new security agreement, but prime minister Clement Attlee was unsuccessful in manoeuvring the British into ANZUS. It is no surprise that the treaty was opposed by Winston Churchill, the opposition leader at the time it was signed, who later made his views known. Menzies recalled:

In England, they weren't very happy about us entering into this with America and New Zealand ... when Winston was prime minister, he bailed me up on it at Downing Street one day and said, 'You know, we take a rather poor view of this. Aren't we in these things?' And I had to explain to him that nobody was more conscious of Great Britain than I was but ... this was a matter of purely Pacific defence and the British presence in the Pacific was a diminishing one. They had quite enough on their own plate without accepting responsibilities for anybody else.[8]

Menzies pointed out that Britain had joined the North Atlantic Treaty Organization (NATO), which did not include Australia. In the Pacific, Australia was one of the 'parties principal' and not 'subordinate' to any other power. Menzies acknowledged that the United States would not involve itself in a war in the Pacific 'without the approval of Congress', but the reality was that it would act to defend Australia if need be.[9] The ANZUS Treaty has provided the foundation for Australia's security since the 1950s. It is a significant achievement of the Menzies government.

Less enduring, however, was the South-East Asia Treaty Organisation (SEATO), an initiative of the United States that also involved Australia, the United Kingdom, France, Pakistan, the Philippines, Thailand, and New Zealand. The initiative came about after the French withdrew from Indochina. Signed in Manila on 8 September 1954, it was designed to be a collective defence arrangement, much like NATO in Europe, to counter aggression in South-East Asia. The treaty was intended to 'promote self-government and to secure the independence of all countries whose people desire it and are able to understand its responsibilities'. It did not specifically refer to 'communist' aggression, but the United States made it clear this was why it became a signatory.

THE French-built Suez Canal in Egypt had opened in 1869 and was operated by an Anglo–French company. The waterway was open to ships from any nation, although Israeli flagged ships had often been blocked by the mid-1950s. On 26 July 1956, Egyptian president Gamal Abdel Nasser announced the nationalisation of the canal. This action was prompted by the United States vetoing a World Bank loan to build the Aswan High Dam on the River Nile; Britain and France had also declined to offer financial support for the dam. In the two years since Nasser had come to power, he had been an outspoken critic of Western colonialism and an advocate for Arab nationalism. He had built new relations with enemies of the West, concluding an arms deal with the USSR, and established diplomatic relations with communist China. Nasser claimed that he needed the funds to build the dam for large-scale irrigation projects, and that the 7 per cent share Egypt received from the Suez Canal's operators was unfair.

Menzies was quick to condemn the 'illegal' nationalisation of the Suez Canal. After attending a crisis meeting with ministers in London on 14 August, he was concerned that, should negotiations fail, a war could break out that somehow involved Australia. That month, Menzies participated in a 22-nation conference in London to examine how nations should respond. It was agreed the canal should remain an international waterway, but Egyptian sovereignty should continue to be respected. British prime minister Anthony Eden and foreign minister Selwyn Lloyd, supported by United States secretary of state John Foster Dulles, asked Menzies to lead a five-nation committee to try to reason with Nasser. Menzies was acutely aware that if he succeeded, his international standing would be significantly enhanced. Menzies' committee proposed that a new international body governed by a treaty would administer the Suez Canal.

Menzies arrived in Cairo on 2 September 1956. He kept a diary of the visit. 'I stepped from the plane into a blaze of searchlights and flashlights so that I had to feel my way down the steps and struggle through this milling mob, being jostled and interrogated in loud voice by any one of 50 or 60 newspaper writers, and microphones being held in front of me in a most sinister fashion,' he wrote. Accompanied by his departmental secretary, Allen Brown, and the head of the Department of External Affairs, Arthur Tange, Menzies met Nasser the following day. 'Nasser is a big man and getting bigger,' he wrote. 'I would judge him to be a man of considerable intelligence. He gave many signs of nervousness which were observed by some members of our party.'[10] Later that evening, Menzies met with Nasser:

> I pointed out to him that, while sovereignty was very important to Egypt, it was equally important to each of the nations I represented, and that we could quite properly regard it as a derogation from

our sovereignty if our conduct of trade and commerce through an international waterway, with its consequent effect upon the living standards of our own people, became subject to the single judgement of one nation.[11]

Nasser sat 'sphinx-like' throughout the meeting. After this first conference concluded, Menzies asked Nasser 'for a purely private talk'. This was a mistake. 'I had noticed that there was a general assumption in the Egyptian press that the London conference had decided against the use of force,' Menzies told Nasser. 'This, I explained to him, was incorrect.' Menzies suggested to Nasser that Britain and France would use force if necessary to retake the Suez Canal. 'I told him that it would, in my judgement, be a mistake for him to assume that the talk of force which had occurred in both England and France was mere bluff.'[12] Menzies thought this thinly veiled threat would give him leverage in his talks with Nasser. This was a grave error of judgement.

Menzies tried to persuade Nasser to allow the Suez Canal to continue as 'an international waterway' that recognised Egyptian sovereignty, but to permit an international body to oversee its operations. Nasser argued this would mean Egypt was subject to foreign occupation. 'You think that an international administration would end the trouble, but I think that an international administration would be the beginning of trouble,' he said. Nasser's adviser, Mohammed Heikal, recalled that Menzies leaned forward over the table and replied, 'Mr President, your refusal of an international administration will be the beginning of trouble.' Nasser told Menzies that he would not be 'threatened', and ended the talks abruptly.[13]

Any hope that Menzies had of persuading Nasser to keep the Suez Canal as an international waterway was, in any event, extinguished when United States president Dwight D. Eisenhower — ahead of a re-election campaign for president — made it clear on 4 September that he thought the dispute should be settled through peaceful means. Menzies' negotiating authority was instantly undermined, and Nasser rejected the proposals. Ten days later, Menzies made another diary note, repeating his earlier observation that Nasser had been 'nervous' when they first met. 'By the time Eisenhower had spoken once and then twice, Nasser's nervousness had disappeared,' Menzies wrote. 'He was in full spate with his phrases about "colonialism" and our chances of a successful negotiation had entirely disappeared. Save us from our friends!'[14]

The situation only further deteriorated. On 13 October, a proposal to establish a Canal Users' Association to safeguard the international use of the waterway was vetoed by the Soviet Union at the United Nations Security Council. Then, on 29 October, a secret plan hatched by Britain, France, and Israel went into effect. Israel invaded Egypt, followed by an ultimatum by Britain and France that Egypt cease hostilities. Nasser rejected their demands. Days later, Britain and France invaded Egypt and occupied the Suez Canal area. The United Nations General Assembly, with United States support, urged them to withdraw from Egypt.

Menzies did not know about the military action in advance, and yet Australia supported the British and French incursions, and then defended them in the United Nations. In short, Menzies sided with the British over the Americans. Dulles, taking a lead from Eisenhower, registered his opposition to the British–French invasion of the canal zone, and urged Britain and France to withdraw. On 6 November, a ceasefire was negotiated. On 3 December, Britain and France began withdrawing their forces. The United Nations sent a peacekeeping force — which did not include Britain and France — but it did not have any role in keeping the Suez Canal open as an international waterway. The result was that Nasser emerged victorious, with his position strengthened and the Suez Canal now operated by a state-owned authority. The resolution of the crisis was particularly humiliating for Anthony Eden, who never recovered; he resigned as prime minister on 9 January 1957.

Menzies' Suez mission was a failure. He was not helped by being kept in the dark by the British and French, but his own judgement was awry. Alan Watt, secretary of the Department of External Affairs (1950–54), offered a damning assessment of Menzies on Suez. 'Australian support for British policy was, therefore, not only ineffective, but damaging to vital Australian international relations with other countries,' he wrote. 'His emotional attachment to Great Britain (where, incidentally, public opinion was seriously split over the Suez issue), his intellectual distrust of paper constitutions and international organisations such as the United Nations, and his instinctive leaning towards "great and powerful friends" clouded his judgment.'[15]

The debacle over Suez still rankled with Menzies many years later. He could not accept that British policy, which he had supported, had failed. Instead, he blamed the United States and the United Nations for intervening when Nasser might have otherwise been removed from office, and the Suez Canal kept as an international seaway. 'After the British and French had intervened with arms at the Canal, the whole matter might have ended up very satisfactorily with the overthrow of Nasser if it hadn't been for the United Nations intervention, and there wouldn't have been an effective United Nations intervention but for the attitude of the United States,' Menzies said. He still defended the British and French use of force, and said Dulles had 'got a few wrong ideas in his mind'.[16]

DURING his second prime ministership, Menzies continued to develop close relationships with British prime ministers. He was already well known in London's political, civil service, and diplomatic circles. These relationships, and those with United States' presidents, were the tangible manifestation of Menzies' continuing belief in 'great and powerful friends' being the cornerstone of foreign policy.

Richard Woolcott, as departmental public information officer, travelled to London and Washington with Menzies in June 1965. 'He did believe in the notion of Australia having "great and powerful friends" in case Australia's security was ever threatened,' Woolcott told me. While travelling between the two cities by plane, he recalled Menzies walking down the aisle and noticing that he was reading an article, but trying to cover it up. 'What are you trying to hide?' Menzies asked. 'It is a comment article to the effect that you are very much focused on England and not so much on the rest of the world,' Woolcott replied. 'Well, I can understand why you are hiding it but it is not entirely true,' Menzies insisted.[17]

Labour leader Clement Attlee had been prime minister in Britain since July 1945, and Menzies knew him from meetings they had had in London during the Second World War. 'With Clem Attlee our contacts were perhaps even better than they were with the Tories,' Menzies reflected. 'I always found him completely helpful and forthcoming. Each time I went to England, they would invite me to go and attend a cabinet meeting and to get my views on various matters.' Menzies had lunch with Attlee at 10 Downing Street in July 1948. On his return to London as prime minister in July 1950, Attlee hosted a dinner for Menzies and invited him to Chequers. A focus of their discussions was accessing capital to fund development projects, and Attlee's proposal for Britain to test atomic bombs in Australia.

Later, as leader of the opposition, Attlee visited Australia in September 1954 at Menzies' invitation. He was hosted at an official reception at Government House, addressed a meeting of ministers, and was guest of honour at a dinner organised by the Labor Party.[18] Reflecting on Attlee in his retirement years, Menzies described him as 'the most laconic of all the great political figures I've known' and 'a great Englishman'.[19]

Winston Churchill returned to the prime ministership in October 1951. Menzies met with Churchill annually, and attended cabinet meetings at 10 Downing Street. On 29 May 1952, for example, Churchill hosted Menzies for dinner at Number 10. Attlee sat to Menzies' right and Churchill on his left. They dined on smoked salmon, spring chicken, and asparagus, with rum baba for desert, washing the meal down with a selection of wines such as Chateau Mouton Rothschild, Taylor, and Martell. Churchill's favourite champagne, Pol Roger, was also served.[20]

Menzies recalled a weekend with Churchill at Chequers in March 1955. Over a cigar and brandy, Churchill asked, 'Do you think I should resign?' Menzies thought he should. 'I think it is a bit unfair to Anthony [Eden],' Menzies replied. 'He has been the bridesmaid for so long.' Churchill said he was contemplating resigning in August or September that year.[21] But Menzies urged him to go sooner rather than later, and said Eden had been 'waiting and waiting and waiting'. Churchill's health was failing, his cabinet was restless, and Menzies might not have been the only one encouraging him to go. Churchill's resignation took effect the following month, in April 1955.[22]

Churchill died, aged 90, on 24 January 1965. Menzies was holidaying in the United States at the time. He liaised with acting prime minister John McEwen, and made arrangements to fly to London, arriving three days before the funeral on 30 January. As the most senior Commonwealth prime minister, and an intimate of Churchill's, he was invited to be one of the 12 pallbearers. After the service, Menzies delivered a eulogy from the crypt of St Paul's, near the tombs of Nelson and Wellington, broadcast live on the BBC. 'Winston Churchill,' he said, 'was not an institution, but a man of wit and chuckling humour, and penetrating understanding, not a man who spoke to us as from the mountain tops, but one who expressed the simple and enduring feelings of ordinary men and women.' Menzies recalled Churchill's wartime leadership: 'In our darkest days, he lit the lamps of hope at many firesides and released so many from the chains of despair. There has been nobody like him in our lifetimes.'[23]

Harold Macmillan was sworn in as prime minister in January 1957, following Anthony Eden's brief prime ministership. A year later, Macmillan visited Australia. The two prime ministers discussed South-East Asia and Britain's entry into the Common Market, but much of the visit looked like a publicity tour.[24] Their relationship later became strained over South Africa and other Commonwealth matters, and Menzies was less than pleased about Macmillan's 'winds of change' speech delivered in Cape Town on 3 February 1960. Although they had a generally warm relationship, in retirement Menzies thought Macmillan had 'a streak of vanity'. Moreover, Menzies found Macmillan to be conceited and patronising and, if that wasn't enough, a bit of a bore. 'Harold, of course, was a rum chap in some ways,' Menzies said. 'His knowledge of European history was profound — so profound that he used to embarrass me a little because talking to me in private or at his house he would be reeling off various events.'[25]

In October 1963, Alec Douglas-Home became prime minister following Macmillan's resignation. Menzies agreed with Douglas-Home that it was up to the British government to determine how and when Southern Rhodesia should become an independent nation, but a number of other Commonwealth members disagreed. Menzies thought Douglas-Home managed to handle discussions on thorny issues between Commonwealth countries more capably than Macmillan. During this time, Menzies was slowly beginning to accept that 'a very different Commonwealth' was emerging from the one he had known and loved for decades, and that his 'somewhat old-fashioned views' could not be imposed on newer members.[26]

A year later, in October 1964, Harold Wilson led Labour back to power, and was in office for the remainder of Menzies' term as prime minister. Menzies had not expected Labour to win the election, and said as much to Douglas-Home in an outgoing letter. When Wilson met the Queen, she asked if he could form a government. 'Yes, of course I can,' he replied. 'Bob Menzies carried on for two years with a majority of only one — I have five'. The Queen liked to repeat this story. When Menzies met Wilson while he was in London for Churchill's funeral, he was encouraged by the British prime minister to commit forces to defend Malaysia. Menzies found Wilson to be 'eminently satisfactory' on issues to do with South-East Asia.[27] Although Wilson supported the United States in Vietnam, he would not commit British troops to the conflict. Wilson raised the idea of Menzies being appointed Lord Warden of the Cinque Ports and, with his agreement, recommended it to the Queen. It was announced in October 1965.

THE Menzies era witnessed significant changes in Australia's international relations. One of the major shifts was forced upon the country when Britain applied to join the European Economic Community in 1961. Britain would now give priority to trade relationships in its own region rather than with dominions such as Australia and New Zealand. Britain would not actually join the common market until 1973, but its foreshadowed move threatened Australia's mineral and agricultural exports, necessitating a search for new markets abroad. Yet Menzies made it clear his heart was always with Great Britain. 'I remained completely aligned to Great Britain because it was our mother country and because it was the country from which every one of our great institutions derived,' he recalled later in life.[28]

Evidence of Menzies' fidelity to Britain is evident in his decision to allow, indeed encourage, the British to undertake atomic weapons' tests in Australia. The first major tests took place on the Montebello Islands, off the coast of Western Australia, in October 1952, and later in May–June 1956. Further tests took place at Emu Field (October 1953) and Maralinga (September–October 1956 and September–October 1957) in South Australia. These tests were carried out in great secrecy, and Australians (including Aboriginal Australians) were not informed of the risks of radioactive contamination. In 1957, the Menzies cabinet considered the idea of Australia developing its own nuclear arsenal, and explored seeking an agreement with the United States to do so. In 1958, Menzies also discussed Australia becoming a nuclear power with British prime minister Harold Macmillan in Canberra. But the United States and the United Kingdom were against any new members joining the nuclear club.

A royal commission chaired by a former Labor MP, and later a judge, Jim McClelland, made damning findings about the British atomic tests in November 1985. Menzies was criticised in the report for too readily acceding to the British request to conduct tests, failing to fully consult his cabinet colleagues, not finalising an agreement before the first tests were carried out, not conducting a thorough examination of the risks of contamination, and failing to put in place adequate safeguards.

The Commonwealth underwent a period of significant change during the 1950s and 1960s. India, though a republic, joined the Commonwealth in 1949. Menzies did not get along with India's prime minister, Jawaharlal Nehru, and privately accused him of wanting to divide the Commonwealth along racial lines. Nehru would not tolerate South Africa's apartheid regime, and clashed with Menzies' view of non-interference in the domestic matters of other countries. Nehru thought Menzies was a mouthpiece for the United States and Britain, and judged his intervention in Suez harshly.

A flashpoint came in October 1960, when Menzies opposed a resolution by non-aligned countries at the United Nations that encouraged United States president Dwight D. Eisenhower to meet with Soviet leader Nikita Khrushchev. Menzies moved an amendment supporting the reinstatement of a summit that also included Britain and France. This led to a savage attack by Nehru on Menzies, accusing him of trying to reconvene the big four powers of an earlier era. 'I hated the sight of Nehru,' Menzies said later, who 'spat almost with hatred ... he was a bad piece of work'.[29] It was understood that Macmillan had asked Menzies to move the resolution, but he revealed in a letter to his wife, Pattie, that it was he who came up with the idea. He made the further point that while his amendment was defeated, the original resolution was withdrawn, so it did have an effect.[30]

On 3 February 1960, Harold Macmillan said the world had to recognise and respond to 'winds of change' that were blowing across the African continent. But Menzies was reluctant to face up to these growing realities. When 69 black protestors demonstrating against new racial segregation laws were shot and killed by South African police in Sharpeville on 21 March 1960, Menzies refused to support international action against South Africa. At the Commonwealth Prime Minister's Conference in London on 3–13 May 1960, Malaysia's prime minister, Tunku Abdul Rahman, urged that a stand be taken against apartheid. But Menzies argued for the principle of non-intervention in another nation's internal affairs. No agreement was reached.

At the Commonwealth Prime Ministers' Conference in London on 8–17 March 1961, South Africa, having become a republic, sought to remain in the Commonwealth. But Canadian prime minister John Diefenbaker was opposed to apartheid, and made his views known; other countries from Africa and Asia also reiterated their criticism of apartheid. South Africa, humiliated, withdrew its application. Menzies thought South Africa had been unfairly treated, and recalled pointing out the racial and ethnic divisions in many Commonwealth countries — Eskimos in Canada, Chinese in Malaya, Tamils in Sri Lanka, and the differences between Pakistan and India. Menzies described Diefenbaker, who visited Australia in December 1958, as 'a dreadful stupid fellow'.[31]

With international opinion increasingly hostile toward South Africa, Menzies spoke about his attitude to apartheid in a speech to parliament on 11 April 1961. 'I am against apartheid,' he said, 'against some of the modern manifestations and practices because they offend the conscience, against it as a basic policy because it seems to me to be doomed to a most terrible disaster.'[32] However, Menzies did not express sympathy for black South Africans being persecuted, nor would he seek to pressure South Africa to change its policy. Menzies was out of step with domestic opinion and the views of some in his cabinet on apartheid. In 1963, at Menzies' insistence, cabinet rejected Garfield Barwick's proposal to limit arms sales to South Africa, to express concerns about apartheid privately to the South African government, and to make a public statement reaffirming the Australian government's 'repugnance' over apartheid.[33]

In retirement, Menzies opposed diplomatic and economic sanctions on South Africa, and the boycotting of touring rugby and cricket teams, and could not bring himself to take an unequivocal and strong moral stand against apartheid or to criticise the white ruling regime. 'I am the last of the Commonwealth men,' he said in 1972.[34]

WHILE Menzies despaired over the future of the Commonwealth, his fondness for the British monarchy never wavered. But he was also out of step with public attitudes towards the monarchy, even though the royal family was widely admired and respected by Australians. In June 1963, the Menzies government announced that the major unit of Australia's new decimal currency would be called the 'royal'. The decision was signed off by cabinet, and the changeover was set for February 1966.[35] There was an immediate public outcry — polls showed a whopping 95 per cent of Australians were against the idea, newspaper editorials lashed the decision, and MPs were inundated with letters registering their opposition. The 'dollar', the most popular choice, had been overlooked. The decision was abandoned in September 1963 — just three months after it had been announced.[36]

On 18 February 1963, Robert Menzies welcomed Queen Elizabeth II to Parliament House in Canberra. In what became a memorable event, long etched into the minds of Australians who saw it on television or heard it on the radio, Menzies fawned over the young Queen. At a gala reception, Menzies glanced at the Queen and quoted the Elizabethan poet Thomas Ford:

There is a lady sweet and kind
Was never face so pleased my mind;
I did but see her passing by,
And yet I love her till I die.

The Queen, the footage shows, uncomfortably winced and then blushed. William Heseltine worked as Menzies' private secretary (1955–59) and the Queen's private secretary (1986–90). 'It was the one time that he had really misjudged his audience, and I thought the Queen was feeling a bit embarrassed about it, too,' he said in an interview for this book.[37] Heseltine made the same point in his Menzies Lecture, delivered in 1989. He showed the Queen his lecture before he delivered it, and she did not object — confirming her visible reaction. None of this, however, diminished the mutual affection between the Queen and Menzies.

A decade earlier, when George VI died on 6 February 1952, Menzies had been chairing a cabinet meeting. The news came from wire services overseas, and spread through a shocked press gallery. Menzies went straight to the House of Representatives. It was 8.50 pm. 'There are grievous reports,' he said. 'I am at present not in a position to make any official statement.' Parliament was adjourned until clarification could be sought; soon, a call came through from the Australian High Commission in London confirming the worst. Twenty minutes later, the House resumed its sitting with the galleries packed, and an ashen-faced Menzies announced the death of the King. 'It is my melancholy task to inform the House the news which ran in rumour a few minutes ago is now officially confirmed,' he said. The following day, 7 February, Menzies and opposition leader H.V. 'Doc' Evatt expressed their sympathies in a 20-minute sitting of the House of Representatives. Menzies was visibly upset, sometimes resting his head in his hands or wiping tears from his eyes. The condolence motion was carried by MPs standing.

Queen Elizabeth II has reigned during the terms of more than a dozen British and Australian prime ministers, not to mention many other Commonwealth leaders over the decades. Of all the Australian prime ministers who have served during her reign, her closest relationship has been with Menzies. When Menzies travelled to London for George V's Silver Jubilee celebrations in May 1935, he met Elizabeth, who was just nine years old.[38] Menzies hosted the Queen during her first tour of Australia as monarch from February to April 1954. 'He had that antipodean flair for striking the right note,' recalled Heseltine. 'He was not unduly deferential but respectful and friendly.' Whereas Churchill displayed 'old-fashioned chivalry', Menzies 'talked seriously' to her without 'false deference'.[39]

The Queen conferred a personal knighthood on Menzies — the Order of the Thistle — in 1963, and appointed him Constable of Dover Castle and Warden of the Cinque Ports in 1965. Menzies wrote an account of receiving his knighthood and left it in his papers at the National Library of Australia. He did not use it in his memoirs. On 11 March 1963, he recalled being 'summoned' to Government House at Yarralumla for an audience with the Queen. 'I want to do something for you,' she said. 'I want to give you something which I alone can give without recommendation or advice. I know you would not wish some political nomination. I want to give you the Thistle.'[40]

Menzies was 'dumbfounded'. He did not seek personal honours, and had said prime ministers should not accept knighthoods while in office. The Queen understood that accepting such an honour could be 'a handicap' for a politician, and said she would not be offended if he declined. Menzies asked to discuss it with his wife, Pattie, and the Queen agreed. Given his surprise, Sir Michael Adeane, the Queen's private secretary, offered him a stiff drink. Pattie urged Robert to accept the honour. He also consulted Country Party leader John McEwen, who agreed he should accept it. That evening, Menzies told the Queen that his answer was 'Yes'.[41] It was an honour too great to refuse.

A private investiture was made on 13 March 1963 in the governor-general's study at Government House. Menzies bowed his knee on the hassock and was touched on each shoulder with a sword by the Queen. Menzies joined 16 other knights outside the royal family. On 1 July 1963, the Queen formally installed Menzies as a Knight of the Thistle in the small Thistle Chapel at High Kirk — St Giles' Cathedral — in Edinburgh. Menzies, dressed in the green mantle of the order and carrying a green hat with a white plume, walked in a grand procession that was met by a fanfare of trumpets as it reached the chapel. As the Queen installed her new knight into Scotland's highest order of chivalry, she pronounced his surname in the traditional Scottish: 'Ming-ees'.[42]

Menzies recalled how different this was compared to when he was given the Order of the Companions of Honour (CH) by her father, George VI, in London. The King had forgotten to invest Menzies following an audience at the Palace. The next day, standing around after lunch, the King approached Menzies 'in the most informal manner' and ushered him to the other side of the room, away from the other guests. 'I made a bit of a blue yesterday,' the King said. 'I didn't give you the CH. Well, here it is anyhow. Put it in your pocket.'[43]

ROBERT Menzies met Harry S. Truman while he was campaigning for re-election in October 1948, and diarised that he was 'a charming man of good sense in conversation'.[44] He had two meetings and a lunch with Truman at the White House on 28 July 1950. The focus of these meetings, according to a State Department memorandum, was Australia's 'need for development' and a request for assistance obtaining international loans to finance key projects. Menzies also emphasised Australia's support for the United States and the United Nations in Korea.[45] Menzies was given the honour of addressing the United States House of Representatives on 1 August 1950.

Menzies and Truman met again for lunch on 19 May 1952; Menzies pushed Truman for a commitment of US troops to South-East Asia, but the president was unmoved.[46] The next day, Menzies met with secretary of state Dean Acheson, telling him that Indochina could not be allowed to fall to the communists. 'He said that if Indo-China were lost, he felt Burma, Thailand and Malaya would almost certainly go with the possible result that Indonesia and even New Guinea might fall with the result of bringing Asian communist forces to the very doorstep of Australia,' Acheson rather alarmingly noted.[47] Menzies' third meeting with Truman was on 20 December 1952, when they had afternoon tea in the president's private study. The ANZUS Treaty was negotiated, signed, and ratified during the Truman administration.

Menzies met with Dwight D. Eisenhower several times during the 1950s, starting with a courtesy call in New York after Eisenhower's election as president, on 17 December 1952. They also met formally at the White House, and enjoyed lunch and dinner, on 14 March 1955. The focus of these discussions was on Chinese aggression in the Asia-Pacific region, and the defence of Taiwan and its Quemoy and Matsu islands. Menzies expressed his alarm about Malaya going communist. He told Eisenhower, 'If the United States gets involved in a great war, [he] could count on Australia being in it too.'[48] Menzies addressed the United States House of Representatives for a second time, on 16 March 1955, during this visit to Washington. He deliberated on the Suez Crisis with Eisenhower on 3 August and 14 September 1956, and the two leaders discussed Nehru's bitter attack on Menzies at the United Nations on 2 October 1960, prior to the US election that year.

Seven months before John F. Kennedy was elected president, Menzies appeared on the 4 April 1960 cover of *TIME* magazine. 'Australia: Things

Are Looking Up Down Under' ran the headline, above an imposing
portrait of Menzies painted by William Dobell. The prime minister had
granted Dobell two sittings, and the final cover image was completed in
a fortnight. An eight-page photo spread accompanied a 5,000-word essay
that purred with approval of Australia's 'coming of age' under Menzies'
'decade of unabashed wooing of free enterprise'.[49] The *TIME* cover story
was a testament to Menzies' profile and standing around the world at the
time, and would have been politically valuable at home. (John Curtin had
appeared on the cover of *TIME*, next to a boxing kangaroo, in April 1944.[50])

Menzies acknowledged that he did not have a high regard for Kennedy
before their first meeting at the White House on 24 February 1961.[51]
Yet they struck up a warm personal relationship, despite a number of
policy differences. At this first meeting, Menzies and Kennedy discussed
China, the 'weakness' of SEATO, and the future of West New Guinea.[52]
Menzies was not successful in persuading Kennedy to have 'sympathy' for
the Dutch and to oppose Indonesian president Sukarno's desire to annex
West New Guinea.[53] They met again, and had lunch, on 20 June 1962.
Although they continued to enjoy cordial relations, Kennedy was not
successful in persuading Menzies to support a 'new Pacific community' to
foster closer cooperation among friends and allies in the region.

Following his Jefferson Oration, delivered at Monticello, Virginia, on
4 July 1963, Menzies talked with Kennedy for the last time on 8 July 1963.
'I don't think that there is a visitor that has more friends in the United
States than the prime minister,' Kennedy said at a lunch.[54] But during this
visit, Menzies was not able to persuade Kennedy to defend Malaysia in its
confrontation with Indonesia. Kennedy believed this was a matter best
managed by Britain and Commonwealth countries.[55] A testament to their
friendly relations was that Kennedy agreed to 'definitely' visit Australia on
a future visit to Asia. He would have become the first sitting president to
do so, but was assassinated on 22 November 1963.[56]

Menzies first met Lyndon Johnson as a senator and then during his
vice presidency. On 24 June 1964, Menzies met Johnson for a private
meeting and a 'stag' lunch with 80 guests at the White House. It was, as
always, a friendly affair. Menzies stressed Australia's commitment to South
Vietnam, and pressed Johnson on the difficulties Australia had with
Indonesian aggression towards Malaysia.[57] Menzies met Johnson again —

just a few weeks after announcing that Australian combat troops would be sent to Vietnam — on 7 June 1965. They walked around the south lawn of the White House, had a meeting in the cabinet room, and then enjoyed lunch in the state dining room.[58] Two days later, Menzies had another breakfast with Johnson.[59] In the evening of 6 July 1965, the following month, Johnson hosted a dinner for Menzies on the second floor of the White House.[60] The legendary Johnson treatment did not diminish when Menzies was out of office. The two lunched together at the White House on 13 December 1966 and again on 25 September 1967.[61] And Johnson met with Menzies in Melbourne on 22 December 1967, prior to the memorial service for Harold Holt.[62]

Menzies also formed a relationship with future president Richard Nixon, who visited Australia as vice president in October 1953. Menzies had extensive talks with Nixon, who also briefed the cabinet, was honoured at a parliamentary luncheon, and was feted at a gala reception at the United States embassy.[63] Nixon, in his book *Leaders*, lavished praise on Menzies as one of 'the ablest' leaders he had ever met. Nixon saw Menzies as a big man on a small stage, endowed with great intelligence, charm, and wit. 'If I were to rate one postwar leader even above the others, it would not be one of the legendary European or American figures,' Nixon wrote. 'It would be Robert Menzies.'[64]

The mutual admiration ended in May 1977, when, during a television interview with David Frost, Nixon disclosed a personal letter that Menzies had sent him. 'Writing as one who has himself had a great deal of experience of the cut and thrust of political campaigning, I am bound to say that I have never known the level of attack to sink so low as it has in your case,' Menzies wrote in August 1973 as the Watergate scandal unfolded. 'In all my life I have treated the press with marked contempt and remarkable success.'[65] Menzies was embarrassed and furious with Nixon. Pattie told the media that her husband believed a 'personal letter should remain personal forever', and was 'disappointed' that Nixon had disclosed it in a television interview broadcast around the world.[66]

WHILE Robert Menzies continued to refer to Australia as 'completely British', and to Australians as 'British people', his government initiated new diplomatic, economic, and cultural links in the Asia-Pacific.[67] There was a recognition at ministerial and departmental level, as well as among a growing number of Australians, that engagement with the region would only become more important in the coming years. Percy Spender and Richard Casey, who both served as external affairs ministers, also recognised and spoke of this shift in 'the centre of gravity of world affairs' to the Asia-Pacific.[68]

The most important initiative was the Australia–Japan Commerce Agreement, principally negotiated by John McEwen, and signed on 6 July 1957 near Tokyo. This agreement cemented Australia's most significant long-term post-war trading relationship. Before the agreement was struck, trade between the two countries substantially favoured Australia: Japan was a large purchaser of Australian goods, especially wool and wheat, but imports of Japanese goods attracted high tariffs and were negligible in comparison. (Australia gave preference to British imports in return for lucrative access to its markets.) McEwen spent several years negotiating the liberalisation of Australia–Japan trade relations. He wanted to guarantee continued access for Australia's wheat and wool exports, primarily, in return for accepting a larger share of manufacturing imports from Japan. The change in Australia's trade was considerable. In 1950, around 30 per cent of Australian exports went to the United Kingdom; by 1965, this had fallen to about 15 per cent.

It is worth noting, however, that other countries negotiated trade deals with Japan in the post-war period. For example, Canada signed a similar agreement with Japan on 1 April 1954 — the Canada–Japan Agreement on Commerce — three years before Australia did. It is also worth noting that Labor, led by H.V. 'Doc' Evatt, unwisely opposed the Australia–Japan Commerce Agreement. McEwen recalled there was 'furious' opposition from manufacturers, but mostly support from the Returned Soldiers' League.[69] The voters were also largely in favour of it, with 38 per cent believing the trade treaty would be good for Australia, and 17 per cent saying it would be bad. By 1963, these figures had changed significantly, with 69 per cent saying the treaty was good, and only 9 per cent believing it was bad.[70]

At a conference of foreign ministers from Commonwealth countries held in Colombo, Ceylon (now Sri Lanka), in January 1950, the

Colombo Plan was formulated. The plan was another major foreign-policy initiative of the Menzies government. It was devised by Percy Spender, the minister for external affairs, to enable the more prosperous Commonwealth members (such as Great Britain, Australia, Canada, and New Zealand) to contribute to the growth of developing countries (such as India, Pakistan, Malaysia, and Ceylon). The concept expanded to include more countries that would receive assistance, and the United States and Japan also agreed to contribute. A key part of the Colombo Plan — initially reported as the 'Spender Plan' — was to provide funding for Asian students to be educated at Australian universities. By the end of the Menzies government, more than 5,000 students had been awarded grants to attend university in Australia.

The Menzies government did not recognise Mao Zedong's communist China. This option was considered very early in the government's first term, and Menzies may have been open to it, but it was out of the question once the Korean War began. The government, however, did authorise the sale of wheat, barley, and flour to China via British-ruled Hong Kong. While there were few politicians urging closer relations with China during the Menzies government, other nations such as France (1964), Canada (1970), and the United Kingdom (1972) established full diplomatic relations with China in this period, and had begun to develop formal relations in the 1950s and 1960s. Within five years of Menzies' retirement, in July 1971, Gough Whitlam led a Labor delegation to China. He was condemned for this by Liberal prime minister Billy McMahon. Later that month, Richard Nixon announced that he would visit China the following year.

Even after the Whitlam government granted diplomatic recognition to China in December 1972, and Whitlam visited the country in October 1973, and Nixon's diplomacy was hailed as a triumph, Menzies still did not support the rapprochement. 'We are nestling down with the communists in China, and Peking and Hanoi ... these are now our friends and, of course, that means we must abandon our old friends,' Menzies said in December 1973.[71] He also wrote to Frances McNicoll about Australia cosying up to 'communist countries' while remaining 'aloof from old allies' such as Britain and the United States. 'That we should be prepared to recognise China on China's terms, which involve the abandonment of Taiwan to their clutches is, I think, bad enough,' he wrote in August 1973.[72]

ONE of the most significant foreign-policy decisions of the Menzies government was to commit combat troops to Vietnam. The United States had been building up its presence in Vietnam since the end of the Second World War, and in July 1962 the Menzies government announced that a 30-man advisory team would be sent to South Vietnam. Australia's 'military instructors' were doubled, then tripled, and by 1965 numbered 100. Military and economic aid was also provided to South Vietnam. In November 1964, conscription (called 'national service') was selectively reintroduced for men turning 20 whose birth dates came up in the so-called 'birthday ballot'. Those called up were required to serve for two years, either at home or abroad, and remain in the reserve army for three more years. Labor leader Arthur Calwell called national service 'the lottery of death'.

On 29 April 1965, the Menzies government announced it would send a combat battalion to South Vietnam. 'The takeover of South Vietnam would be a direct military threat to Australia and all the countries of South and South-East Asia,' Menzies told parliament. More specifically, the reasons for the deployment were a belief in 'the domino theory', which held that communist China would continue its 'downward thrust' through South-East Asia and make Laos, Cambodia, Thailand, Malaysia, Singapore, and Indonesia, and therefore Australia, vulnerable; the desire to help South Vietnam defend its 'democracy'; and the wish to support the United States' effort in Vietnam, given that Australia was an alliance partner. The prime reason, as Menzies argued, was that 'the security of Australia would be at stake if South Vietnam fell'.[73] But the reasons for Australia's involvement in the Vietnam War were flawed from the outset: Australia was never threatened when North Vietnam eventually overran South Vietnam in April 1975; South Vietnam was never a democracy; and the United States did not need Australia to support its military operations.

The official history of Australia's involvement in the Vietnam War does not reflect well on Menzies. Historian Peter Edwards concluded that the decision by the Menzies government to send combat troops to Vietnam was based on 'blind faith' in US military supremacy. There was no real understanding of the conflict, the capacity for strategic goals to be met, or the security implications for Australia. 'Menzies believed that in making the commitment he was simply repeating a winning formula that would achieve military success in Southeast Asia, strengthen the alliance with the United States, and divide the Labor Party's right and left wings,' Edwards wrote. Menzies saw the war as vital to Australia's security, but the manner of the engagement made it harder to exit once the prospect of victory became grim. 'Paying a premium for Australia's strategic insurance with the US was not itself wrong, but should have been handled with a great deal more care,' Edwards concluded.[74] This is a damning judgement of Menzies on Vietnam.

Menzies always said that the decision to send combat troops had been made in response to a formal request from the South Vietnamese government.[75] But as the cabinet papers released thirty years later confirmed, this was false. The decision to send troops was made before there had been a formal request for additional military support from either South Vietnam or the United States. In other words, Australia offered to send troops. A sub-committee of cabinet agreed to offer a combat battalion for Vietnam on 7 April 1965 — three weeks before Menzies' statement to parliament. (There had been discussions with United States officials about possible future troop commitments, but no formal request was made. The Pentagon Papers revealed that on 5 January 1965, President Johnson was informed that the Australian government had indicated it 'might be disposed to participate' in sending 'ground forces' into Vietnam.[76]) In short, Australia invited itself to Vietnam.

The Menzies government saw its commitment as vital to the continued presence of the United States in the region and to Australia's own security needs. Menzies made this clear to cabinet. It was viewed as a down-payment on an insurance policy that would, if necessary, help lock the United States in to the future defence of Australia. On 24 November 1969, Menzies was interviewed at the Lyndon Baines Johnson Presidential Library in Austin, Texas. 'It took us not five minutes to decide that when this thing came to the point of action, we would be in it,' Menzies said, in an unguarded moment. 'We had no hesitation, no doubts, and I've never had any regrets.' And the key reason for sending combat troops? 'It was essential to show that America was not the only country in the world that saw this challenge and was willing to do something about it,' Menzies said. 'It meant showing the flag alongside the United States and showing she wasn't battling this thing out alone.'[77]

Jim Forbes was minister for the army when the decision was made to send combat troops to Vietnam. He stands by the decision, and agreed the main reason was to show America that Australia was 'a dependable ally' and to 'strengthen the alliance' relationship. He does not recall significant debate within the government about the decision to reintroduce national service or to send a combat battalion to Vietnam. 'It wasn't as hard as you might expect it to be,' Forbes said. 'There were a few people who thought we shouldn't do it simply for the reason that it might make it difficult for us as a government, but that didn't represent the majority view.'[78]

Malcolm Fraser, who served as army and defence minister during the Vietnam War, came to view Australia's participation as a misjudgement. 'We accepted, as so many people did around the world, the monolithic view of communism — worldwide, thrusting, controlled by Moscow and Beijing,' Fraser told me. 'But it was a flawed judgement. Menzies wanted, in part, to keep the US engaged in the region. But the US was always going to be involved in our region given the rise of China. It made no difference whether we were involved in Vietnam or not. We underestimated the nationalistic element in the North Vietnamese and the incompetence, the corruption, and the stupidity of the South Vietnamese governments. And we didn't understand the extent of the differences between Russia and China.'[79]

Fraser was, at the time, one of the Vietnam War's most prominent advocates. But, as the war escalated, following Menzies' retirement, Fraser's doubts grew. He was not alone. Harold Holt became increasingly concerned, as did John Gorton and Billy McMahon. They felt Australia was not being given a true picture of what was happening in Vietnam. Indeed, the Johnson administration did not convey its bleak assessments of the war to the Australian government. As early as 1967, the year after Menzies retired, the CIA's most senior analysts told Johnson and defense secretary Robert McNamara that the likelihood of defeat was high and that the US and its allies could withdraw 'without any permanent damage to US or Western security'.[80] Fraser argued that he supported the war based on the knowledge the government had at the time. 'Vietnam was a busted flush by the time we made our major commitments to it,' he said. 'We weren't told about those CIA reports. They were, in part, saying that the bombing won't work, that it's a pretty hopeless task, and that we weren't going to succeed. Johnson wanted political comfort from getting an ally like Australia to join him in a war.'[81] In 1995, McNamara conceded that the war had been 'terribly wrong'.[82]

Garfield Barwick served as minister for external affairs from December 1961 to April 1964. He would not have supported sending conscripts to Vietnam if he had remained in cabinet instead of moving to the High Court. 'I wouldn't have put ground troops in for them,' Barwick told Frances McNicoll. 'I didn't want to have any record of Australians firing on Asians because it is this sort of blood feud that never wears off in history.' He added, 'The other reason why I wouldn't have ground troops in was that we couldn't reinforce our troops from regulars. We didn't have a big enough regular army and that meant we would have to reinforce them from national service, and that would have meant dividing the community.' Barwick talked to John F. Kennedy about Vietnam, and came to the conclusion that the president 'would not have put ground troops in' if he had lived. Barwick's comments constitute an important reflection on Menzies' decision to send combat troops to Vietnam and a valuable insight into Kennedy's thinking about the war.[83]

Richard Woolcott — who was sent to Vietnam to discuss increasing Australia's troop commitment by Harold Holt — also thought Menzies was 'mistaken' over Vietnam. 'Menzies believed in the downward thrust of communism, but it was based on a misunderstanding of what was happening in Vietnam,' he said. 'It did not work out the way he assumed it would.' On their 1965 visit to London and Washington, Menzies told Woolcott that Australia was also in Vietnam to demonstrate its 'worth as an ally'. Woolcott also confirmed that Barwick's views about the folly of Vietnam were expressed to him at the time, corroborating his later interview with McNicoll.[84]

The decision to send combat troops to Vietnam was not just a mistake with the benefit of hindsight. There was strong opposition expressed at the time by many people, including Labor leader Arthur Calwell. 'When the drums beat and the trumpets sound, the voice of reason and right can be heard in the land only with difficulty,' Calwell said on 4 May 1965. 'But if we are to have the courage of our convictions, then we must do our best to make that voice heard ... generations to come will record with gratitude that when a reckless government wilfully endangered the security of this nation, the voice of the Australian Labor Party was heard, strong and clear, on the side of sanity and in the cause of humanity, and in the interests of Australia's security.' Calwell made several startlingly accurate predictions: he said the US would fail to meet its objectives and that it would become 'interminably bogged down in the awful morass of this war' before being defeated or deciding to withdraw.

The Australian newspaper argued that sending troops to Vietnam did not represent the 'enlightened nationalism' the country needed. 'Our long-term interests have been badly served by a politico-military gambit' in Vietnam, an editorial thundered. 'We hold that it will have only insignificant military value, that it deploys our small forces beyond our clear Malaysian commitment and that it tends to widen the war at a time when many of our friends are seeking to bring it to negotiation.' The editorial also addressed the alliance with the United States. 'Uncritical subservience has no place in Australian policy ... it cannot carry with it the guarantee of unalloyed respect. It is too much the act of a toady.'[85] Gallup found that a majority of just 52 per cent of voters supported the decision to send combat troops, and 37 per cent were opposed.[86]

The Holt government escalated the Australian commitment to the war, which was not unpopular through 1966 and 1967, but support had begun to weaken by 1968. The Viet Cong's surprise attacks, known as the Tet Offensive, led many in government to question the likelihood of victory. The United States policy became one of securing 'peace with honour', yet this continued to prove elusive. Demonstrations in Australian cities increased. In early 1968, the Gorton government announced that it would send no more troops to Vietnam; in late 1969, the government announced it would begin withdrawing troops. By late 1972, all combat troops had been withdrawn, and the Whitlam government also recalled the army training team. In the end, 50,000 Australians served in Vietnam, of whom 500 were killed and 2,400 wounded.

By 1985, just ten years after the war's end, the vast majority of

Australians thought it had been a mistake to have sent combat troops to Vietnam. Polls showed that 66 per cent opposed the troop deployment, and only 27 per cent supported it.[87] Further evidence of how badly the conflict was misjudged came just five years after the war, when Vietnam was at war with China. There was no downward thrust of Chinese communism throughout Asia, which was supposed to have endangered Australia. Moreover, China was pursuing its 'reform and opening up' to the West policy under Deng Xiaoping by the late 1970s.

Long into retirement, even after all Australian troops had been withdrawn, Menzies continued to support the discredited 'domino theory' and to defend the war in Vietnam. 'The "domino theory" is dead right, it always was, and how long can South Vietnam survive?' Menzies said in December 1973. 'If they go, Thailand will go. Thailand has no internal capacity for resistance, and then we will get down to a point where jolly old Harry Lee will find himself almost as the remaining bastion against them in Singapore, and this is terrible. And, therefore, what they are doing is increasing the risk of attack on Australia, not eliminating it, as they fat-headedly seem to think or say.'[88] He could not have been more wrong.

CHAPTER 15

Across the Divide:
Evatt, Calwell, and Whitlam

ON 20 June 1951, following the death of Ben Chifley, the Labor caucus elected H.V. 'Doc' Evatt as its leader, unopposed. Arthur Calwell was elected deputy leader, defeating P.J. Clarey, Eddie Ward, and Allan Fraser in a party-room ballot.[1] Robert Menzies did not like Evatt. They had been rivals in the law, and now they were opposed in politics. They had both served in state and federal politics. They were both gifted with great intelligence. They both enjoyed reputations on the world stage. Menzies was a wartime prime minister who had met with presidents and prime ministers. Evatt had been minister for external affairs in the Curtin–Chifley governments, and president of the United Nations General Assembly. They did not enjoy the same kind of respectful relations, or indeed friendship, that existed between Menzies and John Curtin, or Menzies and Chifley. Arthur Fadden recalled 'an atmosphere of coolness and antagonism seemed to descend upon the parliament' when Evatt became Labor leader.[2]

Menzies did, however, have a relatively good relationship with Calwell. He was elected Labor leader on 7 March 1960, after Evatt resigned and left parliament to become chief justice of the New South Wales Supreme Court. In the leadership ballot, Calwell defeated Reg Pollard by 42 votes to 30, and Gough Whitlam was elected deputy leader over Eddie Ward.[3]

Menzies and Calwell had both lived in Melbourne, regularly saw each other at civic and social gatherings, and could put aside politics to have a relaxed discussion about history, literature, and sport. They enjoyed cordial relations for the rest of their lives.

When Gough Whitlam was elected Labor leader on 8 February 1967, Menzies had retired from parliament.[4] But Menzies had been watching Whitlam closely from the time he was elected to the seat of Werriwa in November 1952 with a swing of 12.4 per cent in Labor's favour. He knew Whitlam's father and father-in-law. Menzies and Whitlam had a number of conversations during these years, and a few after Menzies retired as prime minister. However, when Whitlam became prime minister, relations soured. Menzies grew to detest Whitlam and the Labor government, and made this known to the few who visited him and corresponded with him, as well as to his putative biographer, Frances McNicoll.

EVATT was a brilliant lawyer and jurist, a passionate speaker and debater, and a talented writer. He had much in common with Menzies. They were both born in the same year (1894) in small country towns to middle-class parents. They both won scholarships at school, excelled at university, and enjoyed dazzling legal careers. They had both served in state politics and federal politics. They had both been attorney-general. They were both gripped by a vaulting ambition, with a high opinion of their own abilities, and both aspired to be prime minister. And they loathed one another.

But by the time Evatt became Labor leader in 1951, he had worn himself out. ASIO, according to a former senior intelligence officer, believed Evatt had become 'unhinged and unbalanced' and was mentally unstable.[5] Others have also hinted at this. Allan Dalziel, Evatt's private secretary, recalled 'there were those who felt he had burned himself out' during the 1940s while working to establish the United Nations.[6] Evatt's wild mood swings, volcanic temper, and erratic behaviour have long been documented. Menzies once heard a story about Evatt in mid-1955 pacing up and down in the ladies' bathroom at the Hotel Australia in Sydney with his head in his hands, talking to himself and occasionally calling out aloud.[7] Evatt, he was certain, was going mad.

However, Cyril Wyndham, Evatt's press secretary, observed no evidence of mental decline. 'I don't think he was paranoid, but he was erratic — aren't all politicians a bit erratic?' he said. He did concede that Evatt was not the man he once was by the 1950s. Wyndham recalled that before any plane trip, he would be required to purchase two copies of that day's newspapers. One set would be for Evatt to read after take-off; the other set would be scrunched up and placed inside his shirt, trousers, and jacket to ward off the cool air. Many Labor MPs saw Evatt's unpredictable behaviour as a side effect of his genius. But Wyndham was reluctant to diagnose Evatt as mad during his period as Labor leader.[8]

'Evatt distrusted everybody,' Menzies recalled in a previously unpublished interview. 'He was a suspicious man. He could be very rude, and it was no use expecting to be on easy terms with him. No nipping around the back of the Speaker's chair and having a little yarn and a laugh about something, which I could do with Arthur Calwell.' It was more than just a lack of bipartisan courtesy. Menzies did not rate Evatt as a politician or as a parliamentarian. 'He had no instinct for debate at all. He would stand up and put a foot on his chair, and then turn around and make a speech to his own fellows, turning his back on everybody. And he had this mumbling wretched voice, you see, and [if] he had some notes [he] would get lost in them and throw them on one side. It was laughable.'[9]

Evatt had served as a justice of the High Court of Australia from December 1930 until he resigned to contest the federal seat of Barton, in Sydney's south, at the September 1940 election. (He had previously been the state MP for Balmain, in Sydney's inner west, from May 1925 to October 1930.) Menzies believed Evatt resigned from the High Court to re-enter politics with the ambition of becoming prime minister. This is undoubtedly true. It meant that Evatt was a threat to Menzies, even though he did not seem too fazed about the contest. But it was more than just a political contest between two parties and leaders. Menzies thought Evatt was driven by a personal rivalry and jealousy:

He was looking down and seeing me become prime minister and this was no good to him. He had always been a rival of mine and he thought he had got ahead of me when he went on to the High Court and then I found I was prime minister — and he decided he was going to be, so he left the High Court ... John Curtin never trusted him [and] Ben Chifley never trusted him.[10]

'He thought Evatt was a dreadful man,' Heather Henderson, Menzies' daughter, said. 'There was not the faintest skerrick of respect or affection there. But then Evatt's own people didn't like him much.'[11] In Menzies' letters to his daughter, he often referred to 'Brother Bert' dismissively. 'If Brother Bert were not such a warm supporter by sheer inadvertence, we could run into a great deal of trouble,' he wrote in July 1955. 'If he became politically astute for even a couple of weeks, we could be under genuine attack.'[12]

The election on 29 May 1954 was conducted in the wake of the Petrov defections and the subsequent royal commission into Soviet espionage in Australia. The upshot was that Labor won five seats, but lost one, and the Coalition was returned with a majority of seven seats. Overall, Labor gained 50.7 per cent of the two-party-preferred vote. Menzies' victories in 1951 and 1954 formed the building blocks of his longevity. He had defeated Chifley twice and Evatt once, albeit narrowly. But Labor's third election defeat in a row would plunge the party into a period of protracted disunity that would last for a generation. The party split, and bled voters to the Democratic Labour Party, which helped the Liberal–Country coalition remain in power into the 1970s.

ON 3 August 1954, at the first Labor caucus meeting after the election, Evatt faced a leadership challenge from West Australian MP Tom Burke. The challenge came as a shock to most MPs, but Evatt won by 68 votes to Burke's 20.[13] The following month, Evatt was lashed by Victorian MP Bill Bourke, who said he was 'doing the Communists' dirty work'. A motion in caucus to gag Evatt from speaking at the royal commission was defeated.[14] Labor was unsettled, and the divisions among MPs and party officials were about to explode.

Evatt's unstable mind, and the deepening discord in caucus, may have contributed to his decision on 5 October 1954 to issue a statement denouncing the Grouper-dominated Victorian Labor Party state executive as 'increasingly disloyal' — an event now widely seen as forcing the party to split. Two weeks later, on 20 October, Evatt defeated an attempt at a fiery caucus meeting to spill the leadership. The motion was lost on the voices after Eddie Ward called for a formal vote to be taken on a spill motion. Evatt, red-faced and with pen and paper in hand, leapt onto a table and demanded that the names of disloyal MPs be recorded. 'Get their names!' he said. 'Get their names.' The motion was lost 52–28.[15] Although there was no official list of names recorded, among those who voted to open up the leadership to a vote was deputy leader Arthur Calwell, who saw an opportunity to become leader if Evatt fell.[16] Fred Daly, Labor MP for the Sydney seats of Martin (1943–49) and Grayndler (1949–75), recalled the febrile atmosphere. 'It was a bitter debate,' he wrote. 'Insults, interjections and abuse filled the air as emotions and frustrations rose to fever pitch. I doubt if a worse scene has been witnessed in caucus.'[17]

Evatt was losing the plot. The staunchly anti-communist, mostly Catholic members of the party dubbed 'Groupers' were expelled in March 1955. The party split in Victoria and Queensland, and haemorrhaged Catholic voters for decades, but this was avoided in New South Wales due to more effective relationships between the party, the unions, and the church. In Victoria, B.A. Santamaria's shadowy Catholic lay organisation, The Catholic Social Studies Movement, was supported by Archbishop Daniel Mannix with the purpose of fighting communist influence in the Labor Party and the unions. 'The Movement' — later the National Civic Council — was encouraged by Catholic bishops, and had close ties to the party's Industrial Groups. The Movement maintained 'friendly relations' with ASIO, and the two organisations shared intelligence. ASIO also recruited Movement operatives to help penetrate the Communist Party.[18]

Mary Elizabeth Calwell recalled that it was a difficult time for her father, who was Evatt's deputy. They were never close. 'Evatt was secretive and tended to do things on his own without consulting anyone,' she told me. The split over communist influence in the party helped the Coalition to stay in power. 'Menzies was a better politician, but Evatt was a better lawyer,' Calwell said.[19] The party avoided a split in New South Wales because wiser heads prevailed and agreed to accept limited federal intervention. The party executive in Victoria did not accept intervention, and were purged. The upshot is that Menzies exploited the divisions within Labor that could have been avoided with more effective leadership from Evatt and Calwell.

The breakaway Australian Labor Party (Anti-Communist), which became the Democratic Labour Party in 1957 — initially comprising seven former Labor MPs — met on 18 April 1955.[20] It elected Bob Joshua as leader and Stan Keon as deputy leader. The new party was announced to the parliament on 20 April. There had been more drama when Evatt suddenly resigned as leader on 18 April to thwart a vote on a motion of no confidence that had been tabled in caucus. He stood again for leader, and won with 52 votes, easily defeating Calwell (22) and Burke (5).[21]

At the early election on 10 December 1955, the seven rebel MPs who had left the party lost their seats, while Labor won only 45.8 per cent of the two-party-preferred vote to the Coalition's 54.2 per cent. The Menzies government was elected with an increased majority, aided by the flow of preferences away from Labor. These DLP preferences would help the government win more than a dozen seats necessary to stay in office through the 1960s. At the first caucus meeting after the election, on 13 February 1956, Evatt was re-elected Labor leader, having defeated Allan Fraser by 58 to 20 votes.[22]

Ahead of the election on 22 November 1958, Evatt made a spectacular offer. 'I state emphatically, without reservation, that if the DLP leadership requests its supporters to give their second preferences to the ALP, I shall after the elections are won or lost vacate my office as leader and will not nominate as leader,' he said.[23] Evatt's offer to swap his resignation for preferences was rejected by the DLP, and the campaign did not go well for Labor. One of the important factors was the increasing influence of television. Evatt and Calwell did not present well on television, whereas Menzies had transferred his considerable radio-broadcasting skills to the new medium to project a stable, confident, and reassuring presence. The election saw the government win two seats from the opposition, to be easily returned. Menzies had consolidated his position.

On 16 February 1959, at the first caucus meeting after the election, Evatt was challenged by Eddie Ward for leader. He defeated Ward, who had the support of the party's right faction, by 46 votes to 32.[24] Evatt had led Labor to three election defeats in a row, and it was unthinkable that he would be given another chance. He was rescued from inevitable further infighting by the New South Wales Labor government on 9 February 1960, which appointed him as the state's chief justice. After a long and heated cabinet debate, Evatt's nomination was endorsed by eight votes to six, at the urging of premier Bob Heffron.[25] Menzies thought this was an appalling appointment. 'He was ga-ga,' Menzies said, 'going around the bend.'[26] With his health rapidly deteriorating, Evatt stepped down from the Supreme Court in October 1962.

Evatt died three years later, aged 71, on 2 November 1965. Menzies said a notable career in public life had ended, and remembered him as a man of energy and determination.[27] He attended Evatt's state funeral at St John's Church in Canberra on 4 November, and acted as a pallbearer. In retirement, Menzies did not hold back on what he really thought of Evatt. 'He was a dreadful fellow,' Menzies said. 'I think he was a wicked man, a thoroughly bad man.'[28]

THE relationship between Robert Menzies and Arthur Calwell was more mutually respectful. Calwell, aged 63 when he became Labor leader, was two years younger than Menzies. They had known each other while living in Melbourne. They both enjoyed watching Australian Rules Football and cricket. And they had served in parliament together since Calwell's election to the seat of Melbourne in September 1940. Both had served in a wartime government. In opposition, Calwell was deputy leader of the Labor Party from 1951 to 1960, and Labor leader from 1960 to 1967, also leading the party to three election defeats.

Mary Elizabeth Calwell recalled their relationship. 'My father knew Menzies when he was at Melbourne University during World War I,' she said. 'Menzies and [Henry] Bolte were trustees of the Melbourne Cricket Ground, and my father was chairman, and he often had talks with Menzies at Australian Rules football games.'[29] The Menzies and Calwell families had known each other for a long time. Mary Elizabeth remembered meeting Menzies as a young girl in Parliament House. 'You must be like God,' she said to Menzies. He laughed. 'I wish your father thought that,' he replied. She added, 'He and Dad confided in each other ... They were friends.'[30]

As a newly elected Labor MP in 1961, Bill Hayden remembered seeing how well Menzies seemed to get along with Calwell. 'It was the opening of parliament after the election,' Hayden recollected. 'Menzies and Calwell were very friendly with each other. I saw them talking to each other, so I went over to say hello. Arthur introduced me, and Menzies was very courteous and friendly. He had a huge stature in parliament in those days. The only person who could match him in oratory in my time in politics was Gough. I thought a lot of the things said about Menzies were untrue. Politics is tribal. But I liked him and would talk to him now and again, and he was always very courteous to me.'[31]

Menzies described his relationship with Calwell in a May 1972 interview. 'Arthur,' he said, 'was, as he still is, capable of the most eccentric behaviour, and he can say the most dreadful things. He could make an attack on me in the House that I knew he did not mean at all, and in the corridor afterwards he would come up behind me and smack me on the back and say, "You know, old man, it is only politics. You know I don't mean that."' Menzies said Calwell played by the old rules of politics, and some of the attacks stung, but 'at heart he was alright'.[32]

Menzies and Calwell faced off at two elections within two years of each other — in December 1961 and November 1963. The boom in the economy in 1959–60 had been stopped in its tracks with a series of policy changes that induced a credit squeeze. In February 1960, the government had announced a series of measures designed to manage the boom that included ending import licensing, reducing excess liquidity, and halting wage rises. In August 1960, Harold Holt's budget took further steps to curb inflationary pressures by introducing new taxes and spending reductions. Holt announced a series of further deflationary initiatives, such as increased taxes and tighter bank-lending measures, in a mini-budget in November 1960. This suggested that the government had misread the economy just months earlier.

The economy plunged into a recession, businesses collapsed, homeowners defaulted on their loans, and unemployment increased to a post-war high in excess of 3 per cent. Another budget, designed to stabilise policy settings by reducing some taxes and freeing up bank lending, was delivered in August 1961. It was characterised as a 'stay-put' budget in response to the previous 'stop-go' approach to economic policy-making. (Another mini-budget was needed in February 1962 — when unemployment reached 3.5 per cent — to stimulate economic activity.) Strong economic growth continued, fuelled by a mining boom.

The media, especially *The Sydney Morning Herald*, had been scathing of the government's economic management during 1960–61. The *Herald* and *The Australian Financial Review* argued that policy settings were wrong, and thought that a suite of measures to support reflation was needed to deal with the recession and alleviate the continuing effects of the credit squeeze. The *Herald*, for the first time in its history, switched its support to Labor. This decision was forced by its proprietor, Warwick Fairfax, over the objections of managing director Rupert Henderson. John Fairfax & Sons had not only previously offered editorial support to the Liberal Party — and other non-Labor parties — but had also been one of its most regular financial donors. In the first four years of the party's existence, for example, at least £1,450 had been donated by Fairfax to the Liberals — over $100,000 in today's value.[33] Now, albeit briefly, Fairfax was spruiking for Labor.

'*The Sydney Morning Herald* stands today as it has throughout its history for liberal principles,' said the editorial penned by Warwick Fairfax on 1 December 1961. 'Our political principles have in no way changed. Our view of Mr Menzies and his government has indeed changed since having once been supporters of those principles they can, in our view, no longer be trusted to carry them out. Not only have they turned more and more to bureaucratic planning and socialistic methods but the country had been brought to a parlous position.' It said the Coalition offered no remedy for 'stagnation and unemployment' and that Labor should have an 'opportunity' to govern.[34] Further editorials before election day reiterated these points.[35]

Calwell met Henderson at Fairfax's Broadway headquarters in Sydney in October 1961. It was one of several meetings between the two where policy and strategy were discussed in the lead-up to election day. 'Henderson in effect became Calwell's campaign manager, providing hard-headed advice on policy, very reasonable rates for television time, and the writing services of two of John Fairfax's best men,' wrote Gavin Souter. Lou Leck, assistant general manager, and Maxwell Newton, managing editor of *The Australian Financial Review*, wrote speeches for Calwell.[36] (Newton, while a journalist on the *Herald*, had also helped Evatt with speeches during the 1958 election campaign.)[37]

This marriage of convenience was immortalised on the front page of the Rupert Murdoch–owned *Mirror* on 19 November 1961. 'Broadway Melody 1961! (*S.M Herald backs Calwell*)' screamed the headline. A photo showed Calwell's car parked out the front of Fairfax's offices. Below, it said 'Mr. Menzies jilted' and posted a 'wedding notice'. It read: 'Calwell: Henderson. — On November 17, at Broadway, Sydney, the Hon. Arthur Augustus, 65, leader of the federal Labor Party, to Rupert Albert Geary ('Rags '), 65, managing director of John Fairfax and Sons, proprietors of *The Sydney Morning Herald*.' The *Mirror* described the nuptials as 'the strangest and possibly least glamourous of the season' held in the offices of 'the stronghold of Tory opinion in this country', and noted that 'the flowers were pink'.[38]

Calwell's policy speech, delivered in Melbourne on 16 November 1961, promised a return to full employment, new scholarships for school students, and an increase in pensions. Calwell, at the *Herald*'s urging, also pledged, if it were deemed necessary, to reinstate some import controls and to increase tariffs. Calwell thought the campaign had gone well, and was 'quietly confident' Labor would win the election.[39] Graham Freudenberg, who had joined Calwell's staff as press secretary, did not expect Labor to win. 'But we might well have done if the campaign was organised a bit better,' he told me. 'Each state ran their own campaign, so did the unions, there was no full-time federal secretary — so there was no effective organisation at the national level. If we had won seats in Victoria, just one or two, we would have won the election.'[40]

Menzies faced a difficult campaign. He delivered his policy speech at Kew City Hall, which was broadcast live on radio around Australia, on 15 November 1961. He offered a continuation of 'good government' rather than a 'list of promises', defended economic-policy measures over the previous two years, and said Labor was in thrall to the unions and its radical left. It was not one of his better efforts. The *Herald*, perhaps predictably, lashed Menzies for being complacent about the challenges facing the country. But *The Daily Telegraph*, owned by Frank Packer, lavished Menzies with praise for delivering a sound and honest speech.

On polling day, on 9 December 1961, the result was too close to call. Eventually, the Menzies government managed to survive with a one-seat majority, after allocating a Speaker. The government had suffered a sizeable swing against it of 4.6 per cent on a two-party-preferred basis, leaving Labor furious that it had won 50.5 per cent of the two-party vote without securing a majority of seats. The government did, however, lose its majority in the Senate. Just as he had been in 1954, Menzies was lucky. Calwell, like his predecessor Evatt, had come within a whisker of being prime minister.

At one stage, the counting of votes looked so ominous that Menzies thought his government had been defeated, he conceded years later.[41] Jim Killen, who eventually won his Queensland seat of Moreton by just 110 votes, claimed that Menzies had said to him, 'Killen, you are magnificent!' But the story was fiction; Menzies sent no such telegram to Killen.[42] It was also suggested that Killen had been returned with preferences from the Communist Party. In truth, preferences from both the Communist Party and the Democratic Labour Party saved Killen, and the Menzies government, in 1961.[43]

Foreign policy dominated Australian politics in 1962–63. On 17 May 1962, the government announced that the United States would establish a 'naval communications station' at North West Cape in Western Australia. This was a popular stance, with 80 per cent of voters in favour of the idea.[44] However, Labor, concerned about a foreign base being located on Australian soil, was divided. Calwell and deputy leader Gough Whitlam were inclined to support it, provided there was joint control between Australia and the United States. Calwell sought confirmation from the party's federal executive as to whether this position would accord with the party's policy. This turned out to be a mistake, as the matter was referred to Labor's federal conference for determination.

On 21 March 1963, Labor's federal conference met at the Kingston Hotel in Canberra. While the 36 delegates thrashed out Labor policy on the subject, Calwell and Whitlam waited outside. Labor's leader and deputy leader were, at this stage, not members of the federal conference. Close to midnight, *The Daily Telegraph*'s Alan Reid organised for them to be photographed, waiting beneath the lampposts, as the conference determined party policy. The photographs would highlight their exclusion from the conference.

'Arthur Calwell's night watch a sad commentary on the decline in status of Labor's parliamentary leadership', Reid captioned the photos. Although Reid referred to '36 virtually unknown men' (and despite the fact that the conference included one woman), the Liberal Party quickly labelled them the 'faceless men'. By a vote of 19–17, the executive endorsed Calwell and Whitlam's conditional support for the base. The infamous photographs of two impotent leaders unable to attend a meeting of their party's federal conference powerfully underscored Menzies' longstanding argument that Labor was captive to a secretive political machine.

Calwell embarked on a month-long trip through Europe, the Middle East, and the United States in mid-1963. A highlight of his trip was a meeting with John F. Kennedy in the White House. The State Department briefed Kennedy that Calwell could be Australia's prime minister within months. Calwell had a 45-minute meeting with Kennedy on 23 July 1963. What Kennedy told Calwell was alarming. 'In the Far East we have gone far to contain the expansion of Communist China, but a military threat still remains', the president said. 'Thus, the Far East is where the danger of military aggression is most likely in the next 15 years, and Australia and the US should work closely to meeting this threat.' Kennedy told Calwell that a military threat involving China was a clear and probable danger, and that if this eventuated, the two countries had to work closely to contain it. In other words, Australia and the United States could be at war with China.[45]

In September, Menzies announced that Australia would provide military support to Malaysia in its confrontation with Indonesia. The following month, Menzies reached an agreement with the US to purchase two squadrons of F-111 striker bombers. The implication was that these planes could reach Indonesia in the event of any conflict, and possibly carry nuclear weapons. The F-111 deal received maximum news coverage in the months leading up to the election. In a previously unpublished interview, Menzies acknowledged that the planes were purchased in the event of a war with Indonesia:

The experts all agreed we needed a replacement for the Canberra,[46] and what we needed was something peculiarly suited to Australia, and that meant that it must have a long range so that it could go to Indonesia and back again without refuelling ... without it we were a goner. We had no long-range reconnaissance plane, we literally had no means except local fighters to cope with a possible war which involved Indonesia.[47]

On 15 October, Menzies announced that an election would be held on 30 November — a year early. McEwen thought this was too risky. 'He didn't think that we would win,' Menzies later recalled. 'He thought we had not had enough time to recover from the surgical shock of the 1961 election.'[48] But Menzies had learned the lessons of his near-defeat two years earlier. He had stabilised economic policy-making and developed new policies, not least of all state aid for non-government schools, while exploiting the weaknesses within Labor. Calwell again thought victory was all but assured, especially given the closeness of the vote just two years earlier. Labor was ahead in all Gallup polls taken between June 1962 and April 1963, but the polls had levelled by mid-1963.[49] Calwell, now without the *Herald*'s support, was too complacent.

Menzies launched his last general-election campaign as Liberal leader and prime minister at the Kew City Hall in his electorate of Kooyong on 12 November 1963. For the first time, his policy speech was broadcast on television. The centrepiece of Menzies' speech was the provision of a £5 million grant to state governments for building and equipment for the teaching of science, and scholarships for students. There were two other important policy announcements: a new first-home purchase grant scheme, and an initiative that would help increase the availability of housing loans.

A week earlier, on 6 November 1963, Calwell had launched Labor's campaign to an audience of 1,200 people at the Royale Ballroom in Melbourne. It was also broadcast on television. He promised to increase economic growth, impose restrictions on the foreign ownership of companies, introduce measures that made it easier for businesses to win tariff protection, and expand import controls. There would be no 'credit squeeze' or 'boom and bust' management of the economy. He promised a strengthening of defence. And Labor would increase child endowment, introduce free hospital and medical treatment, and provide funds to the states for new school buildings, teacher salaries, and scholarships.[50]

The government was returned with a substantially increased majority, up from two to 22 seats. It was a stunning election result for Menzies, who gained a 3.1 per cent two-party-preferred swing, and again consolidated the Coalition's position. While the assassination of John F. Kennedy a week before the election may have had an impact, it was not critical. This was the view of Calwell's press secretary and speechwriter, Graham Freudenberg. 'We had gone into the campaign with unrealistic hopes,' he said. 'We thought we could win, so did Gough, but we were never going to win. The assassination may have played a role, but it wasn't a decisive factor.'[51]

The truth is that Labor had failed to make the most of the government's precarious one-seat majority after the 1961 election. 'We were in a position to force another election,' recalled Labor MP Fred Daly. 'It was the time for full-scale political war: no "pairs", no leave of absence for ministers, no overseas trips; play it hard and make it impossible for them to govern.'[52] Labor MP Les Haylen agreed. 'We didn't fight,' he lamented, suggesting that Calwell and Whitlam were too busy 'sucking up to the press' and finding ways to cooperate with the government.[53] Labor did not make the most of the disagreements within the Coalition on economic policy, yet the 'faceless men' scandal and Labor's divisions on state aid were successfully exploited by Menzies. Calwell was no match for Menzies.

It is not surprising that Whitlam was eager for Calwell to make way for him to take the leadership of the Labor Party after the 1963 election. He thought he was ready, having been deputy leader since 1960, and after Calwell had led the party to two election defeats. 'He was just so fucking hopeless,' Whitlam told me in May 2007. He believed that if Calwell had vacated the leadership before the 1966 election, he (Whitlam) could have won the 1969 election. Labor would have returned to office three years earlier. 'He just hung on for so long,' Whitlam said of Calwell. 'Evatt had three goes at trying to win an election, so Calwell thought he deserved three goes, too.'[54] If Calwell had stepped down and Whitlam had claimed the leadership — not at all guaranteed — Menzies would have faced Whitlam in his final two years in parliament. Whitlam was nearly 22 years younger than Menzies.

Calwell remained friendly with Menzies after he had retired as prime minister and left parliament in early 1966. 'It was a great disappointment to him that things didn't go his way and, of course, you can understand that and sympathise with [him], but he is alright,' Menzies said.[55] He respected Calwell, but this should not be overstated. Graham Freudenberg said, 'Menzies' principal and dominant attitude was one of condescension, but not contempt, and regularly referred to him as "poor old Arthur".'[56] Journalist Peter Bowers also recalled Menzies referring disparagingly to 'poor Arthur'.[57]

Calwell died on 8 July 1973 in Melbourne. He was 76 years old. 'In private life, we have been good and close friends, and I will miss him very much,' Menzies said in a statement.[58] At 3.45 pm the following day, Menzies sent a message to Calwell's widow. 'My wife and I send you our deepest sympathy,' he said. 'Arthur and I had developed a close friendship as you know. I have been thinking of you for the last two days.'[59] Menzies attended Calwell's funeral service on 11 July 1973. But he was not well enough to go inside; instead, he sat in his car and wept.

WHEN Gough Whitlam led Labor back to power on 2 December 1972, Robert Menzies offered his congratulations. Whitlam replied, offering his predecessor a glowing tribute:

Dear Sir Robert,

I was profoundly moved by your magnanimous message on my election to this great office. No Australian is more conscious than I how much the lustre, honour and authority of that office owe to the manner in which you held it with such distinction for so long. No Australian understands better than you the private feelings of one now facing the change from the years of leading the opposition to the burdens and rewards of leading our nation.

You would, I think, be surprised to know how much I feel indebted to your example, despite the great differences in our philosophies. In particular, your remarkable achievement in rebuilding your own party and bringing it so triumphantly to power within six years has been an abiding inspiration to me.

My wife values deeply the message of goodwill from Dame Pattie. To both of you, may we express our very sincere wishes for health and richly deserved happiness, not only for the new year but for many years to come.

Yours sincerely,
Gough Whitlam[60]

Menzies knew Whitlam's father, crown solicitor Fred Whitlam, and father-in-law, judge Bill Dovey. Fred Whitlam had given Menzies several briefs when he was at the Bar. Menzies had met Bill Dovey when he was also a barrister and worked as a High Court judge's associate. Dovey had written to Menzies to congratulate him on becoming prime minister in April 1939; Menzies' letter of reply was framed and hung on the wall of Dovey's office. Menzies could see that Whitlam was a young man in an old man's party. He was not from a trade union. He was not part of a factional machine. And this university-educated barrister who lived in Sydney's southern and western suburbs was far from working-class. Tall, aloof, and arrogant, he made a striking impression.

But Menzies thought Whitlam got off to a bad start in parliament. 'He began to speak rather too much, I thought, for a new boy,' Menzies said. 'And he then began to make rather nasty speeches. He seemed to be modelling himself on Eddie Ward rather than on the more sober members of the party, and I thought this was a pity.' So Menzies asked Whitlam to come around to the prime minister's office for a talk, and offered him some advice:

Sit down, young Whitlam. I hope you won't mind. You are a new boy here and I am an old scoundrel, from your point of view, but I would like just to give you a little friendly advice ... with your background, you could easily have a substantial middle-class appeal, not a ratbag appeal like Eddie Ward, but a middle-class solid citizens' appeal, but you aren't going the right way about it. You are modelling yourself on him; you are making extravagant charges. You are a bitter disappointment to me, and I do wish for your own sake that you would have another look at it, because I assure you that is not the way to get a real position in this House. If your ambition is to be Eddie Ward's successor, that is a different matter, but it cannot be. You must have higher ambitions than that.[61]

Whitlam apparently appreciated the advice. They shook hands, and Whitlam departed. But Whitlam, it seemed, thought 'the old goat was trying to trick him', and continued his 'foul attacks' in the parliament. Menzies thought Whitlam was trying to commend himself to the left wing of the Labor Party. He predicted that a Whitlam government would be 'a disaster', because 'the truth is not in him and he lacks the elements of decency'.

Menzies became increasingly concerned about the prospect of a Whitlam government. 'If Whitlam carried out one-tenth of the promises that he made in the last two years, then there would be a tremendous inflation in Australia,' he said in a May 1972 interview. 'The whole budget would run so heavily into deficit.' Menzies thought Whitlam was outclassed by the previous generation of Labor leaders, Curtin and Chifley. 'They were an entirely different order of men,' he thought. 'These fellows are not of the same calibre ... I would not be contented with Whitlam as I was with either Curtin or Chifley.'[62]

PART IV

Afternoon Light: 1966–78

CHAPTER 16

The Private Menzies

ROBERT Menzies' daughter, Heather Henderson, sits in her lounge room in a nice house in a quiet, leafy suburb of Canberra. She is surrounded by memories of her father. His paintings, pictures, and books line the walls. Sitting on top of a piano are slides of her father that she glimpses through shafts of sunlight that pour through the windows. There is a large bust of him in the hallway, which she pats on the head while walking past. Few knew Menzies better than his daughter. In recent years, she has collated a book of their letters to each other, and written another filled with anecdotes about both of her parents. They provide a window into the man who still casts a long shadow over Australian politics.

But Henderson is reluctant to talk about her father's political career; she insists that biographers and historians are better suited to assessing his legacy. In August 2014, I persuaded Henderson to talk to me about her father's life. We have talked on the phone several times since then, met occasionally in person, and I conducted another lengthy interview with her for this book in October 2017. 'We had a lot in common,' she said. 'We had the same sense of humour. It was a not uncommon father-daughter relationship. There was a great bond between us. I suppose it was obvious when we were together, particularly at informal gatherings with friends. We could both sort of act the goat together. We understood what we were both talking about.'[1]

Menzies had a commanding presence. He was often portrayed as aloof and arrogant. He could brandish his intellect and cutting wit to devastating effect. He could be imposing, physically and intellectually, and was said to never suffer fools gladly. But how much was the perceived public figure like the private man? 'He was very warm and very soft in lots of ways,' Henderson recalled. 'They thought he was very grand or snooty. When people actually met him, they were surprised he was so human and not at all superior. It didn't matter if it was the Queen or the dustman.'[2]

Henderson was born on 3 August 1928. She has few recollections of her father's early political career in state politics, his move to federal politics, and his first prime ministership. She was at boarding school when her father became prime minister on the eve of the Second World War. 'We were all going to bed in the dormitory,' she remembered. 'The headmistress came in and said, "Heather, your father's been made prime minister." I didn't really know what it meant, but we all got very excited and jumped up and down.'[3]

Henderson was in her early twenties when her father returned to the prime ministership in 1949, and she lived at the Lodge for a period. In 1955, she married diplomat Peter Henderson, after which the couple lived abroad for several years and raised a family. She corresponded and talked frequently with her father while he was prime minister from 1949 to 1966. 'It's not possible to live in a political house like that [the Lodge] without having some interest in politics,' she recalled. 'He would often talk about what was going on. He probably did the talking, and I asked a few questions.'[4]

There was a close and affectionate relationship between Menzies and his only daughter, and they confided in one another. But the same could not be said for Menzies and his two sons, Ken and Ian. Frances McNicoll interviewed Ken about his relationship with his father in 1981. '[It was] a relationship which was always perhaps a little bit studied compared to somebody who was around all the time,' he reflected. 'I don't think he ever really understood the problems involved in being the son of a prominent and great man.' Menzies had a particularly difficult time connecting with Ian, who had 'an epileptic condition', Ken said. The sons did share a common interest in sport with their father, but politics was rarely discussed. 'We are his sons but, you know, [I] never really felt he made any real attempt to get alongside. And certainly [he] was quite lacking in any understanding of the problems involved. He seemed to regard it as containing a lot of privileges but all I can say is that I can't go along with that.' This is an important insight into Menzies' family life.[5]

WHEN the Menzies family moved back into the Lodge in early 1950 — including with their dog 'Ming' — it was still the same modest two-storey home they had occupied from 1939–41. There was a dining room that seated only ten, a sitting room, a billiard room (later converted to another lounge room), a kitchen, and four bedrooms upstairs. It had been largely vacant since mid-1945, as Ben Chifley lived at the Hotel Kurrajong and only went to the Lodge for official functions. (He stayed there overnight only when Elizabeth Chifley was in Canberra.) Menzies would usually return to the Lodge for lunch and dinner, while working long hours. He was never one for excessive physical exercise, but he did enjoy walking, and often did so around the Lodge and in the neighbouring suburbs.

The Lodge was not a very private home, and security in later years only consisted of a single guard in a post near the front gate. A low two-strand wire fence, or hedge, ran around the property, and people could wander in and spot the prime minister and his wife having a cup of tea or coffee on a weekend afternoon. Kids who innocently kicked their balls into the garden retrieved them without any fuss. Bill Fisher, the young son of one of the neighbours, walked up to the front door and pressed the bell one day. 'Hello, Bill, what do you want?' Pattie asked. 'I'm doing a project at school and want to ask Mr Menzies some questions,' he replied. 'We're having lunch, but come in,' she said. Bill was ushered in to meet the prime minister. Bill sat at the table, opened his school book, and began asking questions and writing down the responses in pencil.[6]

On 16 January 1920, prime minister Billy Hughes announced that the federal government would acquire Kirribilli House overlooking Sydney Harbour, rather than see the property subdivided and sold, as the owner, Arthur Wigram Allen, wanted. The Gothic-style villa was originally built in 1854 and adjoined Admiralty House, the Sydney residence of the governor-general. A number of tenants occupied the property in subsequent years, but it was vacant by the mid-1950s and had become derelict. After Eric Harrison raised the idea of preserving the home with

Menzies, it was agreed to make it a guest house for official visitors from overseas, and to make it available for use by the prime minister when he or she was in Sydney. The idea was to essentially replicate Blair House, across the road from the White House, in Washington, D.C. A Georgian-style renovation began in 1957, and Menzies stayed in it overnight for the first time in October that year. The first international guest to stay at Kirribilli House was Japanese prime minister Nobusuke Kishi, in November 1957.

Henderson said that Kirribilli House was not meant to be a new and permanent home for the prime minister. 'It was not until after my father had retired that prime ministers — of both political persuasions — began to regard Kirribilli solely as a residence for prime ministers,' Henderson lamented. 'This is not in accord with the original intention, and I regret it.'[7] Some overseas visitors did occasionally stay there, but since John Howard adopted Kirribilli House as his primary residence as prime minister, it is now widely regarded as the prime minister's Sydney home.

DAME Pattie Menzies, as noted, could be quite demanding of her husband and his ministers, and there were tensions in the marriage from time to time. She was not able to forgive anyone or forget anything that caused her or her husband grief in any way. Menzies always acknowledged Pattie's advice and support. 'I'm a poor judge of character,' he claimed. 'But my wife is never wrong. She is, as you know, full of charm, full of humour, full of patience, has an immense capacity for hard work, and understands human relations far better than I probably ever will.'[8]

Pattie made an enormous contribution to her husband's political career. She hosted many functions at the Lodge, sat on countless platforms as he spoke, was alongside him while dining with prime ministers and presidents, endured nearly four decades of election campaigns, and travelled with him overseas, all while raising their family. John Bunting noted two standout qualities: her sense of style, and the way she always involved herself on any occasion with knowledge, cheerfulness, and class.[9]

William Heseltine was advised when he joined Menzies' office that if Dame Pattie ever rang up with a message for her husband, to deliver it instantly. She had strong opinions, and was not afraid to voice them. But, more than that, she expected her views to be taken seriously and any matters she raised to be acted upon without delay. 'She loomed very large as a figure in the office,' Heseltine said. 'She could make an immense disturbance if she thought she wasn't being given proper attention, and I think she made it quite uncomfortable for Bob at home.'[10]

Life was not always easy for Pattie. She had to help with the cooking, cleaning, and organising of the Lodge. There were dinners, lunches, and meetings with ministers, public servants, diplomats, special guests, and staff. She oversaw renovations and repairs, and expanded the gardens. 'For my mother, it was, looking back, very difficult,' her daughter said. 'These days, I suspect the Lodge is run more like a hotel with a housekeeper, and it's all just done. Whereas in her day, she had to do the running of the house, and the cooking, and find people to do work, and then make sure they did it. So she had a hell of a life.'[11]

ROBERT Menzies had a highly professional relationship with senior public servants and his personal staff. They all respected him and quite a number admired him. He was kindly towards them — although, from time to time, as with most politicians, he outwardly expressed the pressures and strains he was under, and he could lose patience. However, any sign of frustration or temper was usually brief and quickly forgotten. Menzies regularly invited public servants and staff to the Lodge for dinner during the week or for a less formal weekend meeting. He enjoyed playing host, and would often be seen mixing drinks in the pantry and holding court with groups of people, telling funny stories from his time in the law and politics.

Henderson is surprised that ministers and prime ministers today have dozens of staff. When her father travelled overseas, and she sometimes accompanied him, only a couple of staff went along. 'I can't imagine what they all do,' she said. 'Now ministers are surrounded by Yes Men. They employ people who think the same as they do politically. They don't get dispassionate advice. It seems to me they're not listening to their departments as much as they are to the people around them.'[12]

Tony Eggleton worked as Menzies' press secretary in his final year as prime minister. 'Most people saw him as a rather remote sort of figure, but the team around him all had this very warm relationship with him,' Eggleton remembered. 'He went out of his way to be close to his staff and to work well with his staff, and they looked after his interests.'[13] He recalled Menzies inviting staff to join him for dinner at the Windsor Hotel in Melbourne — where he had an apartment — and they would be treated to storytelling, mimicry, and the singing of songs. Sometimes, Menzies would combine all three and regale dinner companions with stories of prime ministers' conferences in London, replete with impersonations of Macmillan or Nehru.[14] Eggleton said staff would also be invited to the Lodge, especially at the end of the year. 'He was very kind to his staff,' he said. 'Every Christmas, he and his dear wife, Dame Pattie, when they were overseas, would pick out distinctive gifts for each of their staffers, so that they had special gifts for them at Christmas.'[15] Every year, Menzies would write to the manager of the parliamentary catering staff to thank him and his employees for the services they had provided him and his office.[16]

Tragedy struck Heseltine when his wife was killed in a car accident. Their car had been hit by a train at a level crossing in Melbourne in June 1957. It was a harrowing time, and he thought he might have to resign from Menzies' staff. But he was touched by the support offered by Allen Brown, his departmental head, and by the prime minister. 'The family were extraordinarily kind,' Heseltine recalled. 'I had been asked to the Lodge for the odd meal and always for a drink before dinner at the Windsor Hotel in Melbourne, and now I was always being asked around to the Lodge. Dame Pattie was always asking if I was looking after myself and feeding myself properly. They were very kind.'[17]

Ray Tracey was the official driver to ten prime ministers. He found Menzies to be a pleasant and kind boss, but not one to relax by playing billiards or cards as he did with Lyons, Curtin, or Chifley. 'I found Mr Menzies a good mixer, moody now and again, but usually good humoured, and always a stickler for promptness,' he recalled of his time driving Menzies between 1939 and 1941. '[My] association with the PM was on a strictly business basis. That doesn't mean that R.G. Menzies was aloof to the point of snobbishness. He was a genial, considerate boss.'[18] Alf Stafford and Ray Coppin, who drove Menzies in his second term as prime minister, found him to be a terrific boss. 'He is the greatest man I have ever driven,' Coppin recalled. 'He is the most human and best towards his staff ... one of his greatest attributes has always been that he is most considerate to the smaller man.'[19]

While Menzies was kindly toward his family and staff, and cordial with his ministers, he had few close friends. Jo Gullett, who had won his father's seat of Henty in 1946, thought Menzies had a distant relationship with his parliamentary colleagues. 'He has few close friends because he has few equals,' Gullett wrote in May 1958. 'He commands more respect than affection.'[20] Frank Menzies, one of his brothers, agreed. 'Bob has lacked that sort of continuing warmth towards people,' he said. 'He lacks friends, you know, and he has all that quality if you meet him at a dinner sitting next to him and find him charming and all the rest of it, but he has always lacked the capacity to get people to come round to him. They have admired him. They have respected him, and they have had to bow to his superior mind and knowledge of things, sometimes with resentment.'[21]

MENZIES' vast collection of 4,000 books, albums, pamphlets, magazines, and student notes is located in the Baillieu Library at the University of Melbourne. It was a gift he made to the university on 28 January 1976. The books at his office in Melbourne and at home in Malvern were to be transferred upon his death, or Pattie's death, or with her consent. The handover of all the books took place on 25 September 1980. The collection reflects the depth and breadth of Menzies' interests — politics, history, poetry, music, literature, art, travel, food, and cricket. There are books by politicians such as Paul Hasluck, Richard Casey, Percy Joske, H.V. 'Doc' Evatt, and Arthur Calwell. There are books from his international contemporaries, and inscribed to him, such as Dwight D. Eisenhower, John F. Kennedy, Lyndon Johnson, Harold Macmillan, and Winston Churchill. The latter presented his biography of Marlborough to Menzies in September 1941, inscribing it: 'To Robert Gordon Menzies, My comrade in anxious days, from Winston Churchill.'[22]

Menzies' student books were initialled 'R.G.M.' Many of his law books have a blue-ink stamp that reads 'Robert G. Menzies, Barrister at Law'. Others have a personal bookplate designed in 1940 that read 'Ex Libris' along the top and 'Robert G. Menzies' at the bottom. In between is a drawing by artist friend Lionel Lindsay featuring a despatch box; a horsehair wig and two shelves of law books; the declaration of war read in September 1939; a decanter of wine; and a sprig of eucalyptus.

Another bookplate designed by Lindsay in 1940 features a boy kneeling by a stream, fishing with a hand reel, who has caught a ceremonial mace that lies beneath the water. (Lindsay and his brother Norman were some of Menzies' artist friends.) A bookplate designed by James Stuart MacDonald has a lady justice statue with scales in one hand and a sword in the other, surrounded by law books, scrolls, and quills.

Menzies liked to read, and indeed reread, novels by Charles Dickens, Conan Doyle, Henry Fielding, Anthony Trollope, and William Makepeace Thackeray. He told Frances McNicoll in a letter that he enjoyed Robert Louis Stevenson's books, and thought it 'silly to think that *Treasure Island* is only a children's book'. Menzies loved William Shakespeare's 'plays and sonnets'. If willing to make 'a concession to romance', he would read Anthony Hope's novels or those written by Alexandre Dumas or Anatole France. Poetry remained a passion. He thought the 'greatest pleasures' came from reading Shakespeare, William Wordsworth, John Keats, and Robert Browning. He thought that Rudyard Kipling, a more modern poet, had been 'seriously undervalued by the critics'.[23]

The sport he loved most of all was cricket. Menzies went to hundreds of matches during his time in politics. He wrote extensively about cricket, penning the odd article or verse, and included a chapter on the sport in his memoirs. He enjoyed talking to cricketers about the game and hosting them for dinners or drinks at the Lodge. In October 1951, he organised the first Prime Minister's XI match at Manuka Oval in Canberra. He selected the teams and always included local players. His inaugural captain was Jack Fingleton, and others in the side included Bill O'Reilly, Neil Harvey, Sam Loxton, and Lindsay Hassett. They played against the touring West Indian cricket team — and the match was drawn. A total of seven matches were held in subsequent years. For the February 1965 match, Menzies persuaded Don Bradman to captain the Prime Minister's XI. The last match was held in December 1965, with Richie Benaud as captain. None of Menzies' Liberal successors had any interest in maintaining the tradition before it was revived by Bob Hawke in January 1984.

When Menzies moved to Melbourne as a schoolboy in 1910, he followed his older brothers in barracking for the Carlton Football Club. 'I became, by derivation and family influence, a Carlton supporter,' he recalled. Although he moved to East Melbourne, Camberwell, South

Yarra, and then Kew, he stuck with 'the old Blues' out of 'personal conviction'. He admired their fighting spirit, their ethos of teamwork, and how they never gave up.[24] There were few things that Menzies enjoyed more in the cooler months, especially before he was prime minister, than watching Carlton play in the Victorian Football League on a Saturday afternoon. He would often go with his sons, Ken and Ian, or brother Syd, and his nephew John, and sit in the stands with a bag of peanuts to watch a game. Menzies would take lunch in the committee room. He was made the number-one ticket holder for Carlton, and later the club arranged for a platform to be raised at Princes Park so that Menzies' black Buick or Bentley could be driven onto it close to the field and he could watch games in comfort from the front passenger seat. 'I think there could be a great future for drive-in football in Melbourne,' he joked.[25] After his first stroke, a special sedan-type chair was made by the club, and he would sit on it and be hoisted up into the stand by several players, from where he could watch the game.

HEATHER Henderson would like today's politicians to learn how her father practised the art of politics. There are many lessons to heed from Menzies, including how to chair a cabinet, manage a party, develop and expound a philosophy, communicate with voters, run a campaign, or develop a policy. Henderson suggests that politicians could learn 'a huge amount' from her father, including the art of oratory, having interests outside politics, enjoying a career before parliament, respecting advice from public servants, and forging friendships across the political divide.

Menzies was a great speechmaker, in parliament, on radio, and on the campaign trail. It was not unusual for him to address thousands of people in a town hall. He enjoyed it immensely. But oratory, Henderson says, is a dying art. 'People listened to what he had to say,' she recalled. 'He had great command over parliament when he got up to speak. He was such an imposing figure. He could communicate a message.'[26] Henderson says people could learn by studying his speeches, including the 'forgotten people' broadcast of May 1942. This speech still remains a touchstone for many Liberals. She would like them to better understand the founding values of the Liberal Party. 'I am concerned that some Liberals are moving away from the principles of the party that my father established in 1944,' she said.[27]

But the most important lesson to learn from her father, Henderson insists, is having a broad range of interests and not being consumed by politics. 'So many of them regard politics as a career,' she said. 'They've never had any experience outside politics. My father had a job first. He was a lawyer. He was always interested in politics, but it was not his sole aim in life.'[28] As we have seen, Menzies loved reading books, and enjoyed watching cricket or football, and spending time with his family.

Building friendships with those on the other side of politics helped her father be a more rounded politician, better able to appreciate different sides to an argument and to respect the different backgrounds and interests of others. It also helped to establish greater comity between politicians. Henderson is disappointed that 'personal abuse' is too often a substitute for reasoned debate today. Menzies would often relax at the end of a day with John Curtin or Ben Chifley. 'He was, on a personal level, very fond of both of them,' Henderson said. 'They each respected each other and what they were doing, what they believed in. They were able to understand that people could have a different point of view.'[29]

Henderson is proud of her father's achievements, such as expanding universities and developing Canberra, but she would also like there to be a more rounded understanding of his personality. 'I would like them to know he was a real human being,' she said. He was loving, caring, and respectful of others. He was a good husband, a loving father, and a doting grandfather. 'I'd like them to know that he was not an ogre,' she said. 'I'd like them to know that he worked prodigiously hard, very long hours. He was a quick thinker. He achieved a lot. People on the whole were increasingly prosperous and comfortable. He was prime minister at a time when Australia was a happy place to live. I would like them to remember him with respect, affection, a smile.'[30]

CHAPTER 17

Menzies in Verse

ROBERT Menzies had a hidden talent that the public rarely saw, even though his family, friends, and political colleagues were keenly aware of it: writing verse. From the earliest age, Menzies liked to compose poems, rhymes, haikus, odes, limericks, and doggerel. It began as a hobby while he was a student, and continued through his time working in the law and in politics. Menzies' flair for simple verse became so well known that he would often delight audiences with his latest writings. He thought there were few things more enjoyable than snatching a moment of time to write verse. Some were typed and kept for safe-keeping, many were quickly disposed of, and others were sent to family, friends, or colleagues for their enjoyment.

He would write at his desk, while travelling on planes or boats, or even during dinners, in parliament, or sitting in a party-room meeting. Many of these were screwed up and dispatched to a waste-paper basket. But some of them — written in longhand on yellow legal pads, scrawled on hotel stationery, or typed by his staff — have survived. Examining hundreds of Menzies' boxes of personal papers at the National Library of Australia has enabled me to rediscover many of them. Others have been located in the papers of his colleagues. And some have been provided to me from the personal collection of Heather Henderson, his daughter, for republication in this book.

'I think it probably came from his love of poetry at school,' Henderson said. 'He always loved poetry, he quoted it all the time, and I think it was just part of him. He always did write little verses. They were just light-hearted things, though. I might sit and do the crossword, and he'd write a little verse. When he was on a ship for about ten days, for a holiday, on the night of the last dinner he would write a little verse about everybody, and he would read it out at the table. It was just fun.'[1]

AS a young girl, Heather kept an autograph book. Her father offered one of the first entries in November 1939:

> To sign your name in a little girl's book
> Is a pleasure The Fairies send;
> For you turn the page, and wherever you look
> You'll see the name of a friend!
> But mine is the name of a friend as well,
> For Heather's a friend to me.
> Though I'm grown, and grey, you can never tell
> How young I can manage to be.
> It may seem funny, but still it's true –
> We're as friendly as bricks and mortar;
> For I am her father — ('How d'you do?) –
> And she is my blue-eyed daughter![2]

On a yellow legal pad, Menzies wrote a ditty for a granddaughter about Christmas:

> Over here, where the squirrels run around
> Up in the trees, and down on the ground
> Picking up food and hiding it away
> For a very great feast on Christmas Day[3]

In 1916, while studying for a law degree, Menzies was editor of the *Melbourne University Magazine*. He wrote several articles of verse for the magazine. Percy Joske thought that two, in particular, while not reaching the heights of great poetry, nevertheless showed 'sensitivity and an appreciation of beauty' as well as 'a facility of rhyme and rhythm':[4]

> So thou art twenty — twenty years gone by,
> And but a brief twelvemonth since last to thee
> We raised the birthday toast; what was to be
> We knew not, and across the world's fair sky
> We saw but Hope's bright blue. Who dared to sigh
> With dull foreboding? — but behold men see
> Grim Mars in dreadful blood-stained majesty,
> And weep to hear the death-gorged Eagle's cry!
> So to unveil the future none may dare;
> Bold would be he who spoke of peace today,
> When a full thousand bugles loudly blare
> And war-wolves roam abroad to hunt their prey.
> Yet, though the clouds have come, to thee we raise
> Another birthday toast — To Happier Days!

Several of Menzies' verses were about the First World War, including an ode to a fallen soldier at Gallipoli:

> His was the call that came from far away —
> An Empire's message flashing o'er the sea —
> The call to arms! The blood of chivalry
> Pulsed quicker in his veins; he could not stay!
> Let others wait; for him the glorious day
> Of tyrants humbled and a world set free
> Had dawned in clouds and thunder; with a glee
> Born not of insensate madness for the fray,
> But rather of a spirit noble, brave,
> And kindled by a heart that wept at wrong,
> He went. The storms of battle round him rave
> And screaming fury o'er him chants its song,
> Sleep, gallant soul! Though gone thy living breath,
> Thou liv'st for aye, for thou has conquered death![5]

That same year, Menzies wrote a song of tribute to Billy Hughes, on behalf of the Student Representatives Council, to the tune of 'PC Forty-Nine':

When Billy went to England he was just a little chap
Who ruled the Labour caucus with his stern parental rap,
But for the other party, well, he didn't care a snap,
    Did little — Billy Hughes
He left Australia far behind, he dared the raging main,
He groaned in agony of spirit and internal pain,
He thought — I'll never hear O'Malley's roosters crow again,
    Thought little — Billy Hughes
Little Billy Hughes
Went to England to expand his martial views,
He stepped ashore at London and he hailed a passing car,
He had his Sunday trousers on, and looked quite 'lah-di-dah',
He called on Mr Asquith who cried 'Hullo, there you are!
    Right welcome, Billy Hughes!' ...[6]

MENZIES thought there should be more humour in politics and the law. He took them seriously, but recognised the lighter side of both professions. He would often entertain gatherings of lawyers, politicians, or journalists with verses he had quickly scrawled on pieces of paper over dinner or had carefully constructed over hours of labour. 'Perhaps we are becoming too prosaic,' he wrote in retirement. 'For busy barristers today there is, conceivably, too much work and too little leisure. So the graces of advocacy and the charms of the forensic life tend to wither away. It is a pity.'[7]

Political adversaries were not spared in Menzies' verse, such as this ode surveying the Labor Party that he delivered to a dinner of journalists in the late 1940s:

All hail, the great CHIFLEY, whom six states obey
Who sometimes baccy takes and sometimes tea.
Fresh from the battle over Bretton Woods;

Fresh from the brawl on Rosie Kelly's good;
Fresh from the caucus and the ALP;
Fresh from launching RIORDAN on the deep blue sea.
How are the boys, my placid Benedict?
Is it still true that JACK LANG has them tricked?
Is BERT behaving? Or are Paraguay
And Chile cooking up a break-away?
And wee JOCK DEDMAN, wi' his tailless shirt.
And cuffless trousers, trailing in the dirt?
Is it the truth that though wee Jock saw reason
To banish iced cakes from the Christmas season,
At Christmas now he gives rewards for failure
To luckless candidates from West Australia?[8]

Menzies penned a short poem to Chifley:

How d'ye do?
Is it true
That the wordy and raucous
Boys of the caucus
At a word, or a sign,
Become noisy, benign,
Noisy as the French would have been if Napoleon had escaped from Elba,
Benign, as if they were listening to Nellie Melba?[9]

And another to H.V. 'Doc' Evatt:

Wee modest crimson-tipped flower,
Why deprecate UN?
Give it a chance, it's bound to grow,
To cut its teeth and learn to grow,
Like grown-up, earthy men.[10]

Some of Menzies' verse could be especially vituperative, and also in
poor taste, such as this written for Arthur Calwell:

As a worker and brother from China, I love you,
But if you <u>will</u> live in Australia, I'll shove you.
I don't like your skin, or your speech, or your race,
But I freely concede you're all right, <u>in your place</u>.
Of course, my dear fellow, if given my choice,
To call you my <u>Brother</u> would make me rejoice,
With my dear colleague Bert, who attends the UN,
I have given great thought to the rights of plain men;
We believe all are equal, all children Divine,
All plainly entitled to sun and to shine.
But the thing you must learn, in a country that's Labour,
Is that no man who's yellow can be a Good Neighbour.
If he's red or just plain pinkish, that's not really sinister,
He may even go on and become a paid minister.
But if Yellow his skin, well, I won't keep him long,
I'll send him to China by way of Hong Kong.[11]

To relieve the tedium of parliament, Menzies would also reach for a piece of paper to write verse while sitting at the table. He was not the only one suffering through dull speeches; so were the clerks, he suggested, in a piece that was published in *The Times* of London:

To the Clerks at the Table.
Two WISE OLD OWLS sat at the table:
Their wigs were grey, their gowns were sable;
They looked so sad, so melancholy,
As if depressed by HUMAN FOLLY,
Around them, carelessly displayed,
Were all their dreadful TOOLS of TRADE,
The STANDING ORDERS, VOTES and MOTIONS,
The STATUTES. MAY, and such like NOTIONS.
The GLASS, with sand so nearly piled,
The RULINGS (wrong), so neatly filed.
The BELLS, to call the MEMBERS in
To tread the paths of VERBAL SIN.

But WISE OLD OWLS must sometimes think!
Of what? of WOMEN? FOOD? or DRINK?
Or are they, as they keep their places,
As really VACANT as their FACES?[12]

The clerks, not to be outdone, returned serve. Their response was published in *The Times* the following day:

If we look glum and vacant stare,
When wigged and seated 'neath the Chair,
Please do not think 'tis Nature's way,
It's rather service for our pay.
For if some thoughts we dare repeat,
We'd find ourselves out in the street.
So time moves on; we leave the MUSE
And lend our ears to Members' views,
We hear their claims, their wants, their quips,
We see their moves, and calls by Whips,
But we don't TALK — So who can label
The inner thoughts of the Clerks at the Table?[13]

Menzies also wrote a ditty for the clerk, Frank Green, reflecting on his attentive style despite the chaos often swirling around him:

When, in some lonely mountain stream,
A trout swims on, in silver dream,
And suddenly snaps an adventurous fly,
From off the mirror of the sky
He hopes that he will not be seen
By the watchful eye of Frankie Green.[14]

Menzies found speaker Archie Cameron's style in the chair to be unnecessarily aggressive. So, after listening to Cameron recite the Lord's Prayer one morning, Menzies scribbled a ditty in pencil that he headlined 'Archie's Lord's Prayer':

Now listen, God, to what I'm saying,
I fear you let your wits go straying,
To tell the truth, I sometimes feel
That I should not make soft appeal
But issue orders in a voice
To make an RSM rejoice
So wake up! God, and make it snappy.
Move to it, it will make me happy.
Get along there with our salvation,
And keep all Members in their station.[15]

Menzies also penned a poem about Canberra, where he had lived for almost two decades but was frustrated by the slow scale of its development:

Ah! Canberra, Ah! Canberra,
What holy peace and quiet there
From dusk to dawn the fountains play
With alcohol on Mugga Way.
Month after month new buildings rise
If not with speed, at least in price.
Year after year the city drowses
Lulled by the lack of shops and houses.
Cicada-like the insistent drone
of Civil Servants on the 'phone
Hums in the background, whilst the purrs
Of kettles, which stenographers
Tend like a sacred flame, combine
To make the perfect anodyne.
Peace, perfect peace? Alas, 'tis fake.
No Eden but conceals its snake.
It would be Paradise on earth
If Parliament could meet in Perth![16]

Journalists and their proprietors were frequent fodder for Menzies' verse. He especially liked to lampoon pressmen. In 1946, he shared a rhyme at a dinner organised by the Australian Journalists' Association:

I often sit below at Question Time
and glaze aloft at the salubrious clime
Where dwell the journalists in their array
Both blind and deaf to everything I say,
The AJA, our daily friends and foes,
up goes the glass, and down the nectar flows.[17]

Sir Frank Packer, whose company owned the Nine Network, *The Daily Telegraph*, and *The Bulletin*, was a friend of Menzies. In 1962, Packer's yacht *Gretel* — named after his wife — was launched by Dame Pattie and competed in the America's Cup. Menzies launched Packer's next yacht, named *Dame Pattie*, which also raced in the America's Cup. Menzies composed a birthday tribute to Packer:

Sixty years young, it's past belief
That your life's course has been so brief.
But as your seniors, we can say
'Good luck, young Frank, for many a day'
A lousy verse, an ill-tuned bell,
That wouldn't have a hope in hell
Of reaching (here let young Clyde laugh!)
The columns of *The Telegraph*.
You are, let's face it, fairly tough.
You can be smooth, you can be rough,
Yet year by year you've done me proud.
Within the limits truth allowed.
There have been times, as you'll remember,
When you've been tempted to dismember
That splendid man, the PMG,
And, just behind him, even me
And sometimes, when it came to taxes,
You've sharpened up your verbal axes,
And then have said, to make amends,
'I can't eviscerate my friends!'
Two friends now think of you with pleasure
And lay up, as a special treasure,

The knowledge that, through thick and thin,
You've done your best to help us win.[18]

Menzies was proud of his parody of how *The Sydney Morning Herald* would report his death. He also wrote a satire about what *The Daily Telegraph* in Sydney would say about him when he was gone:

Well, he's gone.
Do you remember him? He was prime minister.
Not without parts, but unsound on taxation. For some reason or another, he had a puritanical objection to tax evasion. Even by companies.
We stop short of saying that he was born on the wrong side of the blanket. Local tradition forbids that we should take on so technical a point.
But he was born on the wrong side of the border.
Not his fault? No.
Looking back on it all, we say he had his moments.
Indeed, come to think of it, he was, for at least half his time, a good bloke.
And that's something!
Every Australian, imbued with the sporting (if not strictly amateur) tradition, will say to those who have him in hand,
GIVE HIM A GO.[19]

There were frequent diversions from politics that made it into Menzies' verse, such as this on cricket written at the Savoy Hotel in London in 1953:

This is a very solemn night my friends,
Though it may cheer up yet, before it ends.
Here at this miserable board there sit
Men without skills, or eagerness, or wit ...
The gloomy Hassett, sulking in his tent,
Saying: 'That shot was not quite what I meant!'
The ancient Miller, too old now to bustle,
Nursing his something, something, something muscle!

Lindwall with versatility inhuman,
Bowling his slows just faster than Fred Trueman.
Benaud the bold, Benaud the Giant Killer,
Bowls like Doug Ring — but gestures like Keith Miller.
The infant David took a rounded stone,
And smote Goliath through both skin and bone.
With equal art, but much less lethal fun,
Similar things are done by Davidson.
Bill Johnston, smiling darling of Society,
Bowler of lengths and widths a fine variety;
But Tallon always wishes he could know
Whether Bill's going to bowl it fast or slow.
If Ronald Archer were no good at all
Instead of adept with both bat and ball,
I would still cheer him, louder and still faster,
For Queensland lately saved me from disaster![20]
The clutching Tallon oft the Umpire Hails
Before he's actually removed the bails.
(I know that this is libelous, but stay,
I could not get a rhyme another way ...).[21]

IN May 1955, American actress Katharine Hepburn began 'a season
of Shakespeare' in Sydney alongside co-star Robert Helpmann, during
which they performed three of his plays: *The Merchant of Venice, The
Taming of the Shrew*, and *Measure for Measure*.[22] Hepburn visited
Canberra during her tour, and over a 'breezy' lunch with Menzies,
discussed Shakespeare. Menzies suggested the great bard's 'ideas of law'
were flawed and that Shylock should never have been convicted in *The
Merchant of Venice*.

'Why don't you rewrite the trial?' Hepburn cheekily suggested.
Menzies took up the challenge and rewrote 46 lines from one of
Shakespeare's most famous plays. He suggested that the legal battle
between Shylock and Antonio should have been thrown out of court. He
handed Hepburn the rewrite the following day:

If any contract made between two men
Provides the doing of an act of blood
Which leads, or may lead, to a liege's death,
The law of England, which by God's good grace
My author, Mr Shakespeare, makes apply in Venice,
Rejects, on grounds of public policy
The whole arrangement: makes it null and void.

Hepburn's response to Menzies' audacity? 'Mr Menzies is a very wicked man,' she said.[23]

MENZIES did not spare himself from being a target of his verse. In 1961, when there were mutterings in the parliamentary lobbies about when he might retire, he took to rhyme:

Poor old chap, why doesn't he go?
He's had his chips, as he ought to know.
He did quite well for eleven years,
But then he gave us sweat and tears,
And made us yearn for the good old days
When the socialists sang their hymn of praise
To the ration book and the tight control
Of all that a man had, except his soul.
Poor old chap, why doesn't he go?
And give us some pleasure to — don't you know?
One vote up, on the floor of the House,
Why doesn't the old boy show them some nous?
Why not make a spectacular bolt,
Taking with him Spooner and Holt,
Leaving the course quite clear and steady
For our friends Arthur, and Jim, and Eddie?[24]

These jottings show that Menzies did not take politics, nor himself, too seriously. He could be self-deprecatory. They also demonstrate that he had a wide range of interests. His literary endeavours were informed by his extensive reading of novels, plays, and poems. He read history, biography, and politics. And he had several books on sport. There was more than just politics in his life. 'For so many politicians, it is their whole life and they think of nothing else,' Henderson said. 'But it wasn't his whole life.'[25]

CHAPTER 18

Resignation

WHEN Robert Menzies walked into the cabinet room at 10.30 am on Wednesday 19 January 1966, there was a heightened feeling of anticipation that the 16-year continuous reign of Australia's longest-serving prime minister might be about to come to an end. 'Although it has become a good deal known, [I] wish to say I have, after much thought, and even painful thought, [decided] to yield up my post,' Menzies told the cabinet. 'The alternative is to resign now or carry on through the next election and beyond. So, it's now or another three years.'[1]

The cabinet secretary's handwritten notes of the historic meeting, recording the dialogue of ministers, reveal what took place behind closed doors. The record of this meeting has only been available since 2014.[2] 'To tackle another election and a further period [in government] is not my intention,' the 71-year-old Menzies said. 'I feel [I can] come up to the big occasion but not so easily or so often as before. This being so, my time to go is now so that [a] new leader may have the better part of 12 months in order to exhibit his character and [the] character of his government.'[3]

It was in the lead-up to the half-Senate election on 5 December 1964 that Menzies finally decided it was time to retire. 'I went around and I knew that my time was running out on me because I was tired, got easily tired, didn't feel any zip when I was at a meeting,' Menzies later said. 'I then made up my mind that I ought to give it away — and why not? I had had an uncommonly good run. I had no grievances about politics.'[4]

Resignation had been on Menzies' mind for some time. He had planned to retire before the December 1961 election, but the credit squeeze had put the government's survival in jeopardy. 'I am confident that, with united backing on our side, our policy will work out successfully and popular opinion will come back to us,' Menzies wrote to his daughter in January 1961. 'These being our political circumstances, I must clearly defer my hope of retirement and must see the next election through.'[5] In mid-1961, a Gallup poll found that 57 per cent of voters thought Menzies should continue in office, while a not-insignificant 39 per cent said he should retire.[6] After the election, which saw the government narrowly returned, Menzies confessed to being 'singularly depressed', and his retirement plan was again on hold. 'All my plans for a decent retirement, leaving an adequate majority to carry on, seem to have gone down the wind,' he wrote to his daughter in January 1962.[7] Menzies stayed on to fight, and win, the November 1963 election. But nobody can go on forever.

On 8 November 1965, a gala dinner was held in Canberra to celebrate the Liberal Party's 21st anniversary. It was a dinner enveloped in nostalgia about the past and anticipation of the future. Menzies' speech notes provide an insight into how he saw the party's founding, its achievements, and its future. He spoke of the work done at the Canberra and Albury conferences in 1944. Although some had doubted his leadership at the time — 'You'll never win with Menzies' — he had proved them wrong. The party had developed its philosophy and platform. New members had been recruited, and capable candidates enlisted. Labor's 'socialism' became the key issue at the December 1949 election, he said. Menzies identified his major achievements as ANZUS, the Colombo Plan, SEATO, school and higher-education initiatives, boosting defence capability, and national development. The watchwords of his government were 'stability and growth'. He spoke of 'the stirring prospects of the future', and of 'the younger brigade' who would 'have the task and opportunity' of seeing the party to brighter days ahead.[8]

The party, though, was anxious about Menzies' future. A month before the dinner, John Carrick, the New South Wales Liberal Party general secretary, wrote a paper about the next election that was forwarded to Menzies. He argued there were considerable risks for the government. He pointed to policy problems, new electoral boundaries that might make for several tight contests, and the unreadiness of the party organisation to fight another campaign. Leadership was the biggest concern. 'The leadership image of the prime minister, while still particularly strong, is somewhat weakened by the constant public speculation as to his possible retirement,' Carrick wrote. 'There is every indication that the public would wish him to remain as leader so long as his health and inclination permit.'[9] Yet in mid-1965, a Gallup poll had found that 53 per cent of voters thought Menzies should retire, and 43 per cent thought he should continue. In other words, a majority of voters thought Menzies should go.[10]

A month after the 21st-anniversary dinner, Jock Pagan, the federal president of the party, and Philip McBride, the immediate past president, wrote to Menzies. They delicately raised the matter of his retirement. The party unambiguously wanted Menzies to stay. 'In view of all the rumours we hear around the place, is it too late for us to be writing to you on this matter?' they asked. 'Without your so valuable leadership, and highly acceptable public image, the next general election could, we believe, see us in trouble. We do not wish to be regarded as over pessimistic but frankly feel that 1966 could be a bad year for Australia without you to lead it and us.' They got to the point: 'We ask, on behalf of the party, that you seriously consider making yet a further great sacrifice by continuing as our prime minister through another general election.'[11]

But Menzies' mind was made up. On the last day of the parliamentary sittings in December 1965, he hinted that his resignation might be imminent. 'I am very proud to have served in this parliament, because I think it has made its own invaluable contribution to the political history of Australia,' he said. Arthur Calwell noticed that Menzies was looking back, not forward. 'I do not want to peer too far into the future, but I have what Carlyle would have called a preternatural suspicion that things might happen next year,' he said. This prompted Liberal MP William Aston to jokingly interject, 'Are you retiring, Arthur?' Calwell replied, 'I am not retiring, no, neither from the leadership of my party nor from the parliament — but there may be other retirements.' Menzies had told Calwell that he was planning to retire.[12]

Yet it is unlikely that Menzies told any of his parliamentary party colleagues when he planned to go. The first time that deputy leader Harold Holt learned that Menzies was to retire was probably when he announced it at the cabinet meeting on 19 January 1966. The cabinet notebooks reveal Holt was shocked by Menzies' announcement, and utterly clueless as to when his retirement would take place and what the process would be to choose his successor. It is evidence that Menzies was keeping his deputy in the dark.

Menzies had flagged his intentions to retire with his family. 'I remember him coming around to our house and telling us he was going to do it,' daughter Heather Henderson recalled. 'It was only a few weeks before.'[13] On 24 December 1965, the extended Menzies family gathered at the Lodge for a family photo. The next day, they celebrated Christmas. He would almost certainly have told sister Belle and brother Frank about his decision to retire.[14] On 27 December, Menzies had dinner with Jock Pagan at his home in Point Piper.[15] Menzies might have flagged his intentions then.

There had been a clue about Menzies' future plans when, in October 1965, he bought a house at 2 Haverbrack Avenue, Malvern, Victoria, for his post-prime ministerial residence. In June 1966, it was announced that a trust would be established to purchase the house as a permanent home for Robert and Pattie during their lifetimes. Menzies was reluctant at first, but accepted on the proviso that it be sold after his death and the funds given to schools attended by Heather and Pattie. Initially, $100,000 was raised by businessmen and friends led by Sir John Allison.[16]

Another person whom Menzies told was his press secretary, Tony Eggleton. Menzies invited Eggleton to spend a few days with him at Kirribilli House in December 1965. On Boxing Day, they watched the start of the Sydney–Hobart Yacht Race from the lawn sloping down towards the harbour. 'He talked about his retirement,' Eggleton recalled. 'He wanted me to know about it, and we talked about it at length. He was relaxed and reflective. He enjoyed mixing his famous martinis. Sitting on the Kirribilli House veranda, he listened to the sporting broadcasts on the radio and watched the ships and boats going by.'[17]

They discussed the prime ministerial succession. 'Menzies had no doubts about Holt as his successor,' Eggleton said. 'He was keen to note that Harold would finally get his opportunity. He said "Young Harold" would make a good prime minister, and he expected Harold would be strongly supported and endorsed by the parliamentary party. He gave every impression he was very comfortable with his decision to retire and was relishing this down-time prior to the January retirement.' Menzies promised not to make life difficult for his successor. 'Laddie,' he told Eggleton, 'there's no greater has-been than a has-been prime minister.'[18]

ON 10 January, Menzies announced that the Coalition parties would meet on 20 January. 'By this date, I will be in a position to clarify my own intentions,' he said, rather cryptically, 'whichever way my decision goes.'[19] Menzies had lunch with Richard Casey, the governor-general, on Sunday 16 January. He may have signalled his intentions to resign at this time, although Casey made no mention of it in his diary.[20]

When Menzies addressed the cabinet on the morning of 19 January, there were ten other ministers present. Defence minister Shane Paltridge was not there, as he had resigned from cabinet due to illness. He died a few days later. After noting Paltridge's resignation, Menzies made his own statement of resignation. 'I have been 16 years prime minister, and even if one is a great big booby, he tends to overshadow others,' he said. 'So I should go now. I give you all my deep thanks.'

The first to respond was John McEwen. 'As deputy leader and Country Party leader, I express [my] deep thanks and appreciation,' he said. 'We thank you for your leadership and your friendship and your wisdom and guidance. This is a unique period in Australia. I do not expect to see another leader so great. God bless you, old boy — from all of us, thanks.' Holt was caught off-guard. He promised to pay a fuller tribute later. 'You are Australia's greatest son, having led Australia 17 years — its greatest period,' Holt said. 'We have had [the] great privilege [of] working with you and enjoying your friendship. Your standards of cabinet and public service are unequalled.' Menzies was moved. 'I thank you both and you all,' the prime minister said. 'You have all sustained me. But being not yet defunct, I must I suppose get on with the business [of cabinet].'

In another sign that Menzies had not discussed his retirement before the meeting, Holt asked about the 'procedure' regarding the resignation. Menzies said he would announce his resignation at a joint party meeting the following day. The Liberal Party would then meet to elect a new leader. 'Then I will inform [the] governor-general and will, on being asked, advise on [my] successor. [I] would expect that [the] governor-general will ask me to carry on i.e. as caretaker pending [the] formation of a new government.' Paul Hasluck asked about Menzies' seat of Kooyong. Menzies said he would inform his constituency of his intentions, but made it clear that his exit from parliament would soon follow. '[I] do not now want to go [back] into parliament,' he said.

A meeting of all ministers was held the next day, 20 January, at 10.45 am, at which Menzies formally announced his resignation. The lobbies of Parliament House buzzed with the news that was now official. Large crowds had earlier gathered outside to meet Menzies on his arrival at Parliament House at 10.31 am. University students with large fake eyebrows had greeted Menzies with a Union Jack flag and wore 'MING DON'T GO-GO' badges, one of which was pinned on Holt's lapel as he ascended the stairs. They sang several choruses of 'There'll always be a Menzies.' The Coalition parties met at 11.00 am, with Menzies presiding for the last time. He announced his resignation to an emotional gathering of MPs, who knew they were witnessing the end of an era. Later, at a meeting of the Liberal Party, Holt was elected leader. Billy McMahon defeated Paul Hasluck for the position of deputy leader.

'In short, I am tired; my pace has slowed down,' Menzies said in a statement. 'I could not properly continue in office for very much longer and at the same time do justice to the growing problems of the nation.' He spoke of the growing 'complexities' of government, the 'burden' of speechmaking, and the 'strain' of election campaigns. He concluded by thanking Pattie, who had 'made great sacrifices' for what she, and he, believed were in 'the public interest'.[21]

Just before 4.00 pm on 20 January 1966, Menzies sat in the back seat of his black Bentley with its numberplate C-1, and was driven to Government House. He tendered his resignation to the governor-general, Richard Casey, and recommended that Holt be commissioned as prime minister.[22] Casey wrote a brief account of their meeting in his diary: 'RGM called on me at GH and gave me in writing the notification of his retirement, which I acknowledged in writing and asked him to continue in office until next week when the new government would be formed by

Harold Holt. We went on to discuss personalities.' They met for about 50 minutes, and shared a drink and a cigar. The next day, Casey sent a telegram to Buckingham Palace, formally advising of Menzies' retirement and of Holt being his successor.[23]

The letter that Menzies gave Casey on 20 January has been located in his files at the National Library of Australia:

Your Excellency,

I beg to submit my resignation from the office of Prime Minister. I know that you understand my reasons for this. I have had 16 continuous years of office and feel that the time has come to hand over my responsibilities.

I should also inform you that this morning the Right Honourable Harold Holt was chosen unanimously by the Liberal Party to be the leader of that party. I will therefore be advising you to commission him. I should add that it is my understanding that Mr Holt and Mr McEwen have a complete mutual understanding.

I have the honour to be, Sir,

Yours sincerely,

Robert Menzies[24]

Following their meeting, Casey replied to Menzies by letter:

My dear Prime Minister,

I have received with great regret your letter of 20 January, 1966, resigning the office of Prime Minister. Knowing full well and understanding your reasons for this, I accept it.

I accept, too, your advice that I should send for the Right Honourable Harold Holt and, as discussed with you today, I shall see him later this afternoon and invite him to form a government, subject of course to his assurance that he can do this. I am grateful to you for agreeing to remain in office as Prime Minister until such time as I am able to swear your successor.

I am,

Yours sincerely,

Richard Casey[25]

At 12.20 pm the next day, 21 January, Menzies and Holt were photographed together at the Lodge. Menzies gave Holt a friendly pat on the head, and smiled for the press photographers. It was a passing of the baton. And the end of an era.

Eggleton suggested to Menzies that he hold a farewell press conference broadcast on television. 'No, no, laddie,' Menzies replied, 'I don't need to do that.' But eventually Menzies agreed. It was held in the Parliament House dining room at 8.00 pm on 20 January, and was broadcast live on radio and television. Menzies told Eggleton that he needed to have 'a nervous pee' before the press conference. Eggleton could not believe Menzies would be nervous. 'I've always got to have my nervous pee,' he insisted. The timing had to be worked out precisely so that Menzies arrived as the television cameras rolled. Eggleton rehearsed it. Menzies would leave his office at the precise moment, walk via the toilet, and then sit down with the press gallery for the live broadcast.[26]

Menzies' departure was unlike his earlier exit from the prime ministership in August 1941. 'This is something that doesn't happen very frequently — for a man to go out of office under his own steam,' Menzies said to the live audience beneath the glare of bright lights. 'I've gone out of office before today under somebody else's steam, but this time under my own.' He sat at a table and wore a dark double-breasted suit with pocket handkerchief, white shirt, and striped tie. It was a standout performance as Menzies outlined his reasons for going, and deftly handled questions. Asked what he saw as his 'most lasting achievement', Menzies responded with two things: creating the Liberal Party, and the 'fruitful and constant alliance' with the Country Party. He added, on the policy side, the ANZUS Treaty and the expansion of the university sector. Menzies' 50-minute press conference was believed to have attracted the largest television viewing audience on record.[27] 'I must say I heartily enjoyed that conference,' Menzies said later.[28]

Holt, having accepted a commission to form a government, was sworn in as Australia's 17th prime minister in the morning of 26 January 1966 — Australia Day. Robert Menzies' appointment diary notes on this day: 'Sir Robt ceased to be PM'.[29]

Menzies resigned his seat of Kooyong on 17 February 1966; subsequently, Andrew Peacock was chosen as the Liberal candidate to contest the by-election held on 2 April 1966. Peacock had been born into the Liberal Party. His mother and father were prominent Liberals. His maternal grandmother knew Menzies, and was a pioneer in the Australian Women's National League, which merged with the nascent Liberal Party in 1945. Peacock was president of the Victorian Liberal Party (1965–66) and served on the party's federal executive (1964–66). No seat was more prized than Kooyong, the jewel in the Liberal crown. Menzies told Peacock, then a young lawyer and company director, that he favoured Dick Hamer, a Victorian upper-house MP, as his successor. But Hamer turned Menzies down.[30]

Peacock won the preselection contested by nine other candidates, and then the seat at the by-election. He was just 27 years old. Although Peacock was somewhat daunted to be succeeding Menzies, he found the former prime minister to be very supportive during the by-election, and later. 'I was very honoured to be succeeding him,' Peacock told me. 'Menzies was very encouraging and was very good to me. He was a person of huge stature. In terms of political achievements, he is unequalled in Australian history. He had been prime minister, was thrown out, and then formed the Liberal Party. And by 1949, they had won the election and he was prime minister. It was an extraordinary achievement, and he stayed there until he retired at the beginning of 1966. He was just a giant in political terms.'[31]

On 17 March 1966, a tribute dinner was held in Parliament House to honour Menzies. MPs from all parties attended the gala event dressed in their dinner suits while the women wore their finest dresses. Holt said Menzies was unmatched as an orator during his lifetime. Calwell also praised Menzies, and noted the irony that this 'simple Presbyterian' with a Scottish heritage was being feted on St Patrick's Day. In Menzies' address to the 300-plus guests, he acknowledged Dame Pattie, mentioned the great political figures he had served with, such as Lyons, Curtin, and Chifley, and said it was because they respected parliamentary democracy that they succeeded in politics — 'people speaking their minds, disagreeing and fighting their battles, and then accepting, at any rate temporarily, the majority,' Menzies said.[32]

FREED of the burdens of office, Menzies travelled abroad, gave lectures, wrote books, read widely, and watched football and cricket. A series of lectures he gave at the University of Virginia was published as *Central Power in the Australian Commonwealth* in 1967.[33] He remained a well-known and respected figure on the world stage, and continued to be feted by serving and former presidents and prime ministers in the United States and the United Kingdom. He gave the occasional interview on television and radio, wrote for newspapers, and was honoured at Liberal Party gatherings. Menzies also served as chancellor of the University of Melbourne from 1967 to 1972.

Menzies was installed as the 117th Lord Warden of the Cinque Ports and Constable of Dover Castle on 20 July 1966. Dating back to 1066, the post had previously been held by Winston Churchill, William Pitt, the Duke of Wellington, Lord Palmerston, and the Marquess of Salisbury. The installation took place in the Grand Court of Shepway at the ancient Priory of St Martin's in the grounds of Dover College. A procession of around 100 official cars transported guests from Dover Castle to the Grand Court for the historic ceremony. The Royal Marines band played. Barons, earls, commissars, mayors, alderman, and town sergeants were on hand to witness the event. 'So long as I remain mobile enough to be transported across the skies I shall come here every year and have a look at my constituents,' Menzies said.[34]

Menzies made annual visits to see his new constituency between 1966 and 1972. Heather Henderson recalled visiting him at Walmer Castle in Kent, the official residence of the warden. 'He was absolutely thrilled with it,' she said. 'He loved it.' But Menzies did not like dressing up in the Lord Warden of the Cinque Ports uniform made of a blue naval doeskin with gold-embroidered epaulettes and collar, gold-trim trousers, crimson leather belt, white gloves, star and green sash, regulation naval sword, and cocked hat of plush silk and braid. He only did so because the office required it. 'I think it's terrible,' he confessed to a journalist. 'I am sure you must be much more comfortable than I am.'[35] His daughter agreed. 'I never did see him wearing the uniform,' Henderson said. 'Winston loved dressing up; Dad did not.'[36]

Opinion polls showed that Menzies was among the most admired people in Australia in his retirement years. In fact, there were whispers in political circles that he might make a comeback to public office. Dame Mabel Brookes, the president of the Queen Victoria Hospital in Melbourne, wrote a letter to Lyndon Johnson in March 1968 and mentioned that Menzies had been sounded out for the post of governor-general. (Brookes had entertained Johnson when he visited Australia during World War II, stayed overnight at the White House when he became president, and met him on his later visits to Australia as president.) 'A feeling of change is in Canberra,' she wrote to Johnson. 'It is whispered Percy Spender will be the new Governor-General ... the universal wish is that Bob would take it on, but evidently he doesn't want to.'[37]

In any event, Menzies' post-prime ministerial activities were soon curtailed by illness. He suffered a mild stroke in September 1968, and another in November 1971, the latter more serious and requiring a lengthy stay at the Mercy Hospital in Melbourne. Menzies was in no shape to contest another election and continue for another three-year term as prime minister. But his mind remained sharp, even though his body was failing. He even entertained journalists with stories at his hospital bedside, who declared him still to be 'in fine form' despite the stroke.[38] At home, he was regularly attended to by a nurse, and used a wheelchair when he left the house. In his final years, Menzies became somewhat 'gloomier and tetchier', but his strokes 'did not bring about a major personality change', his daughter recalled.[39] In March 1977, Queen Elizabeth II invested Menzies as a Knight in the Order of Australia during the Australia v. England centenary test match at the Melbourne Cricket Ground. It was his last audience with the monarch.

Menzies rejected many requests to cooperate with biographers and historians on their books about his life, the politics of his era, and the record of his government. He disliked Ronald Seth's biography, *R.G. Menzies* (1960), even though he had granted the author an interview while in England. 'He thinks it is a very poor effort,' Frank Menzies recalled.[40] He also did not think much of Kevin Perkins' *Menzies: the last of the Queen's men*, published in 1968. 'It is really atrocious,' Menzies said, having found 'about 100 inaccuracies'.[41] With Menzies' papers restricted to Frances McNicoll, and having given her exclusive interviews, prospective biographers were kept at bay.

Menzies wrote two volumes of memoirs: *Afternoon Light: some memories of men and events*, published in 1967, and *The Measure of the Years*, published in 1970; the former was launched by New South Wales governor Sir Roden Cutler, and the latter by governor-general Sir Paul Hasluck. Menzies wrote the books himself, in longhand, helped with research by Hazel Craig. Some chapters were dictated. He also had secretarial assistance provided by the University of Melbourne. While free of any revelatory details, Menzies' memoirs contain brilliant chapters on his relationships with prime ministers and presidents. His lengthy chapter on Churchill in *Afternoon Light* is superb. Based on early sales and publisher expectations, he thought his first book would sell 50,000 copies.[42] Menzies planned to share the royalties with his family. But after taxes and duties, he did not make as much money as he had hoped.[43]

Menzies spent most of his time either at his 14th-floor office at 95 Collins Street in Melbourne, which he attended several days a week, or at his two-storey home, at 2 Haverbrack Avenue, Malvern. Menzies became somewhat of a neighbourhood celebrity. With so many tourists stopping by to peer into the windows to glimpse the old man in his retirement, Menzies began referring to it as 'Have-a-look-avenue'.

One of the people who visited Menzies in these years was B.A. ('Bob') Santamaria. They would discuss political issues, and deliberate on the past over a drink or two at the end of the day. 'Tell me the three biggest mistakes I ever made,' Menzies asked Santamaria late one afternoon. Although reluctant to do so because 'it was rude', he nominated 'consolidating Canberra as the national capital', which had led to public servants dominating policy development; expanding the university sector when 'there weren't enough good academics' to run them; and, third, creating the Liberal Party. Menzies was astounded, and replied, 'But they're the only three things I ever did!'[44] Menzies took out a subscription to Santamaria's *News Weekly* and sent a further donation to its 'fund' in October 1976. Menzies told Santamaria that there was 'more sound political thinking' in *News Weekly* 'than in any of the newspapers' he subscribed to.[45]

Twelve-year-old Peter Wilmoth started a newspaper, *Our World*, to report on activities in Haverbrack Avenue. 'I would run articles about what kids were doing at school, about sprained fingers, surveys about pets, reviews of television shows, and reports about the pop music scene,' he recalled. But Wilmoth was looking for something bigger. He got a tip from his mother that senior Liberals were visiting the Menzies home, and dubbed the former prime minister the real 'leader of the opposition'. The ABC picked it up, and reported on the comings and goings at the Menzies house in the lead-up to the 1974 election. 'What can you expect of the ABC?' Menzies wrote to his daughter. The boy's father apologised to Pattie.[46]

Menzies maintained a keen interest in politics, although it had changed enormously — and none of it, he thought, for the better. In March 1975, Menzies dictated a note recalling how politicians in the past did their 'homework' on policy issues before speaking to the media. 'Politicians did not speak on matters of policy until they were ripe for the ultimate pronouncement,' Menzies said. 'In my time we had not entered the era in which brash young men shoved their microphones into the teeth of their victims and tried to persuade them to make kerbstone announcements on policy,' he said. 'A public man, who is worth his salt, must do a lot of serious thought and study. It is ridiculous for him to be bashed around by semi-literate people whose qualifications are unknown, but whose vanity knows no bounds.'[47]

More than half a century after he retired, Menzies remains the only Australian prime minister to leave office at a time of his own choosing. Only two other prime ministers could be said to have relinquished office without suffering the ignominy of defeat at the ballot box, being rejected by their colleagues, or losing support on the floor of the parliament: Edmund Barton and Andrew Fisher. Barton resigned as prime minister in September 1903 to join the High Court of Australia. Fisher vacated the prime ministership in October 1915 to take up the post of high commissioner to London.

Yet Menzies should have retired earlier, perhaps shortly after the 1963 election. Polls indicated that a majority of voters thought he should have left office by mid-1965. He was, as he said, tired, and soon suffered a stroke. More importantly, Menzies was increasingly out of step with the views of his colleagues — and indeed voters — on several policy fronts. A departure in 1963 or 1964 would have avoided his being inexorably linked to the disaster of Vietnam. It is telling that the Holt government moved quickly to overturn the Menzies cabinet decision on the White Australia policy and significantly expand the scope of the referendum concerning Aboriginal Australians. Menzies could not bring himself to accept the 'winds of change' sweeping through Africa, and this was particularly evident in relation to apartheid in South Africa. John F. Kennedy was elected United States president in November 1960, and represented a new era of global leadership. Kennedy was born in May 1917; Menzies, in December 1894. It was another sign that, as Kennedy said, the torch had been passed to a new generation.

While Menzies stayed too long, his was nevertheless an exemplary departure from the prime ministership. Menzies was in total command of his party and cabinet when he left. The security of his position was not in doubt. He had the respect of most voters, and exited public life with the tributes and goodwill of the vast majority of Australians. 'As I listened to his reminiscences and his reasons for retiring, I was left in no doubt Menzies was making a sound judgement,' Eggleton recalled of their summer days at Kirribilli House. 'After such a long and successful political career, it was appropriate and admirable that he was handing over the leadership in his own time and in his own way.'[48]

CHAPTER 19

Successors

ROBERT Menzies led the Liberal Party for 21 years. In the ten years that followed his retirement, the Liberal Party cycled through four leaders: Harold Holt, John Gorton, Billy McMahon, and Billy Snedden, before settling on Malcolm Fraser. Stability gave way to a series of short-term leaders who, other than Fraser, lost the confidence of the party room or the voters. In the final decade of his life, Menzies watched in horror as his party was plagued with instability. 'I am witnessing the destruction of the party,' he wrote to his daughter shortly after Holt's death. 'The party which I handed on has become a leaderless rabble, and I have great fears for the future.'[1] Eventually, in 1972, the Coalition tumbled to defeat. In that election — and quite likely in 1969 and 1974 — Menzies could not bring himself to vote for the party that he had led for more than two decades.

On 3 April 1974, Menzies was visited by journalist David McNicoll, and 'granted a lengthy interview' that was published in *The Bulletin* later that month. Menzies lashed Holt for doing 'nothing right', and said his 'besetting sin' was that 'he wanted everybody to love him'. The Liberal grandee reserved his judgement on Gorton, but said McMahon was 'a contemptible squirt' and 'a dreadful little man', and Snedden was 'a hopeless leader'. He expressed admiration for Fraser and Hasluck. The article was explosive.[2] Menzies' family were outraged, and claimed that he had been recorded and quoted without his consent.

The transcript of the interview was later published in full in McNicoll's autobiography, *Luck's a Fortune*, in 1979.[3] In McNicoll's papers at the State Library of New South Wales is a letter he received from Heather Henderson. 'It makes me sad that you in your old age should compound the errors of judgement my father made in his,' she wrote on 15 December 1979. 'His errors were to let you bring the tape recorder after he had asked you not to, and then, believing you to be an old friend, to trust you when he understood it would be used for background only.' Henderson accused McNicoll of 'cold-bloodedly making money' out of her father after his death.[4] McNicoll replied on 9 January 1980, stating he had not broken any undertaking given to Menzies, nor had he taken advantage of him in his old age. 'If I have caused distress I sincerely regret it,' he said. 'I hope you will someday feel regret at the harshness of that statement.'[5]

Following Menzies' death in May 1978, Frances McNicoll — David McNicoll's sister-in-law — wrote an article for *The Bulletin* disclosing snippets of what Menzies had told her about his colleagues in the interviews for her long-planned biography. But his more detailed comments about his successors, from Holt to Fraser, have not been published before. In these assessments about the failures of those who led the Liberal Party after him, Menzies did not hold back.

HAROLD Holt, his long-time deputy, was not up to the job of being prime minister, Menzies thought. 'Harold was a terrific disappointment to me,' he said.[6] 'He wanted to be liked by everybody. In just every matter he could not say something that he thought somebody might dislike.' Menzies thought that 'poor Harold' had 'coasted along on the momentum' the government had when Menzies left, and then, in his second year, 'made every conceivable error'. Holt's handling of the VIP aircraft scandal, especially, shattered Menzies' confidence in him.[7]

Menzies thought Holt had been a good minister and deputy leader. 'As a minister, as a subordinate, he was good,' Menzies said. 'He knew about politics, he knew about the House, he could get on with the Members, and all that kind of thing. As a lieutenant, he was admirable, and I thought he ought to do well.' But Menzies became 'bitterly disappointed' by Holt. 'He didn't realise that the job of prime minister is occasionally to be unpopular, occasionally to do things that some of his people and some of his friends don't like,' Menzies said. 'The result was, of course, that never having any fibre about him, he just fell from one disaster to another.'[8]

This is a harsh assessment, given that Holt had led the Coalition to a landslide election victory in November 1966. Menzies thought Holt might draw on his experience and ask for advice from time to time. 'He would have liked Harold to have been in touch with him a bit more than he was,' Eggleton said. 'I remember on one occasion when Menzies gave me a ring [on the telephone], which was just a sort of general chat, he did intimate that Harold hadn't rung him very much.'[9]

Holt disappeared in the surf at Cheviot Beach, off Portsea, on 17 December 1967. Menzies thought Holt was a deeply troubled man and 'unbalanced' at the time he plunged into the ocean. 'By the time of his famous disappearance, he was a nervous wreck,' Menzies said. 'By about October that year, he was taking sedatives, tablets — what do you call those things — tranquillisers, swallowing them and eating them ... he was all of a twitter.'[10]

Within hours of Holt's disappearance, John McEwen manoeuvred to have himself sworn in as prime minister. Menzies considered that Paul Hasluck was the best person to succeed Holt and encouraged him to nominate for the leadership and to campaign hard for it. On 9 January 1968, the Liberal Party met to choose its new leader. McEwen had placed a veto on Billy McMahon, the deputy leader, who consequently did not contest the ballot. Gorton was the most active in lobbying for party-room support, even at Holt's funeral, while Hasluck made only a perfunctory effort to win over his colleagues. There were four candidates: Hasluck, Gorton, Snedden, and Les Bury. Snedden and Bury were eliminated on the first ballot. In the second ballot, Gorton easily defeated Hasluck by 51 votes to 30.[11]

Hasluck wrote to Menzies shortly after Gorton was sworn in as prime minister. 'Thank you for the encouragement and support that you gave to me,' he wrote. 'I was much more hopeful than the results justified.' Hasluck noted there would be trouble ahead for Gorton. McMahon had 'carried out a brilliantly clever operation', which had benefited Gorton. 'We were moving towards difficult times even before Harold's death,' Hasluck wrote. 'If Harold had lived I think we would have been in a dreadful mess within the next six months.'[12]

Menzies recalled that he always found Gorton to be 'faintly irritating'. Gorton 'wanted to be different' in party-room meetings, and would often express a contrary view, seemingly just for the sake of it. But Menzies' opinion improved as he recognised that Gorton was a man with 'a mind of his own'.[13] Menzies found Gorton to be a diligent minister, but thought he was often reluctant to consult with state governments on education policy because he was 'a unificationist at heart'. There was another problem with Gorton. 'I found he always had some ideas, always quite willing to express them and could express them very well,' Menzies said. 'But he was no lover of the detail. He used to avoid the detail; somebody else could bother about the details.'[14]

In December 1958, Menzies appointed Gorton as minister for the navy. He was then offered the post of ambassador to Washington, but declined — Gorton had bigger ambitions.[15] During the Balaclava by-election in July 1960, Menzies suggested to Gorton that he consider moving from the Senate to the House with the leadership in mind. Menzies thought his political skills could be further developed if he made the switch to the other chamber. 'If you want to see a future as prime minister, you must go into the lower house and face the music,' Menzies instructed. 'You cannot sit aloof and aloft in the Senate, old boy.' Gorton rejected the advice. Menzies believed making Gorton prime minister was a mistake. 'That was a terrible blunder,' he judged. 'He was not prepared to face the music intellectually, in terms of nervous strain, in terms of political battling, which a man has to in the lower house.'[16]

Menzies was shocked to see Gorton say that the prime minister's view should always prevail in cabinet. Menzies' motto was *primus inter pares*, he said. 'I thought this was a denial of cabinet government.'[17] Menzies was also appalled that Gorton edged aside John Bunting to make Lenox Hewitt head of the prime minister's department. Menzies was also cranky when the government cancelled the use of a car and driver for him when in London without telling him — a decision soon reversed. When the Coalition suffered a huge swing of 7.1 per cent against it on two-party-preferred terms at the October 1969 election, Menzies saw it as 'a swing against the prime minister'.[18]

Malcolm Fraser remembered Menzies railing against Gorton. 'He thought that John Gorton was a wild man who was going to destroy the party,' Fraser told me.[19] Doug Anthony also visited Menzies in his retirement years. 'We talked about what was happening in politics, what I was doing in opposition or in government, and he liked me to tell him jokes — even quite rude ones,' he recalled. Anthony was deputy prime minister under Gorton, McMahon, and Fraser. 'He was disillusioned with the Liberal Party in those years, particularly with John Gorton,' Anthony said of Menzies. 'He couldn't stand Gorton's personal behaviour. And he was right about that. It wasn't prime ministerial. But then again, he didn't think many people were as bright and clever as he was.'[20]

After Gorton effectively resigned following a party-room confidence motion being tied at 33–33 on 10 March 1971, McMahon became prime minister. Menzies always had a poor opinion of McMahon. 'He is a fool,' Menzies said.[21] He regarded his successor as untrustworthy, lacking in intellect and judgement, and without any shred of authority, integrity, or credibility. Menzies described McMahon as a 'little brute'.[22]

Menzies had initially been magnanimous when McMahon became prime minister. 'My dear "PM" — Bill,' he wrote to McMahon after they spoke on the phone. 'Old men are soon forgotten, particularly in politics, and both Pat and I were really thrilled to hear from you. You have my warm good wishes as you approach what seems to me the great and difficult task of promoting responsible cabinet government, established on fundamental Liberal principles.' Menzies made a request: that Malcolm Fraser be returned to cabinet.[23] 'He is able, but for the time being it will not do him any harm to remain in [sic] the back benches,' McMahon replied.[24] This would have irritated Menzies. Fraser eventually returned to cabinet in August 1971.[25]

MENZIES became so disillusioned with the Liberal Party that he certainly voted for the Democratic Labour Party in December 1972, and quite possibly also in October 1969 and May 1974. It is likely he gave his preference vote to the Liberal Party. Heather Henderson confirmed to me that her father did not vote Liberal in 1972. 'I can remember him telling us about that,' she said. 'A lot of things were done that he would not have done himself. It's very hard when you've been in a job like that not to be critical of whoever takes over from you. He would sit in front of the television, criticise, and complain about what was being done.' Henderson is reasonably sure that her father strayed only once.[26]

Menzies was not the only former leader who did not vote for his old party. Arthur Calwell did not vote Labor in December 1972. Menzies and Calwell confided their votes to each other. Mary Elizabeth Calwell, his daughter, told me that her father 'was very concerned about the future of the Labor Party under Whitlam's leadership', and she could not be certain who he voted for at that election. 'I don't know,' she conceded. 'He always said to put the communists and the Liberals last. He certainly wouldn't have voted DLP. My father and Menzies were good friends. Whitlam was disloyal to my father, and tried to marginalise him inside the party.'[27]

As Menzies' retirement interviews demonstrate, he did not approve of Gorton, McMahon, or Snedden. It is therefore quite possible that he also did not vote Liberal in either 1969, when Gorton was leader, or 1974, when Snedden was leader. B.A. Santamaria first mentioned Menzies' errant voting in columns for *The Australian* in the 1980s and 1990s — and said he did it twice.[28] Journalist Wallace Brown wrote that Menzies did not vote Liberal in 1969 and 1972.[29] Gerard Henderson says it is likely that Menzies did not vote Liberal in 1972 and 1974.[30] Fraser recalled Menzies' disappointment with the Liberal Party. 'He certainly was disillusioned with the party,' Fraser said. He was in no doubt, however, that Menzies returned to the fold and voted Liberal in 1975 and 1977.[31]

The fact that the Liberal Party suffered a leadership deficit in the aftermath of Menzies' retirement, cascading through Holt, Gorton, McMahon, and Snedden, does not say much for Menzies' capacity to groom and mentor leaders to succeed him. Menzies, in many ways, *was* the Liberal Party. It was always going to be difficult for any successor to step into those shoes. While Menzies cannot be held accountable for the failures of Holt, Gorton, McMahon, and Snedden, it begs the question as to whether he should have done more to prepare them, or others, for leadership. By the late 1960s, the Liberal Party was not exactly flush with talent. Perhaps Menzies should have promoted others from within the party's parliamentary ranks and worked with the party organisation to facilitate the entry of others into parliament who might be future leadership material.

ROBERT Menzies thought Liberal salvation would only come when Malcolm Fraser was made leader. But Fraser, given his role in John Gorton's downfall, remained on the outer of the party. He was seen as aloof, arrogant, and self-centred. Following the election of the Whitlam government, the Liberal Party met on 20 December 1972 to elect a new leader. There were five candidates: Fraser, Gorton, Snedden, Jim Killen, and Nigel Bowen. Early ballots eliminated Killen, and then Gorton and Fraser. A run-off ballot between Bowen and Snedden was tied 29–29. Bruce Graham, the returning officer, then realised he had forgotten to vote. A fifth ballot finally elected Snedden over Bowen by 30–29 votes. (No prize for guessing who Graham voted for.) Snedden was the youngest leader of the party, at the age of 45. Phillip Lynch was elected deputy leader after an exhaustive ballot contested by Fraser, Killen, Andrew Peacock, Don Chipp, and Jim Forbes.[32]

Menzies thought Snedden was a terrible leader. 'The Liberal Party in the federal parliament is completely hopeless and leaderless,' Menzies wrote to Frances McNicoll in August 1973. 'Snedden was quite a good junior minister working under cabinet direction but, as leader of a battered party in opposition, he seems to me to not have a clue.' Menzies was concerned about the Whitlam government's domestic and foreign policies, and considered writing another book that would set out his 'views on some contemporary problems'. He did not think the Liberal Party was capable of effective opposition. 'What state of despair I am in, driven by the incompetence and the lack of courage of my present successors in the federal parliament,' he wrote.[33] He did not get around to writing another book.

Menzies did not like the direction that the Liberal Party was taking. 'I think I have never felt worse about politics,' he wrote to his daughter in April 1974. 'The idiots who now run the Liberal Party will drive me right round the bend.' In Victoria, he railed against Liberals with a small 'l' whom he described as 'Liberals who believe in nothing but who will believe in anything if they think it worth a few votes.' This was not

Menzies necessarily endorsing conservatives within the party, but a reaffirmation that liberalism had to stand apart from Labor's 'socialism' with clear principles and policies so the voters had a choice. He also opposed the Liberal policy of denying supply to Labor — a position he later reversed. 'The House of Representatives is the House that is in charge of the finances of the country,' he wrote to Heather Henderson. 'The Senate can quite properly reject individual bills, but for the Senate to deny supply to the government of the country is a matter without precedent.'[34]

In another previously unpublished interview, in December 1973, Menzies thought the Liberal and Country parties should merge, with Fraser and Anthony as the leadership team. He also suggested that the Democratic Labour Party be invited into the fold, perhaps in coalition, with its leader, Frank McManus, being made a minister. As it happened, McManus lost his Victorian Senate seat at the May 1974 election. (Menzies also suggested 'a political fusion' between the Coalition and the Democratic Labour Party to David McNicoll in April 1974.[35])

> If you could get these parties together, plus the DLP, and have Malcolm Fraser and Doug Anthony, with little Lynch bringing up the artillery at the rear, I think they would sweep the country. And if they did, I would establish a cabinet with [Frank] McManus as a minister, giving the DLP recognition.[36]

Menzies said he 'would not hesitate' to change the leader of the Liberal Party. He thought Snedden's suggestion that the party room elect the ministry was 'idiotic'. He shuddered at the thought that Snedden might actually lead the Liberals back to government and become prime minister.[37] Menzies was so disillusioned with the Liberal Party that he wrote to former minister Hubert Opperman, suggesting, surely in jest, that his party might even make Whitlam its leader. 'I would not put it past the Liberal Party in opposition to offer him the leadership,' Menzies wrote in July 1974. 'In our time, this, of course, would have been unthinkable but, in these days of little "L" Liberals, without any principles whatever, it might happen!'[38]

Menzies went public with a critique of the Liberal Party to mark his 80th birthday in December 1974. 'I was the founder of the Liberal

Party in Australia and have, of course, a personal interest in its future,' he noted. 'Many things that I believed in, and many of the principles which made the Liberal Party, have so far been forgotten or put on one side that I am deeply concerned about the future.' Menzies thought the party was losing its way. 'When we commenced the Liberal Party we had principles,' he said. 'Principles are apparently nowadays things that are not to be insisted upon because to insist upon them is to demonstrate that you are "reactionary" or "conservative". This, of course, is the most pernicious nonsense.'[39]

In the first three years after he retired, Robert Menzies wondered why no Liberal MP had asked for his view on anything.[40] This was probably an exaggeration, but not too much of one. Indeed, journalist Alan Ramsey wrote in September 1968 that Menzies had 'faded into relative insignificance' and become 'virtually a forgotten man'. For most Australians, Ramsey suggested, Menzies evoked 'no reverence, no compassion, no lasting charisma'. Among Liberals, the Menzies era was seen as one to put behind them.[41] One of the few former colleagues who did visit him was Alexander 'Alick' Downer, who had served as minister for immigration (1958–63). He would usually visit Menzies when in Melbourne, and admonished those former colleagues who did not. 'We should all be going and sitting at the feet of Gamaliel,' Downer said.[42] (Gamaliel the Elder was a first-century Jewish rabbi, and member of the Sanhedrin, known for his knowledge and wisdom.)

When the Liberal Party began to reassess the Menzies' legacy in the late 1960s and early 1970s — not always positively — Malcolm Fraser was one of the few who defended him. Fraser was also a regular visitor to Menzies' office and home after his retirement, and stayed in touch with him after he became Liberal leader and prime minister. Fraser learned by studying Menzies in parliament and the party room, and the tutorials continued in his retirement. 'The meetings were really social, because I liked him [and] he was lonely,' Fraser recalled. 'He was good company anyway, and if you picked up something else, well, it was a bonus.'[43]

Menzies disapproved of Fraser's resignation from Gorton's cabinet on 8 March 1971 over a dispute regarding civil-aid policy in Vietnam, and his savage speech which lit the fuse that eventually brought down the prime minister. 'That was a very great tactical error,' Menzies said in a 1973 interview.[44] Menzies issued a statement at the time denying he knew about Fraser's resignation in advance — but he did acknowledge that Fraser mentioned he was going 'to make a statement' about the issue.[45] However, Fraser claimed that he discussed the speech with Menzies in advance and that he 'didn't disapprove' of it.[46] In any event, Menzies saw leadership qualities in Fraser that he saw in nobody else.

After the May 1974 election, Liberal MP Tony Staley began organising support for Fraser to become leader. Fraser kept his distance from the plotting, but did not discourage it. Staley decided to make an appeal to Menzies to support Fraser, and rang him at home in Melbourne. Staley was a little nervous when Menzies answered the phone. Staley said who he was and that he was organising a challenge against Snedden. 'My dear boy, I wish you well,' Menzies responded. 'Fraser is the only one with any hint of statesmanship about him.' Staley was thrilled. But Menzies had not finished. 'Alas, I have to say, you're doomed to fail,' he added. 'Why is that, Sir Robert?' Staley asked. 'They're all so stupid up there,' Menzies said. Staley told me he used Menzies' endorsement to drum up party-room support for Fraser.[47]

Sure enough, Menzies was right. Snedden survived a spill motion to force a leadership ballot instigated by Staley on 27 November 1974. Yet Snedden's days were numbered. Just four months later, on 21 March 1975, a spill motion was successful. Fraser challenged Snedden for the leadership, and won by 37 votes to 27.[48]

On 16 October 1975, the opposition blocked the Whitlam government's supply bills in the Senate. The purpose was to force the government to an election or pressure the governor-general, John Kerr, to dismiss the government and dissolve the parliament. Fraser was not sure how Menzies would react. 'Malcolm, you're going to have to retreat,' Menzies told him on 1 November. 'Sir, I don't know how to retreat,' Fraser said. 'We're right; and we are going to have to give him a lashing, and I believe we will.'[49] Fraser had done his homework, and discovered that Menzies had supported blocking supply in Victoria decades earlier. 'Anyway, he didn't like what we had done, but thought we had no option,' Fraser said.[50]

Doug Anthony also talked with Menzies during the constitutional crisis. During one visit while Menzies was resident at Mount Royal

Hospital in Melbourne, the former prime minister proceeded to 'lecture' Anthony about the irresponsibility of blocking supply. 'You should not be acting like this,' Menzies said. Anthony was riled. He proceeded to litigate the failures of the Whitlam government. 'We can't just sit back and let Australia disintegrate,' he insisted. Menzies stayed silent, mulling it over. As Anthony got up to leave, Menzies looked at him and said, 'Douglas, you've made my day!'[51] Menzies, it seemed, was changing his mind about blocking supply.

On 11 November 1975, Kerr dismissed the Whitlam government. Menzies enthusiastically supported the dismissal. Kerr met Menzies several times at his home, and corresponded with him, after the dismissal. 'Your conduct in this matter has been, in my opinion, beyond reproach,' Menzies wrote to Kerr on 19 November. Menzies said Kerr had 'displayed remarkable moral courage in doing what I believe to have been your duty', and offered his 'congratulations and my profound admiration'. It was the reassurance that Kerr craved. 'Your letter was a great comfort to me,' Kerr replied on 21 November. 'I have, as you would realise, been through a very difficult period but I am in a state of reasonable calm, being convinced that I have done the only thing possible and also that what I have done is right.'[52]

Menzies also provided a political justification for Kerr's actions. In an extraordinary unpublished article written by Menzies in January 1976 that was sent to Kerr, the Liberal Party elder statesman described Whitlam as 'a complete fool' with 'a rather superficial knowledge of the constitution', who was 'a bad loser'. Menzies also ridiculously described Whitlam as 'a kind of Hitler', and his 1975 election campaign launch as 'like a Nuremberg Rally'. Menzies said Fraser had 'saved Australia from disaster'.[53]

After the Queen's visit in March 1977, Kerr confided to Menzies his thoughts about relinquishing the vice-regal post, given the public backlash that he faced. The palace had little respect for Kerr, and the governor-general's relations with Fraser post-dismissal were never warm. Kerr wrote to Menzies, asking 'whether this nation would be helped by a resignation'. This is a remarkable letter. But Menzies told Kerr to hold firm and to banish thoughts of a premature retirement. This advice 'was [an] enormous help to me,' Kerr replied.[54] (Kerr relinquished the vice-regal post in December 1977.)

During the election campaign following the dismissal, Menzies spoke occasionally to Malcolm and Tamie Fraser to offer his support and encouragement, and to give advice on strategy. He could be a hard marker:

You were badly advised about your broadcast the other night. You appeared to be using the 'idiot board' and looking everywhere except into the lens of the camera. You're easily at your best when you are speaking your own words direct to the audience. When, as on the last occasion, you appeared to be reading what somebody else has written, you lose the impact of your own personality. And it is your own personality which will win this election.[55]

He also wrote notes to Tamie during the campaign:

May an old campaigner tell you how much he admires what you have been doing in the course of this campaign. You have not only handled your interviews with great charm and skill, but you have been of tremendous assistance to Malcolm. I am now convinced that he will win on Saturday. I would like you to convey to him my belief that this will be a great personal triumph, a complete vindication of his character and attainments.[56]

Menzies watched the election-night coverage on television at home. He was ecstatic when the Liberals were returned to power. Menzies, however, did not agree with everything that the Fraser government later did. Heather Henderson recalls her father critiquing the Fraser government. 'He did want Fraser to get it, but he found him disappointing,' she recalled. 'I can remember him sitting in front of the television and saying, "Malcolm can do nothing right."'[57]

When Fraser proposed four referendums on 21 May 1977, Menzies made it clear that he disagreed with two of the proposals. First, he spoke out against federal judges having to retire automatically when they reached the age of 70. He noted that some of Australia's finest jurists — Samuel Griffith, Edmund Barton, Isaac Isaacs, Owen Dixon, and John Latham — were older than 70 when they sat on the High Court. Second, he opposed simultaneous elections for the House of Representatives and the Senate. He made a series of public statements condemning the move, which embarrassed Fraser.[58]

ROBERT Gordon Menzies suffered a heart attack while reading in the study of his home at 2 Haverbrack Avenue, Malvern, Victoria, in the afternoon of Monday 15 May 1978. He died in the arms of his doctor, and neighbour, George Morrison. Dame Pattie was also with him at the time.[59] Menzies was 83 years old. He was still seeing friends, family, and colleagues at home and at his office until days before his death. Menzies' appointment diary for that day reads: '4.15 pm — Sir Robert Menzies died peacefully at home.'[60]

Malcolm Fraser issued a statement paying tribute to Menzies. 'All Australians will mourn his passing,' he said. 'Sir Robert leaves an enduring mark on Australian history. His time as prime minister, from 1949–1966, was a time of stability and growth. He was the founder of the Liberal Party. He gave his party and his country strength and inspiration.' Fraser noted his counsel, support, and friendship, and extended his sympathy to Pattie and the Menzies family.[61]

A state funeral was held at Scots Church on Russell Street in Melbourne, beginning at 2.00 pm on 19 May 1978. Scores of politicians from around Australia and representatives from overseas governments joined with family and friends for a solemn service. Prince Charles, representing Queen Elizabeth II, attended. After the funeral, watched by around 100,000 people, Menzies' body was driven to Springvale crematorium, where a private family service took place.

Dame Pattie Menzies moved out of the Malvern home and bought a smaller house in Melbourne, where she lived for many years. She kept largely out of the media spotlight, but was often a guest at government functions and party events. In the last two years of her life, Pattie lived in Canberra to be closer to her daughter. In February 1994, the proceeds from the sale of the Malvern home were donated to Fintona Girls' School and Ruyton Girls' School in Melbourne, which had been attended respectively by Pattie and Heather. Dame Pattie died, age 96, at 7.45 am on 30 August 1995 in Canberra.[62]

Lessons in Leadership

ROBERT Menzies continues to loom large in Australian political life because he defined and dominated an era in Australian politics. He has never been matched for his record term in office or his election victories. And he set the standard against which all subsequent Liberal leaders are judged — but which they can never measure up to. He had authority, credibility, and respect, and he commanded attention. He ran an effective cabinet process, was a skilled administrator of government, and was a shrewd party manager. He had a guiding purpose, espoused a clear philosophy, and used these principles to inform policy development. He was a clever political strategist, a brilliant campaigner, and a persuasive speechmaker. It is understandable that contemporary Liberal leaders are eager to enlist Menzies to their cause. It is also understandable that some Labor leaders seek to delegitimise Menzies' legacy because it remains so important to the Liberal tradition.[1] The continuing debate over Menzies' place in history, his achievements and failures, and his enduring legacy, underscores his significance.

He governed during a period of strong economic growth, low unemployment, increasing wages, rising living standards, and an expanding home-owning middle class. It was a 'golden age' of prosperity and stability, and a continuation of the post-war nation-building ethos. Among his signature policy achievements are the huge expansion of universities and colleges; providing funding to non-government schools, which helped to end the sectarian divide; supporting families with home-savings grants, enhanced child endowment, and new health schemes; developing Canberra into a true national capital; cementing the alliance with the United States with the ANZUS Treaty; and forging new relationships in the Asia-Pacific region with initiatives such as the commerce agreement with Japan and the Colombo Plan.

Menzies, while admired by many world leaders, was less successful on the world stage. He was not able to convince Winston Churchill to reinforce Singapore during the Second World War. Sending troops to Vietnam was a strategic mistake, based on the false 'domino theory', which cost more than 500 Australian lives. He did not persuade John F. Kennedy to support the Dutch retaining West New Guinea, nor to intervene to help defend Malaysia in its confrontation with Indonesia. Menzies said he was 'British to his boot heels', and maintained an Anglophile outlook, even making the Queen blush with his 'I did but see her passing by' reference in 1963. He was one of the few leaders who lamented the waning influence of the Commonwealth. His support for the British in the Suez crisis was humiliating. And it is regrettable that he was reluctant to take a stronger moral and diplomatic stand against South Africa's apartheid policy, as other nations did.

The fear of communism, which was real at home and abroad, was so successfully exploited that it hastened the Labor Party split and helped to keep Menzies in power with the aid of preferences from the Democratic Labour Party. While he may have been helped by dispatching potential rivals such as Richard Casey, Percy Spender, and Garfield Barwick to plum postings at home and abroad, the truth is that they were no match for Menzies. More to the point, Labor's leaders, H.V. 'Doc' Evatt and Arthur Calwell, were no match for Menzies. Yet it is remarkable how close Evatt and Calwell came to leading Labor to victory when they won a majority of the two-party-preferred vote in 1954 and 1961, but not a majority of seats. Menzies' longevity was partly gifted by an opposition plagued by division and saddled with lacklustre leaders. Yet he also learned from his mistakes, and was able to rebuild his political standing, time and time again.

Menzies' policies were central to the shaping of modern Australia, and provided a 'golden era' of prosperity, but much of what he advocated has been left in the past. He was successful in defeating Labor's plans for nationalisation, and promoted liberalism within a conservative policy framework. Paul Kelly's description of the 'Australian Settlement' — Federation-era policies of industry protection, centralised industrial relations, the White Australia policy, state paternalism, and imperial benevolence — remained largely in place.[2] While Menzies championed free enterprise, he practised Keynesian economics, rarely balanced the budget, and expanded the size of government. He had little interest in Aboriginal Australians, the advancement of women, or promotion of the arts. He was a staunch supporter of the White Australia policy. Menzies' Australia is not the Australia of today. His Liberal successors moved quickly with initiatives in these areas of policy ossification. While Menzies was dominant when he retired, and under no pressure to vacate the prime ministership, most voters thought he should have retired earlier than he did. That is why it is best to assess Menzies in his own time.

The aspect of Menzies' legacy that has the most relevance today is his expertise in the art of politics. I identify five key elements of his approach to political leadership. First, he had a deep appreciation and understanding of the institutions of governance. He absorbed the British legal tradition, and admired Westminster parliamentary democracy and representative government. He believed in proper cabinet-government processes. He was an effective chair of cabinet who allowed ministers to have their say and a free rein to work their portfolios, but he could be brutal with those he judged to be poor performers. He respected the public service, and expected frank and fearless advice from it. His hard work, focus, and diligence meant that he was an effective administrator. He was skilled at parliamentary procedure, understood the importance of winning debates in parliament, and knew how to use the chamber for dramatic purposes. He was, after all, a born performer.

Second, he had purpose, belief, and conviction. He knew what he wanted to do, why he wanted to do it, and whom he represented. He had a vision guided by philosophy, principles, and clear values. This informed his approach to policy-making. He was able to work with public servants and ministers, and his party, to design policies, communicate them effectively to voters, and then make sure they were properly implemented.

Third, he understood the importance of party management. He was the principal founder of the Liberal Party. He developed the party's structure, drafted its constitution, vested it with a philosophy, and led it to power and kept it there for 16 years. This gave Menzies immense authority in leading the party. But this alone was not enough to be a good party manager. He developed effective relations with the party organisation, respected the broad membership, and was attentive to the needs of backbenchers, even though he did little to encourage or promote new talent, or to groom leadership successors. He also understood the importance of managing the coalition with the Country Party. He respected its leaders and their views, and made sure that any disagreements on policy, strategy, or personnel were satisfactorily dealt with.

Fourth, and it may be axiomatic for a prime minister, but Menzies was an astute politician. While not always popular — he never won the broad affection of voters — he was respected and admired. He knew that authority mattered more than popularity. He was a good strategist and tactician when it came to the timing of elections, the framing and communication of issues, and exploiting the weaknesses in his opponents. He was often cautious, but knew when to take a principled stand and when to make a pragmatic decision. The mark of any good politician is learning from his or her mistakes. Menzies was able to consolidate after repeated policy and political setbacks, and close election results, throughout his political career. While somewhat aloof and arrogant, perhaps due to his shyness, he maintained the support of his party for more than 20 years.

And, fifth, Menzies understood that politics is about persuasion, and that effective advocacy is based on a mix of logic, reason, and emotion. He was a brilliant orator, a superb parliamentary debater, and without peer on the campaign trail. He used his training as a lawyer, his understanding of history, and his wide reading of literature, poetry, plays, history, and biography to prepare effective speeches, write articles, and develop policies. He was a skilled radio broadcaster, and adapted his speaking style successfully to television, using both mediums to enhance his presentation of political arguments and policy issues to voters.

Menzies believed that politics was an honourable profession that ought to attract the brightest talent the country could offer. He gave up a lucrative career in the law because he believed he had a duty to serve the nation. He was not motivated by an overweening ambition, the accoutrements of office, or, as a kid who grew up in Jeparit, endowed with a born-to-rule mentality. He thought politics should be a battle of ideas rather than a clash of personalities, political slogans, and advertising campaigns. This is not to say that he eschewed political combat, but it was always geared towards a larger purpose. Indeed, he enjoyed genuine friendships on the opposite side of politics. He had a deep commitment to Australia, and his intellect and integrity were never questioned. There was not a hint of scandal when he retired. And he left politics at a time of his own choosing — a feat that none of his successors so far has emulated.

Menzies' most contemporarily relevant legacy was to establish a model for effective leadership that provided stability and unity, with clear policy direction and philosophical conviction, that resulted in continued electoral success and longevity in government. These were the hallmarks of his important and consequential prime ministership, from 1949 to 1966, and underscore how he mastered the art of politics.

Acknowledgements

WRITING a book about Robert Menzies is a daunting prospect. So my deepest appreciation goes to his daughter, Heather Henderson, who hosted me at her home for interviews in August 2014 and in October 2017. We have talked on the phone and corresponded by mail. Heather has been exceptionally generous with her time, and her insights have been invaluable. Her two books, *Letters to My Daughter* (2011) and *A Smile for My Parents* (2013), provide an inimitable window into her father and reveal the real man behind the public stereotype. Heather's approval for me to use her father's unpublished interviews with Frances McNicoll has left me with a debt that I hope I have, if only in part, repaid with this book. I shall always be very grateful.

I am also fortunate to have had the opportunity to interview several of Menzies' ministerial and parliamentary colleagues. To spend a day with Doug Anthony at his farm, Sunnymeadows, in November 2014 was an immense privilege. I conducted a long interview with Doug before and after lunch, and walked around the property with him. We have spoken on the phone many times since. To visit Ian Sinclair at Mulberry Farm in April 2017 and talk about his life in politics was also a great honour. We had a terrific seafood lunch in town, where I saw firsthand what a great politician he still is as many people approached our table to talk to him. We have also spoken on the phone occasionally and exchanged emails. In March 2017, I interviewed John Carrick. This was one of the most moving interviews I have conducted. He provided an invaluable insight into the formation of the Liberal Party and Menzies' leadership. Carrick was a true gentleman of Australian politics, and a man of unimpeachable integrity and extraordinary humanity. I shall never forget it. He died in May 2018. The third still living, but only Liberal, minister from the Menzies government is Dr A.J. 'Jim' Forbes. I visited him at his home in Adelaide in December 2018, where I conducted an interview for this book. It was two days before his 95th birthday. As he sat in his lounge chair, surrounded by books, magazines, and newspapers, we talked about his memories of the Menzies era. It was an afternoon that I shall always treasure.

Another important insight I gained about the Menzies era came from Malcolm Fraser. I interviewed Fraser at his office in Melbourne in September 2002 and April 2013, and on the phone many times. In the years before he died, we spoke occasionally and exchanged text messages. Fraser was very kind to me, and always encouraged my writing and study. Fraser had spent more than a decade in parliament with Menzies. He was one of the few who had a regular dialogue with Menzies in his retirement. I learned a lot from Fraser, and wish he was still with us. I also thank Tamie Fraser for giving me permission to publish a photo of her and Malcolm with Menzies in 1958.

William Heseltine worked as Menzies' private secretary in the 1950s and continued to have an association with him while working for the Liberal Party and at Buckingham Palace in the 1960s and 1970s. It has been terrific to interview Bill on the phone and also twice in person, in September 2015 and June 2017, about his memories of Menzies. Tony Eggleton is perhaps the most important person to serve the Liberal Party who was never in its parliamentary ranks. Tony has also been especially generous in granting me two interviews about his relationship with Liberal leaders in October 2013 and June 2017, and another with Paul Kelly in July 2015. We have also spoken on the phone and corresponded regularly by email, and he provided me with his unpublished memoir.

I would like to thank those who also shared their recollections and impressions of the Menzies era with me for articles in *The Australian*, and for this and previous books, including Tony Abbott, Mary Elizabeth Calwell, Peter Costello, Graham Freudenberg, Jon Gaul, Nick Greiner, Bill Hayden, Lenox Hewitt, Sam Holt, David Kemp, Brendan Nelson, Andrew Peacock, Tony Staley, Richard Woolcott, and the late Cyril Wyndham. I also refer to a memorable conversation I had with Gough Whitlam about Arthur Calwell in May 2007.

I especially thank Henry Rosenbloom for publishing our third book together, and his terrific team at Scribe for their hard work and dedication in making it the best it could be. The Menzies Foundation provided me with access to Frances McNicoll's interviews with Robert Menzies, and I thank Sarah Hardy and Kate Nolan for facilitating this. The staff of the National Library of Australia and the National Archives of Australia have always been helpful in accessing archival material. I want to especially acknowledge Catriona Anderson, Margy Burn, Damian Cole, Duncan Felton, and Kate Boesen at the National Library. I appreciate the assistance of staff at the National Archives, including David Fricker and Louise Doyle, and for allowing me to reproduce several photos from their collection. The Museum of Australian Democracy at Old Parliament House provided funding to compile an index for the book, and for this I am indebted to Daryl Karp and Michael Evans. I appreciate the support of my colleagues at *The Australian*, particularly editor-in-chief Chris Dore, former editor-in-chief Paul Whittaker, and editors John Lehmann and Michelle Gunn, for affording me the time to write books. Picture editor Milan Scepanovic generously sourced several photos from the News Corp archives, and has my further thanks.

Wendy Zanker from the Jeparit and District Historical Society and Wendy Werner from the Wimmera Mallee Pioneer Museum kindly made available several archival records and photos which were useful in the writing of this book. I would also like to acknowledge for their assistance: Manuela Furci (Rennie Ellis Photographic Archive), Jillian Hisock (Royal Historical Society of Victoria), Sally Laming (John Curtin Prime Ministerial Library), Evan Mulholland (Institute of Public Affairs), Caitlin Stone (University of Melbourne), Garry Sturgess (for access to his oral history interviews), Leo Terpstra (Commonwealth Parliamentary Library) and Georgina Ward (University of Melbourne).

My deep gratitude also extends to my friend and colleague Paul Kelly, who has always been encouraging and supportive of my work as a journalist and author. He read the manuscript, and provided many valuable suggestions. Paul set the standard, an impossible one, for writing books on Australian politics. This book is, accordingly, dedicated to him.

John Howard first met Menzies at a cocktail party at the Lodge in 1964. Howard, like Menzies, was not only an astute politician but also a knowledgeable historian of Australian politics. His impressive book, *The Menzies Era* (2014), was an important source while I was writing this book. I could not have been more thrilled when he agreed to read this book in manuscript form and provide me with feedback. I have had the pleasure of discussing politics and interviewing Howard many times at his Sydney office overlooking the city and harbour, and I have drawn on them in this book.

John Nethercote, a renowned expert on all things Menzies, also read the manuscript with an eagle eye, and provided me with exceptionally detailed suggestions, amendments, and corrections. We had several long discussions about Menzies, including for two hours while watching the water lap the shore at Sydney's Double Bay, and also on the phone. Nethercote's own books, including *Menzies: the shaping of modern Australia* (2016), were another indispensable source during the researching and writing of this book.

I was elated when the multi-talented Clive James agreed to read the manuscript and then provided me with useful feedback and encouragement. As a teenager, I was transfixed watching his television series, *Fame in the 20th Century*, and subsequently read his many memoirs, books of essays and poetry. I could not imagine that he would read anything I wrote, let alone allow me to interview him for *The Australian*. I must also thank eminent historian Ian Hancock, who wrote one of the great Australian political biographies on John Gorton, for also reading the manuscript and providing comments. His scholarship on the Liberal Party was essential research for this book. I am also lucky to have two close friends with an interest in politics and history, John Degen and Ben Heraghty, who provided very thoughtful feedback on the manuscript, for which I am also very grateful.

It has been great to talk to my parents, Jeff and Michele Bramston, about their memories of the Menzies era, and I also valued their comments on the manuscript. My amazing children, Madison and Angus, are more knowledgeable about an aspect of Australian politics than they really need to be at their age, and tolerated my occasional absences. They also joined me and my wife, Nicky Seaby, on a roadtrip to Menzies' birthplace, Jeparit, in January 2019. It would have been much harder to write this book without Nicky's loving support. For her astute advice and much-needed reassurance, she has, as always, my endless affection.

Appendix

ON the following pages is an analysis of the August 1943 election campaign written by Robert Menzies. This landmark document, discovered among his papers at the National Library of Australia, and circulated at the time to his parliamentary colleagues, served as a blueprint for the formation of the Liberal Party of Australia the following year. In this document, Menzies articulates the philosophy, structure, and ethos of the new party that, in late 1943, he thought should be named the 'Liberal Democratic Party'.

*C O N F I D E N T I A L.

SOME LESSONS OF THE ELECTION.

It occurs to me that it may be useful to set out, even in a sketchy way, certain impressions that have formed in my mind as a result of the recent disastrous election; because if we are to recover sufficiently to win the next contest I am satisfied that some plain lessons will have to be learned and some very drastic new action taken.

1.   It seems to me that the principal reasons for the Labour victory were:-

    (a)   The prestige of Mr. Curtin, aided as it was by sharp divisions in the Opposition;

    (b)   "Don't shoot Father Christmas";

    (c)   "Why should my son have to go thousands of miles from Australia to defend it?"

At the same time, these are mere assumptions on my part. I would strongly recommend that a small Research Organisation be at once set to work to discover, on the ground level, what were the leading causes of the debacle.

2.   As usual, we were much too late in our selection of important candidates. There can be little doubt that if Captain Gullett had been selected a month earlier he would have won Henty handsomely. There seems equally little doubt that our practice of selecting the Senate team at the very last moment prevents its members from making any sort of individual mark upon the electorate. Usually there is no reason whatever why, when elections come - as this one did- at a normal time, candidates should not be selected at least six months ahead.

3.   I do not know who determines the order of preference to be recommended to the people, but in at least two electorates the recommendation was so fantastic as to be quite unintelligible. The U.A.P. Candidate for Bourke could not possibly win. Apart from whipping up a Senate vote his real function was to direct his second preferences in such a way as to do the greatest dis-service to Labour. Yet his card apparently put Mr. Blackburn last. This will undoubtedly give Mr. Curtin great satisfaction, because it will probably mean the elimination of a Member who would otherwise have continued to trouble him. Similarly in Reid, one learns that the U.A.P. ticket preferred Mr. Morgan to Mr. Lang. This action is beyond my understanding, because there can be little doubt that if Lang were elected he would be a greater menace to the Government than half the Opposition put together.

4.   The Curtin halo, legend, and personality as the public sees them have really been built up by the extraordinarily skilful and devoted services of Mr. Curtin's Press Officer, Mr.D.K. Rodgers. Not only does he understand the kind of thing that people like to read, but his personal contacts with other pressmen are such as to work constantly for his Chief's advantage. On our side we have had painstaking and conscientious but entirely uninspired work. The Leader of the Opposition must be provided with an absolutely first-class press officer. This may very well involve financial assistance from the Party organisations.

5.   Our organisation has completely failed to understand the great importance of State electorates and State elections. At the Victorian general election, for example, Labour Federal Ministers came in droves to take part in the campaign. The U.A.P. organisation not only failed to organise any such campaign but actually failed to produce candidates at all in many electorates which were held by the Party only a few years ago. The effect of this upon Federal electorates should be clear enough. Take Wannon, for example, which until three years ago was held by a U.A.P. Member in the Federal Parliament, and which on this occasion was contested by the sitting Labour Member, a U.A.P. candidate and a C.P. candidate. Wannon includes the State electorates of Warrnambool,Glenelg,

- 2 -

Lowan and Stawell/Ararat (all held by C.P. Members) and Dundas, held by a Labour Member. Only a few years ago Warrnambool and Stawell/Ararat were held by U.A.P. Members, while there has always been a substantial U.A.P. vote in Lowan. Yet I think I am right in saying that in not one of these seats did the U.A.P. even produce a candidate in the State elections!

The Federal electorate of Corangamite is held by Mr.Allan McDonald. Yet an important State seat contained within it, namely, Polwarth - which Mr. McDonald himself represented in the State Parliament - is now handed over to the C.P. without the firing of a shot. The truth is that the State electorates should be, from an organisational point of view, the foundations of the Federal electorates. The U.A.P. will continue to neglect them at its peril.

6.   The wreck produced by the election gives us a great opportunity if we are ready to seize it. The named United Australia Party has fallen into complete disregard. It no longer means anything. Many of my own strongest supporters in my own electorate decline to have anything to do with the Party as such. It is a great misfortune when the name of a political party means nothing. The word Labour does. The name Country Party is self-explanatory. If we are to build a new Party it must have a name which expresses our true and permanent point of view; and having got that name we should not chop and change every few years as we have in the past. My own opinion is that our side of politics should stand for Liberal Democracy. After all, this is one of the natural classifications of political thought, Fascist, Communist and Socialist being among the others. I therefore believe that we should set about establishing a LIBERAL DEMOCRATIC PARTY.

7.   Nothing will destroy us more completely than our continued subservience to the Country Party - which is of necessity sectional and which, in any event, has established itself in Parliament by defeating Members of our own Party. It is one thing to have an alliance with the C.P.; it is another to be annexed by it. The U.A.P. at Canberra signed its own death warrant when it agreed to serve under a C.P. Leader. After all, in the last Parliament we had 40 U.A.P. Members (both Houses) while the C.P. had 15. Under these circumstances, for the U.A.P. to abandon the leadership was to acknowledge its own bankruptcy, and it can scarcely be wondered that the electors took it at its own valuation.

8.   To establish a new party under a new name, it is I think essential to recognise that the new groups and movements which sprang up in the six months before the election (such as the Service & Citizens Party, the Middle Class Organisation, etc.) were all expressions of dissatisfaction with the existing set-up. They provided some valuable elements and in one or two instances put forward excellent candidates. I would like to see the U.A.P. Executives meeting the representatives of these new bodies freely and frankly with a view to the abolition of the existing organisations and the creation of a new one with a clearcut policy.

9.   Any new organisation must in my opinion be set up on an Australian-wide basis. The present system under which no State appears to have any connection with the State next door, except in a sketchy financial way at election time, is unsatisfactory. The Australian Liberal Democratic Party should be just as completely Federally organised as the Australian Labour Party. This means that it must have centrally placed an Executive with a Chief Executive Officer and that under this Central Executive there should be State Executives in each Capital.

10.   Membership of this new organisation should involve the payment of something more than a nominal subscription. One of the most widely accepted criticisms of our Party is that it is run by 'big business'. We lend colour to this theory by the fact that the membership fee is so trifling that the inevitable conclusion is that the real funds come from big subscribers, including the big companies. This belief in turn is supported by the fact that in Victoria, for example, the Party funds are looked after by the National Union which is, so far as I know, a self-appointed body, membership of which seems to belong to the representatives of the largest concerns in the country. If we are to get away from this 'big business' allegation, our organisation must contain a duly elected Finance Committee which will be made up of a variety of people and not merely of one financial section.

- 3 -

11.   The new organisation would require a highly paid
executive head, whose function would be purely organisational. It
I believe, wrong to think that the function of the Chief Executive,
Officer is to be a shrewd and experienced judge of politics.
Organisation is a job all of its own. It requires marked skill and
great energy. No Executive Committee should dream of appointing a
'cheap' man to such a post; on the contrary, his qualifications and
salary ought to be what would be anticipated if he were being
appointed the chief executive officer of a very large business conce
He should have under him, but closely associated with him, a Public
Relations Officer who would be in charge of all literature and
propaganda. Here again the temporary services of some casual journali
would be quite inadequate. Our advertising in the recent campaign wa
deplorable. An effective permanent Public Relations Officer would not
be cheap, for he ought to be a journalist qualified to occupy one of
the first two or three positions in a great daily newspaper.

12.   In addition to the above matters, the new organisation
should aim at placing an agent or representative, a fully salaried man,
in each key electorate. This would not only ensure a complete local
organisation but it would also bring about a much closer association
between the Member or candidate, as the case may be, and the Party which
is supporting him. For this purpose I would regard the key electorates
as including Brisbane and Griffith; Watson, Martin, Parkes, Robertson,
Eden-Monaro; Ballarat, Corio, Wannon; Darwin, Denison; Boothby,
Wakefield; Perth and Fremantle. In some cases, as in Tasmania,
adjoining electorates might be put under one agent.
           I realise that these proposals involve enormous
expenditure, far beyond anything dreamed of in the past; but the
simple fact is that unless we are prepared to spend money, hundreds of
thousands of £s. of it, between now and the next election, we are quit
unlikely to succeed.
           I would like to see in the new organisation a Policy
Committee, including both Parliamentary and non-Parliamentary
representatives, and charged with the duty of constantly revising
and rewtating our political beliefs. At present policies are much too
hastily got up, sometimes at the last moment and without effective
consultation. We have just been witnessing a disastrous example of
this.

13.   The search for new candidates should begin at once. The
defeats we have just experienced at least have one merit, which is that
they open a number of doors through which good men may enter Parliament
in three years' time. The truth is that, while we have had some
grievous losses, we are very well rid of three or four of our defeated
Members and it will be a tragedy if they can come back in three years'
time with a sort of vested right to be once more selected. The
avoidance of this would be one of the great advantages of a new
organisation with no strings on it and no pledges to anybody.

14.   A good Party journal with a wide circulation all over
Australia is also essential. In Sydney, papers like the "Century" and
the "Standard" are very widely read. During the recent campaign I was
much struck by the fact that all over Australia one encountered the
same questions and the same interjections, usually in almost identically
the same language; all of which indicated that the Labour and
Communist party journals were widely circulated and closely read and
put forward similar propaganda in every State. In this as in other
matters we can learn some lessons from our opponents.

15.   The time betweencnow and the next election is already
beginning to run out!

                                        R.G.M.

Notes

Preface: Robert Menzies Unplugged

1 Frances McNicoll, 'Menzies' views on his colleagues', *The Bulletin*, 30 May 1978, pp. 42–47. See also Frances McNicoll, 'Menzies would have really liked it', *The Bulletin*, 25 July 1978, pp. 29–30.

2 Frances McNicoll, 'A new insight into a remarkable statesman', *The Australian Women's Weekly*, 14 July 1982, pp. 10–11.

3 Judith Brett indicates that she is aware of at least one of the McNicoll–Menzies interviews but does not quote from it, presumably because she did not have permission to do so. See Judith Brett, *Robert Menzies' Forgotten People*, Pan Macmillan, Sydney, 1992, p. 299.

4 Valerie Lawson, 'Menzies biography: better late than never', *The Sunday Age*, 30 June 1991, Agenda, p. 9.

5 See Jacqueline Rees, 'Lady McNicoll: study of a prime minister', *The Australian Women's Weekly*, 20 October 1976, p. 9, and Frances McNicoll, 'Little about that remarkably able team, his top public servants', *The Canberra Times*, 15 July 1982, p. 15.

6 See Jill Sykes, 'Menzies biography by Lady McNicoll', *The Sydney Morning Herald*, 25 September 1976, p. 1, and Jefferson Penberthy, 'When will we learn the truth about Menzies?', *The Sydney Morning Herald*, 5 September 1981, p. 39. This article is accompanied by an illustration of McNicoll seated at a desk surrounded by Menzies' papers, which are covered in cobwebs, with a blank 'Chapter 1' in front of her as an admiring portrait of Menzies looks on.

7 Richard McGregor, 'Another author for the life of Menzies', *The Sydney Morning Herald*, 14 January 1984, p. 1.

8 Allan Martin, *Robert Menzies: a life. Volume 1, 1894–1943*, Melbourne University Press, Carlton, 1993, and *Volume 2, 1944–1978*, Melbourne University Press, Carlton, 1999.

9 Ronald Seth, *R.G. Menzies*, Cassell, London, 1960.

10 See chapter 18. Kevin Perkins, *Menzies: the last of the Queen's men*, Rigby, Adelaide, 1968.

11 Percy Joske, *Sir Robert Menzies, 1894–1978: a new, informal memoir*, Angus & Robertson, Sydney, 1978.

12 Cameron Hazlehurst, *Menzies Observed*, George Allen & Unwin, Sydney, 1979.

13 John Howard, *The Menzies Era: the years that shaped modern Australia*, HarperCollins, Sydney, 2014, p. 26.

14 Robert Menzies, Introduction to Billy Hughes' *The Case for Labor*, Sydney University Press, Sydney, 1970 (first published in 1910 by The Worker Trustees), p. vii.

Prologue: Life and Legacy

1 Robert Menzies, *The Measure of the Years*, Coronet, Melbourne, 1970, p. 35. Journalist Alan Reid referred to Menzies as a 'cautious reformer', and argued it was 'nonsense' to regard him as a 'reactionary', nor was it accurate to describe him only as a 'conservative'. See Alan Reid, 'The age of Menzies', *The Bulletin*, 29 January 1966, p. 10.

2 Menzies, *The Measure of the Years*, p. 35.

3 Donald Horne, *The Lucky Country: Australia in the sixties*, Viking, Ringwood, 1964.

4 Scott Morrison, 'Until the bell rings', Speech to the Menzies Research Centre, Albury, 6 September 2018.

5 Seth says Menzies was ten years old (see Seth, *R.G. Menzies*, p. 5.) Menzies recalled that he was ten or 11 years old (see Robert Menzies, *Afternoon Light: some memories of men and events*, Cassell, Melbourne, 1967, p. 316).

6 Menzies, *Afternoon Light*, p. 316.

7 Frances McNicoll note, Papers of Frances McNicoll, MS 9246, Series 3, Box 15, File 93, National Library of Australia, Canberra.

8 However, there were signs that his ambition was fermenting by the time he was a teenager at Wesley College. Percy Joske, a friend of Menzies from those days and later a federal MP, recalled him freely stating his ambition in the schoolyard. 'I intend to be prime minister of Australia,' he said. (See Joske, *Sir Robert Menzies, 1894–1978*, p. 8.)

9 Menzies, *Afternoon Light*, p. 318.

10 Frances McNicoll interview with Robert Menzies, 18 May 1972, Papers of Frances McNicoll, MS 9246, Series 6, Box 15, Files 1–3, National Library of Australia, Canberra.

11 The three surviving ministers are Doug Anthony, Ian Sinclair and A.J. 'Jim' Forbes.

12 The last elections of the Menzies era were the 1964 half-Senate election and the 1963 House of Representatives election. The voting age was then 21.

13 Andrew Roberts, *Churchill: walking with destiny*, Allen Lane, London, 2018, p. 937.

Chapter 1: Jeparit

1 'Jeparit's thistle spire unveiled', *The Canberra Times*, 19 September 1966, p. 1.

2 See 'Jeparit's most famous son returns for spire unveiling', *The Jeparit Leader*, 21 September 1966, p. 1; 'He reached the top ... Jeparit tribute to Sir Robert Menzies', *The Dimboola Banner*, 20 September 1966, p. 1; 'Jeparit honours Sir Robert Menzies', *The Rainbow News*, 22 September 1966, p. 1; '2000 see Jeparit spire ceremony', *The Wimmera Mail-Times*, 19 September 1966, p. 1; 'Jeparit honours its most famous son', *The Age*, 19 September 1966, p. 5.

3 Menzies, *Afternoon Light*, p. 7.

4 Ibid., p. 7.

5 Martin, *Robert Menzies: a life. Volume 1*, p. 7.

6 Ibid., p. 11.

7 John Shaw, 'Ming at the top: the heads that had to roll', *The Sun*, 19 May 1978, pp. 14–15.

Chapter 2: Family

1 Robert Menzies, *The Forgotten People and Other Studies in Democracy*, Angus and Robertson, Sydney, 1943, pp. 3–4.

2 Seth, *R.G. Menzies*, p. 13.

3 Heather Henderson, *A Smile for My Parents*, Allen & Unwin, Crows Nest, 2013, p. 3.

4   Allan Dawes interview with Robert
    Menzies, circa 1951–52, Papers of
    Frances McNicoll, MS 9246, Series
    7, Box 12, File 1, National Library of
    Australia, Canberra.
5   Menzies, *Afternoon Light*, p. 9.
6   Ibid., p. 11.
7   Interview with Lenox Hewitt,
    10 October 2018, via email.
8   'Death of Mr. James Menzies', *The Argus*,
    2 November 1945, p. 3.
9   Menzies, *Afternoon Light*, p. 12.
10 Dawes interview with Menzies,
    1951–52.
11 Menzies, *Afternoon Light*, p. 12.
12 'Mrs. K. Menzies dead', *The Sydney
    Morning Herald*, 1 July 1946, p. 5.
13 Don Whitington, *Twelfth Man?*,
    Jacaranda Press, Ryde, 1972.
14 Frank Menzies, 'Whitington so wrong
    about Menzies home', *The Age*, 30 August
    1972, p. 8.
15 John Hamilton, 'I eloped, says the
    Menzies girl', *The Herald*, 31 August
    1972.
16 Interview with Heather Henderson,
    13 October 2017, Canberra.
17 Martin, *Robert Menzies: a life. Volume 1*,
    pp. 9–10.
18 Joske, *Sir Robert Menzies, 1894–1978*, p. 7.
19 Frances McNicoll interview with Robert
    Menzies, 11 May 1972, Papers of Frances
    McNicoll, MS 9246, Series 6, Box 15,
    Files 1–3, National Library of Australia,
    Canberra.
20 Ibid.
21 Henderson, *A Smile for My Parents*, p. 6.
22 Interview with Heather Henderson,
    13 October 2017, Canberra.
23 Martha Rutledge, 'Green, Isabel Alice
    (Belle) (1893–1984)', *Australian
    Dictionary of Biography*, Australian
    National University, accessed online
    April 2018.
24 Robert Menzies to Belle Green, 7 May
    1965, Robert Menzies Papers, MS 4936,
    Series 40 (1993 Addition), Box 572,
    Folder 3, National Library of Australia,
    Canberra.
25 Interview with Heather Henderson,
    13 October 2017, Canberra.

Chapter 3: Student

1   'Jeparit rolls back the years to 1900',
    The Age, 12 November 1951, p. 4.
2   Henderson, *A Smile for My Parents*,
    p. 14.
3   Ibid., pp. 13–14.
4   McNicoll interview with Menzies,
    18 May 1972.
5   Dawes interview with Menzies,
    1951–52.
6   Seth, *R.G. Menzies*, p. 18.
7   Ibid., p. 32.
8   Dawes interview with Menzies,
    1951–52.
9   Interview with Heather Henderson,
    13 October 2017, Canberra.
10 McNicoll interview with Menzies,
    18 May 1972.
11 Dawes interview with Menzies,
    1951–52.
12 McNicoll interview with Menzies,
    18 May 1972.
13 Ibid.
14 Interview with Heather Henderson,
    13 October 2017, Canberra.
15 Seth, *R.G. Menzies*, p. 29.
16 McNicoll interview with Menzies,
    18 May 1972.
17 Joske, *Sir Robert Menzies, 1894–1978*, p. 9.
18 Ibid., p. 7.
19 Judith Vimpani, *The Houses of R.G.
    Menzies*, Kew Historical Society, 2013.
20 Martin, *Robert Menzies: a life. Volume 1*,
    p. 23.
21 Joske, *Sir Robert Menzies, 1894–1978*,
    p. 21.
22 McNicoll interview with Menzies,
    18 May 1972.
23 Ibid.
24 Frances McNicoll interview with Frank
    Menzies, 16 May 1972, Papers of Frances
    McNicoll, MS 9246, Series 6, Box 15,
    File 5, National Library of Australia,
    Canberra.

25 McNicoll interview with Menzies, 18 May 1972.

26 Gerard Henderson, *Menzies' Child: the Liberal Party of Australia 1944–1994*, Allen & Unwin, St Leonards, 1994, pp. 164–65.

27 Allan Martin, 'Sir Robert Gordon Menzies', in Michelle Grattan (ed.) *Australian Prime Ministers*, New Holland Publishers, Chatswood, 2016, p. 176.

28 McNicoll interview with Menzies, 18 May 1972.

Chapter 4: Barrister-at-Law

1 Menzies, *The Measure of the Years*, p. 229.

2 Seth, *R.G. Menzies*, p. 57.

3 Joske, *Sir Robert Menzies, 1894–1978*, pp. 40–41.

4 Geoffrey Sawer, 'Lawyer', *The Canberra Times*, 21 January 1966, p. 2.

5 Frances McNicoll interview with Robert Menzies, 12 May 1972, Papers of Frances McNicoll, MS 9246, Series 6, Box 15, Files 1–3, National Library of Australia, Canberra.

6 Hazlehurst, *Menzies Observed*, p. 43.

7 Martin, *Robert Menzies: a life. Volume 1*, p. 42.

8 Maie is a variation on May, Pattie's mother's name. See Henderson, *A Smile for My Parents*, p. 190.

9 Vimpani, *The Houses of R.G. Menzies*.

10 The holiday home, which was used by the family for 12 years, was mysteriously destroyed by fire in November 1941. It was not rebuilt and Menzies later sold the property.

11 Sawer, 'Lawyer', p. 2.

12 Sybil Nolan, 'Menzies in Clubland', *Inside Story*, 21 April 2017, accessed online August 2018.

13 Allan Martin, 'Menzies, Sir Robert Gordon (Bob) (1894–1978)', *Australian Dictionary of Biography*, Australian National University, accessed online February 2018.

14 'What election means to party leaders' wives', *The Sunday Herald*, 20 November 1949.

15 Interview with Heather Henderson, 13 October 2017, Canberra.

16 Interview with Heather Henderson, 22 August 2014, Canberra.

17 Ibid.

18 Martin, *Robert Menzies: a life. Volume 2*, p. 367.

19 Interview with Heather Henderson, 13 October 2017, Canberra.

20 Rutledge, 'Green, Isabel Alice (Belle) (1893–1984)'.

Chapter 5: Spring Street

1 Seth, *R.G. Menzies*, pp. 68–69.

2 'The referendum: "No" campaign opened', *The Age*, 17 August 1926, p. 10.

3 Dawes interview with Menzies, 1951–52.

4 Ibid.

5 Menzies, *Afternoon Light*, p. 316.

6 Desmond Robinson, 'Portrait of the artist as a young man', *The Sydney Morning Herald*, 19 December 1964.

7 McNicoll interview with Menzies, 18 May 1972.

8 'East Yarra by-election — voting to-morrow', *The Argus*, 5 October 1928, p. 8.

9 'East Yarra by-election — Mr. Menzies declared elected', *The Argus*, 10 October 1928, p. 8.

10 Robinson, 'Portrait of the artist as a young man'.

11 McNicoll interview with Menzies, 11 May 1972.

12 Ibid.

13 Martin, 'Sir Robert Gordon Menzies', in Grattan (ed.), *Australian Prime Ministers*, p. 181.

14 McNicoll interview with Menzies, 11 May 1972.

15 Ibid.

16 Ibid.

17 Ibid.
18 Ibid.
19 Special Correspondent, 'Sir Robert Menzies', *The Bulletin*, 30 November 1963, p. 15.
20 These remarks vary over the years in their retelling. See Creighton Burns,

'Robert G. Menzies', *The Australasian*, 28 October 1944, p. 16, and 'Merciless Ming', *The Canberra Times*, 26 May 1966, p. 3.
21 McNicoll interview with Frank Menzies, 16 May 1972.

Chapter 6: Canberra

1   McNicoll interview with Menzies, 11 May 1972.
2   Ibid.
3   Martin, *Robert Menzies: a life. Volume 1*, p. 116.
4   Enid Lyons, *Among the Carrion Crows*, Rigby, Adelaide, 1972, p. 55.
5   Shaw, 'Ming at the top: the heads that had to roll', pp. 14–15.
6   'Mr. Menzies deputy leader of U.A.P.', *The Sydney Morning Herald*, 5 December 1935, p. 11.
7   Martin, *Robert Menzies: a life. Volume 1*, pp. 128–29.
8   Frances McNicoll interview with Robert Menzies, 17 May 1972, Papers of Frances McNicoll, MS 9246, Series 6, Box 15, Files 1–3, National Library of Australia, Canberra.
9   Robert Menzies interview with Kenneth Harris, 17 August 1967, Papers of Frances McNicoll, MS 9246, Series 3, Box 5, File 28, National Library of Australia, Canberra.
10 Hazlehurst, *Menzies Observed*, p. 138.
11 Martin, *Robert Menzies: a life. Volume 1*, p. 237.
12 Robert Menzies to Belle Green, 6 August 1938, Robert Menzies Papers, MS 4936, Series 40 (1993 Addition), Box 572, Folder 2, National Library of Australia, Canberra.
13 Ibid.
14 Anne Henderson, *Menzies at War*, NewSouth Publishing, Sydney, 2014, pp. 39–42.
15 Hazlehurst, *Menzies Observed*, p. 155.
16 Martin, *Robert Menzies: a life. Volume 1*, p. 189.

17 Ibid., pp. 256–57.
18 Frank Green, the clerk, is in no doubt that Menzies' speech was 'an attack' on Lyons. See Frank Green, *Servant of the House*, Heinemann, Melbourne, 1969, p. 111.
19 Lyons, *Among the Carrion Crows*, pp. 62, 65.
20 Martin, *Robert Menzies: a life. Volume 1*, pp. 261–62.
21 Green, *Servant of the House*, p. 114.
22 Ibid., p. 116.
23 Enid Lyons, *So We Take Comfort*, Heinemann, Melbourne, 1965, p. 274.
24 'Nation's leader — Page offers seat', *The Sun*, 17 April 1939, p. 3.
25 'Successor to Mr. Lyons — Hughes or Casey?', *The Newcastle Sun*, 8 April 1939, p. 5.
26 'Five for prime minister', *The Sun*, 9 April 1939, p. 2.
27 'Electing new U. A. P. leader — Mr S. M. Bruce as candidate', *The Herald*, 17 April 1939, p. 1.
28 Martin, *Robert Menzies: a life. Volume 1*, p. 267.
29 'Mr. Menzies injures elbow', *Barrier Miner*, 18 April 1939, p. 3.
30 'Mr. Menzies leader of U. A. P. defeats Mr Hughes. Prime minister today. Strange political position', *The Argus*, 19 April 1939, p. 1; 'Four seek party leadership', *The Advertiser*, 19 April 1939, p. 23.
31 'Successor to Mr. Lyons — Hughes or Casey?', p. 5.
32 Kate Menzies, 'Bob was my bravest son, says prime minister's mother', *The Daily Telegraph*, 4 May 1939, p. 8.

33 Interview with Bill Hayden,
    18 September 2018, via phone.
34 Lyons, *Among the Carrion Crows*, p. 60.
35 Ibid., pp. 178–80.
36 McNicoll interview with Menzies,
    11 May 1972.
37 Frances McNicoll interview with Robert
    Menzies, 15 May 1972, Papers of Frances
    McNicoll, MS 9246, Series 6, Box 15,
    Files 1–3, National Library of Australia,
    Canberra.

38 Ibid.
39 Helen Page to Ken Menzies,
    27 December 1979, Robert Menzies
    Papers, MS 4936, Series 11 (1998
    Addition), Box 568, Folder 4, National
    Library of Australia, Canberra.
40 Earle Page, *Truant Surgeon: the inside
    story of forty years of Australian political
    life*, Angus & Robertson, Sydney, 1963,
    pp. 276–77.
41 Page to Menzies, 27 December 1979.

Chapter 7: Wartime Prime Minister

1   Menzies, *Afternoon Light*, p. 14.
2   'Proudest day for PM's parents', *The Daily
    Telegraph*, 4 May 1939, p. 8.
3   Interview with Brendan Nelson,
    1 September 2014, via phone. See also
    Troy Bramston, 'We didn't put our
    democratic traditions on hold 75 years
    ago', *The Weekend Australian*,
    6 September 2014.
4   Robert Menzies to Stanley Bruce, 11
    September 1939, Papers of Frances
    McNicoll, MS 9246, Series 3, Box 11,
    File 85, National Library of Australia,
    Canberra.
5   Robert Menzies to William McMahon,
    24 October 1972, Papers of Frances
    McNicoll, MS 9246, Series 3, Box 5,
    File 29, National Library of Australia,
    Canberra.
6   Frances McNicoll interview with Robert
    Menzies, 18 December 1973, Papers
    of Frances McNicoll, MS 9246, Series
    6, Box 15, File 4, National Library of
    Australia, Canberra.
7   Robert Menzies, 'Secrecy of cabinet and
    other similar discussions', 24 October
    1972, Papers of Frances McNicoll, MS
    9246, Series 3, Box 6, File 42, National
    Library of Australia, Canberra.
8   Allan Martin rationalised his decision
    not to include the letter because he 'did
    not believe it reflected anything other
    than temporary private musings'. See
    Allan Martin (ed. John Nethercote),
    *The 'Whig' View of Australian History
    and Other Essays*, Melbourne University
    Press, Carlton, 2007, p. 141.

9   John Edwards, *John Curtin's War, Volume
    1*, Viking, Sydney, 2017, pp. 156–58.
10 ABC Radio National, *AM*, 19 April
    2001, accessed online July 2018.
11 Interview with Brendan Nelson,
    1 September 2014, via phone.
12 Edwards, *John Curtin's War, Volume 1*,
    pp. 177–8, 239, 246–49.
13 Michael Keenan, 'Menzies: the wartime
    prime ministership, 1939–41' in John
    Nethercote (ed.), *Liberalism and the
    Australian Federation*, The Federation
    Press, Leichhardt, 2001, p. 168.
14 Ibid.
15 Ibid., p. 170.
16 Robert Menzies to Stanley Bruce,
    15 September 1939, *Documents on
    Australian Foreign Policy — Volume 2:
    1939*, Department of Foreign Affairs and
    Trade, accessed online July 2018.
17 Menzies, *Afternoon Light*, p. 18.
18 Don Whitington, *Strive to Be Fair: an
    unfinished autobiography*, Australian
    National University Press, Canberra,
    1977, p. 72.
19 Adele Shelton-Smith, 'Over-the-teacups
    talk about two men', *The Australian
    Women's Weekly*, 28 September 1940,
    p. 8.
20 Clem Lloyd, *Parliament and the Press*,
    Melbourne University Press, Carlton,
    1988, p. 127.
21 'Leadership of the Country Party. Mr.
    Fadden to act', *The Sydney Morning
    Herald*, 16 October 1940, p. 12;
    'Country Party. Tie for leadership. Page

and McEwen. Cameron walks out', *Daily Examiner*, 16 October 1940, p. 5.

22 Percy Spender, *Politics and a Man*, Collins, Sydney, 1972, p. 70.

23 Keenan, 'Menzies: the wartime prime ministership, 1939–41', p. 175.

24 Seth, *R.G. Menzies*, p. 94.

25 Allan Martin and Patsy Hardy (eds.), *Dark and Hurrying Days: Menzies' 1941 diary*, National Library of Australia, Canberra, 1993.

26 Menzies, *Afternoon Light*, p. 45.

27 Robert Menzies, *Speech Is of Time: selected speeches and writings*, Cassell, London, 1958, p. 49. See also Joske, *Sir Robert Menzies, 1894–1978*, p. 115.

28 Interview with Andrew Roberts, 30 November 2018, via phone.

29 Hazlehurst, *Menzies Observed*, p. 207.

30 McNicoll interview with Menzies, 18 May 1972.

31 Ibid.

32 Ibid.

33 Hazlehurst, *Menzies Observed*, p. 225.

34 Ibid., p. 226.

35 Ibid., p. 229.

36 Menzies first met Roosevelt at the White House on 8 August 1935, following his first trip to London.

37 Netherlands (Dutch) East Indies, which is now part of Indonesia.

38 'Time now to tell blunt truth', *The Daily Telegraph*, 27 May 1941, p. 2.

39 McNicoll interview with Menzies, 15 May 1972. See also Menzies, *Afternoon Light*, p. 19.

40 McNicoll interview with Menzies, 15 May 1972.

41 Spender, *Politics and a Man*, p. 158.

42 Robert Menzies to John Curtin, 22 August 1941, in Patrick Weller (ed.), *Caucus Minutes 1901–1949: minutes of the meetings of the federal parliamentary Labor Party — volume 3, 1932–1949*, Melbourne University Press, Carlton, 1975, pp. 285–86.

43 John Curtin to Robert Menzies, 26 August 1941, in Weller, *Caucus Minutes 1901–1949*, pp. 286–87.

44 McNicoll interview with Menzies, 15 May 1972.

45 Hazlehurst, *Menzies Observed*, pp. 237–38.

46 Spender, *Politics and a Man*, p. 71.

47 McNicoll interview with Frank Menzies, 16 May 1972.

48 Henderson, *Menzies at War*, p. 223.

49 'Challenge to Mr. Menzies', *The Sydney Morning Herald*, 28 August 1941, p. 8.

50 Henderson, *Menzies at War*, p. 226.

51 Gavin Souter, *Acts of Parliament: a narrative history of the Senate and House of Representatives, Commonwealth of Australia*, Melbourne University Press, Carlton, 1988, p. 340.

52 Robert Menzies, Press Statement, 28 August 1941.

53 Alan Reid, 'The battle of Canberra', *The Sun*, 31 August 1941.

54 Don Whitington, 'The mistakes that led to Menzies' eclipse', *The Sunday Telegraph*, 31 August 1941.

55 'The prime ministership', *The Sydney Morning Herald*, 29 August 1941, p. 6.

56 Menzies, *Afternoon Light*, p. 57.

57 John Hamilton, 'At 75 Sir Robert looks back', *The Age*, Saturday Review, 20 December 1969, p. 9.

58 Menzies, *Afternoon Light*, p. 57.

59 'Mr. Menzies and New York', *The Age*, 12 November 1941, p. 6.

60 Menzies, *Afternoon Light*, pp. 60–61.

61 David Day, *Menzies and Churchill at War*, Angus & Robertson, North Ryde, 1986.

62 Interview with Heather Henderson, 22 August 2014, Canberra.

63 Malcolm Ellis, 'The mind of R.G. Menzies', *The Bulletin*, 22 March 1961.

64 Alan Reid, 'Prime ministers I have known', *The Bulletin*, 29 January 1980, p. 365.

65 Green, *Servant of the House*, pp. 119–20.

66 Spender, *Politics and a Man*, pp. 49–50.

67 Martin, 'Sir Robert Gordon Menzies', in Grattan (ed.), *Australian Prime Ministers*, p. 186.

68 Paul Hasluck, *The Government and the People, 1939–41*, Australian War Memorial, Canberra, 1952, pp. 565–66.

69 Joske, *Sir Robert Menzies, 1894–1978*, p. 126.

70 Spender, *Politics and a Man*, pp. 152–54.
71 John McEwen, *His Story*, privately published, Canberra, 1983, p. 30.
72 Arthur Fadden, *They Called Me Artie*, Jacaranda, Brisbane, 1969, p. 80.

Chapter 8: 'The Forgotten People'

1   McNicoll interview with Menzies, 18 May 1972.
2   See Judith Brett, 'Menzies' forgotten people', *Meanjin*, Vol. 43, No. 2, June 1984, pp. 253–65.
3   Interview with John Howard, 23 May 2017, Sydney.
4   Menzies, *The Measure of the Years*, p. 8.
5   Robert Menzies, *The Forgotten People*, Robertson & Mullens, Melbourne, June 1942.
6   Robert Menzies, *The Forgotten People and Other Studies in Democracy*, Angus & Robertson, Sydney, 1943.
7   Interview with John Howard, 23 May 2017, Sydney.
8   'Mr Curtin doing a good job', *Australian Gallup Polls*, July–August 1942.
9   Laurie Fitzhardinge, *The Little Digger, 1914–1952: William Morris Hughes —* a political biography, vol. II, Angus & Robertson, Sydney, 1979, pp. 661–62.
10 Edgar Holt, 'Election balance sheet — Robert Gordon Menzies', *The Sunday Telegraph*, 1 August 1943.
11 Martin, *Robert Menzies: a life. Volume 1*, p. 421.
12 'Menzies to lead opposition', *The Courier-Mail*, 23 September 1943, p. 1.
13 Robert Menzies to Lionel Lindsay, 13 October 1943. See 'Billy Hughes had been warned', *The Sydney Morning Herald*, 8 July 1987, p. 3.
14 Robert Menzies, Broadcast — Leading the Opposition, 24 September 1943, Papers of John Cramer, MS 7553, Series 17, Box 20, Folder 1, National Library of Australia, Canberra.
15 Ibid.

Chapter 9: The Liberal Party of Australia

1   Robert Menzies, 'Some lessons of the election', September–October 1943, Robert Menzies Papers, MS 4936, Series 40 (1993 Addition), Box 577, Folder 40, National Library of Australia, Canberra.
2   Robert Menzies, Broadcast — A Liberal Revival, 29 October 1943, in David Furse-Roberts (ed.), *Menzies: the forgotten speeches*, Connor Court (Jeparit Press), Redland Bay, 2017, pp. 17–20
3   William McMahon, 'Record of conversation with Rupert Henderson, 10 August 1978', Papers of William McMahon, MS 3926, Series 19, Box 3, Folder 29, National Library of Australia, Canberra. See also Gavin Souter, *Company of Heralds*, Melbourne University Press, Carlton, 1981, pp. 271–72.
4   'Mr Curtin's popularity maintained', *Australian Gallup Polls*, August–September 1943; 'Curtin and Menzies wanted as party leaders', *Australian Gallup Polls*, August–September 1943.
5   Robert Menzies, Draft Statement, 16 June 1944, Robert Menzies Papers, MS 4936, Series 40 (1993 Addition), Box 573, Folder 1, National Library of Australia, Canberra. See also Robert Menzies, Untitled Document, 16 June 1944, Robert Menzies Papers, MS 4936, Series 40 (1993 Addition), Box 574, Folder 23, National Library of Australia, Canberra.
6   'Liberal policy for non-Labor', *The Age*, 30 August 1944, p. 3.
7   Robert Menzies to Ernest White, 7 September 1944, Papers of Frances McNicoll, MS 9246, Series 3, Box 7, File 53, National Library of Australia, Canberra.
8   Robert Menzies, Opening Speech to the Canberra Conference, Canberra, 13 October 1944, Robert Menzies

Papers, MS 4936, Series 6, Box 418, Folder 64, National Library of Australia, Canberra.

9   Fadden, *They Called Me Artie*, p. 88.

10 Institute of Public Affairs (Victoria), *Looking Forward: a post war policy for Australian industry*, Ramsay Ware Publishing, Melbourne, 1944.

11 Menzies, Opening Speech to the Canberra Conference, 13 October 1944.

12 Robert Menzies, Press Statement, Canberra, 16 October 1944, Robert Menzies Papers, MS 4936, Series 40 (1993 Addition), Box 573, Folder 4, National Library of Australia, Canberra.

13 Menzies, *Afternoon Light,* p. 286.

14 Keith Hancock, *Australia*, Jacaranda Press, Melbourne, 1930 (1966 reprint), p. 194.

15 Speech by Robert Menzies to the Liberal Party of Australia (W. A. Division), 12 May 1970, Robert Menzies Papers, MS 4936, Series 40 (1993 Addition), Box 573, Folder 9, National Library of Australia, Canberra.

16 'Liberals "not each for self"', *The Daily Telegraph*, 1 September 1945, p. 4.

17 Interview with John Carrick, 9 March 2017, Sydney.

18 Dean Jaensch, *The Liberals*, Allen & Unwin, St Leonards, 1994, p. 53.

19 Paul Hasluck, *Sir Robert Menzies*, Melbourne University Press, Carlton, 1980, p. 25–26.

20 Greg Melleuish, *A Short History of Australian Liberalism*, Centre for Independent Studies, Sydney, 2001, pp. 27–28.

21 Interview with Malcolm Fraser, 6 September 2002, Melbourne.

22 Interview with Malcolm Fraser, 16 April 2013, Melbourne.

23 Interview with John Howard, 23 May 2017, Sydney.

24 Interview with Tony Abbott, 23 August 2017, via phone.

25 Troy Bramston, 'Malcolm Turnbull: my government has kept faith with Menzies', *The Australian*, 14 June 2018.

26 Interview with Andrew Peacock, 8 November 2016, via phone.

27 Interview with Nick Greiner, 4 June 2018, Sydney.

28 Interview with Peter Costello, 12 December 2018, Melbourne.

29 Interview with Heather Henderson, 22 August 2014, Canberra.

30 Robert Menzies' Appointment Diary, 16 October 1944, Robert Menzies Papers, MS 4936, Series 13, Box 399, National Library of Australia, Canberra.

31 'Liberal Party is launched at Albury', *The Border Morning Mail*, 15 December 1944, p. 6.

32 Robert Menzies, Opening Speech to the Albury Conference, Albury, 14 December 1944, Robert Menzies Papers, MS 4936, Folder: 'Sir Robert Menzies' Speeches, Statements and Broadcasts', National Library of Australia, Canberra.

33 Interview with David Kemp, 3 October 2014, via email.

34 Menzies was not officially made leader of the party until February 1945. But he was reported as being the parliamentary leader by the time of the Albury conference in December 1944. See Creighton Burns, 'Liberal Party aims to encourage individual initiative', *The Argus*, 19 December 1944, p. 3.

35 Robert Menzies, Closing Speech to the Albury Conference, Albury, 16 December 1944, Robert Menzies Papers, MS 4936, Folder: 'Sir Robert Menzies' Speeches, Statements and Broadcasts', National Library of Australia, Canberra.

36 Robert Menzies' Appointment Diary, 16 December 1944, Robert Menzies Papers, MS 4936, Series 13, Box 399, National Library of Australia, Canberra.

37 'Formal Announcement of New Liberal Party', *The Advocate*, 22 February 1945, p. 2; 'U.A.P. becomes Liberal Party', *The Sun*, 21 February 1945, p. 2.

38 Ian Hancock, *National and Permanent? The Federal Organisation of the Liberal Party of Australia 1944–1965*, Melbourne University Press, Carlton, 2000, p. 81.

39 'Mr. Menzies warmly greeted at Liberal rally', *The Sydney Morning Herald*, 1 September 1945, p 4.

40 'Mr. Chifley wins caucus vote. Will become prime minister today', *The Sydney Morning Herald*, 13 July 1945, p. 1.

41 Robert Menzies, Election Policy Speech, Camberwell Town Hall, 20 August 1946.

42 Interview with Heather Henderson, 22 August 2014, Canberra.

43 Charles Meeking to Robert Menzies, 15 October 1946, Robert Menzies Papers, MS 4936, Series 14, Box 413, Folder 28, National Library of Australia, Canberra.

44 T. Malcolm Ritchie, Report of the Federal Executive Submitted by the Federal President to the Federal Council, 29 October 1946, Robert Menzies Papers, MS 4936, Series 14, Box 412, Folder 18, National Library of Australia, Canberra.

45 Martin, *Robert Menzies: a life. Volume 2*, pp. 61–62.

46 'Bigger vote for Liberals if Menzies not leader?', Australian Gallup Polls, July–August 1947.

47 Robert Menzies, Statement, September 1947, Robert Menzies Papers, MS 4936, Series 14, Box 412, Folder 20, National Library of Australia, Canberra.

48 Ibid.

49 'Menzies and Chifley top leaders' poll', *The Courier-Mail*, 17 December 1947, p. 2.

50 Interview with John Carrick, 9 March 2017, Sydney.

51 McNicoll interview with Menzies, 18 May 1972.

52 Les Haylen, *Twenty Years' Hard Labor*, Macmillan, Melbourne, 1969, p. 31.

53 'Opinion still against banking monopoly', *The Advertiser*, 15 November 1947, p. 4.

54 Martin, *Robert Menzies: a life. Volume 2*, p. 78.

55 Richard Casey to Robert Menzies, 3 November 1947, Robert Menzies Papers, MS 4936, Series 14, Box 410, Folder 3, National Library of Australia, Canberra.

56 Don Cleland to Robert Menzies, 13 January 1949, Robert Menzies Papers, MS 4936, Series 14, Box 412, Folder 19, National Library of Australia, Canberra.

57 Ibid.

58 Clem Lloyd, 'The media', in Scott Prasser, John Nethercote and John Warhurst (eds.), *The Menzies Era: a reappraisal of government, politics and policy*, Hale & Iremonger, Sydney, 1995, pp. 117–18.

59 'How well do you know this man?', Robert Menzies Papers, MS 4936, Series 14, Box 419, Folder 77, National Library of Australia, Canberra.

60 Robert Menzies to Don Cleland, 1 May 1949, Robert Menzies Papers, MS 4936, Series 14, Box 410, Folder 2, National Library of Australia, Canberra.

61 Interview with John Carrick, 9 March 2017, Sydney.

62 Liberal Party membership would peak in the early years of the Menzies government. It reached 198,000 in 1950 but fell to 117,000 by 1965. See Hancock, *National and Permanent?*, pp. 107, 233.

63 Robert Menzies, Election Policy Speech, Canterbury Soldier's Memorial Hall, 10 November 1949.

64 'Liberal-CP victory predicted in final Gallup Poll survey', *The Sun*, 9 December 1949.

65 'Party leaders make last minute appeal to Australian voters', *The Sun*, 9 December 1949, p. 7.

66 'Gallup Poll gives Liberal-CP 50 pc. of federal vote: Labor 40 pc.', *The Sun*, 9 December 1949.

67 Interview with John Carrick, 9 March 2017, Sydney.

68 William McKell to George VI, 26 January 1950, Papers of Sir William McKell, MLMSS 2027, Box 10, State Library of New South Wales, Sydney.

69 Paul Hasluck, *Australian Politics: notes on books*, Papers of Paul Hasluck, MS 5274, Box 39, National Library of Australia, Canberra, pp. 59–60.

70 'Menzies, Holt and the Liberals', *Current Affairs Bulletin*, Vol. 37, No. 9, March 1966, p. 131.

71 McNicoll interview with Menzies, 18 May 1972.

72 Evan Whitton, 'Who really founded the Liberal Party? Menzies' shaky claims', *The Sydney Morning Herald*, 1 August 1981, pp. 37–38.

73 Ibid.

74 Ernest White to Tony Eggleton, 20 December 1979, Papers of Frances McNicoll, MS 9246, Series 3, Box 7, File 53, National Library of Australia, Canberra.

75 Ernest White to Robert Menzies, 4 September 1944, Papers of Frances McNicoll, MS 9246, Series 3, Box 7, File 53, National Library of Australia, Canberra.

76 Menzies, *Afternoon Light*, pp. 289–90.

77 Burns, 'Liberal Party aims to encourage individual initiative', p. 3.

78 Interview with Heather Henderson, 22 August 2014, Canberra.

79 Note by Robert Menzies, Robert Menzies Papers, MS 4936, Series 40 (1993 Addition), Box 577, Folder 39, National Library of Australia, Canberra.

Chapter 10: Friends and Rivals: Curtin and Chifley

1 Menzies, *Afternoon Light*, p. 127.

2 Robert Menzies, 'John Curtin', Robert Menzies Papers, MS 4936, Series 10, Box 354, Folder 1, National Library of Australia, Canberra.

3 Menzies, *Afternoon Light*, p. 127.

4 Ibid., pp. 125–28.

5 McNicoll interview with Menzies, 12 May 1972.

6 Ronda Jamieson interview with Elsie Macleod, 10 May 1994 and 20 February 1995, John Curtin Prime Ministerial Library, Perth.

7 Robert Menzies to John Curtin, 28 June 1945, JCPML00401/52, John Curtin Prime Ministerial Library, Perth.

8 'Parliament pays tribute to Mr Curtin', 6 July 1945, *The Sydney Morning Herald*, p. 5.

9 Fred Daly, *From Curtin to Kerr*, Sun Books, South Melbourne, 1977, p. 32.

10 Menzies, *Afternoon Light*, p. 130.

11 McNicoll interview with Menzies, 12 May 1972.

12 Daly, *From Curtin to Kerr*, p. 105.

13 Ibid., p. 106.

14 David Marr, 'The last waltz', *The Sydney Morning Herald*, Good Weekend Magazine, 9 June 2001, pp. 18–25.

15 Ibid.

16 Clyde Cameron and Daniel Connell, *The Confessions of Clyde Cameron*, ABC Enterprises, Crows Nest, 1990, p. 83.

17 Interview with Heather Henderson, 22 August 2014, Canberra.

18 Robert Menzies to John Curtin, 29 August 1941, JCPML00573/1, John Curtin Prime Ministerial Library, Perth.

19 John Curtin to Robert Menzies, 30 August 1941, JCPML00573/2, John Curtin Prime Ministerial Library, Perth.

20 Robert Menzies, Speech to the National Press Club, Hotel Canberra, 14 September 1964.

Chapter 11: Return to Power

1 John Farquharson, 'Brown, Sir Allen Stanley (1911–1999)', *Obituaries Australia*, Australian National University, accessed online May 2018.

2 Allan Martin mistakenly writes that Menzies was 'commissioned' to 'form a government' on 14 December (see Martin, *Robert Menzies: a life. Volume 2*, p. 129). Menzies was in Melbourne on that date and did not travel to Canberra until 15 December, when McKell asked him to form a government (see 'Menzies commissioned to form govt.', *The Herald*, 15 December 1949, p. 1). But Menzies was not sworn in as prime minister until 19 December.

3 Robert Menzies' Appointment Diary, 15 December 1949, Robert Menzies Papers, MS 4936, Series 13, Box 401, National Library of Australia, Canberra.

4 'Chifley phones Menzies', *The Herald*, 12 December 1949, p. 1; 'Chifley hands in his resignation', *The Herald*, 13 December 1949, p. 1.

5 'Menzies commissioned to form govt.'.

6 Robert Menzies' Appointment Diary, 19 December 1949, Robert Menzies Papers, MS 4936, Series 13, Box 401, National Library of Australia, Canberra.

7 'Ministry sworn in: has first meeting', *The Herald*, 19 December 1949, p. 1.

8 Robert Menzies to William McKell, 17 December 1949, Robert Menzies Papers, MS 4936, Series (2000 Addition), Box 6, Folder 43, National Library of Australia, Canberra.

9 'Mr Fadden named as Treasurer', *The Herald*, 14 December 1949, p. 1.

10 Robert Menzies, 'Cabinet List', Robert Menzies Papers, MS 4936, Series (2000 Addition), Box 6, Folder 43, National Library of Australia, Canberra.

11 Robert Menzies' Appointment Diary, 20 December 1949, Robert Menzies Papers, MS 4936, Series 13, Box 401, National Library of Australia, Canberra.

12 'Govt. "To restore value to money"', *The Daily Telegraph*, 21 December 1949, p. 6.

13 Here, I draw on Robert Manne, 'Revisiting Menzies', *The Age*, 29 November 1999.

14 Robert Menzies, *Mr Prime Minister*, Episode 7: 'Robert Gordon Menzies', ABC TV, 1966.

15 Here, I draw on interviews with William Heseltine and Tony Eggleton. See also John Bunting, *R.G. Menzies: a portrait*, Allen & Unwin, Sydney, 1988, pp. 22–24.

16 Interview with William Heseltine, 11 September 2015, Sydney.

17 Interview with Tony Eggleton, 14 October 2013, Canberra.

18 Stewart Cockburn, Speech to the National Library of Australia Seminar on 'The Legacy of Sir Robert Menzies', 19 November 1994, Canberra.

19 Buzz Kennedy, 'The shy man behind Ming the Merciless', *The Australian*, 16 May 1978, p. 1.

20 Interview with William Heseltine, 22 June 2017, Sydney.

21 Nan Musgrove, 'Five prime ministers were her friends', *The Australian Women's Weekly*, 5 May 1976, pp. 4–5.

22 Will of Robert Gordon Menzies, March 1976, Papers of Frances McNicoll, MS 9246, Series 1, Box 1, File 2, National Library of Australia, Canberra.

23 'Behind the scenes, 1950', Papers of Eileen Lenihan, M3130, Series 2, National Archives of Australia, Canberra.

24 Death Notices, Eileen Lenihan, *The Canberra Times*, 4 September 1990.

25 Fin Crisp, *Australian National Government* (revised edition), Longman Cheshire, 1978, p. 393.

26 Bunting, *R.G. Menzies*, p. 79.

27 Menzies, *The Measure of the Years*, pp. 34–35.

28 Frances McNicoll interview with Robert Menzies, 13 May 1972, Papers of Frances McNicoll, MS 9246, Series 6, Box 15, Files 1–3, National Library of Australia, Canberra.

29 Interview with William Heseltine, 11 September 2015, Sydney.

30 Interview with Lenox Hewitt, 10 October 2018, via email.

31 David Lee, 'Cabinet' in Prasser, Nethercote and Warhurst (eds.), *The Menzies Era*, p. 123.

32 Howard Beale, 'Menzies a leader, not a despot', *The Advertiser*, 29 December 1971, p. 2.

33 Don Whitington, *The Rulers: fifteen years of the Liberals* (revised edition), Lansdowne, Melbourne, 1965, p. 28.

34 Lyons, *Among the Carrion Crows*, pp. 90–91.

35 Menzies, *The Measure of the Years*, pp. 38–39.

36 John Gorton, 'How I became a Menzies man', *The Herald*, 17 May 1978, p. 4.

37 Garfield Barwick, *A Radical Tory: reflections and recollections*, The Federation Press, Sydney, 1995, p. 115.

38 Beale, 'Menzies a leader, not a despot'.

39 Howard Beale, *This Inch of Time: memoirs of politics and diplomacy*, Melbourne University Press, Carlton, 1977, p. 106.

40 Bunting, *R.G. Menzies*, p. 90.

41 Barry York interview with Frank Jennings, Oral History Program, Old Parliament House, 29 October 2007.

42 McNicoll interview with Menzies, 13 May 1972.

43 Ibid.

44 Don Chipp and John Larkin, *Don Chipp: the third man*, Rigby, Adelaide, 1978, p. 54.

45 Frances McNicoll interview with Robert Menzies, 14 May 1972, Papers of Frances McNicoll, MS 9246, Series 6, Box 15, Files 1–3, National Library of Australia, Canberra.

46 Interview with Malcolm Fraser, 6 September 2002, Melbourne.

47 Interview with Doug Anthony, 17 November 2014, Murwillumbah.

48 Interview with Doug Anthony, 20 April 2017, via phone.

49 Interview with Ian Sinclair, 7 April 2017, Taree.

50 Interview with Jim Forbes, 14 December 2018, Adelaide.

51 Alexander Downer, *Six Prime Ministers*, Hill of Content, Melbourne, 1982, pp. 2–3.

52 Chipp and Larkin, *Don Chipp*, pp. 39, 47.

53 Billy Snedden and Bernie Schedvin, *Billy Snedden: an unlikely Liberal*, Macmillan, South Melbourne, 1990, pp. 45–46.

54 James Killen, *Killen: inside Australian politics*, Methuen Haynes, North Ryde, 1985, p. 7.

55 Downer, *Six Prime Ministers*, pp. 4–7.

56 Interview with Lenox Hewitt, 10 October 2018, via email.

57 Interview with Sam Holt, 24 November 2017, via phone.

58 Interview with William Heseltine, 22 June 2017, Sydney.

59 Interview with Heather Henderson, 13 October 2017, Canberra.

60 Fadden, *They Called Me Artie*, p. 111.

61 'Debonair Harold wins — by 2 votes', *The Argus*, 26 September 1956, p. 3.

62 McNicoll interview with Menzies, 13 May 1972.

63 McNicoll interview with Menzies, 14 May 1972.

64 McNicoll interview with Menzies, 18 May 1972.

65 McNicoll interview with Menzies, 14 May 1972.

66 Ibid.

67 McNicoll interview with Menzies, 13 May 1972.

68 Ibid.

69 Robert Menzies, 'Note of conversation between the Prime Minister and the Minister for Labour and National Service, 23 September 1959', Papers of Robert Menzies, Correspondence with William McMahon, M2576/2, National Archives of Australia, Canberra.

70 McNicoll interview with Menzies, 13 May 1972.

71 Interview with Ian Sinclair, 7 April 2017, Taree.

72 McNicoll interview with Menzies, 14 May 1972.

73 Percy Spender, 'Did I fall, or ... was I pushed?', *The Sun*, 30 December 1972, p. 16. See also Spender, *Politics and a Man*, p. 300–02.

74 Barwick, *A Radical Tory,* pp. 199–200.

75 Ibid., pp. 208–09.

76 Robert Menzies, 'Chief Justiceship of the High Court', 27 April 1964, Robert Menzies Papers, MS 4936, Series 10, Box 365, Folder 4, National Library of Australia, Canberra.

77 Frances McNicoll interview with Garfield Barwick, 1981, Papers of Frances McNicoll, MS 9246, Series 6, Box 15, Files 7–19, National Library of Australia, Canberra.

78 Menzies, 'Chief Justiceship of the High Court'.

79 Ray Maley, 'Menzies nips revolt in the bud', *The Argus*, 3 March 1951, p. 3.

80 McNicoll interview with Menzies, 13 May 1972.

81 Ibid.

82 McNicoll interview with Menzies, 14 May 1972.

83 McEwen, *His Story*, p. 73.

84 Interview with Ian Sinclair, 7 April 2017, Taree.

85 Alan Reid, 'After Menzies — who?', *The Bulletin*, 7 August 1965, p. 23.

86 McNicoll interview with Menzies, 14 May 1972.

87 'Australian wanted as next Governor-General', *Australian Gallup Polls*, November–December 1947.

88 Interview with William Heseltine, 11 September 2015, Sydney.

89 McNicoll interview with Menzies, 14 May 1972.

90 Robert Menzies to John McEwen, March 1961, Papers of Robert Menzies, Overseas Visits 1963, M2576/14, National Archives of Australia, Canberra.

91 Martin, *Robert Menzies: a life. Volume 2*, p. 529.

92 McNicoll interview with Menzies, 14 May 1972.

Chapter 12: The Art and Science of Politics

1   Robert Menzies, 'Politics, "Fine Art and Inexact Science"', *The New York Times Magazine*, 28 November 1948, pp. 11, 71, 73–74.

2   Interview with Tony Eggleton, 14 October 2013, Canberra.

3   Special Correspondent, 'Sir Robert Menzies', p. 13.

4   Ibid.

5   Menzies, *The Measure of the Years*, p. 15.

6   Ibid., p. 16.

7   Beale, *This Inch of Time*, p. 32

8   Menzies, *The Measure of the Years*, p. 16.

9   Ibid., p. 17.

10 Howard, *The Menzies Era*, p. 75.

11 Interview with William Heseltine, 22 June 2017, Sydney.

12 Interview with Tony Eggleton, 2 June 2017, Canberra.

13 Interview with Heather Henderson, 22 August 2014, Canberra.

14 Ray Robinson (ed.), *The Wit of Sir Robert Menzies*, Leslie Frewin Publishers, London, 1966.

15 Robert Menzies to Leslie Frewin, 4 April 1966 and Leslie Frewin to Robert Menzies, 18 March 1966, Robert Menzies Papers, MS 4936, Series 10, Box 365, Folder 6, National Library of Australia, Canberra.

16 Fadden, *They Called Me Artie*, p. 111.

17 Interview with Rod Lyall, 9 January 2018, via phone.

18 Jo Gullett, 'Robert Gordon Menzies', *The Observer*, 3 May 1958, p. 167.

19 Interview with John Howard, 8 June 2018, Sydney.

20 Barry Jones, *Knowledge, Courage, Leadership*, Wilkinson, Melbourne, 2016, p. 37.

21 Interview with William Heseltine, 22 June 2017, Sydney.

22 Interview with Tony Eggleton, 14 October 2013, Canberra.

23 Menzies, *The Measure of the Years*, p. 9.

24 Geoff Yeend to Frances McNicoll, 22 July 1982, Papers of Frances McNicoll, MS 9246, Series 1, Box 1, File 2, National Library of Australia, Canberra.

25 McNicoll interview with Menzies, 12 May 1972.

26 See Wallace Brown, *Ten Prime Ministers: life among the politicians*, Longueville Books, Double Bay, 2002, p. 22 and Peter Bowers, 'Silent Menzies and the games he played', *The Sydney Morning Herald*, 17 May 1978, p. 6.

27 Edgar Holt, *Politics Is People: the men of the Menzies era*, Angus & Robertson, Sydney, 1969, p. 129.

28 Cockburn, Speech to the National Library of Australia, 1994.

29 Stewart Cockburn, 'Mr Menzies', Robert Menzies Papers, MS 4936, Series 10, Box 365, Folder 5, National Library of Australia, Canberra.

30 Henderson, *A Smile for My Parents*, p. 56.

31 Yeend to McNicoll, 22 July 1982.

32 Robert Menzies, 'Hughie Dash', 27 June 1960, Canberra.

33 Robert Menzies to Jean Maley, 24 November 1976, Papers of Frances McNicoll, MS 9246, Series 3, Box 11, File 90, National Library of Australia, Canberra.

34 Brown, *Ten Prime Ministers*, pp. 31–32.

35 Interview with Tony Eggleton, 2 June 2017, Canberra.

36 Ibid.

37 Robert Menzies, 'What They Will Say — Sydney Morning Herald', 1960, Robert Menzies Papers, MS 4936, Series 10, Box 354, Folder 2, National Library of Australia, Canberra.

38 Brown, *Ten Prime Ministers*, pp. 18–19.

39 Interview with Jon Gaul, 10 August 2018, Sydney.

40 Rupert Henderson to Robert Menzies, 4 August 1943 and Robert Menzies to Rupert Henderson, 8 August 1943. Robert Menzies Papers, MS 4936, Series 40 (1993 Addition), Box 573, Folder 15, National Library of Australia, Canberra.

41 McNicoll interview with Menzies, 15 May 1972.

42 Ian Fitchett, 'Menzies and his myth', *The National Times*, 11–16 April 1977, p. 28.

43 Interview with Graham Freudenberg, 26 August 2018, Canberra.

44 'Menzies, Calwell popular on TV', *Australian Gallup Polls*, November–December 1963.

45 Henderson, *Letters to My Daughter*, Pier 9, Millers Point, 2011, pp. 68–69.

46 Rob Chalmers, *Inside the Canberra Press Gallery: life in the wedding cake of Old Parliament House*, ANU Press, Canberra, 2011, p. 85.

47 Green, *Servant of the House*, pp. 157–59.

48 Menzies, *Afternoon Light*, p. 304.

49 Harold Holt, 'The Political Situation', 4 February 1957, Robert Menzies Papers, MS 4936, Series 14, Box 410, Folder 1, National Library of Australia, Canberra.

50 Ibid.

51 On 3 April 1957, Menzies surpassed Hughes in serving the longest single term in office. See Hazlehurst, *Menzies Observed*, p. 354.

52 'Liberal Party's ten successful years', *The Sydney Morning Herald*, 16 November 1964, p. 2.

53 Ibid.

54 'Menzies popular as PM', *Australian Gallup Polls*, April–May 1953.

55 'Liberal Party's ten successful years'.

Chapter 13: At Home: Domestic Affairs

1 Reserve Bank of Australia, *Australian Economic Statistics 1949–1950 to 1996–1997*, Occasional Paper No. 8, accessed online August 2018.

2 Henderson, *Menzies' Child*, pp. 147–48.

3 Martin, *Robert Menzies: a life. Volume 2*, p. 143.

4 Howard, *The Menzies Era*, p. 132.

5 Robert Menzies to William McKell, 8 October 1951, Papers of Frances McNicoll, MS 9246, Series 3, Box 3, File 16, National Library of Australia, Canberra.

6 Clyde Cameron, 'None to match him, says a veteran foe', *The Sunday Mail*, 10 April 1988, p. 21.

7 Alan Reid, 'Robert Gordon Menzies', *The Bulletin*, 5 February 1980, p. 41.

8 Robert Menzies to Rupert Henderson, 27 April 1954, Fairfax Media Business Archive, MLMSS 9894, Box 511, State Library of New South Wales, Sydney.

9 Alan Reid to Robert Menzies, 7 May 1954, Fairfax Media Business Archive, MLMSS 9894, Box 511, State Library of New South Wales, Sydney.

10 Rupert Henderson to Robert Menzies,
    30 April 1954, Fairfax Media Business
    Archive, MLMSS 9894, Box 511, State
    Library of New South Wales, Sydney.

11 Howard, *The Menzies Era*, p. 147.

12 William Wentworth, 'Bob's your uncle',
    The Liberals, ABC TV, 1994.

13 Arthur Calwell, *Be Just and Fear Not*,
    Lloyd O'Neil, Hawthorn, 1972, p. 186.

14 Menzies, *The Measure of the Years*, p. 197.

15 Interviews with Cyril Wyndham,
    11 April 2011 and 13 April 2011, via
    phone.

16 Ibid.

17 Troy Bramston, 'Espionage charge denied
    amid questions over Labor leader's
    mental health', *The Weekend Australian*,
    16 April 2011.

18 Menzies, *The Measure of the Years*, p. 81.

19 McNicoll interview with Menzies,
    13 May 1972.

20 Interview with John Carrick, 9 March
    2017, Sydney.

21 Graham Freudenberg, *A Certain
    Grandeur: Gough Whitlam in politics*,
    Macmillan, South Melbourne, 1977,
    p. 25.

22 Elena Douglas, 'Rethinking history:
    stolen legacy', *The Australian Financial
    Review*, 24 January 2014.

23 Menzies, *The Measure of the Years*, p. 89.

24 See Martin, *Robert Menzies: a life.
    Volume 2*, pp. 396–99 and Martin, 'Sir
    Robert Gordon Menzies', in Grattan
    (ed.), *Australian Prime Ministers*, p. 198.

25 Menzies, *The Measure of the Years*, p. 90.

26 Robert Menzies to Allen Fairhall,
    28 April 1956, Robert Menzies Papers,
    MS 4936, Series 40 (1993 Addition),
    Box 574, Folder 18, National Library of
    Australia, Canberra.

27 Allen Fairhall to Robert Menzies,
    4 October 1956, Robert Menzies Papers,
    MS 4936, Series 40 (1993 Addition),
    Box 574, Folder 18, National Library of
    Australia, Canberra.

28 See Troy Bramston, 'Children of the
    revolution', *The Weekend Australian*,
    24 March 2018.

29 Interview with Doug Anthony, 20 April
    2017, via phone.

30 Interview with Ian Sinclair, 7 April 2017,
    Taree.

31 Frances McNicoll interview with Robert
    Menzies, 16 May 1972, Papers of Frances
    McNicoll, MS 9246, Series 6, Box 15,
    Files 1–3, National Library of Australia,
    Canberra.

32 Menzies, *Afternoon Light*, p. 59.

33 Here, I draw on Daniel Oakman,
    Oppy: the life of Sir Hubert Opperman,
    Melbourne Books, Melbourne, 2018,
    pp. 284–86.

34 Martin, 'Sir Robert Gordon Menzies',
    in Grattan (ed.), *Australian Prime
    Ministers*, p. 199.

35 Department of Home Affairs, *Fact
    sheet — abolition of the 'White Australia'
    policy*, accessed online July 2018. John
    Howard writes that 'the Whitlam
    government formally buried the White
    Australia policy' but gives 'the real credit'
    to the Holt government. See Howard,
    The Menzies Era, p. 465.

36 McNicoll interview with Menzies,
    16 May 1972.

37 Ibid.

38 Martin, *Robert Menzies: a life. Volume 2*,
    p. 268.

39 Allan Martin quotes H.C. 'Nugget'
    Coombs on this point. See Martin,
    Robert Menzies: a life. Volume 2,
    p. 569.

40 John Gardiner-Garden, *The 1967
    Referendum — history and myths*,
    Research Brief, Commonwealth
    Parliamentary Library, 2 May 2007, p. 8.

41 McNicoll interview with Menzies,
    18 December 1973.

42 Roberts, *Churchill*, p. 43.

43 Perkins, *Menzies*, p. 253.

Chapter 14: Abroad: Foreign Adventures

1   Pat Farmer, *Menzies: man & myth*, Kangaroo Press, Kenthurst, 1983, pp. 51–52.
2   Owen Harries, 'The men who shaped our place in the world', *The Australian*, 16 January 2005, p. 11.
3   Interview with Richard Woolcott, 15 November 2018, Sydney.
4   Here, I draw on James Curran, 'A brutal lesson in politics from John F. Kennedy', *The Australian*, 21 November 2013. See also Gregory Pemberton, *All The Way: Australia's road to Vietnam*, Allen & Unwin, North Sydney, 1987, pp. 185–86.
5   Max Suich, 'JFK v Murdoch', *The Australian Financial Review*, 10 November 2010.
6   Percy Spender, *Exercises in Diplomacy: the ANZUS Treaty and the Colombo Plan*, Sydney University Press, Sydney 1969, p. 39.
7   Menzies, *The Measure of the Years*, p. 54.
8   McNicoll interview with Menzies, 16 May 1972.
9   Ibid.
10 Robert Menzies, 'Aide-Memoir — 4 September 1956', Robert Menzies Papers, MS 4936, Series 40 (1993 Addition), Box 574, Folder 13, National Library of Australia, Canberra.
11 Ibid.
12 Ibid.
13 'Menzies accused on 1956 Suez clash', *The Sydney Morning Herald*, 28 September 1971, p. 5.
14 Robert Menzies, 'Aide-Memoir — 12 September 1956', Robert Menzies Papers, MS 4936, Series 40 (1993 Addition), Box 574, Folder 13, National Library of Australia, Canberra.
15 Hazlehurst, *Menzies Observed*, p. 207.
16 Menzies interview with Harris, 17 August 1967.
17 Interview with Richard Woolcott, 15 November 2018, Sydney.
18 McNicoll interview with Menzies, 15 May 1972.
19 Menzies interview with Harris, 17 August 1967.
20 Anthony Seldon, *10 Downing Street: the illustrated history*, HarperCollins, London, 1999, p. 144.
21 McNicoll interview with Menzies, 15 May 1972.
22 Ibid.
23 Robert Menzies, *Winston Churchill: a tribute by Sir Robert Menzies*, Wilkie & Co, Melbourne, 1965.
24 Martin, *Robert Menzies: a life. Volume 2*, pp. 370–71.
25 McNicoll interview with Menzies, 15 May 1972.
26 Martin, *Robert Menzies: a life. Volume 2*, p. 493.
27 Ibid., pp. 511–12.
28 McNicoll interview with Menzies, 16 May 1972.
29 Ibid.
30 Henderson, *Letters to My Daughter*, pp. 45–46.
31 McNicoll interview with Menzies, 16 May 1972.
32 Howard, *The Menzies Era*, p. 260.
33 David Tothill, 'Menzies and the South Africans', in Frank Cain (ed.), *Menzies in War and Peace*, Allen & Unwin, St Leonards, 1997, p. 26.
34 McNicoll interview with Menzies, 15 May 1972.
35 Briefing Paper, 'Decimal Currency in Australia', 11 June 1963, Papers of Robert Menzies, Overseas Visits 1963, M2576/20, National Archives of Australia, Canberra.
36 See Adam Harvey, 'The right royal currency coined by Menzies', *The Sydney Morning Herald*, 18 April 1996, p. 7 and Gregory Pemberton, 'Royal rout as public plumped for dollar', *The Australian*, 1 January 1994, p. 6.
37 Interview with William Heseltine, 22 June 2017, Sydney.
38 McNicoll interview with Menzies, 15 May 1972.
39 Interview with William Heseltine, 22 June 2017, Sydney.
40 Robert Menzies, 'Memoirs', Robert Menzies Papers, MS 4936, Series 10,

Box 365, Folder 2, National Library of Australia, Canberra.

41 Ibid.

42 'P.M. installed by the Queen in ancient order', *The Sydney Morning Herald*, 2 July 1963, p. 1.

43 Menzies, 'Memoirs'.

44 Martin, *Robert Menzies: a life. Volume 2*, p. 97.

45 Memorandum of Conversation with Harry Truman and Robert Menzies, 28 July 28 1950, Acheson Papers — Secretary of State File, Harry S. Truman Presidential Library and Museum, Independence, Missouri, United States of America, accessed online August 2018.

46 Martin, *Robert Menzies: a life. Volume 2*, p. 205.

47 Memorandum of Conversation with Prime Minister Robert Menzies of Australia, 20 May 20 1952, Acheson Papers — Secretary of State File, Harry S. Truman Presidential Library and Museum, Independence, Missouri, United States of America, accessed online August 2018.

48 Memorandum of a Conversation, Washington, 14 March 1955, *Foreign Relations of The United States, 1955–57, China, volume II*, accessed online August 2018.

49 'Australia: out of the Dreaming', *TIME*, 4 April 1960, pp. 20–32.

50 'Australia: journey into the world', *TIME*, 24 April 1944, pp. 29–30.

51 Menzies, *Afternoon Light*, pp. 143–44.

52 Memorandum of Conversation, Washington, 24 February 1961, *Foreign Relations of The United States, 1961–1963, volume XXII*, accessed online August 2018.

53 Countries, Australia: General, 1961 — 1 January — 2 March, Papers of John F. Kennedy, Presidential Papers, National Security Files, John F. Kennedy Presidential Library and Museum, Boston, Massachusetts, United States of America, accessed online August 2018.

54 Toasts of the President and Prime Minister Menzies of Australia, Washington, 8 July 1963, Papers of John F. Kennedy, Presidential Papers, President's Office Files, Speech Files, John F. Kennedy Presidential Library and Museum, Boston, Massachusetts, United States of America, accessed online August 2018.

55 Countries, Australia: General, July 1963 — 6–8, Papers of John F. Kennedy, Presidential Papers, National Security Files, John F. Kennedy Presidential Library and Museum, Boston, Massachusetts, United States of America, accessed online August 2018.

56 Howard Beale to Robert Menzies, 25 April 1963, Papers of Robert Menzies, M2576/20, National Archives of Australia, Canberra.

57 President's Daily Diary, 24 June 1964, President's Daily Diary Collection, LBJ Presidential Library, Austin, Texas, United States of America, accessed online August 2018.

58 President's Daily Diary, 7 June 1965, President's Daily Diary Collection, LBJ Presidential Library, Austin, Texas, United States of America, accessed online August 2018.

59 President's Daily Diary, 9 June 1965, President's Daily Diary Collection, LBJ Presidential Library, Austin, Texas, United States of America, accessed online August 2018.

60 President's Daily Diary, 6 July 1965, President's Daily Diary Collection, LBJ Presidential Library, Austin, Texas, United States of America, accessed online August 2018.

61 President's Daily Diary, 13 December 1966 and 25 September 1967, President's Daily Diary Collection, LBJ Presidential Library, Austin, Texas, United States of America, accessed online August 2018.

62 President's Daily Diary, 22 December 1967, President's Daily Diary Collection, LBJ Presidential Library, Austin, Texas, United States of America, accessed online August 2018.

63 'Nixon in Canberra', *The News*, 20 October 1953, p. 1.

64 Richard Nixon, *Leaders*, Warner Books, New York, 1982.

65 Robert Menzies to Richard Nixon, 21 August 1973, Robert Menzies Papers, MS 4936, Series 40 (1993 Addition), Box 574, Folder 19, National Library of Australia, Canberra.

66 'Nixon tells of Menzies' personal letter', *The Canberra Times*, 27 May 1977, p. 1.

67 Howard, *The Menzies Era*, pp. 201–02.

68 Ibid., pp. 212–16.

69 McEwen, *His Story*, p. 54.

70 'Public approves Japanese trade', *Australian Gallup Polls*, November–December 1963.

71 McNicoll interview with Menzies, 18 December 1973.

72 Robert Menzies to Frances McNicoll, 2 August 1973, Papers of Frances McNicoll, MS 9246, Series 1, Box 1, File 5, National Library of Australia, Canberra.

73 Martin, *Robert Menzies: a life. Volume 2*, p. 519.

74 Peter Edwards, *Australia and the Vietnam War*, NewSouth, Sydney, 2014, pp. 285–87.

75 Menzies, *Afternoon Light*, pp. 269–70.

76 *The Pentagon Papers*, accessed online August 2018.

77 Joe Frantz interview with Robert Menzies, 24 November 1969, LBJ Library Oral Histories, LBJ Presidential Library, Austin, Texas, United States of America, accessed online August 2018.

78 Interview with Jim Forbes, 14 December 2018, Adelaide.

79 Interview with Malcolm Fraser, 7 May 2014, via phone.

80 Robert McNamara, *In Retrospect: the tragedy and lessons of Vietnam*, Times Books, New York, 1995, p. 324.

81 Interview with Malcolm Fraser, 7 May 2014, via phone.

82 McNamara, *In Retrospect*, p. 324.

83 McNicoll interview with Barwick, 1981.

84 Interview with Richard Woolcott, 15 November 2018, Sydney. See also Richard Woolcott, *The Hot Seat: reflections on diplomacy from Stalin's death to the Bali bombings*, HarperCollins, Pymble, 2003, p. 76.

85 Editorial, 'Differing with our friends', *The Australian*, 5 May 1965.

86 'Our Vietnam force approved', *Australian Gallup Polls*, July–September 1965.

87 Paul Kelly, 'Labor's strange silence on Vietnam', *The Australian*, 3 May 1985, p. 11.

88 McNicoll interview with Menzies, 18 December 1973.

Chapter 15: Across the Divide: Evatt, Calwell, and Whitlam

1 'Labour's new head: Evatt unopposed', *The Sydney Morning Herald*, 21 June 1951, p. 3.

2 Fadden, *They Called Me Artie*, 135.

3 'Calwell new A.L.P leader', *The Canberra Times*, 8 March 1960, p. 1.

4 Whitlam defeated Jim Cairns, Frank Crean, Fred Daly and Kim Beazley in the leadership contest. See Jon Gaul, 'Mr Whitlam leads ALP', *The Canberra Times*, 9 February 1967, p. 1.

5 Bramston, 'Espionage charge denied amid questions over Labor leader's mental health'.

6 Allan Dalziel, *Evatt: the enigma*, Lansdowne Press, Melbourne, 1967, p. 46.

7 Henderson, *Letters to My Daughter*, p. 12.

8 Interview with Cyril Wyndham, 11 April 2011 and 13 April 2011, via phone.

9 McNicoll interview with Menzies, 12 May 1972.

10 Ibid.

11 Interview with Heather Henderson, 22 August 2014, Canberra.

12 Henderson, *Letters to My Daughter*, p. 5.

13 'Challenge to Evatt as party leader', *The Sydney Morning Herald*, 4 August 1954, p. 3.

14 'Harsh talk in caucus over Evatt', *The Sydney Morning Herald*, 23 September 1954, p. 1.

15 The details of precisely what took place and what was said have been a matter of

debate. Clyde Cameron recalled Eddie Ward shouted, 'Take their names!' Fred Daly said it was Evatt who said, 'Get their names!' See Cameron and Connell, *The Confessions of Clyde Cameron*, pp. 115–16; Daly, *From Curtin to Kerr*, p. 128.

16 This report notes that the vote was 54–28. See 'Evatt wins but big party split', *The Sydney Morning Herald*, 21 October 1954, p. 1.

17 Daly, *From Curtin to Kerr*, p. 128.

18 See Mark Aarons, *The Show: another side of Santamaria's movement*, Scribe, Melbourne, 2017. See also Troy Bramston, 'Catholic spies in ASIO's network, new book alleges', *The Australian*, 11 August 2017.

19 Interview with Mary Elizabeth Calwell, 21 May 2013, Melbourne.

20 The seven Victorian MPs were: Tom Andrews, Bill Bourke, Bill Bryson, Jack Cremean, Bob Joshua, Stan Keon and Jack Mullens. Tasmanian senator George Cole joined the breakaway party in August 1955. Frank McManus was elected to the Senate from Victoria on 10 December 1955.

21 'Surprise caucus ballot solidly backs Dr. Evatt', *The Canberra Times*, 19 April 1955, p. 1.

22 'Overwhelming victory for Dr. Evatt', *The Canberra Times*, 14 February 1956, p. 1.

23 'Would resign for D.L.P. votes says Evatt', *The Canberra Times*, 22 October 1958, p. 1.

24 'Dr. Evatt back as party leader', *The Canberra Times*, 17 February 1959, p. 1.

25 'Dr. Evatt chosen as N.S.W. chief justice', *The Canberra Times*, 10 February 1960, p. 1.

26 McNicoll interview with Menzies, 12 May 1972.

27 'Adjournment tribute to Dr Evatt', *The Canberra Times*, 10 November 1965, p. 2.

28 McNicoll interview with Menzies, 12 May 1972.

29 Interview with Mary Elizabeth Calwell, 2 April 2018, via email.

30 Interview with Mary Elizabeth Calwell, 21 May 2013, Melbourne.

31 Interview with Bill Hayden, 8 September 2018, via phone.

32 McNicoll interview with Menzies, 12 May 1972.

33 Note to Philip Palmer (Company Secretary), 16 September 1949, Fairfax Media Business Archive, MLMSS 9894, Box 512, State Library of New South Wales, Sydney.

34 'Herald's "political principles"', *The Sydney Morning Herald*, 1 December 1961, p. 2.

35 'Labour presents the better case', *The Sydney Morning Herald*, 8 December 1961, p. 2.

36 The speeches included a 'victory' speech ('Our hour has struck indeed … I express our thanks most of all to the electors who have cast a vote of confidence in us') and a 'concession' speech ('We have lost this battle but we shall still win the campaign … our hour will soon strike'). See 'Statement "A"' and 'Statement "B"', Fairfax Media Business Archive, MLMSS 9894, Box 513, State Library of New South Wales, Sydney.

37 Souter, *Company of Heralds*, p. 380.

38 'Broadway Melody 1961! (*S.M Herald backs Calwell*)', *Mirror*, 19 November 1961, pp. 1, 3.

39 Calwell, *Be Just and Fear Not*, p. 210.

40 Interview with Graham Freudenberg, 11 July 2018, via phone.

41 McNicoll interview with Menzies, 15 May 1972.

42 Killen spoke to Menzies on the phone, who rather plainly said: 'Well, laddie, this is good news. I am glad it is over.' See Killen, *Killen*, p. 51.

43 Henderson, *Menzies' Child*, p. 130.

44 'Most favour U.S. radio base', *Australian Gallup Polls*, May–June 1963.

45 See Troy Bramston, 'JFK's meeting with Calwell prompted by Asia concern', *The Weekend Australian*, 12 October 2013.

46 This plane was known as the English Electric Canberra, designed and manufactured in the United Kingdom.

47 McNicoll interview with Menzies, 16 May 1972.

48 McNicoll interview with Menzies, 15 May 1972.

49 'More support for federal CLP', *Australian Gallup Polls*, May–June 1963.

50 'A.L.P. promise of new economic era', *The Canberra Times*, 7 November 1963, p. 1.

51 Interview with Graham Freudenberg, 7 October 2013, via phone.

52 Daly, *From Curtin to Kerr*, p. 161.

53 Haylen, *Twenty Years' Hard Labor*, pp. 130–35.

54 Conversation with Gough Whitlam, May 2007.

55 McNicoll interview with Menzies, 12 May 1972.

56 Interview with Graham Freudenberg, 11 July 2018, via phone.

57 Bowers, 'Silent Menzies and the games he played', p. 6.

58 Robert Menzies, 'Death of Mr A.A. Calwell', 8 July 1973, Robert Menzies Papers, MS 4936, Series (2000 Addition), Box 6, Folder 43, National Library of Australia, Canberra.

59 Robert Menzies, 'Condolence — Calwell', Robert Menzies Papers, MS 4936, Series (2000 Addition), Box 6, Folder 43, National Library of Australia, Canberra.

60 Gough Whitlam to Robert Menzies, 12 December 1972, Papers of Frances McNicoll, MS 9246, Series 3, Box 5, File 28, National Library of Australia, Canberra.

61 McNicoll interview with Menzies, 17 May 1972.

62 Ibid.

Chapter 16: The Private Menzies

1 Interview with Heather Henderson, 22 August 2014, Canberra.

2 Ibid.

3 Ibid.

4 Ibid.

5 Frances McNicoll interview with Ken Menzies, 1981, Papers of Frances McNicoll, MS 9246, Series 6, Box 15, Files 7–19, National Library of Australia, Canberra.

6 Henderson, *A Smile for My Parents*, pp. 91, 94.

7 Ibid., p. 109.

8 Stewart Cockburn, 'Menzies: alone at the top', *The Canberra Times*, 19 December 1964.

9 Bunting, *R.G. Menzies*, p. 137.

10 Interview with William Heseltine, 22 June 2017, Sydney.

11 Interview with Heather Henderson, 22 August 2014, Canberra.

12 Ibid.

13 Interview with Tony Eggleton, 2 June 2017, Canberra.

14 Special Correspondent, 'Sir Robert Menzies', p. 15.

15 Interview with Tony Eggleton, 14 October 2013, Canberra.

16 See, for example, Robert Menzies to H.L. Napthali, 18 December 1942, Betty Hall Collection, National Museum of Australia, Canberra.

17 Interview with William Heseltine, 22 June 2017, Sydney.

18 R.B. Leonard and Ray Tracey, 'I drove the great! With Lyons came laughter to the Lodge', *Daily News*, 15 March 1950, p. 9.

19 Peter Luck, 'The Lodge regrets departure of Sir Robert', *The Canberra Times*, 21 January 1966, p. 3.

20 Gullett, 'Robert Gordon Menzies', p. 165.

21 McNicoll interview with Frank Menzies, 16 May 1972.

22 Caitlin Stone and Jim Berryman, 'The Robert Menzies Collection at the University of Melbourne', *University of Melbourne Collections*, Issue 12, June 2013, pp. 45–50.

23 Robert Menzies to Frances McNicoll, 1 March 1973, Papers of Frances

McNicoll, MS 9246, Series 1, Box 1, File 5, National Library of Australia, Canberra.

24 Robert Menzies, 'Foreword', in Hugh Buggy and Harry Bell, *The Carlton Story: a history of the Carlton Football Club*, Eric White and Associates, Melbourne, 1958.

25 *The Canberra Times*, 4 September 1972, p. 7.

26 Interview with Heather Henderson, 22 August 2014, Canberra.

27 Interview with Heather Henderson, 20 March 2017, Canberra.

28 Interview with Heather Henderson, 22 August 2014, Canberra.

29 Ibid.

30 Interviews with Heather Henderson, 22 August 2014 and 13 October 2017, Canberra.

Chapter 17: Menzies in Verse

1 Interview with Heather Henderson, 13 October 2017, Canberra.

2 Provided to the author by Heather Henderson.

3 Robert Menzies, 'Edwina', Robert Menzies Papers, MS 4936, Series 40 (1993 Addition), Box 574, Folder 15, National Library of Australia, Canberra.

4 Joske, *Sir Robert Menzies, 1894–1978*, p. 11.

5 Ibid., pp. 13, 15.

6 Robert Menzies, 'Billy Hughes', Robert Menzies Papers, MS 4936, Series 10, Box 355, Folders 3–4, National Library of Australia, Canberra.

7 Robert Menzies, 'The lawyer as poet', Robert Menzies Papers, MS 4936, Series 10, Box 365, Folder 3, National Library of Australia, Canberra.

8 Robert Menzies, 'Ode', Robert Menzies Papers, MS 4936, Series 10, Box 355, Folders 3–4, National Library of Australia, Canberra.

9 Robert Menzies, 'To Ben Chifley', Robert Menzies Papers, MS 4936, Series 10, Box 355, Folders 3–4, National Library of Australia, Canberra.

10 Robert Menzies, 'To Bert Evatt', Robert Menzies Papers, MS 4936, Series 10, Box 355, Folders 3–4, National Library of Australia, Canberra.

11 Robert Menzies, 'Arthur Augustus Calwell to Mr Jang', Robert Menzies Papers, MS 4936, Series 10, Box 355, Folders 3–4, National Library of Australia, Canberra.

12 'As it happens', *The Times*, 30 January 1967. See Robert Menzies Papers, MS 4936, Series 40 (1993 Addition), Box 574, Folder 15, National Library of Australia, Canberra.

13 'The Clerk's riposte', *The Times*, 31 January 1967. See Robert Menzies Papers, MS 4936, Series 40 (1993 Addition), Box 574, Folder 15, National Library of Australia, Canberra.

14 Robert Menzies, 'Unnamed', Robert Menzies Papers, MS 4936, Series 10, Box 355, Folders 3–4, National Library of Australia, Canberra.

15 Cockburn, Speech to the National Library of Australia, 1994.

16 Robert Menzies, 'Canberra', Papers of Frances McNicoll, MS 9246, Series 3, Box 2, File 5, National Library of Australia, Canberra.

17 Lloyd, *Parliament and the Press*, p. 171.

18 Robert Menzies, 'For Frank Packer', Robert Menzies Papers, MS 4936, Series 10, Box 365, Folder 5, National Library of Australia, Canberra.

19 Robert Menzies, 'What They Will Say — Sydney Daily Telegraph', 1960, Robert Menzies Papers, MS 4936, Series 10, Box 354, Folder 2, National Library of Australia, Canberra.

20 Menzies wrote: 'Reference to Senate election a few weeks previously'.

21 Robert Menzies, 'Verse by R. G. Menzies, Savoy Hotel, London, June 30, 1953', Robert Menzies Papers, MS 4936, Series 40 (1993 Addition), Box 574, Folder 15, National Library of Australia, Canberra.

22 Bill Strutton, 'Stars of the Old Vic', *Australian Women's Weekly*, 4 May 1955, p. 23.

23 'When Mr Menzies rewrote Shylock scene', *News Chronicle*, 29 August 1956.
24 Yeend to McNicoll, 22 July 1982.

25 Interview with Heather Henderson, 13 October 2017, Canberra.

Chapter 18: Resignation

1 John Bunting, Cabinet Notebook, 19 January 1966, A11099/1/77, National Archives of Australia, Canberra.
2 See Troy Bramston, 'My time to go is now: Menzies' unmatched lesson in how to quit', *The Weekend Australian*, 1 March 2014, p. 21.
3 Bunting, Cabinet Notebook, 19 January 1966.
4 McNicoll interview with Menzies, 15 May 1972.
5 Henderson, *Letters to My Daughter*, pp. 57–58.
6 'At 66 Menzies still wanted', *Australian Gallup Polls*, March–May 1961.
7 Henderson, *Letters to My Daughter*, pp. 84.
8 Robert Menzies, 'Speech Notes for 21st Birthday of Foundation of Liberal Party', 8 November 1965, Robert Menzies Papers, MS 4936, Series 14, Box 411, Folder 15, National Library of Australia, Canberra.
9 John 'Jock' Pagan to Robert Menzies, 18 October 1965, Robert Menzies Papers, MS 4936, Series 14, Box 411, Folder 15, National Library of Australia, Canberra.
10 'LCP voters want Sir Robert', *Australian Gallup Polls*, July–September 1965.
11 John 'Jock' Pagan and Philip McBride to Robert Menzies, 6 December 1965, Robert Menzies Papers, MS 4936, Series 14, Box 411, Folder 15, National Library of Australia, Canberra.
12 Interview with Mary Elizabeth Calwell, 22 April 2018, via email.
13 Interview with Heather Henderson, 22 August 2014, Canberra.
14 Robert Menzies' Appointment Diary, 25 December 1965, Robert Menzies Papers, MS 4936, Series 13, Box 402, National Library of Australia, Canberra.
15 Robert Menzies' Appointment Diary, 27 December 1965, Robert Menzies Papers, MS 4936, Series 13, Box 402, National Library of Australia, Canberra.
16 'This home will be a thanks-offering — Trust to buy Menzies' house', *The Daily Telegraph*, 20 June 1966, p. 3.
17 Interview with Tony Eggleton, 14 October 2013, Canberra; Email from Tony Eggleton to Troy Bramston, 27 February 2014.
18 Ibid.
19 Robert Menzies, Press Statement, 10 January 1966.
20 Robert Menzies' Appointment Diary, 16 January 1966, Robert Menzies Papers, MS 4936, Series 13, Box 404, National Library of Australia, Canberra. See also Richard Casey's Diary, 16 January 1966, Volume 27, Richard Casey Papers, MS 6150, Subseries 4.4, Box 31a, Files 27–30, National Library of Australia, Canberra.
21 Robert Menzies, Press Statement, 20 January 1966.
22 Robert Menzies' Appointment Diary, 20 January 1966, Robert Menzies Papers, MS 4936, Series 13, Box 404, National Library of Australia, Canberra.
23 Richard Casey's Diary, 21 January 1966, Volume 27, Richard Casey Papers, MS 6150, Subseries 4.4, Box 31a, Files 27–30, National Library of Australia, Canberra.
24 Robert Menzies to Richard Casey, 20 January 1966, Robert Menzies Papers, MS 4936, Series (2000 Addition), Box 6, Folder 48, National Library of Australia, Canberra.
25 Richard Casey to Robert Menzies, 20 January 1966, Robert Menzies Papers, MS 4936, Series (2000 Addition), Box 6, Folder 48, National Library of Australia, Canberra.
26 Interview with Tony Eggleton, 14 October 2013, Canberra.

27 'Farewell to the people', *The Sydney Morning Herald*, 21 January 1966, p. 1.

28 McNicoll interview with Menzies, 15 May 1972.

29 Robert Menzies' Appointment Diary, 26 January 1966, Robert Menzies Papers, MS 4936, Series 13, Box 404, National Library of Australia, Canberra.

30 See Troy Bramston, 'Colt from Kooyong on what might have been', *The Weekend Australian*, 17 December 2016, p. 18.

31 Interview with Andrew Peacock, 8 November 2016, via phone.

32 'Sir Robert talks of his devotion', *The Canberra Times*, 18 March 1966, p. 3.

33 Robert Menzies, *Central Power in the Australian Commonwealth*, Cassell, London, 1967.

34 'Sir Robert New Lord Warden', *East Kent Mercury*, 21 July 1966, p. 1.

35 Claude Forrell, 'Sir Robert in Uniform', *The Age*, 16 July 1966, p. 1.

36 Interview with Heather Henderson, 13 October 2017, Canberra.

37 Mabel Brookes to Lyndon Johnson, 2 March 1968, Robert Menzies Papers, MS 4936, Series 40 (1993 Addition), Box 574, Folder 19, National Library of Australia, Canberra.

38 John Fraser, 'Sir Robert's still in fine form', 14 July 1972, *The Sun*, p. 3.

39 Henderson, *Letters to My Daughter*, pp. xv, 244.

40 McNicoll interview with Frank Menzies, 16 May 1972.

41 Robert Menzies to Frances McNicoll, 6 June 1968, Papers of Frances McNicoll, MS 9246, Series 1, Box 1, File 4, National Library of Australia, Canberra. See also Henderson, *Letters to My Daughter*, p. 195.

42 Henderson, *Letters to My Daughter*, p. 167.

43 Belle Green to Robert Menzies, 12 July 1967, Robert Menzies Papers, MS 4936, Series 40 (1993 Addition), Box 574, Folder 25, National Library of Australia, Canberra. See also Henderson, *Letters to My Daughter*, pp. 148, 153.

44 B.A. 'Bob' Santamaria, 'Bob's your Uncle', *The Liberals*, ABC TV, 1994.

45 Robert Menzies to B.A. Santamaria, 12 October 1976, Robert Menzies Papers, MS 4936, Series 40 (1993 Addition), Box 574, Folder 19, National Library of Australia, Canberra.

46 Peter Wilmoth, 'How I got the scoop on Sir Bob', *The Australian*, 5 October 2013.

47 Robert Menzies, 'Draft', 26 March 1975, Papers of Frances McNicoll, MS 9246, Series 3, Box 6, File 42, National Library of Australia, Canberra.

48 Interview with Tony Eggleton, 14 October 2013, Canberra; Email from Tony Eggleton to Troy Bramston, 27 February 2014.

Chapter 19: Successors

1 Henderson, *Letters to My Daughter*, pp. 173, 176.

2 David McNicoll, 'Robert Menzies speaks out', *The Bulletin*, 20 April 1974, pp. 29–31.

3 David McNicoll, *Luck's a Fortune*, Wildcat Press, Sydney, 1979, pp. 203–35.

4 Heather Henderson to David McNicoll, 15 December 1979, David McNicoll Papers, MLMSS 7419, Series 9, State Library of New South Wales, Sydney.

5 David McNicoll to Heather Henderson, 9 January 1980, David McNicoll Papers, MLMSS 7419, Series 9, State Library of New South Wales, Sydney.

6 McNicoll interview with Menzies, 14 May 1972.

7 McNicoll interview with Menzies, 12 May 1972.

8 McNicoll interview with Menzies, 14 May 1972.

9 Interview with Tony Eggleton, 2 June 2017, Canberra.

10 McNicoll interview with Menzies, 14 May 1972.

11 Others recall a closer margin of 43–38. See Jonathan Gaul, 'Gorton's sweeping victory', *The Canberra Times*, 10 January 1968, p. 1.

12 Paul Hasluck to Robert Menzies,
    11 January 1968, Robert Menzies Papers,
    MS 4936, Series 40 (1993 Addition),
    Box 573, Folder 7, National Library of
    Australia, Canberra.
13 McNicoll interview with Menzies,
    14 May 1972.
14 Ibid.
15 Gorton, 'How I became a Menzies man',
    p. 4.
16 McNicoll interview with Menzies,
    14 May 1972.
17 McNicoll interview with Menzies,
    13 May 1972.
18 Robert Menzies to Frances McNicoll,
    31 October 1969, Papers of Frances
    McNicoll, MS 9246, Series 1, Box 1,
    File 4, National Library of Australia,
    Canberra.
19 Interview with Malcolm Fraser,
    6 September 2002, Melbourne.
20 Interview with Doug Anthony, 20 April
    2017, via phone.
21 McNicoll interview with Menzies,
    17 May 1972.
22 McNicoll interview with Menzies,
    18 December 1973.
23 Robert Menzies to William McMahon,
    11 March 1971, Papers of Frances
    McNicoll, MS 9246, Series 3, Box 1,
    File 4, National Library of Australia,
    Canberra.
24 William McMahon to Robert Menzies,
    23 March 1971, Papers of Frances
    McNicoll, MS 9246, Series 1, Box 1,
    File 5, National Library of Australia,
    Canberra.
25 Malcolm Fraser reclaimed his portfolio
    of Education and Science.
26 Interview with Heather Henderson,
    22 August 2014, Canberra.
27 Interview with Mary Elizabeth Calwell,
    25 September 2014, via phone.
28 David Humphries, 'Revealed — how
    Menzies swung against his party',
    The Sydney Morning Herald, 17 April
    2006, p. 4.
29 Brown, Ten Prime Ministers, p. 34.
30 Henderson, Menzies' Child, p. 187.
31 Interview with Malcolm Fraser,
    6 September 2002, Melbourne.

32 David Solomon, 'Snedden faces his first
    problems', The Canberra Times,
    21 December 1972, p. 3. See also Gerard
    Henderson, 'Time has come to end the
    party games', The Sydney Morning Herald,
    13 January 1995, p. 11.
33 Menzies to McNicoll, 2 August 1973.
34 Henderson, Letters to My Daughter,
    p. 167.
35 McNicoll, 'Robert Menzies speaks out',
    p. 29.
36 McNicoll interview with Menzies,
    18 December 1973.
37 Ibid.
38 Robert Menzies to Hubert Opperman,
    8 July 1974, Papers of Frances McNicoll,
    MS 9246, Series 3, Box 5, File 29,
    National Library of Australia, Canberra.
39 Robert Menzies, 'Looking Around At
    80', 12 December 1974, Robert Menzies
    Papers, MS 4936, Series 10, Box 357,
    Folder 'Articles 1974', National Library
    of Australia, Canberra.
40 Henderson, Letters to My Daughter,
    p. 204.
41 Alan Ramsey, 'Menzies: the prime
    minister a nation forgot', The Australian,
    16 September 1968, p. 7.
42 Henderson, A Smile for My Parents,
    p. 188.
43 Interview with Malcolm Fraser,
    6 September 2002, Melbourne.
44 McNicoll interview with Menzies,
    18 December 1973.
45 Robert Menzies, Press Statement,
    9 March 1971, Robert Menzies Papers,
    MS 4936, Series 40 (1993 Addition),
    Box 573, Folder 7, National Library of
    Australia, Canberra.
46 Interview with Malcolm Fraser,
    6 September 2002, Melbourne.
47 Interview with Tony Staley, 23 July 2015,
    Melbourne.
48 Gay Davidson, 'Fraser: no early election',
    The Canberra Times, 22 March 1975,
    p. 1.
49 See Paul Kelly and Troy Bramston,
    The Dismissal: in the Queen's name,
    Penguin Random House, Melbourne,
    2015, p. 301.

50 Interview with Malcolm Fraser,
6 September 2002, Melbourne.

51 Email from Doug Anthony to Troy
Bramston, 7 September 2015.

52 See Troy Bramston, 'Faith, and close
friends, helped Sir John Kerr resist
"hatred of Whitlam"', *The Weekend
Australian*, 13 October 2012. See also
Kelly and Bramston, *The Dismissal*,
pp. 296–97.

53 Robert Menzies, 'Reflections on an
election', 13 January 1976, Papers of
Frances McNicoll, MS 9246, Series 3,
Box 15, File 93, National Library of
Australia, Canberra.

54 Kelly and Bramston, *The Dismissal*,
pp. 296–97.

55 Robert Menzies to Malcolm Fraser,
19 November 1975, Papers of Frances
McNicoll, MS 9246, Series 3, Box 5,
File 29, National Library of Australia,
Canberra.

56 Robert Menzies to Tamie Fraser,
10 December 1975, Papers of Frances
McNicoll, MS 9246, Series 3, Box 5,
File 29, National Library of Australia,
Canberra.

57 Interview with Heather Henderson,
13 October 2017, Canberra.

58 John Monks, 'Vote no! Menzies attacks
age limit for judges', *The Australian*,
23 March 1977, p. 1.

59 'Menzies dead', *The Age*, 16 May 1978,
p. 1.

60 Robert Menzies' Appointment Diary,
15 May 1978, Robert Menzies Papers,
MS 4936, Series 13, Box 529, National
Library of Australia, Canberra.

61 Malcolm Fraser, Statement — Sir Robert
Menzies, 15 May 1978.

62 Henderson, *A Smile for My Parents*,
p. 164.

Epilogue: Lessons in Leadership

1 Here, I draw on Paul Kelly, 'Time to
reconsider the many faces of Menzies',
The Australian, 17 November 1999.

2 Paul Kelly, *The End of Certainty: the story
of the 1980s*, Allen & Unwin, Sydney,
1992.

Select Bibliography

Author interviews

Tony Abbott

Doug Anthony

Mary Elizabeth Calwell

John Carrick

Peter Costello

Tony Eggleton

A.J. 'Jim' Forbes

Malcolm Fraser

Graham Freudenberg

Jon Gaul

Nick Greiner

Bill Hayden

Heather Henderson

William Heseltine

Lenox Hewitt

Sam Holt

John Howard

David Kemp

Brendan Nelson

Andrew Peacock

Ian Sinclair

Tony Staley

Gough Whitlam

Richard Woolcott

Cyril Wyndham

Archives

Cabinet Papers and Cabinet Notebooks, National Archives of Australia, Canberra

Sir Richard Casey Papers, National Library of Australia, Canberra

Sir John Cramer Papers, National Library of Australia, Canberra

John Curtin Papers, John Curtin Prime Ministerial Library, Perth

Fairfax Media Business Archive, State Library of New South Wales, Sydney

Sir John Gorton Papers, National Library of Australia, Canberra

Sir Paul Hasluck Papers, National Library of Australia, Canberra

Harold Holt Papers, National Library of Australia, Canberra

Eileen Lenihan Papers, National Archives of Australia, Canberra

Sir William McMahon Papers, National Library of Australia, Canberra

Sir Robert Menzies Papers, National Archives of Australia, Canberra

Sir Robert Menzies Papers, National Library of Australia, Canberra

David McNicoll Papers, State Library of New South Wales, Sydney

Lady Frances McNicoll Papers, National Library of Australia, Canberra

Sir William McKell Papers, State Library of New South Wales, Sydney

Sir Ernest White Papers, National Library of Australia, Canberra.

Books

Garfield Barwick, *A Radical Tory: reflections and recollections*, The Federation Press, Sydney, 1995

John Bunting, *R.G. Menzies: a portrait*, Allen & Unwin, Sydney, 1988

Howard Beale, *This Inch of Time: memoirs of politics and diplomacy*, Melbourne University Press, Melbourne, 1977

Judith Brett, *Robert Menzies' Forgotten People*, Pan Macmillan, Sydney, 1992

Frank Cain (ed.), *Menzies in War and Peace*, Allen & Unwin, St Leonards, 1997

Arthur Calwell, *Be Just and Fear Not*, Lloyd O'Neil, Hawthorn, 1972

Brian Carroll, *The Menzies Years*, Cassell, Stanmore, 1977

Don Chipp and John Larkin, *Don Chipp: the third man*, Rigby, Adelaide, 1978

John Cramer, *Pioneers, Politics and People: a political memoir*, Allen & Unwin, Sydney, 1989

Fred Daly, *From Curtin to Kerr*, Sun Books, South Melbourne, 1977

Annabelle Dennehy, *A Portrait of Belle: the female Menzies*, Sundance Promotions, Burbank, 2013

Alexander Downer, *Six Prime Ministers*, Hill of Content, Melbourne, 1982

Arthur Fadden, *They Called Me Artie: the memoirs of Sir Arthur Fadden*, The Jacaranda Press, Milton, 1969

Pat Farmer, *Menzies: man & myth*, Kangaroo Press, Kenthurst, 1983

Malcolm Fraser and Margaret Simons, *Malcolm Fraser: the political memoirs*, Melbourne University Publishing (The Miegunyah Press), Carlton, 2010

David Furse-Roberts, *Menzies: the forgotten speeches*, Connor Court (Jeparit Press), Redland Bay, 2017

Frank Green, *Servant of the House*, Heinemann, Melbourne, 1969

Ian Hancock, *National and Permanent? The Federal Organisation of the Liberal Party of Australia 1944–1965*, Melbourne University Press, Carlton, 2000

Paul Hasluck, *The Government and the People, 1939–41*, Australian War Memorial, Canberra, 1952

— *Sir Robert Menzies*, Melbourne University Press, Carlton, 1980

— *The Chance of Politics*, Text Publishing, Melbourne, 1997

Cameron Hazlehurst, *Menzies Observed*, George Allen & Unwin, Sydney, 1979

Anne Henderson, *Menzies at War*, NewSouth Publishing, Sydney, 2014

Gerard Henderson, *Menzies' Child: The Liberal Party of Australia 1944–1994*, Allen & Unwin, St Leonards, 1994

Heather Henderson, *Letters to My Daughter*, Pier 9, Millers Point, 2011

— *A Smile For My Parents*, Allen & Unwin, Crows Nest, 2013

Edgar Holt, *Politics is People: the men of the Menzies era*, Angus & Robertson, Sydney, 1969

John Howard, *The Menzies Era: the years that shaped modern Australia*, HarperCollins Publishers, Sydney, 2014

Percy Joske, *Sir Robert Menzies, 1894–1978: a new, informal memoir*, Angus & Robertson, Sydney, 1978

James Killen, *Killen: inside Australian politics*, Methuen Haynes, North Ryde, 1985

David Lowe, *Menzies and the 'Great World Struggle': Australia's cold war, 1948–1954*, UNSW Press, Sydney, 1999

Enid Lyons, *Among the Carrion Crows*, Rigby, Adelaide, 1972

Allan Martin (with Patsy Hardy), *Dark and Hurrying Days: Menzies' 1941 diary*, National Library of Australia, Canberra, 1993

— *Robert Menzies: A Life. Volume 1, 1894–1943*, Melbourne University Press, Carlton, 1993

— *Robert Menzies: A Life. Volume 2, 1944–1978*, Melbourne University Press, Carlton, 1999

John McEwen, *His Story*, privately published, Canberra, 1983

Robert Menzies, *To the People of Britain at War*, Longmans Green & Co, London, 1941

— *The Forgotten People and Other Studies in Democracy*, Angus & Robertson, Sydney, 1943

— *Speech Is of Time: selected speeches and writings*, Cassell, London, 1958

— *Afternoon Light: some memories of men and events*, Cassell, Melbourne, 1967

— *Central Power in the Australian Commonwealth*, Cassell, London 1967

— *The Measure of the Years*, Coronet, Melbourne, 1970

John Nethercote (ed.), *Menzies: the shaping of modern Australia*, Connor Court, Redland Bay, 2016

Earle Page, *Truant Surgeon: the inside story of forty years of Australian political life*, Angus & Robertson, Sydney, 1963

Kevin Perkins, *Menzies: the last of the Queen's men*, Rigby, Adelaide, 1968

Scott Prasser, John Nethercote and John Warhurst (eds.), *The Menzies Era: a reappraisal of government, politics and policy*, Hale & Iremonger, Sydney, 1995

Ronald Seth, *R.G. Menzies*, Cassell, London, 1960

Billy Snedden and Bernie Schedvin, *Billy Snedden: an unlikely Liberal*, Macmillan, South Melbourne, 1990

Percy Spender, *Exercises in Diplomacy: the ANZUS Treaty and the Colombo Plan*, Sydney University Press, Sydney 1969

— *Politics and a Man*, Collins, Sydney, 1972

Alan Trengove, *Menzies: a pictorial biography*, Nelson, West Melbourne, 1978

Don Whitington, *The Rulers: fifteen years of the Liberals* (revised edition), Lansdowne, Melbourne, 1965

Documentaries

Menzies in Profile, Seven Network, 1964

Mr Prime Minister, ABC TV, 1966

The Liberals, ABC TV, 1994

Howard on Menzies: building modern Australia, ABC TV, 2016

Index